Creating Learning Organizations Through Digital Transformation

Henrique S. Mamede
INESC-TEC, Universidade Aberta, Portugal

Arnaldo Santos
Universidade Aberta, Portugal

A volume in the Advances in Human Resources Management and Organizational Development (AHRMOD) Book Series

IGI Global
PUBLISHER of TIMELY KNOWLEDGE

Published in the United States of America by
IGI Global
Business Science Reference (an imprint of IGI Global)
701 E. Chocolate Avenue
Hershey PA, USA 17033
Tel: 717-533-8845
Fax: 717-533-8661
E-mail: cust@igi-global.com
Web site: http://www.igi-global.com

Library of Congress Cataloging-in-Publication Data

Names: Mamede, Henrique Pereira São, 1965- editor. | Santos, Arnaldo, 1965- editor.
Title: Creating learning organizations through digital transformation / edited by Henrique São Mamede, Arnaldo Santos.
Description: Hershey, PA : Information Science Reference, [2024] | Includes bibliographical references and index. | Summary: "This book presents the essential concepts for understanding the concept of learning organizations, its implementation, and its impact in a global digital transformation context"-- Provided by publisher.
Identifiers: LCCN 2023044074 (print) | LCCN 2023044075 (ebook) | ISBN 9798369305560 (hardcover) | ISBN 9798369305577 (paperback) | ISBN 9798369305584 (ebook)
Subjects: LCSH: Organizational learning. | Employees--Training of--Computer-assisted instruction.
Classification: LCC HD58.82 .C725 2024 (print) | LCC HD58.82 (ebook) | DDC 658.3/124--dc23/eng/20231020
LC record available at https://lccn.loc.gov/2023044074
LC ebook record available at https://lccn.loc.gov/2023044075

This book is published in the IGI Global book series Advances in Human Resources Management and Organizational Development (AHRMOD) (ISSN: 2327-3372; eISSN: 2327-3380)

British Cataloguing in Publication Data
A Cataloguing in Publication record for this book is available from the British Library.

Advances in Human Resources Management and Organizational Development (AHRMOD) Book Series

ISSN:2327-3372
EISSN:2327-3380

Editor-in-Chief: Patricia Ordóñez de Pablos, Universidad de Oviedo, Spain

MISSION

A solid foundation is essential to the development and success of any organization and can be accomplished through the effective and careful management of an organization's human capital. Research in human resources management and organizational development is necessary in providing business leaders with the tools and methodologies which will assist in the development and maintenance of their organizational structure.

The **Advances in Human Resources Management and Organizational Development (AHRMOD) Book Series** aims to publish the latest research on all aspects of human resources as well as the latest methodologies, tools, and theories regarding organizational development and sustainability. The **AHRMOD Book Series** intends to provide business professionals, managers, researchers, and students with the necessary resources to effectively develop and implement organizational strategies.

COVERAGE

- Entrepreneurialism
- Employee Evaluation
- Corporate Governance
- Diversity in the Workplace
- Organizational Behavior
- Human Resources Development
- Organizational Learning
- Collaborative Method
- Recruitment Process
- Coaching and Mentoring

The Advances in Human Resources Management and Organizational Development (AHRMOD) Book Series (ISSN 2327-3372) is published by IGI Global, 701 E. Chocolate Avenue, Hershey, PA 17033-1240, USA, www.igi-global.com. This series is composed of titles available for purchase individually; each title is edited to be contextually exclusive from any other title within the series. For pricing and ordering information please visit http://www.igi-global.com/book-series/advances-human-resources-management-organizational/73670. Postmaster: Send all address changes to above address.

Titles in this Series

For a list of additional titles in this series, please visit:
ttp://www.igi-global.com/book-series/advances-human-resources-management-organizational/73670

The Role of Leaders and Actors in Academy-Business Partnerships Issues of Risk, Trust, Power, Ethics, and Cooperation
Morgan R. Clevenger (Hiram College, USA) Mark Kretovics (Kent State University, USA) and Jessica Shepard Watts (University of North Texas, USA)
Business Science Reference • copyright 2024 • 310pp • H/C (ISBN: 9781668439166) • US $245.00 (our price)

Promoting Value Creation Through Organizational Effectiveness and Development
Thais González-Torres (Rey Juan Carlos University, Spain) and José-Luis Rodríguez-Sánchez (Rey Juan Carlos University, Spain)
Business Science Reference • copyright 2024 • 310pp • H/C (ISBN: 9781668484791) • US $250.00 (our price)

Cases on the Interplay Between Family, Society, and Entrepreneurship
Ethel Ndidiamaka Abe (SashBM LLC, USA) and Isaac Idowu Abe (SashBM LLC, USA)
Business Science Reference • copyright 2024 • 435pp • H/C (ISBN: 9781668487488) • US $240.00 (our price)

Leadership Strategies for Effective Diversity Management
Amdy Diene (Liberty University, USA)
Business Science Reference • copyright 2024 • 300pp • H/C (ISBN: 9798369310502) • US $250.00 (our price)

Women of Color and Hair Bias in the Work Environment
Kula A. Francis (University of the Virgin Islands, US Virgin Islands) and Anna M. Clarke (University of the Virgin Islands, US Virgin Islands)
Business Science Reference • copyright 2024 • 295pp • H/C (ISBN: 9781668487907) • US $245.00 (our price)

IGI Global
PUBLISHER of TIMELY KNOWLEDGE

701 East Chocolate Avenue, Hershey, PA 17033, USA
Tel: 717-533-8845 x100 • Fax: 717-533-8661
E-Mail: cust@igi-global.com • www.igi-global.com

Table of Contents

Detailed Table of Contents

Ecosystem learning is what most educational institutions strive for. However, new theoretical insights on learning have emerged over the past 20 years and a multitude of new digital learning technologies have entered the scene. Consequently, there is a need for new research on ecosystem learning, digital learning technologies and digital transformation. This chapter explores the realization of ecosystem learning through digital learning technologies and digital transformation and analyses and explores the potential of ecosystem learning. The chapter is based on a literature review of theoretical contributions on ecosystems, learning, and digital transformation, and two case studies from the Danish pharmaceutical industry and the Danish insurance industry. Based on the analysis, it was found that ecosystem learning seems to be a successful solution in many industry organizations and the two case studies seem to indicate that multi-tenancy learning platforms and digital transformation initiatives are part of the solution.

The global expansion of COVID-19 has had disastrous consequences, both in terms of health and economics. However, in society and in organisations, we witness positive examples of collaborative and innovative activities. This chapter addresses the problem of how employee response to the COVID-19 calamity through which sudden challenges and opportunities created by digital transformation in learning organisations. Existing research in digital transformation in learning organisations tend to focus on finding out how employees play their vital role in settling their preferences and accustom to unprecedented situation. However, there is enough evidence that researchers have approached the issue generally. Still, from employee perspective very few extant literatures have been available that to specifically digital transformation in learning organisations. The relationships that exist between the COVID-19 crisis and digital transformation in learning yet to explore in different extents and components.

Workplace digital transformation represents a "double disruption": the response to the digital transformation needs of the business, while simultaneously addressing the rapid technological changes that are reshaping work environments. Many organizations' performance and survival challenges require dynamic capabilities and tools to accelerate the acquisition of those capabilities. Considering this context, the idea of the workplace as a valuable learning environment has regained prominence, reflourishing the concept of a learning organization. In today's landscape, learning organizations should devise a technology-based mechanism to advance their organizational learning efforts. Learning technologies are positioned as an enabler that provides learning opportunities. This chapter navigates throughout the diverse learning technologies being used by organizations. In recognition of the vital role successful learning technology implementation plays in organizations, it also assesses the current state of implementations and outlines the primary strategies organizations should prioritize.

In this chapter the authors examine how AI applications support specific learning and training strategies in organizations, empowering individuals to develop their skills, allowing organizations to make data-driven decisions, and ensuring that learning is an ongoing and engaging process. Research shows that AI is an excellent instrument for learning in organizations as it aids in the preparation of instructional materials and helps learners progress in many different ways. So, there seems to be a need for a specific approach to AI pedagogy, which focuses not only on what AI can do but also on which learning activities and learning objectives can be supported by AI applications. As AI technology continues to advance, it will play an even more

In a global context of digital transformation, organisations have been challenged to embrace innovation and new technology and reviewed methodological approaches to enhance their digital learning ecosystems, including a systematic review of the internal value proposition of how people learn, share, and build new knowledge. The relationship between a learning organization, digital transformation, and digital learning is intertwined, as they are all interconnected and mutually reinforcing. Digital learning allows for integrating immersive learning experiences, personalized learning paths, and data-driven insights, which can drive performance improvements and foster innovation within the organization. This chapter aims to resume the main components an organization, and could promote an assessment and apply when designing digital learning content to support a broader digital learning strategy.

This study is concerned with learning organizations' multigenerational workforce and how gamification is essential for digital transformation and digital learning, once learning organizations understand how knowledge growth can affect the organization's long-term success and its culture and innovation. As an essential development and competitiveness, learning organizations are expanding to the digital learning in its culture, for employees develop their own interpersonal and soft skills, through collaborative work and better communication. The main aim of this study is to analyze through a literature review to understand how gamification is a potential problem solver for the multigenerational workforce in its digital learning and development. After a research background and literature review, the analysis shows that organizations with a multigenerational workforce have several benefits—while young employees share their digital skills, older employees share their experience and knowledge. Through gamification, employees increase their motivation, digital skills, and productivity.

In the ever-changing world of professional training, organizations constantly seek innovative methods to boost learning outcomes. A prominent approach gaining traction involves serious games, which merge play and education. Serious games offer immersive learning, encouraging active participation, problem-solving, and skill growth. Unlike conventional methods, they provide a safe space to practice real-world scenarios, fostering decision-making and consequence awareness. Serious games find applications in healthcare, military, engineering, and business. Despite benefits, evaluating and adapting serious games remains challenging. Effective assessment measures are needed, catering to diverse learners. The framework for adaptive serious games (F4ASG) aims to tackle these issues. Based on literature amd expert standpoints, the F4ASG is detailed, outlining dimensions and aspects. It's exemplified shedding light on improvements. An experiment demonstrates F4ASG's efficacy in real-world training. Design, participants, data collection, and analysis are explained, followed by result discussions.

To gain a competitive advantage in dynamic and complex environments, organizations are continuously seeking strategies. One such strategy is the emergence of learning organizations, which foster collective and collaborative learning. Effective communication plays a vital role within learning organizations as it facilitates the efficient exchange of knowledge and information. Moreover, with the advent of digitization, social media has become a widespread mode of communication even within the workplace. This chapter analyzes the impact of social media on intra-organizational communication in learning organizations. It explores how managers can choose appropriate communication platforms and discusses the potential positive and negative implications of social media on various aspects of learning organizations such as organizational effectiveness, structure, pattern, and content of communication. The researchers have proposed a model to assist managers in selecting suitable social media platforms based on situational demands. Furthermore, the chapter highlights areas for future research.

Preface

Welcome to *Creating Learning Organizations Through Digital Transformation*, a comprehensive exploration edited by Henrique S. Mamede and Arnaldo Santos. In today's ever-evolving landscape, organizations must adapt, innovate, and flourish within the global context of Digital Transformation.

Within this transformative environment, the significance of cultivating new contexts, innovative scenarios, and dynamic learning spaces has become increasingly apparent. Our collective consciousness has recognized the pivotal role of digital learning spaces, particularly within a Learning Organization (LO) framework. In an LO, individuals perpetually expand their capacities to achieve desired outcomes, fostering organic thinking patterns while cultivating a culture of continuous learning.

The bedrock of knowledge within these organizations lies in the amalgamation of data and information culled from digital content and sophisticated information systems. These resources' adept management and utilization demand specialized skills, driving the need for adeptness in their application. Embedded within the sphere of cutting-edge technologies like context-aware and immersive learning, personalized learning environments and artificial intelligence, these spaces redefine the learning process and its evolution.

This compilation stands as a guiding beacon, illuminating essential concepts that unravel the fabric of the Learning Organization, its implementation, and its profound impact within the global tapestry of digital transformation.

In presenting this book, we aim to catalyze and fortify ongoing research endeavours in constructing a robust Learning Organization within the landscape of Digital Transformation. This compilation caters to a diverse audience, encompassing researchers entrenched in Learning Organizations and Digital Transformation alongside practitioners and professionals seeking to integrate or apply these principles and concepts within real-world contexts.

The thematic spectrum covered in this book encompasses pivotal domains:

- People Capacities, Profiles, and Management
- Digital Contents

- Learning Technologies
- Learning Evaluation

We sincerely thank the contributors whose expertise and dedication have enriched this volume. May this compilation serve as a reservoir of knowledge and a catalyst for transformation, guiding individuals and organizations towards a future where learning is both perpetual and transformative.

ORGANIZATION OF THE BOOK

Chapter 1: Ecosystem Learning through Digital Transformation

Henrik Simonsen's chapter delves into the evolving landscape of ecosystem learning amidst the emergence of new digital learning technologies. This exploration spans theoretical insights, culminating in a deep analysis of ecosystem learning's potential. Supported by case studies from the Danish pharmaceutical and insurance industries, it unravels the success of ecosystem learning within organizational contexts, showcasing multi-tenancy learning platforms and digital transformation initiatives as integral components.

Chapter 2: Retorting to the COVID-19 Calamity: The Swift Turn Towards Digital Transformation in Learning Organizations

Praveen Kakada's chapter sheds light on the swift adaptation of learning organizations in response to the COVID-19 crisis. Focused on employees' roles and preferences amidst unprecedented challenges, this exploration highlights the underexplored nexus between the pandemic crisis and digital transformation within learning organizations.

Chapter 3: Revealing the Essentials of Learning Technologies: Guiding Learning Technologies Implementation in a Learning Organization

Helena Ferreira's contribution navigates the domain of workplace digital transformation, emphasizing its parallel response to business needs and technological shifts. With a spotlight on Learning Organizations, this chapter elucidates the pivotal role of Learning Technologies in fortifying organizational learning efforts. It offers insights into current implementations and strategic priorities for organizations.

Chapter 4: AI Transformation for Learning in Organizations

Authored by José Bidarra and Cláudia Neves, this chapter investigates AI applications' role in bolstering organizational learning strategies. It examines AI's contributions to skill development, data-driven decision-making, and continuous learning, advocating for a humanistic approach to integrating AI within pedagogy.

Chapter 5: Learning Technologies: Chatbots to Support Personalized Learning

The collaborative work by Daina Gudoniene, Tomas Blazauskas, Rita Butkiene, Lina Ceponiene, and Evelina Staneviciene spotlights chatbots as personalized learning assistants. Focusing on their impact on educational quality and student support, it assesses chatbot functionalities based on six parameters, emphasizing their communication and interaction capabilities.

Chapter 6: Learning Analytics Impact for Learning Evaluation in the Context of Creating Learning Organizations

João Dias' exploration delves into learning analytics' significance in evaluating learning within organizations undergoing digital transformation. Examining its potential to inform decision-making and enhance learning outcomes, this chapter presents case studies to underscore successful implementations and outlines future directions in the field.

Chapter 7: Designing Digital Learning Content to Support a Corporate Digital Learning Strategy

Lucia Moreira's chapter unravels the intricate relationship between digital learning content and organizational digital strategies. It emphasizes integrating immersive experiences and data-driven insights within digital learning ecosystems, fostering performance improvements and innovation.

Chapter 8: The Potential of Gamification in the Multigenerational Learning Organizations

Iolanda Bernardino's study scrutinizes the intersection of gamification and multigenerational learning within organizations undergoing digital transformation. It highlights gamification's role in fostering digital skills, motivation, and productivity and elucidates how diverse generations contribute to a dynamic learning culture.

Chapter 9: Improving Learning and Engagement in Professional Training Using Serious Games

Authored by Alvaro Pistono, this chapter explores the integration of Serious Games in professional training for enhanced learning outcomes. It presents a Framework for Adaptive Serious Games (F4ASG) and demonstrates its efficacy in real-world training scenarios.

Chapter 10: Organizational Communication: The Impact of Social Media as a Mode of Communication on Learning Organizations

Divya Suresh and Ujjal Mukherjee's chapter examines social media's influence on intra-organizational communication within learning organizations. Exploring its implications on organizational effectiveness, communication patterns, and managerial strategies, it proposes a model to aid managers in selecting suitable social media platforms.

Chapter 11: Didactic Knowledge (DK) eLearning Optimizing Digital Strategies for the Continuous Pedagogical Training of Trainers

Authored by Daniela Barros, Ana de Jesus Ferreira Nobre, Antonio Chenoll Mora, and Paula Valente da Silva, this chapter scrutinizes digital strategies for continuous pedagogical training in vocational settings. It fills the research gap in vocational training's digital transformation, emphasizing the need for innovative strategies facilitating effective learning paradigms.

IN SUMMARY

As we draw the curtains on this meticulously curated compendium, *Creating Learning Organizations Through Digital Transformation,* we find ourselves immersed in a narrative that transcends conventional learning and organizational evolution paradigms.

This collaborative endeavour, spearheaded by esteemed scholars and experts, unveiled an intricate tapestry woven from digital transformation and organizational learning threads. Each chapter serves as a testament to digital technologies' profound impact and potential in fostering learning ecosystems within organizations navigating the tumultuous seas of change.

From the exploration of ecosystem learning to the swift adaptation prompted by the COVID-19 crisis, from the pivotal role of learning technologies to integrating AI and chatbots for personalized learning experiences, these chapters resonate as guiding beacons illuminating the path toward transformative organizational learning.

The holistic approach embedded within these chapters transcends mere technological discourse; it encapsulates the essence of human-centric learning, emphasizing the convergence of technology and humanity in creating enriched learning environments. The chapters underscore the essence of fostering engagement and innovation, whether through gamification fostering multigenerational learning or the integration of serious games in professional training.

Moreover, the discourse on communication through social media within learning organizations and the innovative strategies proposed for continuous pedagogical training in vocational settings further accentuate the multifaceted nature of digital transformation in learning.

This compendium serves as a repository of knowledge and a catalyst for progressive thought, urging us to traverse the uncharted territories of digital transformation within organizational learning.

As editors, we are grateful to the erudite contributors whose intellectual prowess has enriched this compendium. May this culmination of insights and scholarly explorations serve as a cornerstone for scholars, practitioners, and visionaries alike, embarking on a journey to shape the learning organizations of tomorrow in an ever-evolving digital landscape.

In the digital transformation continuum, let these pages stand as a testament to the endless possibilities and the unwavering resilience of human ingenuity in fostering learning organizations that thrive amidst change and transformation.

Warmest regards,

Henrique S. Mamede
INESC-TEC, Universidade Aberta, Portugal

Arnaldo Santos
Universidade Aberta, Portugal

Chapter 1
Ecosystem Learning Through Digital Transformation

Henrik Køhler Simonsen
Copenhagen Business School, Denmark

ABSTRACT

Ecosystem learning is what most educational institutions strive for. However, new theoretical insights on learning have emerged over the past 20 years and a multitude of new digital learning technologies have entered the scene. Consequently, there is a need for new research on ecosystem learning, digital learning technologies and digital transformation. This chapter explores the realization of ecosystem learning through digital learning technologies and digital transformation and analyses and explores the potential of ecosystem learning. The chapter is based on a literature review of theoretical contributions on ecosystems, learning, and digital transformation, and two case studies from the Danish pharmaceutical industry and the Danish insurance industry. Based on the analysis, it was found that ecosystem learning seems to be a successful solution in many industry organizations and the two case studies seem to indicate that multi-tenancy learning platforms and digital transformation initiatives are part of the solution.

1. INTRODUCTION AND PROBLEM

Theoretical considerations on learning organizations (Senge, 1990), experiential learning (Kolb, 1984) and action learning (Revans, 1982) remain relevant for modern organizations - even in the "age of AI" (Gates, 2023).

Learning agility, learning ability and the ability to change and adapt are crucial for organizations because learning is the precondition for innovation, business

DOI: 10.4018/979-8-3693-0556-0.ch001

development, and survival, and in an increasingly complex disruptive business environment (Christensen, 2013) based on exponential digital technologies (Downes & Mui, 2000), organizational learning and innovation performance are crucial disciplines.

The pivotal question is how organizations realize that potential. Research combining theories on ecosystems (Adner, 2012), cf. (Simonsen 2019, 2020, 2021) and (Simonsen & Walther, 2021), digital transformation (Vial, 2019) and action learning (Revans, 1982, 2011) and digital learning (Salmon, 2013) and (Clark & Mayer, 2016), seem to indicate that part of the solution is ecosystem learning accelerated by digital transformation initiatives.

The purpose of this chapter is to explore the holy trinity of ecosystem theory, learning theory and digital transformation further. The research objective of this chapter is consequently to analyse, discuss and reflect on the concept of ecosystem learning (Simonsen, 2019) as a tool to create not only learning organizations but also entire learning industries. The chapter will address the following research questions:

- what characterizes ecosystem learning?
- how does ecosystem learning facilitate organizational and industry learning?
- how is ecosystem learning achieved through digital transformation and digital learning?

Companies and organizations spend huge amounts of money on different types of employee training and competence development, but in fact most organizations are mere victims of what might be called the great training robbery. Training and competence development no doubt have a positive effect, however, researchers have so far not been able to empirically demonstrate to which degree, cf. (Garavan et al., 2020), who report on the training effectiveness based on a very comprehensive literature review.

Consequently, there is a need for additional research and new and more holistic approaches in this area to make sure that training efforts lead to function-specific and value-adding knowledge, skills and character, cf. (Fadel et al., 2015:78). The purpose of this chapter is to do just that and focus on ecosystem learning.

2. METHODOLOGY AND DATA

This paper subscribes to a constructionist research philosophy (Saunders et al., 2019), which entails that an interpretative and social-constructivist analysis of the two cases from the corporate educational sector has been applied.

The first methodological approach taken is a thematic analysis of relevant literature, cf. (Saunders et al., 2019) focusing on a combinatorial approach to selected theories on ecosystems theory, cf. for example (Adner, 2012) and (Weill & Woerner, 2018), on learning theory cf. for example (Revans, 1982, 2011), (Kolb, 1984), (Salmon, 2013), (Fadel et al., 2015) and (Simonsen, 2019) and on digital transformation and digital business models, cf. (Vial, 2019), (Weill & Woerner, 2018), and (Simonsen, 2020, 2021).

The second methodological approach taken is a case study presenting key findings from two live cases from the Danish corporate sector, in which the author of this chapter has played a role. The chapter thus draws on case data from two comprehensive live case studies. The first case study is from the Danish pharmaceutical industry where the first ecosystem learning model was developed and implemented by the industry association's learning department in 2008-2014. The case will be referred to as (ATRIUM). The second case study is from the Danish insurance industry where the second ecosystem learning model is being implemented by the industry association's learning department in 2022-2023. The case will be referred to as (FOAK).

3. UNDERSTANDING ECOSYSTEMS, LEARNING AND DIGITAL TRANSFORMATION

This section of the chapter offers a thematical analysis of relevant theoretical literature combining three overall theoretical areas: ecosystem theory, learning theory and digital transformation. The three theoretical gear wheels form the theoretical basis of this chapter.

3.1. Ecosystem Theory

The first part of the theoretical foundation is the concept of ecosystems and adoption chains as suggested and successfully demonstrated by (Drucker, 1994), (Osterwalder & Pigneur, 2010), (Osterwalder et al., 2014), (Adner, 2012) and (Weill & Woerner, 2018) to be able to develop an understanding of the concept of ecosystems.

It all starts with Milton Friedman, who is quoted to have said "the business of business is business" and that is no doubt true. But then again. Time has shown that there is so much more to it. Drucker, for example, presents the notion of "the theory of the business", cf. (Drucker, 1994), which in so many ways is the predecessor of modern business model research. Drucker explored how organizations work and why some succeed while others fail. Drucker argued that all organizations are based on a specific set of assumptions about its market and customers etc. and this is often referred to as "the theory of the business". In continuation of that this chapter uses the valuable theoretical considerations on value-creation and business models and the seminal theories "value proposition canvas" and "business model canvas" cf. for example (Osterwalder & Pigneur, 2010) and (Osterwalder et al., 2014). The two canvases suggested by (Osterwalder & Pigneur, 2010) and (Osterwalder et al., 2014) have been hugely successful all over the world and are also relevant for this discussion. Because an ecosystem learning model is also based on value-creation focus and a clear focus on the right value proposition to the individual partners in an ecosystem.

This leads to perhaps the two most important theoretical contributions when trying to understand ecosystem learning models. The first one is (Adner, 2012). The seminal book by Ron Adner called "The Wide Lens" has also had a huge impact on innovation and business modelling. (Adner, 2012) makes a very strong case for applying a wide-lens perspective on both innovation and business strategy. Adner argues that it is not only about execution. It is about conceiving and applying ecosystem ideas and principles. Adner's understanding of ecosystems is later explored further and was five years later called "ecosystem as structure" cf. (Adner, 2017). In fact, (Adner, 2012) talks about "internal and external ecosystems all around you" and suggests three steps. First, it is about "seeing the ecosystem", cf. (Adner, 2012:13-79), next it is about "mapping the ecosystem", cf. (Adner, 2012: 83-160) and finally "winning the game" by changing the game and reconfiguring the ecosystem to work for you, cf. (Adner, 2012: 161-234) and Adner even presents "five levers of ecosystem reconfiguration" as shown below (Adner, 2012: 176-178):

- *Separate – what can be separated?*
- *Combine – what can be combined?*
- *Relocate – what can be relocated?*
- *Add – what can be added?*
- *Subtract – what can be subtracted?*

According to Adner applying the five levers will create a new blueprint for the ecosystem where most bottlenecks are eliminated, paving the way for a successful ecosystem. As will appear below Adner's understanding of an ecosystem as "ecosystem as structure" is quite useful for the understanding of ecosystem learning models because it is in fact about changing the game and making sure that all parties stand to gain.

Finally, the other seminal theory on ecosystems is the digital business model framework developed and presented in the very famous book "What's your digital business model", cf. (Weill & Woerner, 2018). Based on an empirical analysis involving many businesses, the two authors found that digitization is changing business models on two dimensions: from value chains to ecosystems and from a fuzzy understanding of customer needs to a well-defined and clear understanding of their needs.

This is shown in the digital business model framework, which clearly shows that an ecosystem approach seems to be much stronger than existing business models. The digital business model framework consists of four distinct business models as illustrated below, cf. (Weill & Woerner, 2018:7-8):

- *Supplier – producer that sells through other enterprises.*
- *Omnichannel – integrated value chain that creates multiproduct, multichannel experiences to address life events.*
- *Modular producer – provider of plug-and-play products or services.*
- *Ecosystem driver – organizer of an ecosystem, a coordinated network of enterprises, devices, and customers to create value for all participants.*

The digital business model framework is extremely useful in this analysis because it empirically demonstrates that "moving right and up" in the framework – that is – securing maximum control of the entire business design of the ecosystem (price, quality, participants etc.) and securing maximum knowledge of the end customer (identity, purchase history etc.) is the right thing to do. In other words, according to this framework an organization should strive to become "ecosystem driver". As will appear later, this very approach was in fact used in both case studies.

3.2. Learning Theory

The chapter furthermore draws on theoretical contributions on several theoretical contributions from the realm of learning. The first extremely important concept of relevance for the design of ecosystem learning models is the theoretical concept "action learning", cf. (Revans, 1982) and (Revans, 2011). The concept of action learning was first mentioned in a report on the British coalmining industry in 1945 and assumes that the best learning occurs when learners actively engage in problem-solving and reflection and that learning takes place when learners apply what they have learned by working with real-life problems or cases. Revans "resisted any single definition of action learning" according to (Pedler, 2016:9), but after almost 30 years he did formulate the "learning equation", which in all its simplicity is thought-provoking and very useful. In the seminal book ABC of Action Learning (Revans, 2011), Revans formulated the *"learning equation"* as follows (Revans, 2011:8-10):

$$L = P + Q$$

So according to (Revans, 2011) learning (L) takes place when programmed knowledge (P) is facilitated by questioning insights (Q). Revans elaborated on the learning equation by defining 20 assumptions of action learning, including the following selected assumptions *"1. Learning is cradled in the task", "2. Formal instructions are not enough", "4. Learning involves doing", "9. Learning as re-interpretating past experience", "10. The contribution of peers", "14. Learning with and from each other"*, cf. (Revans, 2011: 8-11). The analysis and discussion below will show that ecosystem learning models are based on a bit more complex learning equation.

Action learning is pivotal for ecosystem learning and plays a dominant role in corporate or industry learning. As will be demonstrated later through the cases, action learning is indeed what takes place in both cases and facilitates value-adding, function-specific learning. Action learning is not a new idea, as the ancient Greek writer Sophocles (5th century BCE) said: *'One must learn by doing the thing, for though you think you know it, you have no certainty until you try'.*

In relation to action learning, concepts like "organizational learning", "single-loop – double learning", "experiential learning", "the learning organization", "situated learning", and "core competences" cf. (Argyris & Schøn, 1978), (Argyris, 1990, 1991), (Kolb, 1984), (Senge, 1990), (Lave & Wenger, 1991), and (Prahalad & Hamel, 1990) remain relevant. As will appear later from the cases all these concepts and theories can in fact be used to explain how ecosystem learning is based on ideas such as double loop learning (Argyris & Schøn, 1978), "situated learning" (Lave & Wenger, 1991) and the "learning organization" (Senge, 1990).

The third element of the learning theory section is theories on digital learning, which to a very high extent in fact is an important element of digital transformation, see 3.3 below. As will appear later, many digital learning theories and approaches do qualify as digital transformation processes and the concept of Virtual Action Learning in fact combines action learning with digital learning, cf. also (Dickenson et al., 2010), who define virtual action learning as *"action learning which takes place in a virtual environment... via a range of enabling, interactive and collaborative communication technologies*".

Also (Laurillard, 2002, 2012) and later (Fung, 2014) are very important as these contributions have influenced the way we teach and learn at many institutions of higher education in Europe. Fung's work for example, paved the way for the concept of a "Connected Curriculum", which later was perfected by (Perovic & Young, 2015), who designed a 90-minute hands-on workshop approach to curriculum design. This work is very relevant for the development of an ecosystem learning model, as it includes thoughts on how to include external stakeholders in learning, cf. (Fung, 2014: 4-5) who defines the connected curriculum framework as *"a framework designed to be a catalyst for sharing excellent practices already taking place in higher education institutions and stimulating new creative ideas for enriching the curriculum and the wider student experience"*. Later (Fadel et al., 2015) introduced the "4D Framework", which now seems to be the preferred learning design architecture in the world as it encompasses *"Knowledge, Character, Skills and Meta-Learning"* and prepares learners for the 21st century, cf. (Fadel et al., 2015: 78).

Another very relevant part of this theory section, are the very useful theoretical contributions on digital learning and teaching. Here especially two seminal books are crucial. The first is (Salmon, 2013), which has been the foundation of most first-generation digital learning and teaching. Gilly Salmons Five Stage Model and Carpe Diem approach provide a framework for a structured approach to online learning and is used internationally as a useful scaffold for a structured use of what Salmon calls "e-tivities", cf. (Salmon, 2013: 5-35). The second seminal book is "e-Learning and the Science of Instruction" by (Clark & Mayer, 2016). Clark & Mayer's book is also very useful as it presents proven guidelines on how to design modern learning resources applying a total of 67 guidelines, (Clark & Mayer, 2016: 396-401).

Finally, the scalability possibilities of digital learning need to be addressed, cf. (Simonsen, 2019, 2020 and 2021). Digital learning resources inherently have some important transformative characteristics. Development of digital learning resources can be based on the simple but very important principles of specialization and division of labour, which means we will be able to benefit from economies of scale, reduce costs and increase output. The learning value chain can thus be divided in three or four expert roles each specializing in this role. Furthermore, digital learning can be scaled. This means we can scale scarce teaching resources such as hyper specialist roles. If for example we need to educate millions of people fast in a profession with scarce teaching resources, the only viable solution is digital learning, cf. (Simonsen & Walther, 2021) for different scalability models. In summary, digital learning is inherently scalable and is in fact a very good example of digital transformation, which is the topic of the next subsection.

3.3. Digital Transformation

Finally, the chapter draws on theory on digital transformation (DT) and digital business models (DBM). First, it is necessary to define what is understood by DT. Defining DT is no doubt a daunting task as demonstrated by (Vial, 2019), who reviewed 282 works on digital transformation and found 23 unique definitions of DT, cf. (Vial, 2019:120). This chapter will be using a definition offered by (Vial, 2019:121) as follows: *"a process that aims to improve an entity by triggering significant changes to its properties through combinations of information, computing, communication, and connectivity technologies"*.

This conceptual definition is relevant and appropriate for this analysis, as the definition is suitable for identifying and discussing the properties of digital transformation facilitating successful change in an organization.

The analysis and discussion will also draw on established theoretical considerations on concepts like digital strategies for disruptive technologies such as (Christensen, 2013), whose definition and understanding of the concept of "disruption" has had a huge influence in the fields of innovation and business. In this chapter, the concept of "disruption" does play a role, because a learning ecosystem model is in fact seen as an incumbent business model, which in fact challenges existing business models. Another aspect of interest is the concept *"Law of Disruption"* as coined by (Downes & Mui, 2000). (Downes & Mui, 2000) argue that the law of disruption means that technologies are inherently exponential, and that societies, organizations and people develop incrementally. This perspective is also crucial for this discussion as the combination of a disruptive business model with disruptive technologies, such as digital learning technologies, together become the secret sauce that many organizations are looking for.

(Simonsen, 2020, 2021) and (Simonsen & Walther, 2021) discuss the huge potential of combining digital learning technologies with digital transformation approaches and make a very strong case for the disruptive potential of building digital learning on the principles of specialization and scalability. As will appear later, this also seems to play an important role for the understanding of disruptive ecosystem learning models. Finally, seminal theories on digital business models and ecosystems are included as demonstrated by (Weill & Woerner, 2018). (Weill & Woerner, 2018) present a very useful digital business model based on ecosystem theory, and this approach also plays an important role in the understanding of digital transformation.

4. PRESENTING THE TWO CASE STUDIES

This section of the chapter outlines two specially selected case studies of interest for this discussion. The first case study describes the business model or the learning ecosystem model from the Danish pharmaceutical industry.

5. TOWARDS AN UNDERSTANDING OF ECOSYSTEM LEARNING MODELS

This first part of this section addresses the first research question *"what characterizes ecosystem learning"?* Obviously, the discussion draws on theoretical considerations and on insights and experiences from the two case studies.

As is the case in many innovation projects the role of technology has also played a defining role in the development of the ecosystem learning model below and it

Table 1. Case study overview of ATRIUM

Logo	atrium
Link	https://www.atriumcph.com/
Professional area	Pharmaceutical industry
Industry characteristics	A large proportion of the learners in the pharmaceutical industry already have different types of MSc educations from primarily the scientific, technical, engineering, or medical fields. The other group of learners typically have other types of educations from various fields and have been reschooled at Atrium. Atrium offers industry-recognized educational programmes designed for pharmaceutical representatives, market access professionals and of also scientifically grounded programmes on regulatory affairs, pharmaceutical, research & development and good manufacturing processes. Atrium's industry-recognized programmes are seen by the industry as "license to operate" and a degree from Atrium is a prerogative for working in the pharmaceutical industry. The Danish pharmaceutical industry is also characterized by the fact that staff are constantly required to maintain training standards, which means that companies have large training budgets for both internal and external training.
Degree of regulation	The pharmaceutical industry is highly regulated by both national and international guidelines.
Ownership	Atrium is owned by the industry organization The Danish Association of the Pharmaceutical Industry (Lif). Lif is owned by the 41 member companies some of which include some of the world's largest pharmaceutical companies.
Business model	The business model might be described as an internal group-based business model. Profits made by the educational department Atrium are channelled back to the Lif Group. The underlying idea is to use the strong position held by the Lif Group to sell educational services to the pharmaceutical industry and to create a strong ecosystem. The profits made are then used to run the Danish Association of the Pharmaceutical Industry, which effectively is a powerful lobby organization.
Partners/ecosystem	Atrium is part of a very strong and almost impenetrable ecosystem. The first partner in the ecosystem setup are the 41 pharmaceutical industries. These pharmaceutical industries populate the Board and several important advisory boards in the different areas. Experts from the pharmaceutical industries are also affiliated with Atrium as external teachers and programme managers. The second partner in the ecosystem are the Danish Medicines Agency (DMA), the Danish Health Authority (DHA) and other official authorities in the health and pharmaceutical fields. These official bodies populate advisory boards and are widely used as external teachers and programme managers at Atrium. The third partner in the ecosystem are the patient organizations. Board members from the patient organizations have increasingly been involved in Atrium's operations and experts from the patient organizations are affiliated with Atrium as external teachers and programme managers. The fourth partner in the ecosystem is the parent company Lif, which is a very powerful industry organization in Denmark. Rumour has it that Lif has been the author of large parts of the health programmes of different governments throughout the last 25 years. Lif and Atrium together are the ecosystem driver and to a very high degree dictate both business design and customer relations. The physical manifestation of this role can be seen in the Life Science House which is the physical campus of Atrium. Stakeholder analyses show that the 6P understanding still holds. The following six Ps are part of Atrium's stakeholder landscape: Prescribers (medical doctors), Producers (pharmaceutical companies), Providers (pharmacies), Patients (patient organizations), Politicians (Key Opinion Leaders and Regulators) and the Press.

Table 2. Case study overview of FOAK

Logo	FORSIKRINGS AKADEMIET
Link	https://www.forsikringsakademiet.dk/
Professional area	Insurance industry
Industry characteristics	Many of the learners in the insurance industry have no formal academic educations such as a bachelor or a master. Instead, they hold professional educations such as certified claims adjusters etc. FOAK is de facto the only institution of education for the insurance industry and in fact FOAK holds a monopoly position in the Danish insurance or pension industry. FOAK is the only place where learners in the 139 member companies can be licensed to operate as most of the companies require their staff to hold certificates or diplomas from FOAK. FOAK's educations are recognized in the industry. y as the industry standard and are seen as "license to operate". FOAK's highest levels of education equal a bachelor's degree and all FOAK's educations have in fact been accredited by the Danish Accreditation Institution and the NQF. As was the case with the pharmaceutical industry, the insurance industry is also highly regulated and training standards in fact dictate the training standards required in the industry.
Degree of regulation	The insurance industry is regulated by both national and international guidelines.
Ownership	FOAK is a Danish limited company (A/S) owned by the 139 insurance and pension companies in Denmark.
Business model	Customers from the 139 member companies buy entire education programs, courses, conferences, seminars etc. from FOAK. Each member company gets an annual discount based on the total amount it has spent at FOAK. This way the companies enjoy considerable shareholder benefits. The profits are thus partly channelled back to the shareholders in the form of reduced prices on function-based training and partly on running the entire academy on behalf of the entire industry.
Partners/ecosystem	FOAK is part of a very strong and almost impenetrable ecosystem. The first and most important partner in the ecosystem are the 139 insurance and pension companies, which 70 years ago decided to establish the Insurance Academy (FOAK). The companies are also shareholders in FOAK and populate the Board and all professional advisory boards. Insurance experts from the many shareholding companies are affiliated with FOAK as external teachers and examiners. The second partner in the ecosystem is FOAK itself. FOAK is a quite powerful company and plays a dominant and trendsetting role for all companies in the industry. FOAK is the only place staff can be trained and FOAK plays a monopoly role in the training area.

might even be argued that the learning management system used seems to be the facilitator unfolding the digital transformation.

Figure 1. Digital business model (DBM) framework, cf
(Weill & Woerner, 2018: 8)

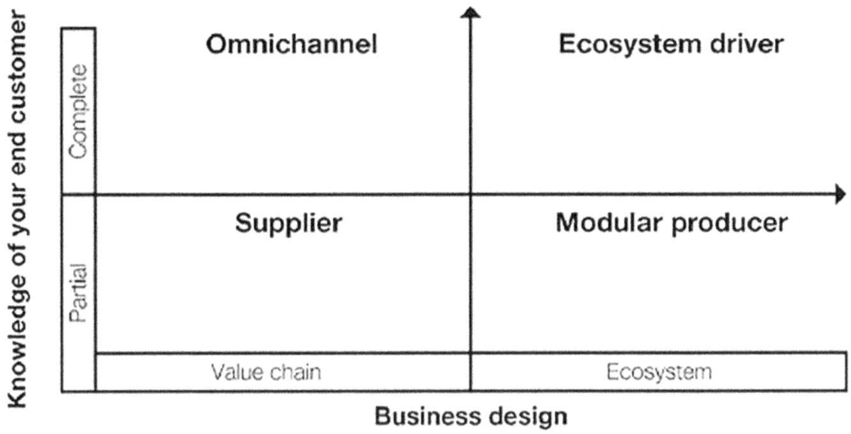

Teece for example, views an ecosystem as a *"community of organizations, institutions, and individuals that impact the enterprise and the enterprise's customers and supplies"*, cf. (Teece, 2007: 1325). Teece thus views the ecosystem as an economic community of interacting actors that all affect each other through their activities, considering all relevant actors beyond the boundaries of a single industry.

Teece's definition is no doubt useful, but it is argued that it should be extended when it comes to discussing ecosystem learning models. Ecosystem learning models are also based on transformative digital learning technologies and job function-focused digital learning theories and content, cf. for example (Salmon, 2013) and (Simonsen & Walther, 2021). Adner uses the expression *"ecosystem as structure"*, cf. (Adner 2007), which in fact might be more relevant for this discussion.

Adner also argues for the *"five levers of ecosystem reconfiguration"*, cf. (Adner, 2012:176-178) and as will appear from the suggested model below, I have used the *"combine"* and *"add"* levers. Finally, Weill & Woerner's digital business model framework is extremely useful when answering the research question. As is the case with both case studies the two industry organizations seek to become the drivers of the ecosystem, which can be illustrated by means of Weill & Woerner's digital business model framework, cf. (Weill & Woerner, 2018: 8):

Weill & Woerner researched many companies and found that most companies can be characterized by means of the 2X2 framework as shown in Figure 1. On the vertical axis we have "Knowledge of your end customer" and on the horizontal axis we have "Business Design" (that is influence on the ecosystem, prices, contracts, architecture etc.).

By means of all these theoretical considerations the first elements of an ecosystem learning model are revealed. Both ATRIUM and FOAK seek to be the ecosystem drivers of the ecosystem. FOAK for example has to some extent been an ecosystem driver for many years as it has used its own tailor-made and very customer-centric learning management platform for many years. However, it was not until the company decided to invest in a multi-tenancy learning management platform that the degree of business design influence increased dramatically, placing it in the ecosystem driver quadrant in Figure 1.

Another important element in our understanding of ecosystem learning models is the power of the right pedagogic choices. Both ATRIUM and FOAK are industry organizations educating people for specific job functions. This means that we need to apply the right learning theories. At FOAK for example, the learning philosophy upon which all teaching activities rest, is based on "action learning", cf. (Revans, 1982, 2011), "social learning", cf. (Salmon, 2013) and (Fung, 2014) and workplace learning (which theoretically is referred to as "situated learning, cf. (Lave & Wenger, 1991). Finally, all teaching activities are based on real-life examples from the insurance and pension fund companies, in other words, job function-relevant cases and examples are used. Finally, FOAK totally dominate the "ecosystem driver" quadrant as it also has its own monopoly publishing unit, publishing the authoritative learning materials in the insurance and pension fund fields.

In conclusion, and to understand ecosystem learning and answer the first research question all these theoretical considerations and insights may be expressed in the ecosystem learning equation as follows:

EL = ASKC

Based on this study, ecosystem learning (EL) equals acquired skills, knowledge, and character (ASKC).

- Skills are defined as *"How we use what we know"*.
- Knowledge is defined as *"What we know and understand" and*
- Behaviour is defined as *"How we behave and engage in the world"*.

The elements skills, knowledge and behaviour are all important elements of the seminal 4D Framework model by (Fadel et al., 2015:78) and are used here to explain the complexity of what ecosystem learning is. Skills, knowledge, and behaviour can be acquired through formal education (such as an entire education or degree), training (such as on-the-job training or an online course) or mere life experience (which is acquired through working with and solving problems). The last and perhaps most important element of ecosystem learning is meta-learning, cf. (Fadel et al., 2015:78), which is defined as *"How we reflect and adapt"*. So professional

Figure 2. Ecosystem learning model for FOAK

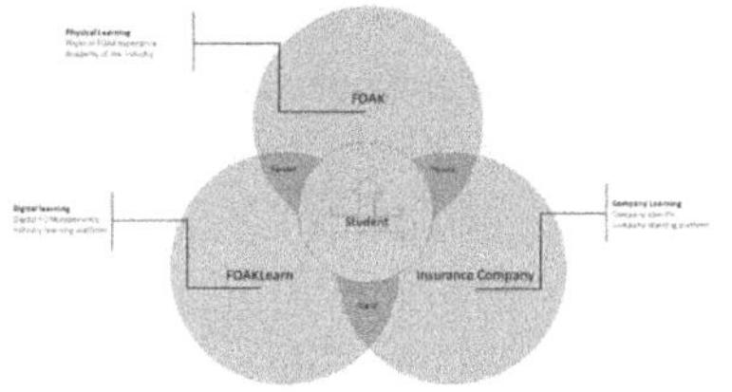

ecosystem learning aims at providing learning with the necessary skills, knowledge, behaviour, and meta-learning abilities to be able to operate in a professional arena.

However, it is not as simple as that. The acquired skills (AS) are acquired in an ecosystem, based on three overall elements: learning theories, digital tools, and capability utilization, which might be expressed as follows:

ASKC = (AL+SL+WL+FC) x (PLT+DLT) x (PCT+DCT+CT)

In other words, this means that acquired skills (AS) are acquired through action learning (AL) + social learning (SL) + workplace learning (WL) + job function-related learning content (FC) x physical learning technologies (PLT) + digital learning technologies (DLT) x physical capability transfer (PCT) + digital capability transfer (DCT) + content transfer (CT).

When both expressions are combined, FOAK's ecosystem learning equation can thus be expressed as follows:

EL = ASKC x (AL+SL+WL+FC) x (PLT+DLT) x (PCT+DCT+CT)

In practice, a simple ecosystem learning model for FOAK may thus look like this:

As will appear, the model developed for FOAK might be described as *"ecosystem as structure"*, cf. (Adner 2017) as it both encompasses the physical academy campus, the 139 insurance and pension fund companies and the digital academy campus FOAKlearn. This simple ecosystem learning model ensures that the student can both acquire the required skills through physical learning at the insurance academy FOAK, as company or workplace learning in the 139 insurance and pension fund companies or as digital learning at the digital campus FOAKlearn.

This second part of this section addresses the second research question *"how does ecosystem learning facilitate organizational and industry learning"?*

First, we need to take a closer look at concepts like *"organizational learning"*, cf. (Argyris & Schøn, 1978), the *"learning organization"*, cf. (Senge, 1990) and *"communities of practice"*, cf. (Wenger, 1998).

Argyris & Schøn identified two types of learning – single-loop learning and double-loop learning. Single-loop learning occurs when an organization detects and corrects a mistake without changing its underlying policies and objectives, but double-loop learning occurs when an organization questions and modifies its policies and objectives considering the mistake made. It is argued that the type of ecosystem learning proposed above does safeguard effect double-loop learning, as students work with real-life examples and cases enabling them to question and modify the processes already in place. This is in fact done through "social learning" and *"communities of practice"* as suggested by (Wenger, 1998) as all learning at FOAK takes place in small teams. Building communities of practice and facilitating social learning also supports organizational learning and "externalization" of the acquired skills, as described in the seminal SECI-model, cf. (Nonaka, 1994).

Finally, ecosystem learning facilitates organizational or even industry learning because it allows organizations or even industries to acquire new skills rapidly and effortlessly. As Weill & Woerner point out, a digital competitive advantage is often acquired by focusing on the customer experience including for example *"including digitized business processes that the customer uses"*, cf. (Weill & Woerner, 2018:67), which means that the platform upon which organizational learning takes place is crucial. As already indicated, technology plays a crucial role in the suggested ecosystem learning model. The use of a multi-tenancy learning management platform such as Moodle Workplace is pivotal for enabling all insurance and pension fund companies access to a digital insurance academy.

In conclusion, the answer to the second research question is that ecosystem learning dramatically facilitates and supports organizational learning or even industry learning, because of its multi-disciplinary focus on both ecosystem theory, learning theory and transformative digital technologies.

The third and final research question is *"how is ecosystem learning achieved through digital transformation and digital learning"?*

The transformative nature of digital technology is crucial and as will appear from Vial's definition above, digital transformation is about triggering significant changes to processes by combining new information and facilitating access and use of new information by means of new technologies. This is exactly what takes place when a multi-tenancy learning platform is used. The advantage of using a multi-tenancy learning management platform is that it can easily be scaled to meet the needs of your own organization and the other partners of the learning ecosystem. Some of the benefits of a multi-tenancy learning platforms include:

- Segregation of Data: Each tenant's data, including user accounts, courses, content, and progress, is kept separate from others. This ensures data privacy and security for each organization. This advantage is very important in the FOAK case study, which uses Moodle Workplace.
- Centralized Management: Despite separate data, the platform provides a centralized management interface that allows administrators from each organization to manage their respective content, users, and settings. This

is also seen the FOAK case study as FOAK offers many courses in what is called Shared Space. These courses can be accessed by all subscribing insurance and pension fund companies. However, all subscribers can also design and access their own courses at their own Tenant.

- Cost Efficiency: By sharing the same infrastructure, hardware, and software resources, the cost of maintaining and hosting the platform can be significantly reduced compared to each organization running its own separate system.
- Scalability: The platform can be easily scaled to accommodate the growing user base of multiple organizations without the need for major overhauls or additional infrastructure investment. This is in fact also seen in the FOAK case study, as specific tenants are rented out to trusted partners outside the insurance industry.
- Customization: Depending on the platform's design, each tenant might have the ability to customize their branded learning environment, upload their own content, and configure settings according to their requirements. This is also the case in the FOAK case study as several of the 139 shareholding companies have started customizing their own tenant installations.
- Collaboration and Sharing: In some cases, the platform might provide opportunities for collaboration and sharing of resources between tenants, fostering a sense of community and knowledge exchange.
- User Management: Each organization can manage its own users, assign roles, track progress, and monitor engagement within their courses and training programs.
- Integration: The platform can often integrate with other tools and systems used by the organizations, such as HR systems, content management systems, and analytics tools. This in fact is also one of the very important features of FOAKlearn as all HR managers can access exam and test results directly from their own tenants.
- Updates and Maintenance: Platform updates, improvements, and maintenance tasks can be handled centrally, ensuring that all tenants benefit from the latest features and security enhancements.
- Support: Technical support and assistance can be provided to tenants from a centralized support team, reducing the burden on individual organizations.

The multi-tenancy platform combined with the right learning philosophy can thus be used by both individual companies and entire industries to support organizational learning and attain ecosystem learning benefits, because the very scalability of multi- tenancy platforms enables industries to pool their innovation investments and speed up development processes significantly. As soon as a course is done it can be published in the Shared Space of the multi-tenancy platform allowing

Figure 3. Multi-tenancy learning platform model for FOAK

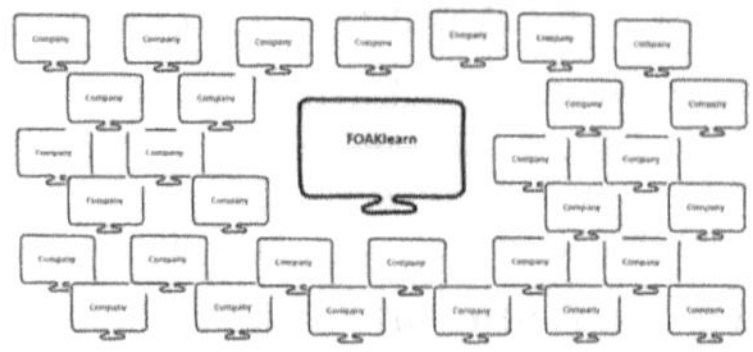

all subscribing companies to access it. The scalable nature of digital learning is also part of the solution as pointed out by for example (Salmon, 2013), who also includes what resembles elements of social learning or communities of practice in her Five Step model. The concept of scalability in digital learning is also discussed by (Simonsen & Walther, 2021), who make a strong case for division of labour, specialization, and scalability.

The practical manifestation of the digital transformation model used in the multi-tenancy learning platform in the Danish insurance sector may be illustrated like this:

The multi-tenancy learning platform in the Danish insurance sector is a Moodle Workplace platform, which to a very high extent enables all partners in the learning ecosystem to co-innovate and share training materials while at the same time ensuring total autonomy for the individual insurance company. The multi-tenancy model shown in Figure 3 also facilitates easy and quick dissemination of crucial new courses and learning, for example in connection with new regulatory changes affecting the entire industry. As will appear, FOAK may thus be described as an ecosystem driver by establishing FOAKlearn. FOAK's Board of Directors has tasked FOAK to organize the ecosystem and by investing in the multi-tenancy learning platform FOAKlearn, FOAK so to speak becomes the ecosystem driver, cf. (Weill & Woerner, 2018: 8) with a view to creating value for all partners in the ecosystem.

6. CONCLUSION AND FUTURE PERSPECTIVES

The research objective of this chapter was to explore the potential of learning ecosystems. The two cases from two different industries, seem to indicate that ecosystem learning is an effective way of creating learning industries and learning organizations and that some of the facilitators of ecosystem learning models include cross-industry collaboration, ecosystem collaboration, common industry training standards and common industry regulations.

The theoretical review and discussion combined with empirical insights from the two cases showed that ecosystem learning is based on both ecosystem theory, learning theory and digital transformation theory. The analysis demonstrated that establishing successful learning ecosystems are based on an in depth understanding of ecosystems and especially of "ecosystems as structure", cf. (Adner, 2017). An ecosystem is not just a group of companies working together. It is about a value-creating structure benefitting all parties and where capabilities are transferred back and forth in a learning-focused exchange system.

The analysis also demonstrated that learning ecosystems do in fact facilitate both industry learning and organizational learning, cf. (Senge, 1990). The cases and the theoretical discussion combined showed that the mere structured cooperation between industry organizations, training academies, companies, regulators, and key opinion leaders supported by a learning focused exchange system of different types of capabilities in fact support learning in entire industries and learning in organizations.

Finally, the analysis clearly showed that the most important catalyst in building learning ecosystems is digital transformation through a structured use of digital tools and digital learning technologies. The establishment of learning ecosystems is naturally dependent on complex digital learning technologies such as for example multi-tenancy learning management systems by improving processes by triggering significant changes through digital tools.

In conclusion, the theoretical and practical contributions of this chapter was the ecosystem learning equation and the ecosystem learning model. Ecosystem learning models are very strong exchange systems and will probably continue to play an important role in building learning industries and learning organizations for many years to come.

7. REFERENCES

Adner, R. (2012). *The Wide Lens – What Successful Innovators See That Others Miss*. Penguin.

Adner, R. (2017). Ecosystem as structure: An actionable construct for strategy. *Journal of Management*, *43*(1), 39–58. doi:10.1177/0149206316678451

Argyris, C. (1990). *Overcoming organizational defences*. Allyn & Bacon.

Argyris, C. (1991). Teaching smart people how to learn. *Harvard Business Review*, *69*(3), 99–109.

Argyris, C., & Schon, D. (1978). *Organizational learning: A theory of action approach*. Addison-Wesley.

Christensen, C. (2013). *The Innovator's Dilemma: When New Technologies Cause Great Firms to Fail*. Harvard Business Review Press.

Dickenson, M., Burgoyne, J., & Pedler, M. (2010). Virtual action learning: Practices and challenges. *Action Learning*, *7*(1), 59–72. doi:10.1080/14767330903576978

Downes, L., & Mui, C. (2000). *Unleashing the Killer App: Digital Strategies for Market Dominance* (Revised Edition). Harvard Business Review Press.

Drucker, P. F. (1994). The Theory of the Business. *Harvard Business Review*, (Sept-Oct), 95104.

Fadel, C., Trilling, B., & Bialik, M. (2015). *Four-Dimensional Education: The Competencies Learners Need to Succeed.* Center for Curriculum Redesign.

Fung, D. (2014). *Connected Curriculum: Transforming education at University College London.* UCL Academic Committee paper. UCL. https://www.ucl.ac.uk/teaching-learning/connected-curriculum/resources.

Garavan, T. N. (2020). The Current State of Research on Training Effectiveness. In *Learning and Development Effectiveness in Organisations*. Palgrave Macmillan. doi:10.1007/978-3-030-48900-7_5

Gates, B. (2023). The Age of AI has begun. *GatesNotes*. <gatesnotes.com/The-Age-of-AI-Has-Begun>

Kirkpatrick, D. L. (1987). Evaluation of training. In R. L. Craig (Ed.), *Training and development handbook: A guide to human resource development* (pp. 301–319). McGraw-Hill.

Kolb, D. A. (1984). *Experiential learning: Experience as the source of learning and development* (Vol. 1). Prentice-Hall.

Laurillard, D. (2002). *Rethinking university teaching: a conversational framework for the effective use of learning technologies* (2nd ed.). Routledge Falmer. doi:10.4324/9780203160329

Laurillard, D. (2012). *Teaching as a design science: building pedagogical patterns for learning and technology*. Routledge.

Lave, J., & Wenger, E. (1991). *Situated Learning: Legitimate Peripheral Participation*. Cambridge University Press. doi:10.1017/CBO9780511815355

Nonaka, I. (1994). A dynamic theory of organizational knowledge creation. *Organization Science*, *5*(1), 14–37. doi:10.1287/orsc.5.1.14

Osterwalder, A., & Pigneur, Y. (2010). *Business Model Generation: A Handbook for Visionaries, Game Changers, and Challengers*. John Wiley & Sons, Inc.

Osterwalder, A., Pigneur, Y., Bernada, G., & Smith, A. (2014). *Value Proposition Canvas: How to create products and services customers want*. John Wiley & Sons, Inc.

Perovic, N., & Young, C. (2015). Rapid and creative course design: as easy as ABC? In: Procedia - Social and Behavioral Sciences, 228, 390 – 395.

Prahalad, C. K., & Hamel, G. (1990). 'The Core Competence of the Corporation'. *Harvard Business Review*, (May/June), 79–91.

Revans, R. W. (1982). *The origin and growth of action learning*. Chartwell-Bratt.

Revans, R. W. (2011). *The ABC of Action Learning*. Gower Publishing.

Salmon, G. (2013). E-tivities - the key to active online learning. Routledge.

Saunders, M. N. K., Lewis, P., & Thornhill, A. (2019). *Research Methods for Business Students* (8th ed.). Pearson.

Senge, P. (1990). *The Fifth Discipline: The Art and Practice of the Learning Organization*. Doubleday.

Simonsen, H. K. (2019): From Ego-based to Eco-based Online Learning: Presentation of a Model for Eco-based Online Learning. At *Promoting Online Training Opportunities for the Workforce in Europe*. Europea. https://publications.europa.eu/en/publication-detail/-/publication/812aeaf7-dccd-11e8-afb3-01aa75ed71a1

Simonsen, H. K. (2020). *Forsøg med uddannelsesdigitalisering og uddannelsesformater* (H. K. Simonsen, Ed.). Samfundslitteratur.

Simonsen, H. K. (2021). *Forsøg med uddannelsesdigitalisering og hybride formater* (H. K. Simonsen, Ed.). Samfundslitteratur.

Simonsen, H. K., & Walther, L. R. (2021). Fleksible og skalerbare undervisningsmodeller. In H. K. Simonsen (Ed.), *Forsøg med uddannelsesdigitalisering og hybride formater* (pp. 145–160). Samfundslitteratur.

Teece, D. J. (2007). Explicating dynamic capabilities: The nature and microfoundations of (sustainable) enterprise performance. *Strategic Management Journal*, *28*(13), 1319–1350. doi:10.1002mj.640

Turner, M. E. (Ed.). (2001). Communities of Practice: Learning, Meaning, and Identity. Cambridge University Press.

Vial, G. (2019). Understanding digital transformation: A review and a research Agenda. *The Journal of Strategic Information Systems*, *28*(2), 118–144. doi:10.1016/j.jsis.2019.01.003

Weill, P., & Woerner, S. (2018). *What's Your Digital Business Model? Six Questions to Help You Build the Next-Generation Enterprise*. Harvard Business Review Press.

Chapter 2
Retorting to the COVID-19 Calamity:
The Swift Turn Towards Digital Transformation in Learning Organizations

Praveen Kakada
https://orcid.org/0000-0002-9010-1539
Vellore Institute of Technology, India

ABSTRACT

The global expansion of COVID-19 has had disastrous consequences, both in terms of health and economics. However, in society and in organisations, we witness positive examples of collaborative and innovative activities. This chapter addresses the problem of how employee response to the COVID-19 calamity through which sudden challenges and opportunities created by digital transformation in learning organisations. Existing research in digital transformation in learning organisations tend to focus on finding out how employees play their vital role in settling their preferences and accustom to unprecedented situation. However, there is enough evidence that researchers have approached the issue generally. Still, from employee perspective very few extant literatures have been available that to specifically digital transformation in learning organisations. The relationships that exist between the COVID-19 crisis and digital transformation in learning yet to explore in different extents and components.

DOI: 10.4018/979-8-3693-0556-0.ch002

1. INTRODUCTION

The growing importance of digital transformation in learning organisations is widely acknowledged, and organisations all over the world see it as both a risky experience and a lucrative opportunity (Silva, Ribeiro, & Ferreira, 2020; Livari et al., 2020). It poses disruptive difficulties and vast potential in the modern business environment, which is marked by growing complexity and dynamicity. Undoubtedly, a big change that contradicts what we previously considered to be true regarding our economy's state and market conditions has occurred in 2023. As a result, in order to address the issue, we must consider novel methods for leading both our organisations and ourselves. To do this, one strategy is to consider the promise that digitalization presents, another of our time's most significant developments (Kronbald, 2020; Kronblad and Pregmark, 2020).

By making immaterial communication and services instantly accessible worldwide, digitalization opens a place for solutions in contrast to COVID-19, which closes borders and controls the movement of people and things. Entrepreneurial initiatives (Fredberg and Pregmark, 2018), the creation and management of digital innovation (Nambisan et al., 2017), (Dahlander and Wallin, 2020; Kronblad and Pregmark, 2021) and others have noted that COVID-19 responses and their innovative opportunities, particularly learning organisations, are crucial for organisations during times of change and can become useful instruments for minimising existing COVID-19 consequences. Furthermore, recent research has shown that COVID-19 has accelerated the workplace's digital transition (Kudyba, 2020; Leonardi, 2020; Osterwalder, 2011; Teece and Linden, 2017).

1.1 Background and Context of the COVID-19 Pandemic

To address the COVID-19 challenge, organisations commonly use digital interventions, although they do so in a number of ways. There are various organisational characteristics, and each one is specifically sensitive to COVID-19's impacts. It is based on organisational characteristics as well as the advantages and disadvantages that come with digitalization. This contributes to the ongoing scholarly discussion of digital transformation and new business model innovation by illuminating how different responses to COVID-19 distress are possible in learning businesses according to the materiality/immateriality characteristics of modern business models. The course of the digital revolution is currently being changed by digital models (Kronblad & Pregmark, 2019; Moore & Tambini, 2018; Kudyba, 2020). Technology has always had a significant impact on how society is shaped and how society advances. This has received extensive technological paradigm documentation. It has been a driving factor in past industrial developments as the spread of new technology, which is seen as both an opportunity and a threat, has revolutionised society, the economy, the labour market, and the market. Digitalization, however, is unlike from earlier industrial transformations in that it necessitates the use of numerous new technologies (Dahlander and Wallin, 2020).

1.2 Impact of the Pandemic on the Education Sector

The global education industry was severely and unprecedentedly affected by the COVID-19 pandemic's emergence. Millions of children, teachers, and educational institutions were impacted by the pandemic, which forced widespread school closures and interfered with traditional face-to-face learning. The disruption of learning, the switch to emergency remote learning, issues with equity and the digital divide, social and emotional effects, challenges with teacher professional development, and issues with assessment and evaluation are just a few of the major effects of the pandemic on the education sector (Garcia & Lee, 2020; Moore & Tambini, 2018; Kudyba, 2020). The shift to remote learning has disturbed all of these techniques. Alternative methods had to be investigated by educators, including online exams, open-book tests, and project-based evaluations.

1.3 Need for Digital Transformation in Learning Organizations

The pandemic's effects on the educational landscape brought to light the urgent necessity for learning organisations to undergo digital transformation. The term "digital transformation" describes the blending of cutting-edge teaching and learning methods with digital technologies. In order to maintain educational continuity, be flexible and adaptable, improve engagement and interaction, have access to global resources, be ready for the digital age, and address equity and inclusion, learning organisations must adopt digital transformation (Doe, 2021; Kronblad & Pregmark, 2019). The digital divide can be closed and educational equity can be supported by digital transformation. Learning organisations may guarantee that all students have an equitable learning experience by granting equal access to technology and digital learning materials.

The impact of the COVID-19 pandemic on the education sector underscores the importance of digital transformation in learning organizations. Embracing digital technologies and innovative strategies can enhance educational resilience, provide equitable learning opportunities, and prepare students for success in the digital age (Garcia & Lee, 2020). It requires a collaborative effort among policymakers, educators, and stakeholders to create a supportive and inclusive digital learning environment that empowers students to thrive in an ever-changing world.

This study like to discuss how different organisations are using cutting-edge digital solutions to the COVID-19 crisis at the conclusion of this session. We'd also like to discuss whether these solutions are equally viable for all types of organisations and whether they will have an impact on how the general digital transformation unfolds within learning organisations. In conclusion, improving one's understanding of how digital transformation works in learning organisations has theoretical as well as practical implications. Even if only temporarily, the COVID-19 outbreak has increased usage of digital technology. Nobody, however, can predict how the workplace will change quickly as it transitions to digital work or how the number of digital job types will increase. So, this raises the question: Has the COVID-19 outbreak sped up the digital transformation in learning organisations? The two primary research questions in this chapter are as follows:

RQ1. What is the relevance of digital transformation?

RQ2. What is the role of digital transformation in learning organisations.?

2. DIGITAL TRANSFORMATION ISSUES AND STRATEGIES IN LEARNING ORGANISATION

In addition, change is occurring faster and in larger leaps. In especially for learning organisations, many researchers argue that digital transformation takes into account internal, external, and holistic firm dimensions and is linked to a fundamental shift in achieving a competitive advantage (Reis et al., 2018). Even as a subset of transformation, it has been considered (Ross et al., 2017; Kronblad and Pregmark, 2019). Consequently, the three dimensions of digital transformation can be described as internal, external, and holistic. Internally, the term refers to the shaping of operations, organisational structures, and work processes. Externally, the term focuses on digitally enhancing the customer experience and value proposition. There are several problems and solutions; some of them are covered here.

A. Using e-learning tools and platforms

Learning institutions can use powerful LMS platforms as central centres for organising educational content, delivering online courses, monitoring student progress, and facilitating communication between teachers and students. Learning organisations can provide interesting and dynamic learning materials that accommodate different learning styles by creating digital learning content, such as interactive e-books, films, quizzes, and simulations. Utilising OER, or open educational resources, can lower costs and increase access to high-quality learning materials for both students and teachers (Hess et al., 2016),

B. Blended learning approaches

Learning institutions can encourage students to independently research course materials online before class using this strategy. In order to promote deeper comprehension, classroom time is then used for engaging conversations, problem-solving, and hands-on activities (Bughin et al., 2018). A rotational paradigm that alternates between traditional face-to-face classroom instruction and online learning activities can be used by learning organisations. This enables a healthy mix of face-to-face communication and independent online learning (Iivari et al., 2020). This method involves having students switch between various learning stations, including digital ones where they can interact with online content, digitally collaborate, or take online tests.

C. Virtual classrooms and online collaboration

Learning organisations can conduct live virtual classes using video conferencing services, enabling real-time communication between instructors and students. Group conversations and virtual office hours are also supported by these systems (Westerman, Bonnet, & McAfee, 2014). To encourage cooperation and involvement among students, learning organisations can use collaborative tools like shared document editors, online whiteboards, and platforms for group projects (Kaufman & Horton, 2015). Learning organisations can give lectures, seminars, and workshops to a larger audience, including students, parents, and the community, by hosting webinars and webcasts.

D. Interactive learning activities and game-based learning

The motivation and engagement of students in digital learning activities can be increased by using gamification components like badges, prizes, and progress tracking. Giving students access to interactive simulations enables them to investigate real-world situations, carry out experiments, and apply theoretical ideas in real-world situations, encouraging active learning (Kohli, & Melville, 2019). Students who explore VR and AR technology can become fully immersed in virtual worlds, improving their comprehension of difficult subjects and producing memorable learning experiences (Sahoo & Dhir, 2021).

3. CHALLENGES AND OPPORTUNITIES OF DIGITAL TRANSFORMATION IN LEARNING ORGANISATIONS

The acquisition, sharing, and application of knowledge are being revolutionised by the digital transformation, which has a significant impact on learning organisations. While there are many prospects for improving organisational performance and learning outcomes thanks to digital transformation, there are also many obstacles that must be overcome for its successful implementation. Organisations looking to use digital technologies to build vibrant, dynamic learning environments must comprehend and navigate these difficulties. Here are some of the major issues that learning organisations face when they undergo digital transformation.

3.1 Sudden Transition to Remote Learning Organisational Culture

Significant problems were presented to learning organisations around the world by the abrupt move from traditional face-to-face learning to remote or online learning: To fit online platforms, teachers have to quickly modify their teaching strategies. They had to overcome the difficulty of adapting lesson plans and teaching techniques to engage pupils successfully in a virtual environment (Bulger et al.,2020). To deliver online education, learning organisations had to find and use the best digital technologies and platforms. This includes interactive instructional resources, video conferencing software, and learning management systems. It became crucial to keep students interested in virtual classes (Huang, & Shang, 2019). Teachers had a difficult time retaining students' interest and motivation during online sessions because of potential distractions at home and the lack of face-to-face contacts. Traditional evaluation techniques had to be reimagined for online learning. Learning organizations faced the challenge of conducting fair and effective assessments, including online exams, quizzes, and projects, while addressing concerns related to academic integrity.

3.2 Connectivity and Infrastructure Issues

Students didn't all have the same access to modern technologies and dependable internet connections. Getting access to online educational resources was more difficult for households in rural areas and those who were economically underprivileged (McKinsey & Company, 2020). Many students did not have access to the computers, tablets, or cell phones needed to take part in online classes. Some students found it difficult to stay on top of their schoolwork without their own devices. Students and teachers have trouble accessing online content, taking part in live classes, and turning in assignments in areas with patchy or inconsistent internet service.

3.3 Training and Upskilling of Educators

Many teachers lacked prior online teaching expertise and needed instruction in using technology, running virtual classes, and creating interesting online learning environments. Teachers required direction on how to modify their lesson plans for online learning environments, including methods for encouraging student involvement and collaboration. Some instructors struggled to explore online resources and use technology successfully for teaching because they lacked fundamental digital literacy abilities (Kalyuga, & Dörney, 2021).

3.4 Making Sure Everyone Has Equal Access to Digital Learning

Despite the pandemic, learning institutions had to figure out how to guarantee that all students had equal access to educational possibilities. Existing educational disparities were made worse by the switch to online schooling. Students from underprivileged backgrounds had trouble using online resources and taking part in online classes (Law & Soh, 2019). Learning institutions required to provide accessible digital content and make sure that online platforms were inclusive in order to meet the needs of students with disabilities. During the epidemic, some students needed special assistance, such as access to therapy services or help resolving socioeconomic issues (Pasmore et al., 2019; World Economic Forum, 2020).

Here are some of the key opportunities associated with digital transformation in learning organisation.

1. *Advancing Technological Integration:* The COVID-19 pandemic accelerated the adoption of digital technologies in education. Learning organizations have the opportunity to build upon this momentum and further integrate technology into their teaching practices. They can explore innovative tools, platforms, and learning management systems to enhance the learning experience and create more engaging and interactive virtual classrooms.
2. *Personalized Learning Experiences:* With digital transformation, learning organizations can offer personalized learning experiences tailored to each student's needs, preferences, and learning pace. Adaptive learning technologies can be utilized to analyse students' performance data and provide customized learning paths, ultimately improving learning outcomes.
3. *Global Reach and Collaboration:* Digital learning has the potential to transcend geographical barriers and enable collaboration between students, educators, and experts worldwide. Learning organizations can leverage this opportunity

to foster cross-cultural exchanges, virtual study programs, and international collaborations, enriching the educational experience for students.

4. *Data-Driven Decision Making:* With the integration of digital technologies, learning organizations can gather valuable data on student performance, engagement, and learning preferences. They can use this data to make informed decisions, improve instructional practices, and optimize learning content for better student outcomes.
5. *Education-Industry Partnerships:* Digital transformation aligns education with the demands of the modern workforce. Learning organizations can collaborate with industries to design curricula that equip students with relevant digital skills and knowledge, enhancing their employability.
6. *Continuous Improvement and Adaptation:* Digital learning enables real-time feedback and evaluation. Learning organizations can use this data to continuously improve their educational offerings, ensuring that the learning experience remains relevant, engaging, and responsive to changing needs.

4. DRIVERS OF SWIFT DIGITAL TRANSFORMATION

Digital tools and resources are widely accessible, which allowed learning organisations to easily make the switch to online learning environments.

4.1 Accessibility and the Advancement of Technology

Rapid digital transformation was facilitated by the development of digital technologies and the availability of sophisticated online tools. These technical developments were used by learning organisations to quickly adopt new teaching techniques and put into place efficient online learning strategies. Cloud-based platforms, online collaboration tools, and e-learning software all played a key role in the advancement of remote learning (Saberi, Kouhizadeh, & Sarkis, 2020). Many areas' internet infrastructure improvements have made it possible for online interactions to run more smoothly and have lessened connectivity issues for both teachers and pupils. Learning organisations were able to hold virtual lessons and smoothly share educational resources because to faster and more dependable internet connections.

4.2 Shift in Pedagogical Approaches

The shift towards student-centred learning strategies was driven by the pandemic. Learning institutions have come to see the value of individualised learning environments where students can advance at their own rate and receive specialised help. The emergence of blended learning methods, which combine both in-person and online components, was prompted by the requirement for flexibility and adaptation (Vial, 2020). Utilising digital tools to increase learning opportunities, blended learning enabled learning organisations to maximise the advantages of in-person interactions. To engage students and improve learning results in the digital age, educators have embraced cutting-edge teaching techniques including flipped classrooms, virtual labs, and interactive multimedia content.

4.3 Support From Educational Policymakers and Institutions

During the pandemic, numerous governments understood the importance of digital transformation in education and offered support through funds and legislation designed to improve technology integration in educational institutions. In order to gain access to educational resources, platforms, and tools, educational institutions cooperated with technology businesses, creating a favourable atmosphere for the digital transition (Lacity, Khan, & Yan, 2020). Educational institutions and policymakers provided guidelines and resources to help teachers adjust to online teaching strategies and design successful online learning experiences.

4.4 Necessity-Driven Innovation

The COVID-19 epidemic sparked a digital transition in learning organisations by pressuring them to move swiftly in response to the new situation. Digital technology was more quickly adopted because of the need to maintain educational continuity during the crisis. (Cline, & Williamson, 2020). Learning organisations understood how crucial it was to develop resilience and adaptation to deal with upcoming uncertainty. The advent of digital transformation made it possible to continue learning despite difficult circumstances (Forbes, 2021). The pandemic's rapid digital transformation experience revealed the long-term durability of digital learning practises, inspiring learning organisations to adopt them beyond the crisis.

5. NAVIGATING THE DIGITAL TRANSFORMATION JOURNEY

Learning organisations should establish a clear vision and strategy before starting the digital transformation journey. This entails laying out a plan for implementation, specifying intended objectives, and setting concrete goals. For successful digital adoption, all stakeholders must be involved, including teachers, students, administrators, parents, and policymakers. Stakeholders who are actively involved in the transformation are more likely to support it and help make it a success (Zhu,

& Kraemer, 2015). It is crucial to provide educators with thorough professional development and training. This involves instruction in the use of digital tools, pedagogical strategies for online instruction, and dealing with any difficulties that may arise with the incorporation of technology.

5.1 Addressing Obstacles and Reducing Risks

Learning organisations should identify students without access to the required technology and internet connectivity and offer the necessary resources or help to guarantee equitable access to digital learning. When integrating digital learning, it is essential to emphasise data privacy and security. Learning institutions should take the necessary precautions to protect sensitive student data and guarantee compliance with data protection laws. The quality of digital learning platforms and material should be monitored and evaluated by learning organisations through established processes. The whole learning experience will be maintained and improved via frequent evaluations and feedback loops. (Saebi & Foss, 2015).

5.2 Increasing Digital Citizenship and Literacy

To give students the knowledge and abilities to appropriately use the digital world, it is crucial to incorporate digital literacy into the curriculum. This includes instructing children on how to evaluate online content critically, safeguard their digital identities, and act responsibly online. Learning institutions should promote a culture of moral behaviour online and sensible technology usage (Silva, Ribeiro, & Ferreira, 2020). This includes tackling problems like online etiquette, plagiarism, and cyberbullying. It is crucial to teach parents and the larger community about digital citizenship and literacy. Learning institutions can hold workshops and offer materials to enable parents in assisting their children in their digital learning.

6. ADVANTAGES OF DIGITAL LEARNING

Students who are unable to physically visit a campus can still engage in classes and educational programmes thanks to digital learning. Students who reside in rural places or have limited mobility would especially benefit from this.

6.1 Flexibility and Accessibility

Students have the freedom to access instructional materials and content through digital learning whenever it is convenient for them. Students now have more freedom to manage their study schedules because they can participate in learning activities whenever and wherever they want. Digital platforms can be altered to suit different learning preferences and styles. To meet their unique needs and learning pace, students can select from a variety of learning resources, approaches, and formats (Galer, 2021).

6.2 Experiences With Personalised Learning

Adaptive learning technologies, which analyse student performance and customise information to address individual strengths and weaknesses, are frequently used in digital learning platforms. This individualised strategy improves student engagement and learning effectiveness. The student is put in the centre of the educational experience through digital learning (Yusoff & Rejab, 2021). The curriculum is flexible enough to allow students to move through it at their own pace, concentrating on the subjects that need more attention and omitting material they have already mastered. Students can comprehend their performance and pinpoint areas for development thanks to the immediate feedback provided by digital exams. Real-time tracking of student progress by learning organisations enables prompt intervention and support.

6.3 Expanded Learning Opportunities

Beyond traditional textbooks, the range of educational resources available through digital learning is vast. To further their comprehension of ideas, students can access multimedia materials, online libraries, instructional films, and interactive simulations. Students from various regions can collaborate and engage more easily thanks to digital tools. Cross-cultural interactions and a variety of viewpoints are made possible via online conversations and virtual classes (Zhu & Kaplan, 2020). Beyond traditional education, digital learning offers ongoing skill improvement. Throughout their lives, both professionals and students can access online resources to learn new skills or explore new interests.

7. RECOMMENDATIONS AND IMPLICATIONS FOR THE LEARNING ORGANISATIONS

Beyond traditional textbooks, the range of educational resources available through digital learning is vast. To further their comprehension of ideas, students can access multimedia materials, online libraries, instructional films, and interactive simulations. Students from various regions can collaborate and engage more easily thanks to digital tools. Cross-cultural interactions and a variety of viewpoints are made possible via online conversations and virtual classes. Beyond traditional education, digital learning offers ongoing skill improvement. Throughout their lives, both professionals and students can access online resources to learn new skills or explore new interests.

To prepare students with the digital skills and competencies needed for the future labour market, learning institutions may need to modify their curricula. Data literacy, coding, digital communication, and online collaboration might be highlighted as a result. The digital era necessitates ongoing education. Learning institutions may promote a culture of lifelong learning by giving students chances to keep up with the latest information and skills throughout their careers. Addressing the digital divide becomes increasingly important as digital learning becomes more commonplace. Every student should have equitable access to technology and internet connectivity, according to learning organisations. By putting an emphasis on inclusive design principles, educational platforms and material may be developed that are accessible to students with disabilities and meet their wide range of learning needs. Promoting digital literacy among students from marginalized backgrounds will empower them to navigate the digital landscape effectively.

It is essential to put the right ideas and suggestions into practise if learning organisations are to successfully manage the difficulties and take advantage of the opportunities brought about by digital transformation. Organisations may increase the effect of digital transformation initiatives and develop vibrant, stimulating learning environments by implementing these methods. Here are several important fixes and suggestions. In this chapter, we provide an integrative framework that classifies and summarises the digital transition in learning companies based on prior research. We contend that many learning organisations need a framework like this. Establish specific targets and goals that are in line with the organization's overall learning and development strategy for digital transformation activities. To pinpoint the precise areas where digital transformation may offer value and address organisational difficulties, do a detailed needs assessment. Make a strategy that outlines the order of digital activities, resource allocation, and execution schedules. We hypothesise that digital transformation in learning organisations serves as a set of components for the success of learning organisations during and after the COVID-Pandemic since our initial analysis was unable to find evidence indicating that a common technical intervention plays a crucial role in the process.

8. FUTURE OUTLOOK FOR LEARNING ORGANIZATIONS IN THE DIGITAL AGE

This section's subheading focuses on learning organisations' prospects for the future as they embrace digital transformation in the post-pandemic period. It addresses how technology can be used by learning organisations to address current problems and promote continual progress. It also discusses the possible long-term effects of digital learning on the education industry. Learning organisations can use data analytics and artificial intelligence (AI) and machine learning (ML) to customise each student's learning experiences. In order to improve learning results, adaptive learning platforms can examine student data, pinpoint learners' strengths and weaknesses, and give personalised content and recommendations. Collaborative learning opportunities will continue to be made possible by digital transformation. Learning organisations will use social learning platforms, online forums, and collaborative tools to encourage peer interaction, knowledge sharing, and group problem-solving. In order to make educated judgements about learning programmes, the effectiveness of the material, learner engagement, and skill gaps, learning organisations will rely on data analytics. Organisations will be able to continuously improve learning programmes and match them with business objectives (Osterwalder, 2011).

Building Resilience: In order for learning organisations to respond to unanticipated disruptions, the conclusion might emphasise the significance of creating resilience. Education systems' resilience can be significantly improved through digital transformation.

Embracing Innovation: To improve the learning experience, learning organisations are urged to embrace innovation and investigate cutting-edge technologies. Technology advancements like augmented reality, virtual reality, and artificial intelligence have the potential to significantly transform education (Leonardi, 2020).

Strengthening Partnerships: Collaboration and collaborations among educational institutions, tech firms, and decision-makers are essential for a successful digital transformation. The conclusion might emphasise the value of encouraging such alliances to build an environment favourable of education.

9. CONCLUSION AND CALL TO ACTION

The way learning organisation's function and provide educational and training experiences is being revolutionised by digital transformation. Personalization, mobile learning, immersive technology, collaboration, data-driven decision making, and a continuous learning culture are the future trends in digital transformation. These developments highlight the significance of utilising digital tools, technology, and data to develop learner-centric experiences, improve engagement and knowledge retention, and match learning objectives with organisational objectives. Learning institutions that embrace digital transformation and adjust to these trends will be better able to fulfil the changing requirements of students, maximise learning outcomes, and promote innovation and success in the digital age. The chapter ends with a summary, its contribution to the learning organization's digital transformation, and a road map for further research.

The conclusion can include a call to action, urging participants in the education system to adopt certain actions to promote digital transformation and spur progress. Investing in Technology Infrastructure: Educational institutions and policymakers may be asked to make investments in technology infrastructure to ensure that all students have fair access to digital learning. Professional Development for Teachers: The need for ongoing professional development and training for teachers to improve their digital abilities and pedagogical knowledge may be emphasised in the conclusion. Promoting Digital Literacy: To build responsible digital citizens, the call to action may call for a coordinated effort to promote digital literacy among students and the larger community. The result may stimulate additional investigation and assessment of the effects of digital learning on student outcomes, educational equity, and teaching practices.

REFERENCES

Bughin, J., Hazan, E., Lund, S., Dahlström, P., Wiesinger, A., & Subramaniam, A. (2018). *Skill Shift: Automation and the Future of the Workforce*. McKinsey Global Institute.

Bulger, S. M., Bright, A. D., & Richards, A. (Eds.). (2020). *Building the Agile Business through Digital Transformation*. Kogan Page Publishers.

Cline, M., & Williamson, D. (2020). Drivers of digital innovation and transformation in U.S. hospitals: A mixed methods study. *Health Care Management Review*, *45*(4), 309–316.

Dahlander, L., & Wallin, M. (2020). Why now is the time for 'open innovation. *Harvard Business Review*. https://hbr.org/2020/06/why-now-is-the-time-for-open-innovation

Forbes. (2021). Digital Transformation Trends 2021: CEOs Prioritize Customers, But Speed Is Key. *Forbes*.

Fredberg, T., & Pregmark, J. E. (2018). Organization renewal through corporate entrepreneurship: When the seed changes the soil [Emerald, Bingley, UK.]. *Research in Organizational Change and Development*, *26*. doi:10.1108/S0897-301620180000026003

Galer, I. (2021). E-Learning in Education: Analysis of Advantages and Disadvantages. *Comparative Professional Pedagogy*, *11*, 41–44.

Hess, T., Matt, C., Benlian, A. & WiesböCk, F. (2016). Options for formulating a digital transformation strategy. *MIS Quarterly Exclusive, 15*(2).

Huang, R., Shang, K. C., & Yu, P. P. (2019). Opportunities and Challenges in Digital Transformation of Learning Environments. *Journal of Educational Technology & Society*, *22*(1), 37–51.

Iivari, N., Sharma, S., & Ventä-Olkkonen, L. (2020). Digital transformation of everyday life – how COVID-19 pandemic transformed the basic education of the young generation and why information management research should care. *International Journal of Information Management*, *55*, 102183. doi:10.1016/j.ijinfomgt.2020.102183 PMID:32836640

Kalyuga, S., & Dörney, Z. (2021). Digital Transformation in Higher Education: Challenges and Opportunities for Implementation of AI and Data-Driven Analytics. *Computers in Human Behavior*, *118*, 106663.

Kaufman, I., & Horton, C. (2015). Digital transformation: Leveraging digital technology with core values to achieve sustainable business goals. *The European Financial Review*, (December– January), 63–66.

Kohli, R., & Melville, N. P. (2019). Digital Transformation and Information Systems Research: A Productivity Perspective. *Management Information Systems Quarterly*, *43*(1), 1–21.

Kronblad, C., & Pregmark, J. E. (2019). Beyond digital inventions – diffusion of technology and organizational capabilities to change. In M. Corrales, M. Fenwick, & H. Haapio (Eds.), *Legal Tech* (pp. 123–146). Smart Contracts and Blockchain.

Kronblad, C., & Pregmark, J. E. (2021). *How Covid-19 Has Changed the Digital Trajectory for Professional Advisory Firms, COVID-19 and the Future of the Service Industry Post-Pandemic: Insights and Resources*. Springer.

Kudyba, S. (2020). COVID-19 and the acceleration of digital transformation and the future of work. *Information Systems Management*, *37*(4), 284–287. doi:10.1080/10580530.2020.1818903

Lacity, M., Khan, S. U., & Yan, A. (2020). The Digital Transformation of Business Process Services. *MIS Quarterly Executive*, *19*(3).

Law, E. H., & Soh, P. C. (2019). Challenges and Opportunities of Digital Transformation: A Service Ecosystems Perspective. *Journal of the Association for Information Systems*, *20*(1), 4.

Leonardi, P. M. (2020). COVID-19 and the new technologies of organizing: Digital exhaust, digital footprints, and artificial intelligence in the wake of remote work. *Journal of Management Studies*, *58*(1), 249–253. doi:10.1111/joms.12648

McKinsey & Company. (2020). *Digital Transformation: Improving the Odds of Success*. McKinsey & Company.

Moore, M., & Tambini, D. (2018). *Digital Dominance: The Power of Google, Amazon, Facebook, and Apple*. Oxford University Press.

Nambisan, S., Lyytinen, K., Majchrzak, A., & Song, M. (2017). Digital innovation management: Reinventing innovation management research in a digital world. *Management Information Systems Quarterly*, *41*(1), 223–238. doi:10.25300/MISQ/2017/41:1.03

Osterwalder, A. (2011). *Businessmodel generation*. Alex Oster Walder. https://alexosterwalder.com/books.html

Pasmore, W., Winby, S., Mohrman, S. A., & Vanasse, R. (2019). Reflections: Sociotechnical systems design and organization change. *Journal of Change Management*, *19*(2), 67–85. doi:10.1080/14697017.2018.1553761

Reis, J., Amorim, M., Melão, N., & Matos, P. (2018). Digital transformation: a literature review and guidelines for future research. In Á. Rocha, H. Adeli, L. P. Reis, & S. Costanzo (Eds.), *Trends and Advances in Information Systems and Technologies. Advances in Intelligent Systems and Computing* (Vol. 745). Springer. doi:10.1007/978-3-319-77703-0_41

Ross, J., Sebastian, I., & Beath, C. (2017). How to develop a great digital strategy. *MIT Sloan Management Review*, *58*(2), 7–9.

Saberi, S., Kouhizadeh, M., & Sarkis, J. (2020). Blockchain technology and its relationships to sustainable supply chain management. *International Journal of Production Research*, *58*(7), 2063–2085.

Saebi, T., & Foss, N. J. (2015). Business Models for Open Innovation: Matching Heterogeneous Open Innovation Strategies with Business Model Dimensions. *European Management Journal*, *33*(3), 201–213. doi:10.1016/j.emj.2014.11.002

Sahoo, N., & Dhir, A. (2021). Digital Transformation: Challenges, Opportunities, and Lessons Learned from COVID-19. *Journal of Enterprise Information Management*, *34*(4), 747–768.

Silva, L. L., Ribeiro, M. M., & Ferreira, C. F. (2020). Digital Transformation Leadership and Navigating the Digitalization Process. *Computers in Human Behavior*, *111*, 106414.

Teece, D. J., & Linden, G. (2017). Business models, value capture, and the digital enterprise. *Journal of Organization Design*, *6*(1), 8. doi:10.118641469-017-0018-x

Vial, G. (2020). Data-Driven Decision-Making and Management. *California Management Review*, *62*(1), 49–71.

Westerman, G., Bonnet, D., & McAfee, A. (2014). Leading Digital: Turning Technology into Business Transformation. *Harvard Business Review Press.*

World Economic Forum. (2020). *Top 10 Emerging Technologies of 2020*. World Economic Forum.

Yusoff, M. S. B. M., & Rejab, M. R. M. (2021). Advantages and Challenges of E-learning During the Pandemic in Malaysia. *International Journal of Academic Research in Business & Social Sciences*, *11*(4), 51–59.

Zhu, E., & Kaplan, A. (2020). Advantages and Disadvantages of Online Education During the COVID-19 Pandemic: Longitudinal Case Study. *Journal of Medical Internet Research*, *22*(10), e20107.

Zhu, K., & Kraemer, K. L. (2015). Post-adoption Variations in Usage and Value of E-business by Organizations: Cross-country Evidence from the Retail Industry. *Information Systems Research*, *26*(1), 173–192.

Chapter 3
Revealing the Essentials of Learning Technologies:
Guiding Learning Technologies Implementation in a Learning Organization

Helena Ferreira
https://orcid.org/0000-0001-7516-4171
Universidade Aberta, Portugal & Universidade de Trás-os-Montes e Alto Douro, Portugal

ABSTRACT

Workplace digital transformation represents a "double disruption": the response to the digital transformation needs of the business, while simultaneously addressing the rapid technological changes that are reshaping work environments. Many organizations' performance and survival challenges require dynamic capabilities and tools to accelerate the acquisition of those capabilities. Considering this context, the idea of the workplace as a valuable learning environment has regained prominence, reflourishing the concept of a learning organization. In today's landscape, learning organizations should devise a technology-based mechanism to advance their organizational learning efforts. Learning technologies are positioned as an enabler that provides learning opportunities. This chapter navigates throughout the diverse learning technologies being used by organizations. In recognition of the vital role successful learning technology implementation plays in organizations, it also assesses the current state of implementations and outlines the primary strategies organizations should prioritize.

DOI: 10.4018/979-8-3693-0556-0.ch003

INTRODUCTION

The increased usage of information technologies and data constitutes crucial challenges in different aspects of an organization (Kutzner et al., 2018). In the wake of the pandemic, an organization's ability to adapt quickly to supply chain disruptions, time to market pressures, and rapidly changing customer expectations, has become critical (The Enterprisers Project, 2020). Over 85% of organizations identify increased adoption of new and frontier technologies and broadening digital access, as the trends most likely to drive transformation in their organization (Di Battista et al., 2023).

The reimagination of the business in the digital age is what we call Digital Transformation (DX). Academic literature describes DX as the process where digital technologies play a central role in the creation as well as the reinforcement of disruptions taking place at the society and industry levels (Vial, 2019). DX is a new development model that calls for redefining relationships between organizations, their stakeholders and clients, and reviewing previous approaches to offering services and products (Zaoui & Souissi, 2020). DX definitions vary depending on perspectives, but what all these definitions have in common is the technology as the main driver of a relevant change, the customer experience innovation and also a change that concerns the internal organizational processes.

While prior theory on Information Systems (IS) can inform the study of DX, recent research suggests that digital transformation is a process of deep, structural change that occurs through the integration of multiple technologies and fundamentally redefines organizational value and identity (Trenerry et al., 2021). Deloitte, in the 2023 Global Human Capital Trends survey (2023) presented that 90% of surveyed business leaders believe that using such technology to improve work outcomes and team performance is very important to their organization's success. Despite IS research has made significant contributions to support transformations, the work of implementing and adapting to the massive changes that go along with digital transformation falls to everyone: The workplace is not oblivious to the technology's evolution and for this reason, DX is also a people subject (The Enterprisers Project, 2020).

Technology is disrupting job tasks and occupations and the increased automation is creating changes in skill requirements for roles. Identifying these skills and reskilling the workforce is an important focus for organizations (Mondal, 2021). Workplace Digital Transformation represents a "double disruption" (KPMG, 2021): the demand to respond to the digital transformation needs of the business while simultaneously addressing the rapid and extensive technological changes that are radically reshaping work environments. Technology is evolving from helping workers produce outputs to enabling humans and teams to focus on outcomes and making work better (Deloitte,

2023). New initiatives, new technologies, and new strategies are all required, but if the company's workforce does not have the right skills, it is extremely hard to succeed. Employers estimate that 44% of workers' skills will be disrupted in the next five years and that 6 in 10 workers will require training before 2027. Besides it, only half of workers have access to adequate training opportunities (Di Battista et al., 2023). Despite the increased adoption of technology in workplaces, the quality and style of the professional relationships will continue to be important to support its transformation. Specifically, high-quality leadership and team members' exchange, positively promote innovative work behaviors, while misalignment between new technologies and established team identities can lead to resistance (Trenerry et al., 2021). Managers need to manage hybrid teams, providing work flexibility and ensuring employee well-being. At the same time, organizations are asking managers to do even better with existing responsibilities, such as managing changes, hiring critical talent and driving productivity (Gartner, 2023).

Due to the increased need for upskill/reskill along with the growing new competence requirements, the idea of the workplace as a valuable learning environment has regained significant prominence. The concept of Learning Organization (LO) flourished in the 1990s, stimulated by Peter M. Senge's The Fifth Discipline (Senge, 1990). Senge, defined the LO as the place where people continually expand their capacity to create the results they truly desire, where new and expansive patterns of thinking are nurtured, where collective aspiration is set free, and where people are continually learning how to learn (Senge, 1990, p. 14). "Learning Organization" is still an appropriate and widely used term to describe an organization that prioritizes and values continuous learning and improvement.

Throughout the years, several researchers made significant contributions to the study of learning organizations. In today's landscape, learning organizations should foster human-machine collaboration. These organizations should devise a technology-based mechanism to advance their organizational learning and development efforts. For better production of organizational learning, different databases and knowledge management systems should be developed to capture, store, disseminate, and share organizational knowledge and experiences among knowledge workers (Kang et al., 2021).

The learning technology layer is full of different acronyms, tools, and platforms, and the enormous market for training and learning tools is fragmented. Today, there are more than 200 Learning Management Systems (LMS) vendors, more than 30 Learning Experience Platforms (LXP), and thousands of vendors who build collaboration tools, mobile learning tools, content development tools, and analytics tools. Roughly, 12% of the $240 billion corporate training market is spent on tools (Taylor, 2017).

Without considering the epitome of the LMS, no discussion of learning technologies would be complete. An LMS is a software application or web-based technology used to plan, implement and assess a specific learning process (Taylor, 2017, p.57). LMS are used to track, record, and report learning data. They deliver and manage all types of content, including video, courses, and documents (Cooke, 2021). LMS is part of the tech-ecosystem of the majority of the organizations and for several years, it was the name used to describe the corporate learning system. In an attempt to provide a fresh perspective, around 4 or 5 years ago, some newer systems focused on the user experience, and social or informal learning, resulting in additional classifications such as Next Gen Learning Environment (NGLE) and Learning Experience Platforms (LXP) (Training Magazine Network, 2022). LXP has presented a next front end to the plethora of available learning opportunities and, at first, looked more modern - a cleaner, more consumer-grade user experience. With LXP, learners receive personalized content recommendations. They can also be given the option of adding content they believe is relevant to their learning experience. LXPs put the user in charge of command and control (Tassetto, 2019).

Learning Content Management Systems (LCMS) have gained popularity in the workplace due to their numerous advantages. These systems offer employees flexible access to learning content, irrespective of their location, gender, or cultural background. Furthermore, e-learning systems facilitate learning while also facilitating the creation, sharing, and transfer of knowledge within organizations. LCMS empowers organizations to globally update their capabilities and consistently deliver high-quality learning materials in various formats (Yoo & Huang, 2016). However, it is crucial to acknowledge the drawbacks of digital content. For instance, the current completion rate for Massive Open Online Courses (MOOCs) averages as low as 15%, rendering training budgets inefficient and costly (Tassetto, 2019). In addition, from a top-down perspective, delivering current curriculums and content throughout the entire organization is a challenging task, especially at a pace that matches the rapid changes occurring in the business and industry landscape. Organizations need to shift the corporate mindset from one of waiting to be taught, toward a culture of daily learning that is autonomous and self-directed (Betts, 2020).

With the advent of affordable and widespread virtual reality technology and the proliferation of smartphones capable of supporting augmented reality, opportunities for improving how we learn were disclosed. The use of virtual reality technology has been shown to increase learners' engagement and focus, while the immersive and interactive environment encourages the learners to become active learners (Bazavan et al. 2021). Mixed Reality (MR) is an extension of Augmented Reality (AR) that combines the overlay of virtual and real elements to create a hybrid and interactive environment (Marr, 2021). MR is similar to AR, since it partially immerses the users, but the main difference with AR is that MR enables the interaction of the user with the digital contents (Mourtzis et al., 2022). The usage of immersive training environments to prevent risks and establish a culture of prevention in accordance with safety rules is an opportunity in expansion. MR technology- based Occupational Safety and Health training enables trainees to explore hazardous situations without exposure to real-life threats (Li et al., 2022). When using MR in training, the applications facilitate spatial vision, that is, allow the user to visualize three-dimensional shapes or arrangements that may be complex to understand). Besides it, allow users to interact with virtual elements, both those that represent real and tangible objects as well as those that represent abstract concepts or intangible realities, and simulate the operation of real devices or installations, such as machines, tools or entire laboratories (Extremera et al., 2022). Another key benefit of using MR-based training is that it can be implemented and is useful in environments that are very difficult and pose a threat in traditional training. Despite some reservations with the impact of training using AR or MR, research has shown that AR systems performed better in immediate and long-term recall after training when compared to traditional training methods like video training and training through printed text instructions (Doolani et al., 2020).

Another area of great advancement to the learning technology landscape is artificial intelligence (AI). AI adoption in corporate learning has been steadily increasing, with organizations recognizing its potential for enhancing employee training and development. For Learning & Development (L&D) teams, AI-powered efficiency increases will be felt most keenly in the realms of administration, personalization, and content generation (Fissel, 2023).

Providers are adding AI advancements to their learning systems to streamline personalized capabilities based on existent data such as employee skills, current skill requirements for the organization's job roles and industry, and individual employee aspirations. For instance, the AI-enhanced Learning Management System (LMS), an upgraded version of the existing LMS, or a Learning Experience Platform (LXP), introduces substantial improvements to the L&D process. It achieves this by tailoring learning journeys, personalizing messages, and automating the display of curated content. AI-driven training serves as a prompt for learners, leading them through their learning path, or utilizing search engines to assist those who prefer to explore existing content. This approach simplifies and enhances learning journeys for employees (Ogibowski, 2023). AI is not just transforming the learning experience for learners; it's also influencing learning technology providers who are integrating generative AI capabilities into their systems. This integration automates authoring and editing functions, presenting an opportunity to augment and streamline learning efforts. AI generative systems bring the ability to build learning programs fully automatically from existing high quality content, and to deliver these programs to learners via individually personalized journeys. Automated mapping and contextualization removes the need of building learning paths into courses by hand or quizzes, while adaptive learning engines can guide the learner through this network of content. Competency guides, skills models can be generated based on the internal information of the organization (Ogibowski, 2023). A niche of learning vendors are building their entire platforms on AI-enabled cores creating learning technologies that are data-centric. Such systems can perform deep learning, natural language processing, and large language models (LLMs) in their core, extending functionality to build models that accommodate thousands to tens of thousands of data elements. Those systems can support decision makers, by analyzing the data and delivering a layer of predictive analytics that supports data driven decisions.

In many cases, generative AI system capabilities will be consumed via APIs (application programming interface), meaning there is little control over and transparency into the operations and development of the system. Furthermore, Generative AI systems in the future might be trained on data generated from the current crop of systems, amplifying existing ethical issues. Because of that, ethics and safety should be a top priority in the design, development, and deployment of any AI system (Szabadi, 2023). To respond to ethical or legal issues, organizations should develop policies around intellectual property related to products built from generative AI to protect themselves from potential pitfalls, like copyright violations (PricewaterhouseCoopers, 2023). Scrutiny from regulators will intensify as these use cases become widespread and affect people in meaningful ways. The same happens on the IS side, in the cybersecurity field. Implementing robust cybersecurity protections is crucial to protect their systems and stakeholders (Szabadi, 2023).

The world of learning technology in the twenty-first century remains filled with caveats, concerns, and various unknowns. Some raise cautionary fags over the cost justifiability of different technologies, tools and applications. Others sound alarms over their practical implications. Still, others ask whose needs are being served and for what purposes they adopt or integrate a particular technology tool or application (Bonk & Wiley, 2020). Although technology is pervasive in the workplace supporting the creation of a LO, work productivity and engagement could remain unchanged if employees have a low acceptance of technology. This unfavorable outcome becomes a reality when organizations think that merely building technological systems is good enough to make their employees use those (Yoo & Huang, 2016). Understanding how organizations are navigating the integration of these learning technologies is a highly valuable assessment because it provides significant insights into the strategies and approaches organizations are employing in this regard. Especially when organizations have not achieved the planned benefits from their investment in technology. While it is easy to point the finger at technology, it is not software, which is the problem, but how it has been implemented. Research indicates that more than over 50% of Information Systems (IS) projects exceed their allocated budgets and timelines, and fall short of expected outcomes (Mandal & Pal, 2015).

In 2022, the "Learning Technologies Implementation" written online survey was created to understand organizations' strategies for implementing learning technologies. It was conducted targeting organizations (public or private) with a Learning & Development function. The respondents have responsibilities or were the decision-makers in the implementation of learning technologies, and/or were knowledgeable in the implementation of the learning technologies field. The survey covered organizations with headquarters localized in 12 countries from all over the world. Switzerland, Belgium, Portugal and the US represent 47.8% of the answers. From the 22 answers received several conclusion were possible to be taken.

Organizations typically have an average of at least three learning technologies. There is no definite market trend that identifies what is the next learning technology that an organization should implement, instead, organizations are creating a tailor-made learning technology ecosystem based on the lessons learnt and best practices from the previous implementation. In general, the adoption of learning technologies extends beyond the confines of specific industries, illustrating a broad implementation that is not limited to any particular sector. Even in traditional business models like Manufacturing or the Chemical Industry, where conventional learning approaches might be anticipated, there are examples where LXPs, or Virtual Reality (VR) are being employed. However, there is a tendency of high tech companies to be more innovative in learning technologies implementations being the early adopters of AI driven platforms and MR. When analyzing the challenges that organizations are addressing, the implementation of learning technologies is not primarily driven by cost reduction or resource optimization, nor because the existing systems do not comply with needs the current. Rather, organizations are actively seeking technology that aligns with their "people-centered" objectives and engagement strategies. An interesting trend is that simultaneously, organizations are also pursuing the engagement of their employees in their learning initiatives. This is a noteworthy finding because, despite the strategies to reskill and upskill the workforce, organizations still pursue a fundamental aspect of a LO: engaging employees in their learning journey. Certainly, the implementation of learning technologies can enable LO, however it is essential to know in advance the learning engagement level to define the needed efforts and actions during a technology implementation. Let us consider a LXP implementation as an example: in an organization where the learning engagement is low and prescriptive, more efforts are needed to put the employees in the driver's seat of their development. On the opposite side, if the engagement for learning is already high, it indicates a robust learning culture within the organization, making the necessary behavioral change less heavy. In terms of their impact, learning technologies contribute to increased efficiency, productivity, and profit, where each employee takes part in the knowledge and experience-sharing process and feels ownership and accountability for the organization's accomplishments (Balavadze & Zhgenti, 2018). Organizations consider the overall company growth rate, the employee performance and morale, the team and individual performance, and the technology usage as indicators to measure the impact of the learning technology implementation. The identification of these indicators when correlated with the leadership's satisfaction with the implementation reveals a positive correlation. This tendency can be a result of the routine established to communicate the maintained oversight and consistent measures of the anticipated impact. When assessing the satisfaction of the project team with the implementation, they tend to maintain. This could be attributed to their active participation in the implementation process and their access to information throughout it. Positive evaluation regardless of whether specific metrics were or not identified. A current fit in the modern workforce does not mean a slowdown in the learning technologies implementation. The adoption of learning technologies follows an iterative pattern, as organizations continually strategize for subsequent implementations to enhance their learning technology initiatives.

Therefore, a question arises: "What strategies should organizations consider to ensure the successful implementation of learning technologies?

Structured and robust planning is essential, and it starts even prior to selecting the learning technology. A proper strategy is required that enables the analysis of the three critical dimensions for successful implementations: Challenges, Technologies and Impact. To align business needs with the capabilities that the technology will facilitate is the case for change needed to every implementation. Before the implementation, the organization must first budget for the entire process, including technological acquisition, implementation, and execution. Additionally, it is crucial to proactively identify the metrics and expected impact, gain the buy-in and ownership of the leadership team, and secure approval for all planned elements.

When planning the implementation *per se,* there are two main areas to consider:

- The creation of the project team with the needed skills, including technical and change management expertise as well as to establish a comprehensive governance to operate;
- The identification of the key stakeholders, including business leaders, who need to be engaged throughout the implementation and a communication plan for both the project kick-off and ongoing communication with them.

Regular meetings should be held with the project team, encompassing both internal stakeholders and the external provider. Throughout the entire project, a continuous feedback loop should be maintained, with special attention given to the pilot phase. The implementation may consider a kick-off pilot with select end users to perform adjustments before a global implementation. This includes developing an evaluation plan for post-kick-off assessment.

When assessing the potential learning technology partner, it is vital to prioritize the employee's experience. Factors to consider include the provider's experience in similar projects, the benefit of their software features, their ability to explore solutions beyond their own, their readiness to adjust to predefined business and technical requirements, as well as their post-implementation support and services. If possible, to get the feedback from other clients will give a realistic perspective on their service.

Currently, plenty of new learning technologies can accelerate the nurturing of the Learning Organization needed of today rapid changes. In some cases, learning technologies can guide the evolution of the learning strategy itself. Nevertheless, in today's dynamic landscape, where technology advances rapidly, learning strategies are intricately linked with the identification and implementation of technologies. Technology adoption and strategy renewal need to emerge in parallel and inform one another. An organization cannot devise a new strategy without assessing the real potential of new technologies and its ability to acquire the necessary skills and resources. Conversely, it cannot adopt every new piece of digital technology without a strategic plan to leverage it (Bughin et al., 2019). Strategy implementation is a critical component of why some organizations outperform others, as even a well-formulated strategy cannot guarantee success until it is effectively implemented (Tawse & Tabesh, 2021).

REFERENCES

Balavadze, T., & Zhgenti, T. (2018). The Bank of Georgia Learning Hub. *International Journal of Advanced Corporate Learning, 11*(1), 5–9. doi:10.3991/ijac.v11i1.9367

Bazavan, L. C., Roibu, H., Petcu, F. B., Cismaru, S. I., & George, B. N. (2021). Virtual Reality and Augmented Reality in Education. *Proceedings of the 2021 30th Annual Conference of the European Association for Education in Electrical and Information Engineering, EAEEIE 2021*. IEEE. 10.1109/EAEEIE50507.2021.9531005

Betts, B. E. N. (2020). Are LXPs the Next Best Thing? *TD: Talent Development, 74*(1), 30–35. https://widgets.ebscohost.com/prod/customerspecific/ns000290/authentication/index.php?url=https%3a%2f%2fsearch.ebscohost.com%2flogin.aspx%3fdirect%3dtrue%26AuthType%3dip%2cshib%2cuid%26db%3da9h%26AN%3d140964999%26lang%3dpt-pt%26site%3deds-live%26scope%3dsite

Bonk, C. J., & Wiley, D. A. (2020). Preface: Reflections on the waves of emerging learning technologies. In Educational Technology Research and Development, 68(4). doi:10.100711423-020-09809-x

Bughin, J. R., Kretschmer, T., & van Zeebroeck, N. (2019). Experimentation, Learning and Stress: The Role of Digital Technologies in Strategy Change (SSRN Scholarly Paper N.o 3328421). doi:10.2139/ssrn.3328421

Deloitte. (2023). 2023 Global Human Capital Trends. *Deloitte Insights*. https://www2.deloitte.com/us/en/insights/focus/human-capital-trends.html#get-connected

Di Battista, A., Zahidi, S., Rayner, M., Li, R., Leopold, T., Hasselaar, E., & Grayling, S. (2023, April 30). The Future of Jobs Report 2023. World Economic Forum. https://www.weforum.org/reports/the-future-of-jobs-report-2023/

Doolani, S., Wessels, C., Kanal, V., Sevastopoulos, C., Jaiswal, A., Nambiappan, H., & Makedon, F. (2020). A Review of Extended Reality (XR) Technologies for Manufacturing Training. Technologies, 8(4). *Technologies*, *8*(4), 77. Advance online publication. doi:10.3390/technologies8040077

Extremera, J., Vergara, D., Rodriguez, S., & Davila, L. P. (2022). Reality-Virtuality Technologies in the Field of Materials Science and Engineering. *APPLIED SCIENCES-BASEL, 12*(10), 4968. doi:10.3390/app12104968

Fissel, J. (2023). Taming the AI Beast: How Artificial Intelligence Can Optimize L&D. *Employee Learning & Development Excellence*, *10*(7), 38–42.

Gartner. (2023). *Managers are cracking - and more training won't help*. Gartner. https://www.gartner.com/en/human-resources/trends/managers-are-cracking-and-more-training-wont-help

Holden, G. (2021). *The Enterprise Project What is digital transformation?* Enterprise Project. https://enterprisersproject.com/what-is-digital-transformation

Kutzner, K., Schoormann, T., & Knackstedt, R. (2018). *Digital Transformation in Information Systems Research: A Taxonomy-Based Approach to Structure the field.*

Li, C. H. J., Liang, V., Chow, Y. T. H., Ng, H.-Y., & Li, S.-P. (2022). A Mixed Reality-Based Platform towards Human-Cyber-Physical Systems with IoT Wearable Device for Occupational Safety and Health Training. *Applied Sciences (Basel, Switzerland)*, *12*(23), 23. doi:10.3390/app122312009

Mandal, A., & Pal, S. (2015). Identifying the Reasons for Software Project Failure and Some of their Proposed Remedial through BRIDGE Process Models. *International Journal on Computer Science and Engineering*, *3*, 118–126.

Marr, B. (2021). *The Important Difference Between Augmented Reality And Mixed Reality*. Bernard Marr. https://bernardmarr.com/the-important-difference-between-augmented-reality-and-mixed-reality/

Miller, S. (2014). *Why E-HR Projects Fail to Deliver Business Benefits*. Legal Island. https://www.legal-island.com/articles/uk/features/hr/2014/june/why-e-hr-projects-fail-to-deliver-business-benefits/

Mondal, T., (2021). Three Strategies To Leverage Skills As The New Currency To Create Organizational Agility. *Forbes*. https://www.forbes.com/sites/forbeshumanresourcescouncil/2021/03/16/three-strategies-to-leverage-skills-as-the-new-currency-to-create-organizational-agility/?sh=1bd5662f28a1

Mourtzis, D., Angelopoulos, J., & Panopoulos, N. (2022). Closed-Loop Robotic Arm Manipulation Based on Mixed Reality. Applied Sciences (Switzerland), 12(6). *Applied Sciences (Basel, Switzerland)*, *12*(6), 2972. doi:10.3390/app12062972

Ogibowski, V. (2023). Learn Smarter with AI-Powered Learning. *Employee Learning & Development Excellence*, *10*(7), 29–32.

PricewaterhouseCoopers. (2023). *Generative AI tools push new boundaries for responsible AI*. PwC. https://www.pwc.com/us/en/tech-effect/ai-analytics/business-impacts-of-generative-aitools.html

Senge, P. M. (1990). *The Fifth Discipline: The Art and Practice of the Learning Organization*. Doubleday.

Szabadi, A. (2023, janeiro 5). *ChatGPT Will Change Many Things—But It Won't Change Everything*. BCG Henderson Institute. https://bcghendersoninstitute.com/chatgpt-will-change-many-things-but-it-wont-change-everything

Tassetto, J.-M. (2019). *The Rise of The Learning Experience Platform (LXP/LEP)*. Credit Control, 40(3/4).

Tawse, A., & Tabesh, P. (2021). Strategy implementation: A review and an introductory framework. *European Management Journal*, *39*(1), 22–33. doi:10.1016/j.emj.2020.09.005

Training Magazine Network. (2022). Don't Get Left Behind: Understanding & Succeeding with Tomorrow's L&D Ecosystem. *Training Magazine Network*. https://www.trainingmagnetwork.com/events/3197?gref=calendar

Trenerry, B., Chng, S., Wang, Y., Suhaila, Z. S., Lim, S. S., Lu, H. Y., & Oh, P. H. (2021). Preparing Workplaces for Digital Transformation: An Integrative Review and Framework of MultiLevel Factors. *Frontiers in Psychology*, *12*, 620766. https://www.frontiersin.org/articles/10.3389/fpsyg.2021.620766. doi:10.3389/fpsyg.2021.620766 PMID:33833714

Vial, G. (2019). Understanding digital transformation: A review and a research agenda. *The Journal of Strategic Information Systems*, *28*(2), 118–144. doi:10.1016/j.jsis.2019.01.003

Yoo, S. J., & Huang, W. D. (2016). Can E-Learning System Enhance Learning Culture in the Workplace? A Comparison among Companies in South Korea. *British Journal of Educational Technology*, *47*(4), 575–591. doi:10.1111/bjet.12240

Zaoui, F., & Souissi, N. (2020). Roadmap for digital transformation: A literature review. *Procedia Computer Science*, *175*, 621–628. doi:10.1016/j.procs.2020.07.090

Chapter 4
AI Transformation for Learning in Organizations

José Bidarra
https://orcid.org/0000-0002-2082-5996
Universidade Aberta, Portugal

Cláudia Neves
https://orcid.org/0000-0002-8175-4749
Universidade Aberta, Portugal

ABSTRACT

In this chapter the authors examine how AI applications support specific learning and training strategies in organizations, empowering individuals to develop their skills, allowing organizations to make data-driven decisions, and ensuring that learning is an ongoing and engaging process. Research shows that AI is an excellent instrument for learning in organizations as it aids in the preparation of instructional materials and helps learners progress in many different ways. So, there seems to be a need for a specific approach to AI pedagogy, which focuses not only on what AI can do but also on which learning activities and learning objectives can be supported by AI applications. As AI technology continues to advance, it will play an even more significant role in shaping the future of learning and development in the organizations, but this should always follow a humanistic perspective and a critical approach.

DOI: 10.4018/979-8-3693-0556-0.ch004

1. INTRODUCTION

The purpose of this chapter is to analyze and discuss AI transformation in terms of pedagogical and technological applications for learning, and to answer the overall question: how do AI applications support specific learning and training strategies in organizations?

Learning organizations are dynamic entities that prioritize continuous learning, adaptation, and growth as part of their core values. While the concept of a learning organization is immensely beneficial, it is not without its challenges. But there are several obstacles that organizations face when striving to become learning organizations. For example: resistance to change, learning overload, individuals' engagement, insufficient and inadequate learning infrastructures, cultural resistance, among others.

Despite these challenges, the pursuit of becoming a learning organization remains essential in today's fast-paced, knowledge-driven world. Overcoming these obstacles demands patience, perseverance, and a commitment to fostering a culture of learning and improvement at all levels of the organization. In the end, the benefits of a learning organization, such as increased innovation, improved problem-solving, and enhanced adaptability, make the journey worthwhile.

In today's rapidly evolving world, staying competitive and adaptable is paramount, and AI plays a pivotal role in achieving this. AI is widening the possibilities for the way organizations approach learning as an ongoing, engaging process. As AI technology continues to advance, it will play an even more significant role in shaping the future of learning in organizations.

Namely, there seems to be a need for a specific approach to AI pedagogy, which focuses not only on what AI can do but also on which learning activities and learning objectives can be supported by AI applications. We are now beginning to understand the potential, as well as the social and ethical implications of AI. Nonetheless, what is clear is that the topic of AI in learning is too important to be left to engineers and entrepreneurs. Instead, it is critical that educators, learning scientists, and other stakeholders engage, to ensure that the AI applied in educational contexts best supports the learners and the learning (Zawacki-Richter et al., 2019).

Firstly, we have to understand what Artificial Intelligence (AI) is today, explaining how AI seeks to simulate human intelligence processes through machines, enabling them to learn, reason, make decisions, and solve problems. The concept of Machine Learning is crucial, as it is one of the main areas of AI that focuses on creating algorithms and models capable of learning from data and improving their performance over time without requiring any additional programming. Another significant aspect is the connection with Artificial Neural Networks, which are models inspired by the structure and functioning of the human brain, and are essential in many AI applications today, such as computer vision, natural language processing, and games. Natural Language Processing (NLP) is a subfield of AI that focuses on the interaction between computers and humans through human language, allowing machines to understand, interpret, and generate text. Additionally, another subfield of AI that involves algorithm development is Computer Vision, which employs techniques to enable machines to "see" and interpret images and videos, enabling applications such as object recognition and pattern detection.

The potential of Artificial Intelligence took a long time to be fully explored. Many recent advancements have yet to reach widespread use. However, AI-driven systems are increasingly being implemented in schools, colleges, and universities, as well as in training programs. While many people fear that AI in education means the replacement of teachers by robots, the reality is less dramatic. The connection between AI and Education is also more complex than is generally assumed. A commonly used approach involves learning with AI, learning about AI, and preparing for AI (Holmes et al., 2019). Learning with AI (often referred to as "Artificial Intelligence in Education" or "Learning with AI") involves learner-centered applications (such as intelligent tutoring systems, dialogue-based tutoring systems, exploratory learning environments, automated text assessment, and conversational agents); institution-focused AI (for recruitment, scheduling, and other administrative applications); and, in more theoretical terms, AI focused on the teacher (although there currently seem to be few examples of this type). The connection between AI and education also entails learning about AI (how it works) and how to prepare for AI (the impact of AI on humans, raising ethical, bias, fairness, and manipulation questions).

Educational robotics has long been developed as a tool for learning, with applications in science, technology, mathematics, computer science, and other school subjects in recent years. Similarly, AI has been applied in domains such as physics, mathematics, programming, and reading. Typical examples often include intelligent tutoring, knowledge representation, autonomous agents, and natural language processing. AI in education has also been used to enhance the efficiency of teaching and optimize resources. Some examples include iTalk2Learn, Third Space Learning, Duolingo, Thinkster Math, and EdTech Foundry. In many cases, AI in education has significantly improved students' learning environments and classroom interaction at universities. In recent times, differentiated and individualized learning has become the focus, and teachers' workloads have been reduced with the support of AI technologies like ChatGPT. This is a rapidly evolving field that requires ongoing updates by educators, students, and learning organizations.

It is also essential to have an understanding of Ethics and Responsibility in AI, particularly in the research and application of AI that can have consequences in terms of privacy, security, and social impact. There are many ethical issues related to the application of Artificial Intelligence (AI) for learning. First and foremost is privacy and data protection, which concerns the collection and storage of data for personalized learning purposes. It is essential to ensure that data is protected from unauthorized access and that learners have control over their personal information and data.

On the other hand, AI algorithms are influenced by the data collected during their training, which can result in discriminatory or unfair decisions. Similarly, the implementation of AI technologies can exacerbate inequalities if they are not accessible to all the learners, especially those with limited resources. It is crucial to ensure that AI does not increase digital exclusion and that everyone can access learning opportunities.

Also, the opacity of AI algorithms can generate distrust and make it difficult to understand decision-making processes. AI systems for organizations must be transparent and capable of explaining their recommendations understandably for all the stakeholders. Who is responsible when an AI recommendation leads to a negative outcome? It is essential to establish clear accountability for AI systems and ensure that they are designed to make ethical decisions. The main factor here is perhaps "trust in AI" (Gillespie et al., 2023), but also important are access to AI by citizens and the (ethical) integration with normal human life.

2. THE GLOBAL AI TRANSFORMATION

The extensive survey by Zawacki-Richter et al. (2019) provides a useful context for AI in Education and Training. According to the authors, the birth of AI dates back to the 1950s when John McCarthy organized a two-month workshop at Dartmouth College in the United States. In the workshop proposal, McCarthy used the term "artificial intelligence" for the first time in 1956 (Russell & Norvig, 2010, p. 17): "The study [of artificial intelligence] should proceed on the basis of the conjecture that every aspect of learning or any other feature of intelligence can in principle be so precisely described that a machine can be made to simulate it. An attempt will be made to find out how to make machines use language, form abstractions and concepts, solve problems now reserved for humans, and improve themselves."

A comprehensive definition of AI was provided by Baker and Smith (2019): "Computers performing cognitive tasks, usually associated with the human mind, especially learning and problem-solving" (p. 10). These authors explain that AI does not refer to a single technology but is a comprehensive term describing various technologies and methods such as machine learning, natural language processing, data analysis, neural networks, or generative algorithms. Nonetheless, machine learning is crucial as a process of AI systems for supervised and unsupervised classification and sampling, for example, predicting the probability of a student dropping out of a course or being admitted to a program, or identifying topics in written works. Popenici and Kerr (2017) define machine learning "as a subfield of artificial intelligence that includes software capable of recognizing patterns, making predictions, and applying newly discovered models to situations that were not included or addressed in its initial design" (p. 2).

Artificial Intelligence (AI) has already significantly altered organizations, societies, and individuals. In many cases, it can exhibit substantial analytical capacity based on large volumes of data and a learning process that enables it to predict changes in its external environment. During AI's formative years, the focus of algorithms was generally limited to supervised and unsupervised learning, inspired by biological organisms and the physical properties of nature, and then computationally establishing a response to solve problems within a data universe (Kar, 2016). However, traditional AI algorithms require structured data both for model construction and information processing. These older, established AI algorithms, such as neural networks, generative algorithms, decision trees, random forests, support vector machines, k-means clustering, and many others (Duan et al., 2019), were severely limited in their capabilities due to these constraints.

Recent AI algorithms, which have evolved over time, have become capable of processing data more naturally, making it possible to extract unstructured data such as raw text and images. AI algorithms designated as "deep learning" and "reinforcement learning" have evolved into specific algorithms such as convolutional neural networks and recurrent neural networks, gaining prominence for their ability to analyze images, audio, and even video (LeCun et al., 2015). Furthermore, industrial needs involving text extraction and Natural Language Processing (NLP) have multiplied, leading to the development and growth of algorithms that can work with unstructured data. Algorithms like Bidirectional Encoder Representations from Transformers (BERT), Long Short-Term Memory (LSTM), and language models have gained prominence in recent applications (Guan et al., 2019, Kushwaha and Kar, 2021).

Many of these algorithms heavily depended on two resources: (1) large volumes of data to train and operate the algorithms and (2) highly complex computational resources to deploy and run the algorithms. However, real-world applications did not always have access to high-level computational resources. Over time, new AI models were developed and adopted, such as federated learning and "tiny" machine learning algorithms, for industrial applications (Li et al., 2020a, Li et al., 2020b). Many of these applications worked in scenarios where data was not initially available to train these algorithms, a problem referred to as the "cold start problem." If data wasn't available, how could these applications learn patterns and predict future trends? These limitations led to the development of reinforcement learning algorithms that gained prominence in both marketing and financial management applications (Singh et al., 2022a, Singh et al., 2022b).

Current news from around the world make us aware that AI is not as sophisticated as many argue. For example, that "AI is better than humans at image recognition". Several experiments show the opposite (https://neurosciencenews.com/ai-image-recognition-21513/). Another is that "AI doesn't need people". But again, this is not true. There are AI companies based in developing countries (https://time.com/6247678/openai-chatgpt-kenya-workers/) where workers spend their entire day online identifying and labeling objects ("here is a person", "here is a car", "here is another person"). But humans are also needed to design the neural network and write the algorithms that train that network.

In parallel with the continuous development of AI algorithms, there has been an increase in the number of studies related to chatbots in the literature (Lokman and Ameedeen, 2018). These chatbots typically use natural language processing (NLP) to respond to user queries, transferring them to the best sets of available responses in the system. To provide real-time feedback, chatbots adopted language models along with deep learning to handle NLP challenges (Bellegarda, 2004, Melis et al., 2017, Kushwaha and Kar, 2021). The recent launch of OpenAI's ChatGPT demonstrates a significant expansion of chatbot capabilities through the integration of deep learning and language models based on the Generative Pre-training Transformer (GPT) architecture (Radford et al., 2018). Language models attempt to predict the probability of a word sequence typical of a human interaction and present the most likely response through generative and discriminative algorithms, often applying deep learning and transformer-based neural network architectures (Bengio et al., 2000, Bellegarda, 2004, Vaswani et al., 2017). ChatGPT uses a combination of unsupervised pre-training and supervised fine-tuning to generate responses similar to those of humans and provide information on topics that appear to be from a human expert. It is a language model based on billions of parameters, trained on a diverse set of naturally sourced data from various internet sources such as web pages, books, research articles, and social media conversations. While current language models generally employ deep learning subjected to supervised learning, future evolutionary models may be built based on reinforcement learning (Uc-Cetina et al., 2022).

The recent global and widespread transformation imposed by ChatGPT has demonstrated a tremendous variety of use cases for this technology in organizations, including software development and testing, poetry, essays, business letters, and contracts (Metz, 2022, Reed, 2022, Tung, 2023). However, it has also raised a series of concerns related to the difficulty of distinguishing human authorship from AI authorship within academic communities, reigniting the debate about more traditional human activities (Else, 2023, Stokel-Walker, 2023). These challenges arise because ChatGPT, and others such as Bard and Claude, may result in both positive and negative impacts on the society in which we live, so there must be some precaution in the application and use of the technology.

3. PEDAGOGY AND AI TOOLS

In the context of academic learning there are two main issues to be resolved: (1) Current AI tools, like other digital technologies, are primarily viewed and used instrumentally, obscuring its fundamental role as a constitutive factor of human perception and experience (Hillman & Säljö, 2016; Malafouris, 2013; Säljö, 2019), and (2) predominant pedagogical approaches denote a uniformizing character, usually centered on the instructor, implying a limited view of instruction that disregards other types of learning situated outside these restrictive boundaries (Pargman, 2019; Selwyn et al., 2020).

These issues make it essential to understand and legitimize other "spaces of possibility" (Selwyn, 2020). As a way to contribute to the improvement of learning processes, Hatch et al. (2021) highlight the importance of breaking down barriers between learning "inside" and "outside" of the institution, allowing students to pursue their interests. Gee (2018) argues that the most powerful learning experiences for young people have been found in experiences and environments outside the traditional school system, developing practices rarely used in traditional schools.

Considering the typical characteristics of AI that may be applied to the specific domains of education and training, there are many ways to approach the selection and use of the tools for successful learning experiences. In a recent report, Baker and Smith (2019) address educational AI tools from three different perspectives: a) student-centered, b) teacher-centered, and c) system-centered. Tools aimed at students are software applications that students use to learn a subject, such as adaptive learning management systems or personalized Intelligent Tutoring Systems (ITS). Teacher-centered systems are used to support the teacher and reduce their workload by automating tasks such as administration, assessment, feedback, and plagiarism detection. These tools can also provide information on students' learning progress so that the teacher can proactively guide them. System-centered tools are those that provide information for administrators and institutional-level managers, such as monitoring student dropout patterns. The same approach would apply to the context of organizational training of human resources.

Intelligent Tutoring Systems (ITS) can be used for teaching. Based on learning models, generative algorithms, and neural networks, ITS can make decisions about a student's learning path, identify the content to be selected, provide cognitive support, and promote dialogue with the student. ITS has enormous potential, especially in large-scale organizations and distance education institutions that offer training and courses to thousands of learners, a situation where individual tutoring is impossible. Research shows that learning is a social exercise; interaction and collaboration are at the heart of the learning process (Jonassen, Davidson, Collins, Campbell, and Haag, 1995).

However, online collaboration needs to be facilitated and moderated (Salmon, 2000). AI in education can contribute to collaborative learning by supporting group-adapted teaching based on recognized learning models, facilitating online group interaction, or summarizing discussions that can be used by a human tutor to guide learners. Finally, also leveraging ITS, Intelligent Virtual Reality (IVR) may be used to engage and guide learners in authentic virtual reality-based learning environments and games. Virtual agents can act as tutors, facilitators, or peers, for example, in virtual or remote labs (Perez et al., 2017).

With the advancement of AI in education (AIEd) and the availability of large volumes of student data, it becomes possible to analyze learning processes. Luckin et al. (2017) recognize a "renaissance in assessment" (p. 35). They believe that AI can provide real-time feedback and assessment. Instead of stopping teaching to assess students, AIEd can be incorporated into learning activities for continuous analysis of student performance. Algorithms have been used to predict the probability of a student failing a task or dropping out of a course with a high level of accuracy (e.g., Bahadır, 2016).

The recent emergence of Chatbot systems known as Large Language Models (LLMs), such as ChatGPT, Bard and Claude, brings a more practical and real perspective on AI usage. For example, incorporating ChatGPT into higher education teaching practices can significantly enhance the learning experience for both students and teachers. By generating educational materials, creating discussion topics, providing personalized feedback, and supporting active and collaborative learning, ChatGPT empowers teachers to interact with students more effectively and provide a deeper understanding of subjects. In this regard, as AI technologies continue to evolve, educators must stay informed and adapt their teaching methods to make the most of these powerful tools. However, like all tools, there are also disadvantages, such as:

- ChatGPT's knowledge base (version 3.5) only extends up to September 2021, which means it may not have the most up-to-date information on certain topics;
- Since ChatGPT is trained on internet data, it can inadvertently reproduce biases and distortions existing in the data used for its training, requiring the users to be aware of the issue and always verify the information;
- While ChatGPT can generate human-like responses, it may occasionally produce factually incorrect or inappropriate content, requiring supervision and discernment by human instructors;
- ChatGPT lacks emotional intelligence or empathy, which can be a limitation when discussing sensitive topics or providing emotional support to learners.

4. PEDAGOGICAL STRATEGIES

Pedagogical strategies are also relevant, and AI tools should be aligned with them, as previously mentioned (Holmes et al., 2019). The UNESCO publication "Understanding AI and Education" (2021) clearly illustrates the educational potential of AI through various application scenarios. The topics and examples presented are adapted from this source.

4.1 Intelligent Tutoring Systems (ITS)

Of all the educational applications of AI, ITS have been researched the longest (over 40 years). They are the most common AI applications in education and have been tested by more students than any other. Additionally, ITS have attracted the highest level of investment and interest from major technology companies worldwide and have already been adopted by organizations worldwide.

In general, ITS work through step-by-step tutorials that can be customized for each student or trainee, covering topics in structured disciplines like accounting, mathematics or physics. The system determines an optimized learning path through learning materials and activities, using subject matter expertise to respond to student questions and performance. This approach can also be implemented in learning management systems such as Moodle and Open edX or platforms like Khan Academy.

As users progress through learning activities, the system relies on operation records and machine learning to automatically adjust the difficulty level and provide hints or guidance based on the student's strengths and weaknesses, ensuring efficient topic learning. Some ITS also capture and analyze data on the student's emotional state, including monitoring their gaze to determine the level of attention.

However, while it may seem like an interesting model, it's important to recognize that the pedagogical assumptions embedded in ITS and their typical knowledge transmission approach ignore other possibilities valued by the Education Sciences, such as collaborative learning, exploratory learning, and productive failure, for example. In particular, the "personalized learning" provided by ITS merely selects paths within the programmed content, rather than promoting the student's problem-solving abilities.

4.2 Dialogue-Based Tutoring Systems

Dialogue-based tutoring systems (DBTS) use natural language processing and other AI techniques to simulate a dialogue between a human tutor and the student as they progress through their online tasks. Initially more common in the field of Computer Science, DBTS have more recently appeared in other less structured domains. DBTS take a Socratic tutoring approach, using AI-generated questions instead of guidance instructions, allowing for a conversation where students can discover appropriate solutions to problems on their own. The goal is to encourage students to develop knowledge for a deep understanding of the topic, rather than the superficial understanding that may result from some ITS. Currently, there are relatively few DBTS in use. The most widely tested one is AutoTutor (Graesser et al., 2001). Watson Tutor is a well-known commercial system developed by IBM and Pearson Education.

4.3 Exploratory Learning Environments

An alternative to the step-by-step approaches of ITS and DBTS is provided by Exploratory Learning Environments (ELEs). These adopt a constructivist philosophy: instead of following a step-by-step sequence, as in the "knowledge transmission" model favored by ITS, students are actively encouraged to construct their knowledge by exploring the learning environment and making connections with the existing knowledge. The role of AI in ELEs is to minimize the cognitive overload often associated with exploratory learning by providing automated guidance and feedback based on collected data and machine learning. This feedback includes error recognition and proposes alternative approaches to support the learners as they explore the solutions. In reality. Examples include 'ECHOES' (Bernardini et al., 2014), 'Fractions Lab' (Rummel et al., 2016), and 'Betty's Brain' (Leelawong and Biswas, 2008).

4.4 Automatic Text Assessment

Instead of just promoting academic work on computers through adaptive support, Automatic Text Assessment (ATA) uses natural language processing and other AI techniques to provide automatic feedback on writing. Typically, there are two overlapping approaches to ATA: formative ATA, which allows the learners to improve their writing before submission, and summative ATA to facilitate automatic grading of writing afterward.

In practice, most ATAs focus on grading rather than feedback; they were primarily designed to reduce assessment costs and can be considered components of instructional management. However, since its introduction, summative ATA has been controversial. For example, it has been criticized for giving credit to students for superficial features like sentence length, even if the text doesn't make sense. These systems are also unable to assess creativity. Summative ATA also does not address academic tasks that may involve easily accessible "deep-fake" essays - essays written by AI technologies. These essays are likely challenging to detect, even for Turnitin. Finally, using AI to assess tasks also doesn't recognize the value of assessment. While assessment can be time-consuming and tedious, it can also be the best opportunity for the instructor to understand the learner's skills.

4.5 Language Learning and Reading through AI

Language learning and reading tools increasingly use AI in their approach. For example, some use personalized learning paths in the style of ITS, leveraging AI-enabled voice recognition. Typically, voice recognition is used to compare student production with recordings of native speakers to provide automatic feedback that helps the learner improve pronunciation. Other uses of machine translation include helping students read learning materials in other languages and enabling learners from different cultures to interact more easily with each other. Some systems automatically detect and analyze reading skills to provide individualized feedback to students. AI applications for language learning and reading include AI Teacher, Amazing English, Babbel, and Duolingo.

4.6 Intelligent Robots

The use of AI-integrated robots, often referred to as "intelligent" robots, is also used in education, especially in educational environments for children with learning difficulties or disabilities. For example, humanoid robots with speech capability have been used with students with special needs on the autism spectrum, providing predictable mechanical interactions instead of human interactions, which can be confusing for these students. The goal is to develop communication and social interaction skills. Another example is telepresence robots for students who cannot attend school due to illness, humanitarian crises, or other reasons, allowing them to access a classroom. A third example is the use of humanoid robots like Nao or Pepper in kindergarten classes in Singapore to teach young children programming languages and other STEM disciplines.

4.7 Learning Agents

It's possible to learn a topic more deeply and with better retention by teaching it to others, a learning method known for a long time. This effect has been explored by various AI approaches. For example, in "Betty's Brain" students are encouraged to teach a virtual student named Betty about a river ecosystem. In another example, from a Swedish research project, students teach a virtual agent the rules of a mathematics-based educational game. A third example, from Switzerland, involves young children teaching handwriting to a humanoid robot, an approach that has been shown to stimulate metacognition, empathy, and self-esteem.

4.8 VR and AR Applications

Virtual Reality (VR) and Augmented Reality (AR) are two related innovations that have been applied in educational contexts and are often combined with machine learning and other AI techniques to enhance the user experience. VR has been used in teaching various subjects, from elementary education to astronomy, biology, geology, and industry. VR headsets provide an immersive experience that excludes the physical world, allowing users to feel like they've been transported to other real-world environments or imagined worlds (such as the surface of Mars, the interior of a volcano, or a human uterus with a developing fetus). Some VR innovations use AI techniques to control realistic avatars, enable voice control through natural language processing, or generate complete environments from a few initial images.

On the other hand, AR overlays computer-generated images onto the user's real-world view (like a fighter pilot's visor). When a smartphone camera is pointed at a specific QR code, a 3D human heart in AR can be revealed, allowing for detailed exploration. AR can also include image recognition and tracking through AI processes. This is the technology that enables some apps like Instagram or Snapchat to add bunny ears or cat whiskers to people's images.

4.9 Learning Network Organizers

Learning Network Organizers (LNOs) are AI tools that allow networked learners and instructors to organize learning activities. LNOs typically match participants based on their availability and areas of expertise to facilitate coordination and cooperation. An example is "Third Space Learning," which connects UK students at risk of failing in math with math tutors from other countries. Another example is the "Smart Learning Partner," which involves an AI-driven platform that allows students to choose and connect with a human tutor via mobile, similar to a dating app, to receive personalized support.

4.10 Collaborative Learning through AI

Collaborative learning, in which students work together to solve problems, is known to improve learning outcomes. However, effective collaboration among learners can be challenging to achieve. In this regard, AI can transform collaborative learning in several ways: a tool can help connect remote learners; it can identify the most suitable people for specific collaborative tasks and group them appropriately; or it can actively contribute to group discussions as a virtual agent. Although specific examples have not been identified, this is currently an area of interest.

4.11 Instructors and AI

Despite the potential to empower instructors, the use of AI tools to improve teaching processes has so far received much less attention than AI systems for students. Currently, researchers and computer scientists tend to think about developing applications for instructors to use at the end of the process, such as dashboards to display student data. However, this is likely to change. Many AI applications for instructors can help reduce workload by automating tasks such as assessment, plagiarism detection, administration, and feedback. It is often argued that this could free up time for teachers to invest in other tasks, such as providing more effective individual support to students. While this may have some benefits in contexts where instructors are scarce, the goal of eliminating the need for human teachers reveals a fundamental misunderstanding of their essential social role in the learning process.

5. TOWARDS A STRATEGY FOR AI IN LEARNING ORGANIZATIONS

As previously mentioned, any emerging technology, especially applications involving AI, can raise new ethical and legal questions, such as those related to social responsibility or decision-making. The ethics of artificial intelligence has received significant attention from researchers (e.g., Boddington, 2017; Floridi, 2019; Jobin et al., 2019; Whittaker et al., 2018; Winfield and Jirotka, 2018) both in Europe and around the world (e.g., the European Union, 2019; the UK House of Lords, 2018; UNESCO, 2019; and the World Economic Forum, 2019), with numerous other initiatives on AI ethics emerging in recent years (e.g., the Ada Lovelace Institute, 2019; AI Ethics Initiative, 2017; AI Now Institute, 2017; DeepMind Ethics & Society, 2017; Future of Life Institute, 2013).

All these efforts primarily focus on the collected data (involving issues like informed consent, data privacy, and data collection biases) as well as how this data is analyzed (involving issues like bias, transparency, and statistical apophenia - for example, finding patterns where there are no significant patterns). The Montreal Declaration for the Responsible Development of Artificial Intelligence (2018), for instance, offers a comprehensive approach involving ten principles centered around human well-being, respect for autonomy, privacy protection, solidarity, democratic participation, fairness, diversity, prudence, responsibility, and sustainable development. Currently, no such statement exists specifically for the ethical issues raised by AI in education (IAED).

The ethics of pedagogy, including the choice of the pedagogical model were discussed by Shiohira & Holmes (2023); almost all commercial AI-based learning tools adopt an effective behaviorist or instructivist pedagogy. This approach to teaching and learning prioritizes memorization over critical thinking. AI systems can also take power away from teachers, often turning them into mere "facilitators", i.e., those who connect the equipment and maintain classroom behavior. But human instructors do much more than that.

The ethics of educational data and learning analytics has been the subject of research (e.g., Ferguson et al., 2016; Slade and Prinsloo, 2013; Potgieter, 2020), covering a wide range of topics that cannot be fully summarized here. But several aspects can be considered, first: "the ethical and privacy aspects of learning analytics are varied and change as data use reveals information that was previously inaccessible" (Ferguson et al., 2016, p. 5). Second, the ethics of learning analytics involves various types of issues, including but not limited to informed consent and privacy, data interpretation, data management, and perspectives on data (e.g., institutional vs. individual); it can also include much broader issues like power relations, surveillance, and the purpose of education (Slade and Prinsloo, 2013). Third, it has been argued that "educational data mining is not the superconductor of truth that some of its advocates believe... and the transformative impact it will have on students' autonomy is a cause for concern" (Potgieter 2020, pp. 3, 6).

Some research has also focused on ethical issues in related areas such as user data modeling, e-learning environments, and intelligent agents. For example, in user data modeling, there are concerns about the security and privacy of this data (e.g., Schreck, 2003), the possibility of inspection (e.g., Zapata-Rivera and Greer, 2004), and individual privacy (e.g., Kobsa, 2007). More recently, dedicated workshops have been held at prominent conferences (e.g., FairUMAP, in Mobasher et al., 2020), with significant contributions exploring issues like fairness (Sacharidis et al., 2020), transparency (Schelenz et al., 2020), and bias (Deshpande et al., 2020). Researchers in the e-learning domain are also concerned with the ethical issues raised by the systems they build, including issues of fairness, diversity, surveillance, consent, identity, and confidentiality, as well as student privacy: "when an observer [which could be an automated system] monitors..." (Anwar and Greer, 2012, p. 63). However, it's notable that other e-learning researchers seem more interested in the ethical practices of students, such as copying and cheating in learning (e.g., Gearhart, 2012).

Finally, researchers and computer scientists developing intelligent agents like chatbots are also increasingly focused on the ethical issues raised by their work (e.g., Murtarelli et al., 2020; Richards and Dignum, 2019). More recently, the

World Economic Forum launched "RESET" - a framework and set of principles for governing the responsible use of conversational AI (WEF, 2020) - which, although focused on healthcare, has clear potential for application in the ethical issues of intelligent agents in education. The RESET principles focus on safety, beneficence, effectiveness, data protection, humanization, responsibility, transparency, fairness, explainability, integrity, and inclusivity.

Other important ethical concerns of AI in education revolve around computational approaches. How should data be analyzed, interpreted, shared, and used? Just like biases (conscious or unconscious) that can negatively impact students' civil rights, caution must be exercised regarding issues related to gender, age, race, social status, income inequality, and more. Finally, as the Facebook and Cambridge Analytica scandal demonstrated, data is always vulnerable to hackers and manipulation: "it is impossible to have privacy and personal control over large-scale data, so it is crucial that the uses to which data will be subjected are ethical - and that ethical guidelines are clearly understood" (Tarran, 2018, pp. 4–5).

However, the ethics of AI in education and training cannot be reduced solely to issues of data or computational approaches (Holmes et al., 2019). Research also needs to explicitly consider the ethics of instruction, which, although the subject of decades of research, is often overlooked. For example, research needs to explicitly address issues such as: (1) the purpose of learning (e.g., preparing students to pass exams or helping them fulfill their full potential), (2) the choice of pedagogy (mostly following a single theoretical approach, e.g. instructionalism or behaviorism, challenged by the educational sciences), (3) the role of technology in relation to teachers (replacing or complementing human functions), and (4) access to education (often seen through the ethical dimension of justice and equity). Furthermore, there is still limited research on what teachers and students expect from AI systems - such as requirements regarding student autonomy and privacy, on which teachers and students may not agree (Holstein et al., 2019). Looking at the corporate world, when organizations aim at behavioral changes, such as "leading" individuals to take a certain action, the entire sequence of pedagogical activities enhanced by AI needs to be ethically justified.

6. AI RESHAPING ROLES AND PROCESSES IN LEARNING ORGANIZATIONS

As previously mentioned, AI has emerged as a disruptive force in organizational learning, transforming the way individuals' access, engage with, and benefit from learning content. The multifaceted impact of AI on the learning process, encompassing both formal and informal educational settings, opens up to a world of opportunities and challenges posed by the integration of AI technologies into learning organizations.

One of these opportunities and/or challenge is related to the importance of tailored learning experiences and the AI's ability to create individualized learning paths for individuals thus increasing engagement and knowledge retention. The work of Baker & Siemens (2014) explores how data mining and learning analytics, often powered by AI, can be used to create personalized learning experiences for students. Their work provides valuable insights into the role of artificial intelligence in tailoring learning experiences to the needs of individual learners. They emphasize how AI can analyze data, adapt content, and provide real-time feedback to create more effective and engaging learning experiences.

Through advanced algorithms, AI systems can analyze an individual's learning history, preferences, and performance to recommend customized learning paths. This personalization ensures that individuals receive content and training that are directly relevant to their needs, thereby increasing engagement and knowledge retention.

On the other hand, AI tools have the potential to allow us to develop a more adaptive learning process, because learning systems can adjust the difficulty of content based on an individual's progress and performance (Siemens, 2005). These systems continuously assess an individual's performance and knowledge, adapting the learning materials to match their needs and obstacles. This dynamic approach ensures that individuals are neither overwhelmed nor under-challenged, promoting continuous growth.

But as Roschelle, J., Lester, J. & Fusco, J. (2020) highlighted, technology's impact on education (and learning) is often to amplify impacts, regardless of whether the impacts are intended. In order to be prepared for unintended impacts, it is crucial to rethink the role of human intelligence (the educators, leaders, decision makers and the learners) in the learning process with AI tools. Educators and trainers, for instance, need to adapt their teaching strategies to AI technologies, but they also should explore the transformative power of AI in learning as a way to revolutionize learning processes, making them more efficient, personalized, and impactful for both individuals and organizations.

There is a vast potential of AI in personalizing learning (Baker & Siemens, 2014), making education accessible (Holmes, Bialik & Fadel, 2023), improving skills assessment (Meyer, 2022), and facilitating data-driven decision-making (Siegel, 2013). As AI continues to evolve, the works of these authors provide a solid foundation for educators and organizational leaders looking to harness the transformative power of artificial intelligence in learning environments.

It is important for learners to understand that they also play a crucial role in the development and application of AI in several ways. Learners contribute to AI by generating data through their interactions with educational platforms, online courses, and digital learning materials. This data, including user behavior and performance data, is invaluable for training AI algorithms and improving the quality of AI-driven educational tools. Learners also provide insights into what works and what doesn't, learners can influence the ongoing development of AI systems in education. In this way they can collaborate with educators and content creators to design and develop AI-enhanced learning materials.

But it is very important to realize that as AI continues to shape the learning landscape, learners need to develop critical thinking skills and an understanding of AI's limitations, biases, and ethical considerations. This awareness empowers learners to be responsible users of AI technologies and informed contributors to discussions about AI in the learning process (Gašević, Siemens & Sadiq, 2023).

Learners are not passive recipients of AI in education; they are active participants and contributors. Their input, feedback, and engagement are essential for the responsible and effective integration of AI in educational settings. Moreover, learners who develop AI-related skills and awareness can also benefit from AI's capabilities in their lifelong learning journeys.

In this context, the relationship between pedagogy and AI must be one of collaboration and augmentation, hence AI has the potential to enhance and optimize pedagogical practices by offering new tools and capabilities that can benefit educators, instructors and learners. However, the effective and responsible use of AI in education requires careful consideration of ethical, privacy, and equity concerns. The ethical and societal challenges associated with AI adoption in learning needs careful consideration and regulation. The role of educators and policymakers in guiding the responsible integration of AI into learning environments will be crucial in harnessing the full potential of these transformative technologies.

7. CONCLUSION

In general, research shows that AI is an excellent instrument for learning in organizations as it aids in the preparation of instructional materials and helps learners progress in many different ways. So, for instruction and learning, AI is not a just a way of "cheating" as it provides the means to build summaries, show examples, create simulations and develop practice. It turns out that everyone must cultivate AI literacy to be able to perform on the job and be effective citizens in this world, but this should always follow a humanistic perspective and a critical approach.

The inappropriate use of AI for learning can affect the autonomy and the ability to make informed decisions. It is important to balance the use of AI with the need for critical thinking and learning success. For this purpose, we offer six recommendations:

Table 1. Recommendations

	Recommendations	Stakeholders
1	Emphasize the valued role of human instructors	Leaders, Instructors
2	Provide technical and pedagogical support to instructors	Leaders, Instructors
3	Associate AI tools with an accepted pedagogical model	Instructors, Students
4	Design and deliver instruction using ethical AI principles	Instructors, Students
5	Address issues of safety and privacy of AI use	Leaders, IT Staff
6	Notify users of specific guidelines and precautions	Leaders, IT Staff

In conclusion, the role of artificial intelligence in learning within organizations is transformative. It empowers individuals to develop their skills, allows organizations to make data-driven decisions, and ensures that learning is an ongoing, engaging process. As AI technology continues to advance, it will play an even more significant role in shaping the future of learning and development in the organizations.

REFERENCES

Anwar, M., & Greer, J. (2012). Facilitating trust in privacy-preserving E-learning environments. *IEEE Transactions on Learning Technologies*, *5*(1), 62–73. doi:10.1109/TLT.2011.23

Baker, R., & Siemens, G. (2014). *Educational data mining and learning analytics.* Cambridge University Press., doi:10.1017/CBO9781139519526.016

Bellegarda, J. R. (2004). Statistical language model adaptation: Review and perspectives. *Speech Communication*, *42*(1), 93–108. doi:10.1016/j.specom.2003.08.002

Bengio, Y., Ducharme, R., & Vincent, P. (2000). A neural probabilistic language model. *Advances in Neural Information Processing Systems*, *13*, 1–7.

Bernardini, S., Porayska-Pomsta, K., & Smith, T. J. (2014). ECHOES: An intelligent serious game for fostering social communication in children with autism. *Information Sciences*, *264*, 41–60. doi:10.1016/j.ins.2013.10.027

Boddington, P. (2017). *Towards a code of ethics for artificial intelligence research.* Springer. doi:10.1007/978-3-319-60648-4

Christensen, C. M., Horn, M. B., & Johnson, C. W. (2008). *Disrupting Class: How Disruptive Innovation Will Change the Way the World Learns.* McGraw-Hill.

DeepMind Ethics & Society. (2017). https://deepmind.com/about/ethics-and-society

Deshpande, K. V., Pan, S., & Foulds, J. R. (2020). Mitigating demographic Bias in AI-based resume filtering. Adjunct Publication of the *28th ACM Conference on User Modeling, Adaptation and Personalization*, (pp. 268–275). ACM. 10.1145/3386392.3399569

Duan, Y., Edwards, J. S., & Dwivedi, Y. K. (2019). Artificial intelligence for decision making in the era of Big Data – evolution, challenges and research agenda. *International Journal of Information Management*, *48*, 63–71. doi:10.1016/j.ijinfomgt.2019.01.021

Else, H. (2023). Abstracts written by ChatGPT fool scientists, 423-423. *Nature*, *613*(7944), 423. doi:10.1038/d41586-023-00056-7 PMID:36635510

European Union. (2019). *Ethics guidelines for trustworthy AI*. Independent High-Level Expert Group on Artificial Intelligence. European Union. https://ec.europa.eu/digital-single-market/en/news/ethics-guidelines-trustworthy-ai

Ferguson, R., Brasher, A., Clow, D., Cooper, A., Hillaire, G., Mittelmeier, J., Rienties, B., Ullmann, T., & Vuorikari, R. (2016). *Research evidence on the use of learning analytics: Implications for education policy*. ORO. http://oro.open.ac.uk/48173/

Floridi, L. (2019). Translating principles into practices of digital Ethics: Five risks of being unethical. *Philosophy & Technology*, *32*(2), 185–193. doi:10.100713347-019-00354-x

Gašević, D., Siemens, G., & Sadiq, S. (2023). Empowering learners for the age of artificial intelligence. *Computers and Education: Artificial Intelligence*, *4*, 100130.

Gearhart, D. (2012). Lack of Ethics for eLearning: Two sides of the ethical coin. *International Journal of Technoethics*, *3*(4), 33–40. doi:10.4018/jte.2012100103

Gee, J. P. (2018). Affinity spaces: How young people live and learn on line and out of school. *Phi Delta Kappan*, *99*(6), 8–13. doi:10.1177/0031721718762416

Gillespie, N., Lockey, S., Curtis, C., Pool, J., & Akbari, A. (2023). *Trust in Artificial Intelligence: A Global Study*. The University of Queensland and KPMG Australia. doi:10.14264/00d3c94

Graesser, A. C., VanLehn, K., Rosé, C. P., Jordan, P. W., & Harter, D. (2001). Intelligent tutoring systems with conversational dialogue. *AI Magazine*, *22*(4), 39.

Graham, J. (2018). *Meet the robots teaching Singapore's kids tech*. aPolitical. https://apolitical.co/solution_article/meet-the-robots-teaching-singapores-kids-tech/

Guan, C., Wang, X., Zhang, Q., Chen, R., & He, D. Xie, & X., M. (2019). Towards a deep and unified understanding of deep neural models in NLP. In *International conference on Machine Learning* (pp. 2454–2463). http://proceedings.mlr.press/v97/guan19a/guan19a.pdf.

Hatch, T., Corson, J., & Van den Berg, S. G. (2021). *The Education We Need for a Future We Can't Predict* (1st ed.). SAGE Publications.

Hillman, T., & Säljö, R. (2016). Learning, knowing and opportunities for participation: Technologies and communicative practices. *Learning, Media and Technology*, *41*(2), 306–309. doi:10.1080/17439884.2016.1167080

Holmes, W., Bialik, M., & Fadel, C. (2019). *Artificial Intelligence in Education: Promises and implications for teaching and learning*. Center for Curriculum Redesign.

Holmes, W., Bialik, M., & Fadel, C. (2023). Artificial intelligence in education. In *Data ethics: building trust: how digital technologies can serve humanity* (pp. 621–653). Globethics Publications. doi:10.58863/20.500.12424/4276068

Holstein, K., McLaren, B. M., & Aleven, V. (2019). Designing for complementarity: Teacher and student needs for orchestration support in AI-enhanced classrooms. In S. Isotani, E. Millán, A. Ogan, P. Hastings, B. McLaren, & R. Luckin (Eds.), *Artificial Intelligence in Education* (Vol. 11625, pp. 157–171). Springer International Publishing AG. doi:10.1007/978-3-030-23204-7_14

House of Lords. (2018). *Ai in the UK: Ready, Willing and Able*. House of Lords. https://publications.parliament.uk/pa/ld201719/ldselect/ldai/100/100.pdf

Jobin, A., Ienca, M., & Vayena, E. (2019). Artificial intelligence: The global landscape of ethics guidelines. *Nature Machine Intelligence*, *1*(9), 389–399. doi:10.103842256-019-0088-2

Kar, A. K. (2016). Bio inspired computing–a review of algorithms and scope of applications. *Expert Systems with Applications*, *59*, 20–32. doi:10.1016/j.eswa.2016.04.018

Kobsa, A. (2007). Privacy-enhanced web personalization. In P. Brusilovsky, A. Kobsa, & W. Nejdl (Eds.), *The Adaptive Web: Methods and Strategies of Web Personalization* (Vol. 4321, pp. 136–154). Springer. doi:10.1007/978-3-540-72079-9_4

Kushwaha, A. K., & Kar, A. K. (2021). MarkBot – A Language Model-Driven Chatbot for Interactive Marketing in Post-Modern World. *Information Systems Frontiers*. doi:10.100710796-021-10184-y

LeCun, Y., Bengio, Y., & Hinton, G. (2015). Deep learning. *Nature, 521*(7553), 436–444. doi:10.1038/nature14539 PMID:26017442

Leelawong, K., & Biswas, G. (2008). Designing learning by teaching agents: The Betty's Brain system. *International Journal of Artificial Intelligence in Education, 18*(3), 181–208.

Lokman, A. S., & Ameedeen, M. A. (2018). Modern chatbot systems: A technical review. *Proceedings of the Future Technologies Conference*. Springer, Cham. 10.1007/978-3-030-02683-7_75

Luckin, R., Cukurova, M., Baines, E., Holmes, W., & Mann, M. (2017). *Solved! Making the case for collaborative problem- solving*, London, Nesta. https://www.nesta.org.uk/report/solved-making-the-case-for-collaborative-problem-solving/

Malafouris, L. (2013). *How Things Shape the Mind A Theory of Material Engagement* (1st ed.). The MIT Press Cambridge. doi:10.7551/mitpress/9476.001.0001

Mayer, R. (2022). Instructional media and instructional methods in digital language learning: Are we asking the right questions? *Bilingualism: Language and Cognition, 25*(3), 396–397. doi:10.1017/S1366728921000559

Melis, G., Dyer, C., & Blunsom, P. (2017). *On the state of the art of evaluation in neural language models*. arXiv preprint, arXiv:1707.05589.

Metz, A. (2022). 6 exciting ways to use ChatGPT – from coding to poetry. *TechRadar*. https://www.techradar.com/features/6-exciting-ways-to-use-chatgpt-from-coding-to-poetry

Mobasher, B., Kleanthous, S., Ekstrand, M., Berendt, B., Otterbacher, J., & Shulner Tal, A. (2020). FairUMAP 2020: The 3rd Workshop on Fairness in User Modeling, Adaptation and Personalization. Proceedings of the *28th ACM Conference on User Modeling, Adaptation and Personalization*, (pp. 404–405). ACM. 10.1145/3340631.3398671

Murtarelli, G., Gregory, A., & Romenti, S. (2020). A conversation-based perspective for shaping ethical human–machine interactions: The particular challenge of chatbots. *Journal of Business Research*. doi:10.1016/j.jbusres.2020.09.018

Pargman, C. T. (2019). Unpacking Emergent teaching Practices with Digital Technology. In C. T. Pargman & I. Jahnke (Eds.), *Emergent Practices and Material Conditions in Learning and Teaching with Technologies* (1st ed., pp. 33–51). Springer Netherlands. doi:10.1007/978-3-030-10764-2_3

Potgieter, I. (2020). Privacy concerns in educational data mining and learning analytics. *International Journal of Information Ethics, 28*. https://informationethics.ca/index.php/irie/article/view/384. doi:10.29173/irie384

Radford, A., Narasimhan, K., Salimans, T., & Sutskever, I. (2018). *Improving language understanding by generative pre-training*. Preprint. https://paperswithcode.com/paper/improving-language-understanding-by

Reed, L. (2022). *ChatGPT for Automated Testing: From conversation to code*. Sauce Labs. https://saucelabs.com/blog/chatgpt-automated-testing-conversation-to-code

Richards, D., & Dignum, V. (2019). Supporting and challenging learners through pedagogical agents: Addressing ethical issues through designing for value. *British Journal of Educational Technology, 50*(6), 2885–2901. doi:10.1111/bjet.12863

Roschelle, J., Lester, J., & Fusco, J. (Eds.). (2020). AI and the future of learning: Expert panel report [Report]. *Digital Promise*. https://circls.org/reports/ai-report

Rummel, N., Mavrikis, M., Wiedmann, M., Loibl, K., Mazziotti, C., Holmes, W., & Hansen, A. (2016). Combining exploratory learning with structured practice to foster conceptual and procedural fractions knowledge. C. K. Looi, J. Polman, U. Cress, and P. Reimann (eds.), *Transforming Learning, Empowering Learners: The International Conference of the Learning Sciences (ICLS) 2016*. Singapore, International Society of the Learning Sciences.

Sacharidis, D., Mukamakuza, C. P., & Werthner, H. (2020). Fairness and diversity in social-based recom- mender systems. Adjunct Publication of the *28th ACM Conference on User Modeling, Adaptation and Personalization*, (pp. 83–88). ACM. 10.1145/3386392.3397603

Säljö, R. (2019). Materiality, Learning, and Cognitive Practices: Artifacts as Instruments of Thinking. In C. T. Pargman & I. Jahnke (Eds.), *Emergent Practices and Material Conditions in Learning and Teaching with Technologies* (pp. 21–32). Springer. doi:10.1007/978-3-030-10764-2_2

Schelenz, L., Segal, A., & Gal, K. (2020). Best practices for transparency in machine generated personaliza- tion. Adjunct Publication of the *28th ACM Conference on User Modeling, Adaptation and Personalization*, (pp. 23–28). ACM. 10.1145/3386392.3397593

Schreck, J. (2003). *Security and Privacy in User Modeling* (Vol. 2). Springer. doi:10.1007/978-94-017-0377-2

Selwyn, N. (2020). Approches critiques des technologies en éducation: Un aperçu. *Formation et Profession*, *27*(3), 6. doi:10.18162/fp.2019.579

Selwyn, N., Nemorin, S., Bulfin, S., & Johnson, N. (2020). The "obvious" stuff: Exploring the mundane realities of students' digital technology use in school. *Digital Education Review*, *37*(37), 1–14. doi:10.1344/der.2020.37.1-14

Shiohira, K., & Holmes, W. (2023). Proceed with Caution: The Pitfalls and Potential of AI and Education. In D. Araya & P. Marber (Eds.), *Augmented Education in the Global Age*. Routledge.

Siegel, E. (2013). *Predictive Analytics: The Power to Predict Who Will Click, Buy, Lie or Die*. John Wiley & Sons, Inc.

Siemens, G. (2005). Connectivism: A Learning Theory for the Digital Age. *International Journal of Instructional Technology and Distance Learning*, *2*. https://www.itdl.org/Journal/Jan_05/article01.htm

Singh, V., Chen, S. S., Singhania, M., Nanavati, B., & Gupta, A. (2022). How are reinforcement learning and deep learning algorithms used for big data-based decision making in financial industries - A review and research agenda. *International Journal of Information Management Data Insights*, *2*(2), 100094. https://www.sciencedirect.com/science/article/pii/S2667096822000374. doi:10.1016/j.jjimei.2022.100094

Singh, V., Nanavati, B., Kar, A. K., & Gupta, A. (2022). How to maximize clicks for display advertisement in digital marketing? A reinforcement learning approach. *Information Systems Frontiers*, 1–18. doi:10.100710796-022-10314-0

Slade, S., & Prinsloo, P. (2013). Learning analytics ethical issues and dilemmas. *The American Behavioral Scientist*, *57*(10), 1510–1529. doi:10.1177/0002764213479366

Smith, J. (2022). Applications of artificial intelligence in educational management. *Educational Technology Research and Development*, *70*(2), 457–478. 10.100711423-022-09981-1

Stokel-Walker, C. J. N. (2023). ChatGPT listed as author on research papers: Many scientists disapprove. *Nature*, *613*(7945), 620–621. doi:10.1038/d41586-023-00107-z PMID:36653617

Tarran, B. (2018). What can we learn from the Facebook—Cambridge Analytica scandal? *Significance*, *15*(3), 4–5. doi:10.1111/j.1740-9713.2018.01139.x PMID:32536948

Tung, L. (2023). ChatGPT can write code. Now researchers say it's good at fixing bugs, too. *ZDNet.* https://www.zdnet.com/article/chatgpt-can-write-code-now-researchers-say-its-good-at-fixing-bugs-too/

Uc-Cetina, V., Navarro-Guerrero, N., Martin-Gonzalez, A., Weber, C., & Wermter, S. (2022). Survey on reinforcement learning for language processing. *Artificial Intelligence Review*, 1–33. doi:10.100710462-022-10205-5

UNESCO. (2019). *Artificial intelligence in education: Challenges and opportunities for sustainable development.* UNESCO. https://unesdoc.unesco.org/ark:/48223/pf0000366994

Université de Montréal. (2018). *Declaration of Montréal for a responsible development of AI.* Université de Montréal. https://www.montrealdeclaration-responsibleai.com

Vaswani, A., Shazeer, N., Parmar, N., Uszkoreit, J., Jones, L., Gomez, A. N., & Polosukhin, I. (2017). *Attention is all you need. 31st Conference on Neural Information Processing Systems*, Long Beach, CA, USA.

Whittaker, M., Crawford, K., Dobbe, R., Fried, G., Kaziunas, E., & Mathur, V. MyersWest, S., Richardson, R., Schultz, J., & Schwartz, O. (2018). AI now report 2018. AI Now Institute: New York University.

Winfield, A. F. T., & Jirotka, M. (2018). Ethical governance is essential to building trust in robotics and artificial intelligence systems. *Philosophical Transactions. Series A, Mathematical, Physical, and Engineering Sciences, 376*(2133), 20180085. doi:10.1098/rsta.2018.0085 PMID:30323000

World Economic Forum. (2019). *Generation AI.* WEF. https://www3.weforum.org/docs/WEF_Generation_AI_%20May_2019_Workshop_Report.pdf

Zapata-Rivera, J.-D., & Greer, J. E. (2004). Interacting with inspectable bayesian student models. *International Journal of Artificial Intelligence in Education, 14*(2), 127–163.

Zawacki-Richter, O., Marín, V. I., Bond, M., & Gouverneur, F. (2019). Systematic review of research on artificial intelligence applications in higher education – where are the educators? *International Journal of Educational Technology in Higher Education, 16*(1), 1–27. doi:10.118641239-019-0171-0

Chapter 5
Learning Technologies:
Chatbots to Support Personalized Learning

Daina Gudoniene
Kaunas University of Technology, Lithuania

Tomas Blazauskas
Kaunas University of Technology, Lithuania

Rita Butkiene
Kaunas University of Technology, Lithuania

Lina Čeponienė
Kaunas University of Technology, Lithuania

Evelina Staneviciene
Kaunas University of Technology, Lithuania

ABSTRACT

The aim of the chapter is to present the learning technologies helping students to get high-quality personalised assistance in the learning process. Digital transformation in education makes a huge impact on the quality of education; however, authors are focusing on the chatbots that can be used for providing personalised support and guidance to students in education. Moreover, chatbots can help to improve academic performance and reduce the number of drop out students. The authors will discuss the chatbot aspects based on the 6 main chatbot parameters that determine design and development presented by Kumar: (1) knowledge, (2) services, (3) goals, (4) input processing, (5) human aid, and (6) building open-source or closed platforms. These parameters convey that a chatbot can fulfil numerous communication and interaction functionalities based on needs, platforms, and technologies.

DOI: 10.4018/979-8-3693-0556-0.ch005

1. INTRODUCTION

Educational chatbots are digital tools designed to assist learners in various educational settings. These chatbots use natural language processing (NLP) and machine learning algorithms to simulate human conversation and respond to user queries in a way that facilitates learning. They can be integrated into various educational platforms such as learning management systems, educational apps, and websites to provide learners with a personalised and interactive learning experience.

Educational chatbots can be used for a variety of purposes, including:

Student support: chatbots can be used to assist students with answers questions about learning material.

Administrative support: chatbots can be used support learners on administrative issues.

Personalised learning: chatbots can be used to provide personalised learning experiences by tailoring content and lessons to individual student needs and abilities.

Student engagement: chatbots can be used to increase student engagement by providing interactive and gamified learning experiences.

Tutoring: chatbots can be used to provide students with tutoring services by answering questions and providing feedback on assignments. Chatbots can help with homework, test preparation, and etc.

Mentoring: chatbots can be used to provide mentoring or coaching services to users by suggesting personlaysed feedback and offering insights into specific areas of interest, and providing guidance on how to achieve learning goals.

Scaffolding (challenge support): chatbots can be used to provide support or guidance to users as they complete a challenging task or process. Scaffolding refers to guidance to help users navigate through a process or complete intended tasks.

Student mental health support: chatbots can be used to provide students with support for their mental health and wellness, including resources for stress management and coping strategies.

Distance learning: chatbots can be used in distance learning to provide students with instant access to information and support, regardless of their location in the real time by assuring synchronous feedback.

Library assistance: chatbots can be used to help users to access and utilise different library resources and services. Library chatbots can be integrated into library websites, social media platforms, or messaging apps to provide quick and convenient assistance to library patrons. Library chatbots can help users with a variety of tasks, such as finding books or articles, accessing databases, reserving meeting rooms, and getting information about library hours and events. Chatbots can also answer frequently asked questions about library policies and procedures.

Cultural support: These chatbots are designed to help users learn about different cultures and languages. They can provide historical and cultural context, offer language lessons, and even provide travel recommendations.

Thus, different educational chatbots can help learners with a range of tasks and offer recommendations based on the learner's interests and learning needs and experience. The benefits of educational chatbots are numerous, including increased student engagement, improved learning outcomes, and personalised learning experiences. They also provide a scalable and cost-effective solution to educational institutions that may struggle to provide individual attention to each student. With the continued advancement of machine learning and NLP technologies, educational chatbots are poised to become an increasingly important part of the educational landscape. The authors discuss the main aspects of chatbot design and development in the first chapter and in the second chapter we speak about possible chatbot scenarios for education. The third chapter presents the practical implementation of the discussed chatbot strategies. Finally, authors present conclusions of their findings by analysing effective chatbot implementation for personalised learning approach.

2. CHATBOT DESIGN AND DEVELOPMENT ASPECTS

Benoti et al. (2018) discuss that adoption of educational chatbots is on the rise due to their ability to provide a cost-effective method to engage students and provide a personalised learning experience. Another author Winkler & Söllner (2018) discusses the online classes that include many students where individual support from educators to students is challenging.

Fermoaga et al. (2018) introduce Chatbots as real-time educational assistants for the teacher - they are designed to distribute interactivity with students and to manage it at an individual level. This approach adds a highly increased degree of interactivity and personalization to the learning experience, aspects which are critical from the student's point of view as each individual has its own learning and understanding capabilities.

Chalves &Geros (2021) and Gonda &Chu (2019) speak about chatbots as a learning resource, creating conversational bots as a supplement for teaching assistant training courses.

Luo et al. (2022) and Mafra et al. (2022) discussed chatbots development processes by defining requirements for the development of useful and usable chatbots.

Rediscovering the use of chatbots in education was discussed by Pérez et al. (2020). However, Binkis et al. (2021) say that a Chatbot refers to software that can perform services based on commands or answers given by a user during an

Figure 1. Chatbots parameters

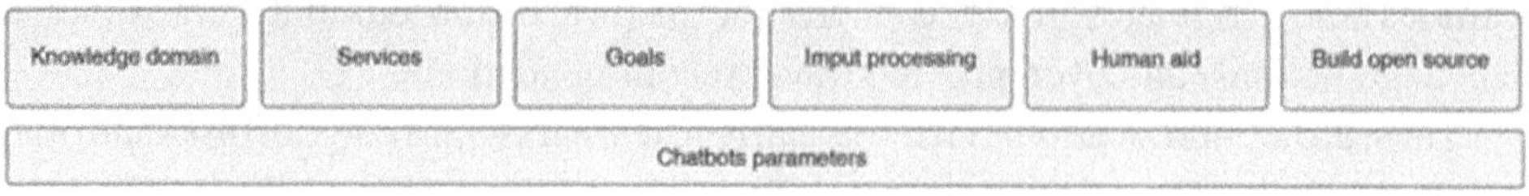

online conversation. The Chatbots are applied in different areas ranging from pure entertainment solutions to learning support systems.

Another authors Bahja et al. (2020) discuss a user-centric approach which enables developers to consider the following: learners' and teachers' technological skills and competencies, attitudes, and perceptions and behaviour; conceptual concerns, such as pedagogical integration on online platforms, assessment procedures, varying learning culture and lifestyles; technical concerns, such as privacy, security, performance, ubiquity; and regulatory concerns, such as policies, frameworks, standards, ethics, roles and responsibilities have.

Okonwo & Ibijola (2021) say that chatbot technology has the potential to provide quick and personalised services to everyone in the sector, including institutional employees and students.

Moreover, many authors discuss security issues related to the chatbot design and implementation. Hasal et al. (2021) present the main findings on the main concerns that are rather about the user's data stored on the backend side and its usage, as chatbots generate enormous amounts of data about users. Regulations such as GDPR strictly define data manipulation methods, but not everybody lives in the EU under the jurisdiction of GDPR regulations for data protection.

In many cases, chatbot design and development strategies depend on the target's needs. According to Adamopoulou and Moussiades (2020), there are six main chatbot parameters (Figure 1).

That determines design and development considerations: (1) knowledge domain - open and closed domains, (2) services - interpersonal, intrapersonal, and inter-agent chatbots, (3) goals - informative, chat-based, or task-based, (4) input processing and response generation - rule-based model, retrieval-based model, and generative model, (5) human aid and (6) build - open-source or closed platforms.

Adamopoulou and Moussiades (2020), also present chatbot categories (Figure 2).

The main aim a chatbot aims to achieve classifies them in Informative, that-based conversational, and task-based chatbots.

Figure 2. Chatbot categories

Chatbot Categories		
	Knowledge domain	Generic
		Open Domain
		Closed Domain
	Service provided	Interpersonal
		Intrapersonal
		Inter-agent
	Goals	Informative
		Chat based/Conversational
		Task based
	Response Generation Method	Rule based
		Retrieval based
		Generative
	Human-aid	Human-mediated
		Autonomous
	Permissions	Open-source
		Commercial
	Communication channel	Text
		Voice
		Image

2.1. Knowledge Domain

The knowledge domain is based on the knowledge the Chatbot accesses. There are two types of domains; the open and the closed domains. Sandu et al. say (2019) that the open domain Chatbots address general topics and respond appropriately to general questions. The bots in the closed domain address specific knowledge domains and may fail to respond to questions from other domains. Nimavat et al. (2017) say that classification based on the knowledge domain considers the knowledge a chatbot can access or the amount of data it is trained upon. Open-domain chatbots can talk about general topics and respond appropriately, while closed-domain chatbots are focused on a particular knowledge domain and might fail to respond to other questions. A chatbot can access a range of knowledge, which determines its Knowledge Adamopoulou & Moussiades (2020) discuss chatbots that can answer any user question from whichever domain are called Generic chatbots.

2.2. Services

The service-based Chatbots are categorised into those that offer interpersonal, intrapersonal and inter-agent services. Nimavat et al. (2017) mentioned classification based on the service provided considers the sentimental proximity of the chatbot to the user, the amount of intimate interaction that takes place, and it is also dependent upon the task the chatbot is performing. Interpersonal chatbots lie in the domain of communication and provide services such as Restaurant booking, Flight booking, and FAQ bots. They are not companions of the user, but they get information and pass them on to the user. They can have a personality, can be friendly, and will probably remember information about the user, but they are not obliged or expected to do so.

2.3. Goals

The goal-based Chatbots are further categorised under the informative, conversational and task-based Chatbots. Nimavat et al. (2017) present a classification based on the goals the primary goal chatbots aim to achieve. Informative chatbots are designed to provide the user with information that is stored beforehand or is available from a fixed source, like FAQ chatbots. Chat-based/Conversational chatbots talk to the user, like another human being, and their goal is to respond correctly to the sentence they have been given. Task-based chatbots perform a specific task such as booking a flight or helping somebody. These chatbots are intelligent in the context of asking for information and understanding the user's input.

2.4. Input Processing

Chatbots based on the input method and the responses generated. According to Sandu &Gine (2019) there are Chatbots that accept input, and process and generate output in natural language, and others that are rule-based as they process input based on rules. Other Chatbots in this category are a hybrid as they use natural understanding and rules to process input and generate output. Another author Nimavat et al. (2017) presents a classification based on the input processing and response generation method that takes into account the method of processing inputs and generating responses. There are three models used to produce the appropriate responses: rule-based model, retrieval-based model, and generative model.

2.5. Human Aid

Nimavat et al. (2017) present another classification for chatbots that considers the amount of human-aid in their components. Human-aided chatbots utilise human computation in at least one element from the chatbot. Crowd workers, freelancers, or full-time employees can embody their intelligence in the chatbot logic to fill the gaps caused by the limitations of fully automated chatbots.

Adamopoulou and Moussiades (2020) present another classification for chatbots that considers the amount of human aid in their components. Human-aided chatbots utilise human computation in at least one element from the chatbot. Crowd workers, freelancers, or full-time employees can embody their intelligence in the chatbot logic to fill the gaps caused by the limitations of fully automated chatbots.

2.6. Building Open Source or Closed Platforms

Adamopoulou and Moussiades (2020) present that chatbots can also be classified according to the permissions provided by their development platform. Development platforms can be open-source, such as RASA (https://rasa.com), or can be of proprietary code such as development platforms typically offered by large companies such as Google or IBM. There many open platforms that provide the chatbot designer the opportunity to intervene in most aspects of implementation. Moreover, there are many closed platforms, typically acting as black boxes, which may be a significant disadvantage depending on the individual project's requirements.

3. CHATBOTS SCENARIOS

Sandu & Gide (2019) present that chatbots have been in use for educational purposes for quite some time. These Chatbots can be categorised into those with education intentionality and those without. Chatbots without education intentionality are used in administrative tasks such as student guidance and assistance. Chatbots with education intentionality are used in fostering teaching and learning. Cahn (2021) says that within this category, there are Chatbots which provide the framework of the learning process, that is, select and arrange content to fit the students' needs and speed as well as help in reflection and learning motivation. These bots act as a learning companion which provides dialogue, collaboration and reflection. Furthermore, there are exercise and practice Chatbots that present a stimulus in question form, to which the student provides an answer that is assessed by the Chatbot which then provides feedback.

Chatbots have been in use for educational purposes for quite some time. These Chatbots can be categorised into those with educational intentionality and those without. Chatbots without education intentionality are used in administrative tasks such as student guidance and assistance. Chatbots with education intentionality are used in fostering teaching and learning.

Cahn (2017) discusses that within this category, there are Chatbots which provide the framework of the learning process, that is, select and arrange content to fit the students' needs and speed and help in reflection and learning motivation.

We planned to use 4 chatbot scenarios directly related to the study process, that could assure better quality of education and instruments for using intelligence technologies in education by developing virtual assistant i.e.

1) chatbot for course guidance and support,
2) chatbot for content material support,
3) chatbot for assessment,
4) chatbot for individual tasks support.

The first scenario is intended for a course guiding and support and would be designed to assist students in navigating their educational pathway. The chatbot would be available any time and accessible from any device. It would be developed with a range of features to support students in achieving their academic goals. Some of the features that a course guidance and support chatbot might include (see Figure 3):

Course recommendations: The chatbot could suggest courses based on a student's interests, academic history, and career aspirations.

Enrollment assistance: The chatbot could help students enrol into the courses, answer questions about enrollment requirements, and provide guidance on how to register for classes.

Course scheduling: The chatbot could help students schedule courses in a way that fits their availability, and ensure they are taking the appropriate courses to meet their degree requirements.

Study support: The chatbot could provide tips and resources to help students study effectively, manage their time, and prepare for exams.

Academic counselling: The chatbot could offer advice and support for students who are struggling academically, and connect them with appropriate resources such as tutoring services or academic advisors.

Career guidance: The chatbot could provide information about career options related to different courses, and connect students with career counsellors for more personalised guidance.

A course guidance and support chatbot would be a valuable resource for students, providing them with quick and convenient access to information and support that can help them succeed in their academic pursuits.

The second scenario related to the chatbot for content material support would be used to assist students with the material covered in their courses and might include (see Figure 4):

There are several important issues related to the content material support:

Figure 3. A course guiding and support

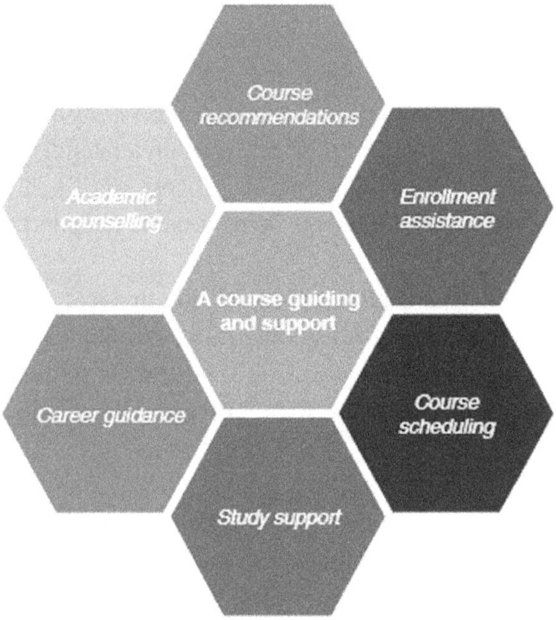

Figure 4. Content material support

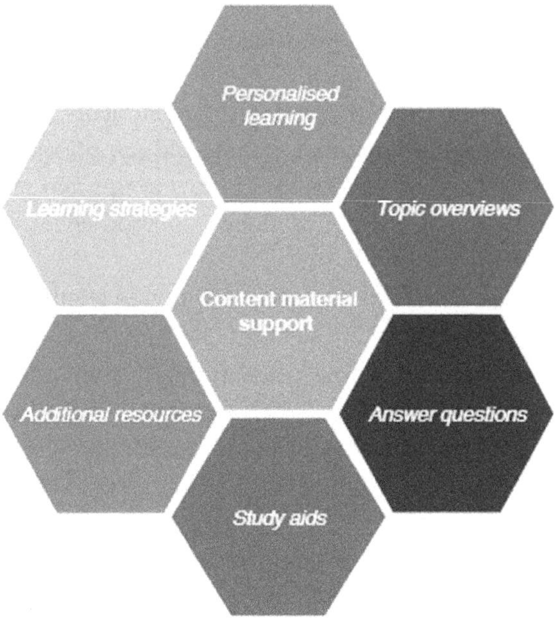

Topic overviews: The chatbot could provide overviews of the topics covered in a course, breaking down complex concepts into easy-to-understand language.

Answer questions: The chatbot could answer specific questions about course material, providing students with quick and accurate responses to their inquiries.

Study aids: The chatbot could provide students with study aids such as flashcards, summaries, and quizzes to help them reinforce their understanding of course material.

Additional resources: The chatbot could suggest additional resources such as textbooks, articles, and videos that can help students deepen their understanding of course material.

Learning strategies: The chatbot could provide tips and strategies for learning and retaining course material, such as note-taking techniques and memory aids.

Personalised learning: The chatbot could customise its responses based on a student's specific needs and learning style, providing personalised support to help them succeed.

A content material support chatbot would be a importnat for students who want to enhance their learning experience and succeed in their courses. It would provide quick and convenient access to information and resources that can help students understand and retain course material more effectively.

The third scenario is related to the support in assessment tools and would be designed to assist students in preparing for exams, quizzes, and other assessments. This type of chatbot would be especially useful for students who struggle with test anxiety, need additional support outside of the classroom, or who want to improve their performance on assessments. Some features that an assessment chatbot might include (see Figure 5):

Test preparation: The chatbot could provide students with test preparation resources such as study guides, practice exams, and sample questions.

Test-taking strategies: The chatbot could provide tips and strategies for taking exams, such as time-management techniques or approaches for tackling essay questions.

Feedback and reflection: The chatbot could provide feedback and reflection on student performance.

Test anxiety support: The chatbot could provide strategies for managing test anxiety and reducing stress before and during exams.

Personalised learning: The chatbot could customise its responses based on student's specific needs and learning style, providing personalised support to help them succeed on assessments.

Progress tracking: The chatbot could track a student's progress over time, providing insights into their strengths and weaknesses and suggesting areas where they might benefit from additional support.

Figure 5. Support in assessment tools

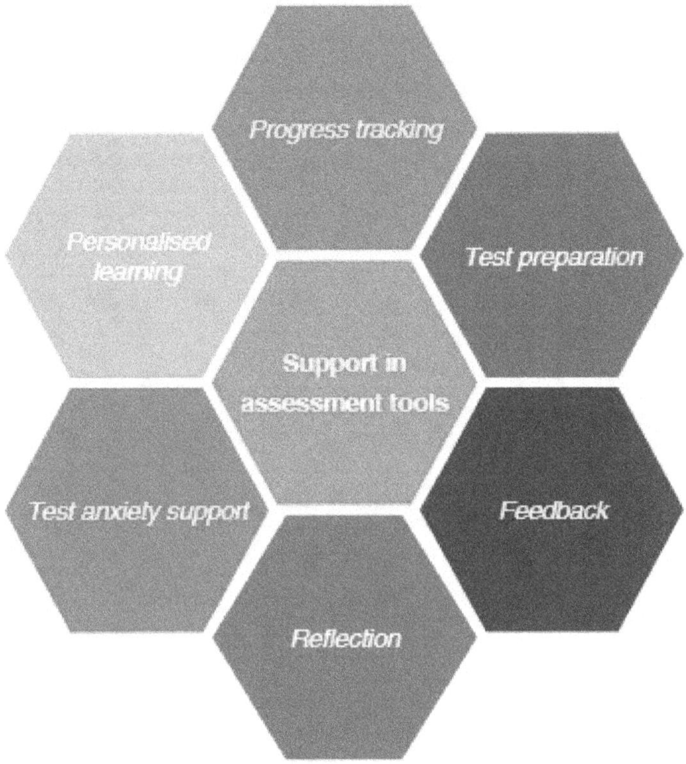

An assessment chatbot would be a valuable resource for students who want to improve their performance on exams and quizzes. It would provide quick and convenient access to information and resources that can help students feel more confident and prepared, and ultimately achieve better results on their assessments.

A chatbot designed to provide **individual task support** would be used to assist students with specific tasks related to their academic work. This type of chatbot would be especially useful for students who need help with tasks outside of the classroom, such as research, writing assignments, or formatting papers. Some features that an individual task support chatbot might include (see fig. 6):

Research support: The chatbot could provide assistance with research tasks such as finding sources, evaluating information, and organising research materials.

Writing support: The chatbot could provide guidance on writing tasks such as brainstorming, outlining, drafting, and revising essays and other written assignments.

Formatting support: The chatbot could provide guidance on formatting papers according to specific guidelines, such as APA or MLA style.

Figure 6. Individual task support

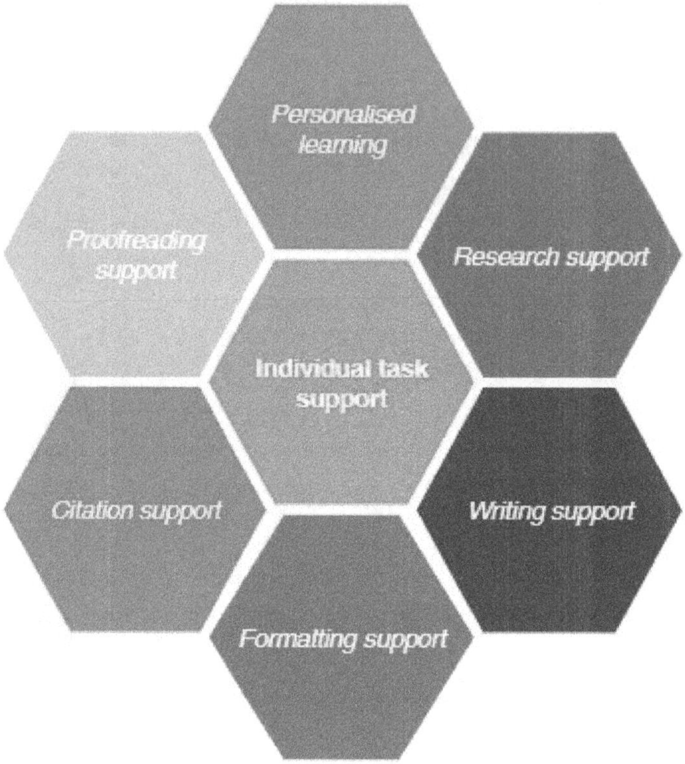

Citation support: The chatbot could assist students with citing sources in their work, including generating bibliographies and correctly formatting in-text citations.

Proofreading support: The chatbot could provide assistance with proofreading and editing written work, including identifying errors and suggesting improvements.

Personalised learning: The chatbot could customise its responses based on student's specific needs and preferences, providing personalised support to help them succeed.

An individual task support chatbot would be a valuable tool for students who need help with specific tasks related to their academic work. It would provide quick and convenient access to information and resources that can help students complete their work more efficiently and effectively.

3.1 Examples of the Personalised Learning Approach

The methodology which we follow while designing a chatbot is depicted in Figure 3.

Figure 7. Chatbot design methodology

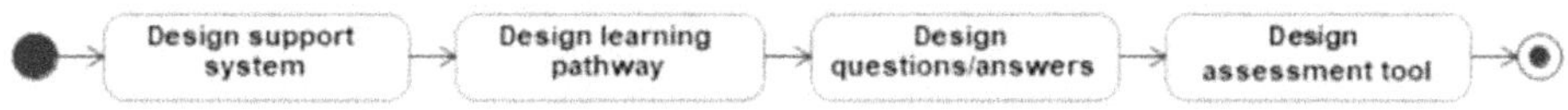

We design a support system which needs to be consistent with other parts of the system. Usually, there is a momental job because the support system can be reused in other chatbots. Sometimes the chatbot support systems will differ a bit if different interactions are planned for chatbots.

During the next step, we design a learning pathway. This is a pedagogical activity. We prepared a scenario where the quiz is related to a conversation when a chatbot has the purpose of asking self-assessment questions.

Having a learning pathway implemented, we can design the conversations or dialogues for chatbots. Finally, we design questions and the answers for chatbot to speak (and write) and the responses to learners.

After preparing the information for the chatbot we develop an assessment tool and all the assessed activities will be available for the teacher to review in a learning management system.

3.2 Personalised Learning Scenarios Implementation

First, we developed scenarios useful for all teachers implementing chatbots in education.

Moreover, a personalised learning pathway is considered to be one of the most effective ways to learn new skills and to reach learning outcomes. Using artificial intelligence (AI) and machine learning (ML) in the educational process is one of the most important trends of modern education which can provide learners flexibility of learning, assuring support any time, based on the personal needs of each learner. Kuhail et al.(2022) say in systematic review that most of the chatbots used a predetermined conversational path, and more than a quarter utilised a personalised learning approach that catered to students' learning needs, while other chatbots used experiential and collaborative learning besides other design principles. Moreover, more than a third of the chatbots were evaluated with experiments, and the results primarily point to improved learning and subjective satisfaction. Challenges and limitations include inadequate or insufficient dataset training and a lack of reliance on usability heuristics.

We are focusing on the developed scenarios (see chapter above) and scenarios implementation into practice. We are using Moodle environment for the chatbots

Figure 8. Personalised learning scenarios

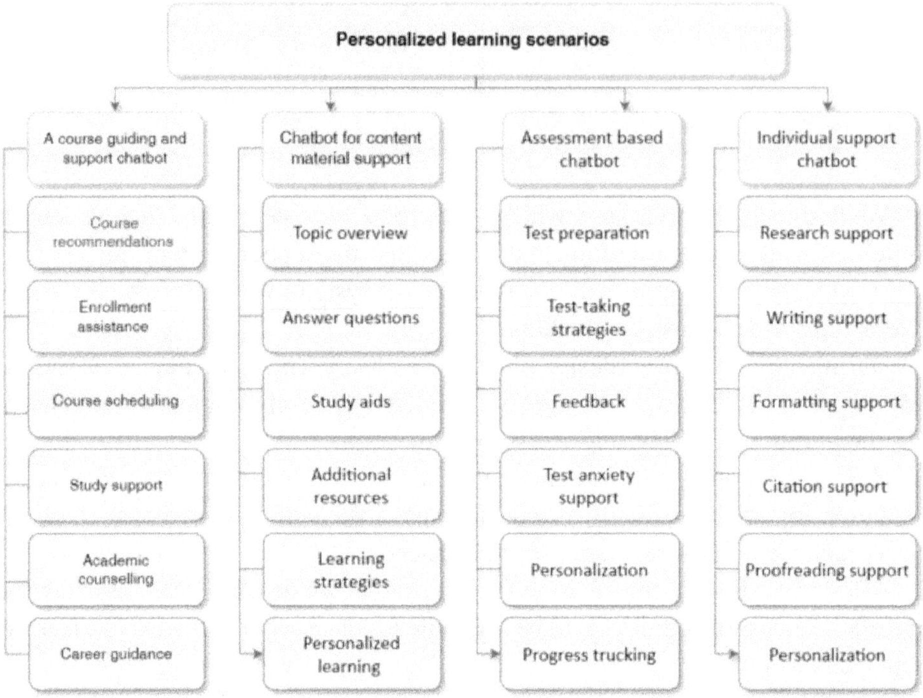

integration and delivery learning modules based on personalised learning scenarios (Figure 4).

During the next step, we are integrating the chatbots into Moodle courses. Our chatbots can be integrated into Moodle's environment either as a custom menu item or as a widget inside an HTML block.

The system follows a set of commands, and the general recommendation process starts by first, fetching data from the database (F), then suggesting relevant learning resources or asking for missing feedback (R) and finally, keeping traces of computed recommendations for further analysis or similar queries (T) (Figure 9).

We presented a dialogue system and proposed a new recommendation approach for the Moodle environment related to the personalised learning approach, based mainly on the development and use of an implemented chatbot (Figure 10).

The important aspect is that the availability of an open popular platform that appears to be an almost perfect environment for chatbots implementation and suggestion for personalised learning.

Figure 9. Chatbots on the platform

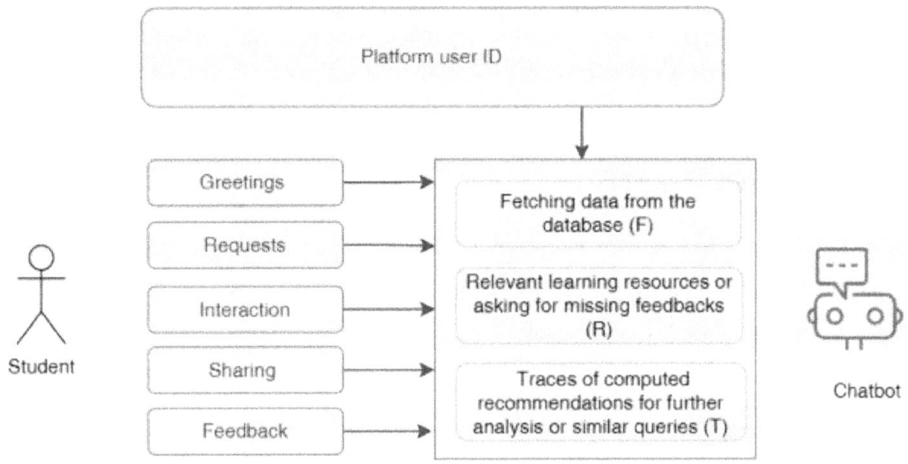

Figure 10. Chatbot implementation in the virtual learning environment

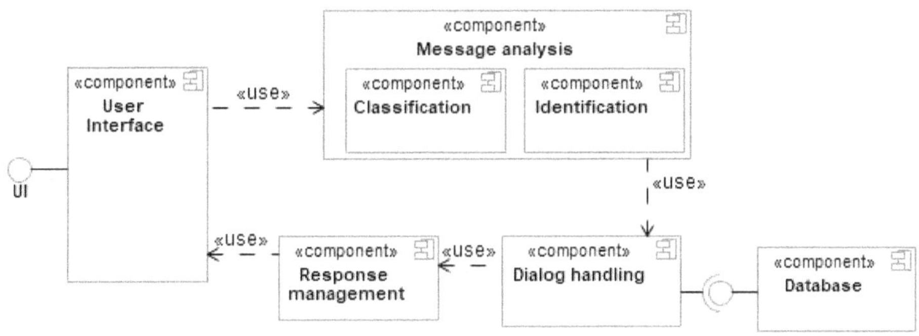

4. CONCLUSION

The advancements in technology to enrich learning in higher education is a result of the push and pull of the needs of the learner and the availability of the technology.

Chatbots help to improve teaching and learning in higher education.

Artificial intelligence as e-learning support has captured the interest of many researchers for its many applications to be used in education for personalised learning approaches.

In total three privileged didactic uses for the platform's bot can be highlighted: lectures, recovery actions and ways of deepening.

Chatbots can have some limitations that could be resolved with specific programming from the beginning, carried out by professionals. It seems necessary to have a department dedicated to technological development, working together with faculty, specialised in the design and implementation of this type of tool.

ACKNOWLEDGEMENT

The case is prepared in the frames of the Erasmus + project "ASSISTANT - Challenge Based Learning in AI Enhanced Digital Transformation Curricular" No. 2022-1-LT01-KA220-HED-00008655.

REFERENCES

Adamopoulou, E., & Moussiades, L. (2020). An overview of chatbot technology. In I. Maglogiannis, L. Iliadis, & E. Pimenidis (Eds.), *Artificial intelligence applications and innovations. AIAI 2020. IFIP advances in information and communication technology* (Vol. 584, pp. 373–383). Springer. doi:10.1007/978-3-030-49186-4_31

Bahja, M., Hammad, R., & Butt, G. (2020). A User-Centric Framework for Educational Chatbots Design and Development. In C. Stephanidis, M. Kurosu, H. Degen, & L. Reinerman-Jones (Eds.), Lecture Notes in Computer Science: Vol. 12424. *HCI International 2020 - Late Breaking Papers: Multimodality and Intelligence. HCII 2020*. Springer. doi:10.1007/978-3-030-60117-1_3

Benotti, L., Martnez, M. C., & Schapachnik, F. (2018). Atool for introducing computer science with automatic formative assessment. *IEEE Transactions on Learning Technologies, 11*(2), 179–192. doi:10.1109/TLT.2017.2682084

Binkis, M., Kubiliūnas, R., Sturienė, R., Dulinskienė, T., Blažauskas, T., & Jakštienė, V. (2021). Rule-Based Chatbot Integration into Software Engineering Course. In A. Lopata, D. Gudonienė, & R. Butkienė (Eds.), *Information and Software Technologies. ICIST 2021. Communications in Computer and Information Science* (Vol. 1486). Springer. doi:10.1007/978-3-030-88304-1_29

Cahn, J. (2017). *CHATBOT: Architecture, design, & development*. University of Pennsylvania School of Engineering and Applied Science Department of Computer and Information Science.

Chaves, A. P., & Gerosa, M. A. (2021). How should my chatbot interact? A survey on social characteristics in human–chatbot interaction design. *International Journal of Human-Computer Interaction*, *37*(8), 729–758. doi:10.1080/10447318.2020.1841438

Fernoagă, V., Stelea, G. A., Gavrilă, C., & Sandu, F. (2018). Intelligent Education Assistant Powered by Chatbots. *eLearning & Software for Education, 2*.

Gonda, D. E., & Chu, B. (2019, December). Chatbot as a learning resource? Creating conversational bots as a supplement for teaching assistant training course. In *2019 IEEE International Conference on Engineering, Technology and education (TALE)* (pp. 1-5). IEEE. 10.1109/TALE48000.2019.9225974

Hasal, M., Nowaková, J., Ahmed Saghair, K., Abdulla, H., Snášel, V., & Ogiela, L. (2021). Chatbots: Security, privacy, data protection, and social aspects. *Concurrency and Computation*, *33*(19), e6426. doi:10.1002/cpe.6426

Kuhail, M. A., Alturki, N., Alramlawi, S., & Alhejori, K. (2023). Interacting with educational chatbots: A systematic review. *Education and Information Technologies*, *28*(1), 973–1018. doi:10.100710639-022-11177-3

Kumar, J. A. (2021). Educational chatbots for project-based learning: Investigating learning outcomes for a team-based design course. *International Journal of Educational Technology in Higher Education*, *18*(1), 65. doi:10.118641239-021-00302-w PMID:34926790

Luo, B., Lau, R. Y., Li, C., & Si, Y. W. (2022). A critical review of state-of-the-art chatbot designs and applications. *Wiley Interdisciplinary Reviews. Data Mining and Knowledge Discovery*, *12*(1), e1434. doi:10.1002/widm.1434

Mafra, M., Nunes, K., Castro, A., Lopes, A., Oran, A. C., Braz, G. Junior, ... Rivero, L. (2022). Defining Requirements for the Development of Useful and Usable Chatbots: An Analysis of Quality Attributes from Academy and Industry. In *International Conference on Human-Computer Interaction* (pp. 479-493). Springer, Cham. 10.1007/978-3-031-05412-9_33

Nimavat, K., & Champaneria, T. (2017). Chatbots: An overview types, architecture, tools and future possibilities. *Int. J. Sci. Res. Dev.*, *5*, 1019–1024.

Okonkwo, C. W., & Ade-Ibijola, A. (2021). Chatbots applications in education: A systematic review. *Computers and Education: Artificial Intelligence*, *2*, 100033. doi:10.1016/j.caeai.2021.100033

Pérez, J. Q., Daradoumis, T., & Puig, J. M. M. (2020). Rediscovering the use of chatbots in education: A systematic literature review. *Computer Applications in Engineering Education*, *28*(6), 1549–1565. doi:10.1002/cae.22326

Sandu, N., & Gide, E. (2019, September). Adoption of AI-Chatbots to enhance student learning experience in higher education in India. In *2019 18th International Conference on Information Technology Based Higher Education and Training (ITHET)* (pp. 1-5). IEEE.

Winkler, R., & Söllner, M. (2018). Unleashing the potential of chatbots in education: A state-of-the-art analysis. In *Academy of management annual meeting (AOM)*. AOM. 10.5465/AMBPP.2018.15903abstract

Chapter 6
Learning Analytics Impact for Learning Evaluation in the Context of Creating Learning Organizations

João Tiago Dias
https://orcid.org/0000-0002-0686-7540
Open University, Lisbon, Portugal

ABSTRACT

This chapter explores the mission and concerns surrounding learning analytics and its significance in learning evaluation in creating learning organizations through digital transformation. It provides an overview of the current learning analytics landscape, emphasizing its potential to drive data-informed decision-making and enhance learning outcomes. The chapter addresses the importance of leveraging learning analytics within the broader context of digital transformation initiatives, highlighting the need to evaluate learning outcomes in digital environments. It underlines the importance of learning evaluation and the role of learning analytics frameworks in collecting and analyzing data and delves into the potential benefits and challenges of implementing learning analytics, highlighting the impact on learning. It also discusses the need for addressing gaps and improving the effectiveness of learning analytics. A couple of case studies are presented to showcase successful implementations and conclude with future directions and predictions for the field.

DOI: 10.4018/979-8-3693-0556-0.ch006

BACKGROUND

According to Agarkar (Agarkar, 2019) "Learning may be described as an 'individual's construction, stemming from an experiential journey, internal to the individual, and leading to a relatively consistent alteration in behavior". Consequently, learning empowers the person to adjust to a particular circumstance and thus assumes the incorporation of the situation's structure and comprehension. This journey results in a relatively enduring shift in one's actions. In essence, this process equips the individual to acclimate to a specific circumstance, assuming a foundational grasp and assimilation of that circumstance. The creation of this knowledge framework can manifest in various manners and by employing diverse approaches. For instance, we can acquire knowledge through traditional means like informative lectures, learn through experimentation and learning from mistakes, uncover insights through independent exploration, understanding concepts by practical application, or even stumble upon understanding accidentally.

Nevertheless, owing to the emergence of technology, this learning process has experienced substantial transformations, encompassing alterations in both learning methodologies and the evaluation of that learning. Innovative technological environments harbor the potential for substantial advancements in training and education, supplying to the necessity of refining skills and keeping knowledge up to date. This domain is currently experiencing a rush in growth, propelled by remarkable developments and progress, all enabled by the integration of technology.

In recent years, Digital Transformation has exerted significant influence on the economy, business operations, and education. It has emerged as a central theme in corporate strategy due to its capacity to generate value. Digital Transformation is characterized by the convergence of advanced technologies and the fusion of physical and digital systems. It carries profound implications for companies compelled to adapt to the new reality of a globalized world. Efficiency and effectiveness in information, services, and personalized experiences are essential for stakeholders. The global pandemic has highlighted the importance of agility with digital technologies making leaders in education and policymakers to be under pressure to embrace a structured approach to transformation facilitated by digital innovation. It brought decision-makers across various sectors to actively seek a clear understanding of digital transformation within intricate systems (McCarthy et al., 2023) .

Also referred by per Baig et al. (2020), the economic landscape has experienced a substantial evolution, primarily driven by the emergence of the COVID-19 virus, also known as SARS-CoV-2. This evolution has notably affected the process of digital transformation, particularly in the scope of business models, where digitalization has become a decisive focus. Many companies have found their sustainability and survival under scrutiny. In response to government-imposed health restrictions,

Digital Transformation has emerged as a lifeline for business continuity. Through digital channels, companies have been able to market their products and provide services that would have otherwise been inaccessible due to government constraints at the onset of the pandemic (Almeida et al., 2020).

With this changing in mind, educational purposes have been transformed along the way. This Digital Transformation have empowered organizations to integrate technology-driven learning platforms in multiple ways, promoting enhanced accessibility to schools, lessons, and degree programs for learners, enabling students to engage in learning from any location, at any time, and using various devices. The adoption of digital tools and technologies involves a revaluation and streamlining of business processes. This includes the effective use of learning management systems (LMS) and other digital platforms (such as gamification tools, adaptive learning platforms or even virtual and augmented reality tools) to optimize the delivery of educational content and efficiently manage student progress (Ewing & Cooper, 2021; McCarthy et al., 2023).

Digital learning also fosters easier collaboration among educators and students. Teachers can easily create and manage groups through learning platforms, facilitating seamless communication and collaboration not only between students and teachers but also among peers. The integration of new services, technologies, and competencies within educational systems also plays a crucial role in enhancing education outcomes. Digital learning platforms offer personalized learning experiences, adaptive assessments, and real-time feedback, resulting in more effective learning for students.

Finally, digital transformation necessitates strategic responses from organizations aiming to redefine their value creation pathways while addressing structural changes and organizational barriers. This involves embracing new digital technologies to enhance teaching and learning outcomes (McCarthy et al., 2023).

McCarthy (McCarthy et al., 2023) considers that customer expectations play a critical role in driving digital transformation (DT) within larger organizations. Recognizing the drivers and markers for transformative change within an educational context and then crafting a well-informed DT strategy, supported by relevant examples, can simplify the collective understanding crucial for successful change management. In the scope of education, DT involves revisioning how to integrate individuals, data, and processes to foster improved environments for students, educators, parents, and system leaders in today's digital-first landscape, while also preparing for future innovations and challenges.

This transformation may necessitate restructuring both formal and informal learning settings, as well as reimagining educational content and its delivery. Additionally, there's a critical need to focus on talent and talent management within educational institutions and systems, beginning from recruitment, hiring, and onboarding, to fostering engagement based on strengths, managing performance, and facilitating career development, all the way to ensuring a positive exit experience. The key to ensuring a satisfactory experience for all stakeholders starts with identifying the primary stakeholder, a process that is often simpler in the business sector. Corporations prioritize customer needs and experiences, making enhanced talent management and organizational development central objectives (McCarthy et al., 2023).

In a learning-oriented organization, the responsibility for evaluation is distributed among all members. The assessment of learning holds significant value for organizations due to: the validation of training programs and enriching educational offerings for their workforce; an initial learning assessment establishes a valuable baseline for evaluating progress in learning practices. However, ongoing assessment must be integrated into the organizational learning process, crucially aligning with evolving company vision and strategy; organizational learning enhances operational efficiency, enabling organizations to thrive in a dynamically changing environment; providing learning opportunities as an employee benefit improves job satisfaction, boosts retention rates, and facilitates upskilling, ultimately benefiting the organization's bottom line; embracing a learning organization framework cultivates an environment that nurtures innovative and expansive thinking patterns; it encourages collective aspirations and installs a continuous learning mindset among individuals (Schwartz & Rist, 2017; Suswanto et al., 2021) .

As so, Learning Evaluation becomes crucial for Learning Organizations under Digital Transformation as they need to cultivate a culture of shared responsibility for evaluation and persistently measure their learning initiatives over time. By doing so, they can foster a vibrant learning organization culture, ultimately creating a more joyful and productive workplace.

UNVEILING THE MISSION AND PURPOSE OF LEARNING ANALYTICS

In this new digital era, innovative methods for creating value have emerged, particularly through optimizing performance and enhancing company profitability using data analysis. Educational institutions and organizations possess an unprecedented wealth of data. This abundance provides a unique opportunity to gather valuable insights into the learning process and its outcomes. Recognizing the importance of adapting to a globalized and interconnected world, both professional and educational learning communities emphasize the delivery of training and learning programs through virtual learning environments.

Data is considered among the most vital assets a company or organization generates and possesses, defining its distinctive qualities. Utilizing data, organizations can precisely identify the root causes of problems and inefficiencies. Moreover, data enables companies to visualize relationships among variables across various locations, departments, and systems in a comprehensive manner (Kleimola & Leppisaari, 2022).

To tackle this challenge, learning analytics (LA) plays a crucial role in identifying and validating significant measures of overall learning phenomena. It also promotes evidence-based practices and interventions, which were often impractical until recent years. Although LA holds promise in measuring and leveraging the development of generic competences, further research and development are essential to gain a deeper understanding of not only its potential benefits but also its limitations as a vital component of learning and comprehensive competence development within Learning Organizations going under Digital Transformation.

Focusing on what Learning Analytics means, we can understand it resides at the intersection of education and data science, constantly evolving. Reviewing Greller and Drachsler (Greller & Drachsler, 2012) definition of Learning Analytics:

"Learning Analytics (LA) is defined as measuring, collecting, and reporting data related to learners and learning environments to understand and improve learning and the surrounding environment".

Fundamentally, it involves the systematic collection, analysis, and interpretation of data generated throughout the learning journey. This data incorporates various facets of student engagement, behaviour, interactions with educational resources, and performance. The primary objective of Learning Analytics is to provide meaningful insights from this data, informing decisions and enriching the learning journey (Tsai et al., 2020). Below in figure 1, we have the critical dimensions of learning analytics by Greller (Greller & Drachsler, 2012):

The central mission of Learning Analytics is to facilitate tailored learning experiences. By examining individual learner data, instructional institutions can customize educational content and methodologies to meet each student's unique

Figure 1. Critical dimensions of learning analytics

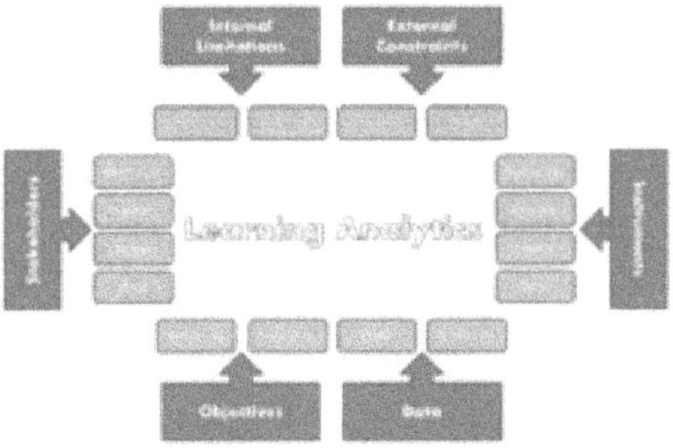

needs, fostering heightened engagement and superior learning outcomes (Greller & Drachsler, 2012).

According to Lodge (Lodge et al., 2018), Learning Analytics empowers institutions to discern patterns of student engagement and disengagement. Understanding the circumstances surrounding disengagement enables timely intervention by educators, thereby significantly enhancing the overall learning experience. It also empowers educators and administrators with data-driven insights. By utilizing data to shape decisions regarding curriculum design, teaching methodologies, and resource allocation, institutions can make informed choices that optimize the educational process. Furthermore, it cultivates a culture of continuous improvement within educational organizations. Through regular data analysis and assessment of learning outcomes, institutions can identify areas for enhancement and innovation, crucial for adapting to the evolving needs of learners in the digital age.

When implementing Learning Analytics models there are some goals to be achieved. It will assist in monitoring the progress of individual learners and entire classes. This monitoring can pinpoint struggling students requiring additional support and highlight areas necessitating instructional material refinement. It will forecast learner behaviour and outcomes. For instance, it can predict students at risk of dropping out or failing a course, allowing timely educator intervention and support provision. Educational institutions can optimize resource allocation based on data-driven insights. For example, if analytics reveal that a particular instructional method is more effective, resources can be reallocated to prioritize its implementation. It also revolutionizes traditional learning evaluation methods. It advocates for a more nuanced and comprehensive assessment of learning outcomes, incorporating not only test scores but also engagement, behaviour, and other data points. This approach offers a holistic view of student progress, facilitating more accurate and actionable insights that drive improvements in teaching and curriculum design (Kew & Tasir, 2021; Lodge et al., 2018).

In essence, Learning Analytics has the potential to reshape traditional paradigms of learning evaluation, providing a comprehensive, nuanced assessment of learning outcomes. By considering a broader spectrum of data points, it offers a holistic understanding of student learning, fuelling precise insights for refined teaching methodologies and curriculum enhancements, playing a critical role in modern education. As Learning Organizations embark on their digital transformation journeys, Learning Analytics emerges as an indispensable tool in their arsenal to reshape learning and education to its full potential.

THE SIGNIFICANCE OF LEARNING ANALYTICS FOR LEARNING EVALUATION

In today's scenario, technology's rapid evolution and the growing complexity of learning underline the necessity for superior analytical tools to effectively assess and evaluate learning outcomes. Traditional evaluation methods often prove inadequate in offering timely, actionable insights into both student performance and the effectiveness of instructional approaches (Ifenthaler & Yau, 2020). Learning Analytics has emerged as a transformative instrument, providing a data-driven avenue to enhance the evaluation and assessment of learning. It has a crucial role in delivering real-time feedback, identifying knowledge gaps, monitoring learner advancement, facilitating adaptive learning, and fostering a culture of constant enhancement within instructional institutions. Business organizations and educators alike seek advanced analytical instruments to comprehend learners' challenges and gaps carefully, enabling them to make more informed decisions and enhance the efficacy of the teaching and learning processes. The inclusion of an efficient and user-friendly learning analytics tool holds immense value for all stakeholders (Dias & Santos, 2022).

Kleimola (Kleimola & Leppisaari, 2022) refers that Learning Analytics provides educators and educational institutions with the means to acquire real-time information on student engagement and performance. By analysing this data, educators can pinpoint struggling students and rapidly intervene, while also adjusting instructional methods instantly based on real-time feedback. This formative assessment approach not only elevates learning outcomes but also empowers educators to tailor their teaching strategies precisely to meet their students' needs.

Additionally, Learning Analytics serves as a bridge between formative and summative evaluations. Formative assessments focus on ongoing learning processes and enable instructional adjustments, while summative assessments evaluate overall learning outcomes. Learning Analytics offers a continuous flow of data that informs both types of evaluation. Educators can monitor learners' progress over time, facilitating the assessment of whether learning objectives are being achieved and where modifications are required.

A prominent advantage of Learning Analytics is its ability to identify knowledge gaps among students. Through the analysis of their interactions with learning materials, quizzes, and assignments, educators can pinpoint areas where students struggle or fail to grasp crucial concepts. This data-driven insight allows for targeted interventions, such as providing extra resources or reevaluating the curriculum to effectively address these gaps. Furthermore, it also supports instructional interventions by assisting educators in making well-informed decisions. By analysing student performance data, instructors can tailor their teaching methods to suit the diverse needs of their students. For example, if the data indicates that a particular group of learners excels in a specific area, educators can challenge them with advanced materials, while simultaneously providing additional support to those who require it (Dias & Santos, 2022; Ifenthaler & Yau, 2020).

Adaptive learning, a pedagogical approach that tailors learning experiences to individual learner needs and preferences, is greatly facilitated by Learning Analytics. Learning Analytics plays a pivotal role in enabling adaptive learning by continuously gathering and analysing data on each student's progress, strengths, and weaknesses. This data can be utilized to design personalized learning pathways, ensuring that students receive content and resources that align with their unique learning styles and pace. Moreover, Learning Analytics encourages data-driven decision-making in educational institutions. By analysing trends and patterns in data, administrators can make informed choices regarding curriculum development, resource allocation, and instructional strategies. This evidence-based approach fosters continuous improvement within learning organizations, resulting in enhanced learning outcomes and heightened student satisfaction (Dias & Santos, 2022; Kleimola & Leppisaari, 2022).

To unlock the full potential of Learning Analytics, institutions must thoughtfully select an appropriate framework or model. Various frameworks are available, each with its own set of advantages and limitations. Educators and administrators should carefully consider factors such as the institution's goals, the types of data to be collected, and the technical capabilities of their systems when choosing a framework that aligns with their specific needs (Macfadyen, 2022).

Instructors strive to find effective learning models in this digital environment. Online education is well-known for its interactivity and the ability to blend various teaching and learning strategies, with the Learning Management System (LMS) playing a central role in both online and offline training. Furthermore, organizations utilize LMSs to ensure that both new and existing employees possess the necessary skills and competencies. They recognize the potential of their training platforms to enhance continuous learning, emphasizing compatibility and adaptability (Dias & Santos, 2022).

According to Bradley (Bradley, 2021), we can understand that a Learning Management System is a web-based application designed to manage learning content, student interaction, assessment tools, progress reports, and student activities. Therefore, Learning Management Systems (LMS) play a critical role in data collection throughout the learning process. These systems record student interactions with course materials, assessments, and collaborative tools, generating a rich dataset that offers valuable insights into student behaviour and performance. This dataset serves as the foundation for Learning Analytics.

Collecting data is merely the initial step. The true value of Learning Analytics lies in the analysis and interpretation of this data to derive actionable insights. Educators can leverage these insights to provide early alerts for at-risk students, offer personalized recommendations to learners, and optimize their training paths. Additionally, instructors can enhance their teaching effectiveness by incorporating evidence-based insights from Learning Analytics.

By understanding the importance of Learning Analytics in the context of learning evaluation, educators and institutions can unlock the full potential of data-driven education.

CROSSING THE CHALLENGES AND GAPS IN LEARNING ANALYTICS

Within the continuously shifting terrain of education, the combination of technology has sparked a revolution. Learning Analytics, a domain leveraging data's potential to enrich educational results, has emerged as a formidable asset for educational institutions and organizations.

According to Dias and Santos (Dias & Santos, 2022), it becomes evident that the integration of a Learning Analytics Framework within Learning Management Systems yields significant advantages for learners, educators, and organizations alike. Given the evolving landscape of learning and its escalating significance across learners, educators, and particularly within organizations, the implementation of a targeted Learning Analytics Framework within Learning Management Systems stands out as a highly endorsed approach in the literature. A Learning Analytics model facilitates comprehensive data collection and analysis from various sources, enabling the prediction of learning outcomes and student retention. It achieves this by enhancing early warning and recommendation systems, providing personalized guidance, feedback, and support to learners. Simultaneously, it equips teachers and instructors to gain deeper insights into their learners' needs and potential, enabling timely intervention during the learning journey, which will deeply impact the success of Learning Evaluation.

A notable benefit of this implementation is the path it creates for systematically refining, assessing, and enhancing instructional effectiveness through the integration of interactive technologies. This holistic approach enhances the teaching and learning experience, bridging knowledge gaps, and fostering a positive student attitude making them to improve in what they feel they have more difficulty to execute. Personalized analysis of students' learning paths and behaviour patterns helps them recognize the adjustments they can make to enhance their study progress. The data generated from these analytical tools holds immense value for organizations, acting as a catalyst to guide senior management in making informed decisions that bolster organizational capacity in Learning Analytics. This, in turn, amplifies the efficacy of Learning Management Systems, thereby enhancing teaching and learning outcomes.

Considering these numerous benefits, a thoughtfully designed Learning Analytics framework has the potential to supply learners with a tailored learning experience and enhance future e-learning courses. It achieves this by aiding instructors in comprehending the learner's journey and facilitating the attainment of their learning objectives (Dias & Santos, 2022).

Although not only benefits are found when implementing Learning Analytics models. Comprehending the progression of online education and learning analytics within specific contexts unveils various challenges that demand attention when conceiving and executing a Learning Analytics (LA) Framework in an educational or organizational setting. These challenges stem from the rapid advancements in technology and the evolving needs of diverse stakeholders. Attending these challenges demands a nuanced understanding of their significance and the specific contexts of implementation.

A significant obstacle to overcome is the necessity to craft a meticulous instructional design that ensures the competence of newly trained learners, given its profound impact on learner behaviour. Consequently, a critical task involves identifying and seamlessly integrating advanced instructional methods and appropriate evaluation techniques to support student engagement and enhance the efficacy of the learning journey. This situation may inadvertently result in a lack of regular supervision, making it difficult to guide learners effectively and provide them with nuanced feedback for adjusting their learning paths appropriately.

Therefore, when devising an LA framework, it is vital to incorporate predefined rules linked to users' learning styles and deploy adaptable, intuitive analytical tools. These tools could contain simple yet powerful visualizations and suggestions of pedagogical actions. Such measures are crucial to ensure that the framework supplies to the needs of all stakeholders, offering actionable insights that foster an effective learning environment, keeping students engaged and aligning with course-specific contexts.

Moreover, meticulous handling of data manipulation and analysis is essential to stop misinformation or inaccurate inferences in prediction models, like algorithmic biases and wrong interpretability of analytics, impacting negatively on data-driven decision-making. Equally important is enhancing the digital competencies of teaching staff, enabling more informed decision-making processes and robust feedback mechanisms. Additionally, assisting learners in following acquired knowledge thoroughly poses a notable obstacle that guarantees attention.

Addressing the shift from traditional diverse learning to online education is a critical concern, potentially requiring a transformation in organizational culture and management models, emphasizing the value-adding role of Learning Analytics. Another significant gap lies in the limited scalability or replicability of these frameworks across diverse scenarios, impeding their widespread adoption and delaying the management of new knowledge.

Lastly, the lack of meticulous attention to designing instructional conditions can significantly impede the deployment of the framework, potentially leading to over or underestimation of specific predictors and consequently distorting the analytical outcomes (Dias & Santos, 2022).

One important issue to mention, regards the privacy and ethics to data security, transparency, algorithmic biases, and the limitations of data-driven decision-making. There must be implemented some strategies to achieve successful implementations of the LA models. The existing challenges and gaps in the field of Learning Analytics underscore the necessity for ongoing research and heightened awareness. Given the rapid evolution of this domain, staying informed about best practices, emerging technologies, and ethical considerations is essential for progress and efficacy.

According to Tsai (Tsai et al., 2021), a primary concern within the department of Learning Analytics turns around privacy breaches and ethical dilemmas associated with the collection, storage, and use of data. As instructional institutions assemble extensive data on learner´s learning behaviours, ensuring the utmost sensitivity in handling this information becomes imperative. Safeguarding learner privacy stands as a principal objective. In the absence of adequate safeguards, the misuse of such data can have profound and far-reaching consequences. Data security is closely interlinked with privacy concerns. Instructional institutions serve as custodians of sensitive information, declaring them susceptible to cyberattacks. Breaches in data security could lead to the exposure of personal and academic data, paving the way for identity theft and other malicious activities. Also, transparency in Learning Analytics is vital for building trust among stakeholders. Transparency leads to openly discussing data collection and usage, as well as the algorithms and methodologies utilized for analysis. Institutions need to provide lucid guidelines detailing how data is employed to enhance learning outcomes.

To mitigate these risks, institutions must invest in robust cybersecurity measures. Also, regular audits, encryption, and stringent access controls are fundamental elements of a thorough data security strategy. Additionally, ensuring that staff members are well-versed in cybersecurity best practices is crucial in minimizing vulnerabilities. Institutions must institute clear policies and guidelines governing data collection and usage. Learners should be provided comprehensive information regarding the data being collected and its intended usage. Consent mechanisms should be firmly established, granting individuals control over the extent to which their data is utilized for analytical purposes. Finally, transparent practices effectively relieve concerns regarding invasive surveillance and misuse of data, fostering a sense of trust among those impacted by Learning Analytics (Tsai et al., 2021).

Deho (Deho et al., 2022) refers another major concern related to biased algorithms used for data analysis which can perpetuate inequality and discrimination. Moreover, the interpretability of analytics holds immense significance. Stakeholders must possess the ability to comprehend how decisions are arrived at based on data to ensure fairness and equity. Mitigating algorithmic biases necessitates the use of diverse and unbiased data samples during model training. Additionally, there should be a priority on developing machine learning models that are interpretable, providing insights into the decision-making process.

While Learning Analytics possesses the potential to revolutionize education, it is not without its limitations. Relying solely on data-driven decision-making, without balancing it with human judgment, can lead to a one-size-fits-all approach to education or instruction, inadvertently neglecting the individual needs of learners.

IMPLEMENTING LEARNING ANALYTICS

According to Rienties (Rienties et al., 2017), implementing Learning Analytics effectively, requires addressing a range of challenges and obstacles. Instructional institutions must allocate resources to reinforce technology infrastructure, provide training in data literacy, and seamlessly integrate analytics into existing educational frameworks. Additionally, cultivating a culture that prioritizes data-driven decision-making and fosters innovation is crucial.

Achieving a successful implementation of learning analytics models involves a series of essential steps and techniques (Macfadyen, 2022). Some examples of successful implementations of learning analytics models depart from these general steps:

First Step is Defining Clear Policy Objectives - Prior to implementing learning analytics within your organization, it's crucial to define precise policy objectives. This initial step aids in comprehending your organization, assessing its readiness for change, and pinpointing the necessary resources and stakeholders vital for successful implementation.

Second Step regards Contextual Mapping - Mapping the context demands identifying the purposes of learning analytics and the key stakeholders involved. This mapping process helps in understanding the specific context in which learning analytics will be applied and identifies the stakeholders whose roles will be impacted by the implementation.

Third Step is to Identify Learning Analytics Goals - The identification of learning analytics goals involves outlining the intended goals and objectives of the learning analytics implementation. This step is vital in determining the data that must be collected and analysed to achieve the desired educational outcomes.

Fourth Step is to Leverage Data Science and Qualitative Analysis - Successful implementation of learning analytics models require expertise in areas such as data science and qualitative analysis. Proficiency in these domains is essential for collecting and analysing data, providing valuable insights into student learning patterns and performance.

Fifth Step is to Apply Information Visualization and Data Mining - Information visualization and data mining are pivotal techniques for uncovering significant patterns within learning analytics data. Employing these techniques facilitates the identification of trends and patterns related to student learning behaviour and performance.

Sixth Step is to Categorize Learning Analytics Models - Categorizing learning analytics models based on their objectives and identifying their relevant components aids in understanding the diverse types of learning analytics models. This categorization enables insights into how these models can be utilized to achieve specific educational outcomes.

Seventh Step is to Utilize Predictive Models - Constructing predictive models through machine learning methods using historical data from prior course presentations enables the prediction of student performance. These models can identify students who might require additional support, enhancing proactive intervention strategies.

By following these steps and utilizing the mentioned techniques, organizations can effectively implement learning analytics models to enhance educational processes and outcomes.

Several organizations and educational institutions have demonstrated successful implementations of Learning Analytics. For example, IBM Watson's AI-driven solutions (*IBM Watson*, 2011) have been instrumental in tailoring learning experiences within the education sector. We could also mention, for example, LinkIt. LinkIt (*LinkIt*, 2010) is a data analytics company that provides insights into student performance and progress. Their platform uses data visualization and predictive analytics to help educators make data-driven decisions.

Another good example is the Open University (UK). The Open University UK (Rienties et al., 2017) stands out among a select few institutions for its explicit and systematic documentation of learning designs on a significant scale. Leveraging advanced analytical techniques on extensive and detailed datasets, the Open University has been delving into the intricate realm of instructional practices. It has not only provided empirical evidence but also conceptual insights into how learning design profoundly shapes student behaviour, contentment, and academic performance. Learning Design, the methodological approach pioneered and practiced by the Open University (OU), is characterized as a "methodology empowering educators and designers to make informed decisions when creating learning activities and interventions. It is pedagogically driven, optimizing the use of appropriate resources and technologies" (Rienties et al., 2017). In essence, LD places emphasis on 'students' engagement in learning,' shifting the focus from 'teachers' actions' or 'course content.' Within the OU, there is a growing acknowledgment that LD serves as a vital catalyst for effective learning, recognizing its critical role in steering educational outcomes.

These implementations offer valuable insights into the significance of collaboration among data scientists, educators, and administrators. Furthermore, the iterative nature of Learning Analytics emphasizes the importance of continuous enhancements and adaptations based on feedback and the evolving landscape of education.

CONCLUSION

In the early years of this century, the rapid expansion of information and communication technology marked a significant transformation. Digital technology became paramount across various domains, particularly in work environments and formal as well as informal education. This shift paved the way for e-Learning, emerging as a powerful educational tool and a viable alternative to traditional learning methods.

The escalating demand for learning solutions has placed considerable pressure on businesses to meet these needs. Consequently, this has exposed certain knowledge gaps, a revelation substantiated by numerous studies. As a response, there is a growing necessity for more efficient analytical tools that are user-friendly yet capable of offering precise insights to trainers. These insights are pivotal for tailoring instructional designs to learners' unique paths, fostering higher engagement and value in their training experiences and a critical step for Learning Evaluation.

The global implementation of e-Learning technologies has become imperative for enhancing the knowledge base of organizations, a need underscored prominently during the recent Covid-19 pandemic, prompting widespread adoption by major corporations. Many strategic e-Learning platforms were carefully chosen to address this priority. These platforms boast features such as comprehensive data analysis, drawing from multiple sources to forecast learning outcomes and student retention. They enhance early warning and recommendation systems, ensuring personalized feedback and guidance along the learners' educational journeys, pinpointing areas that must be improved. This, undoubtedly, holds immense significance for any organization and its evidence-based decision-making, amplifying the potential and value of every employee for the business.

However, deploying such technology within organizations poses challenges, as highlighted in various research endeavours. Researchers have pointed out critical obstacles and inhibitors, particularly in crafting personalized instructional designs that ensure learning proficiency across diverse scenarios. These difficulties lead to limited use, indicating a pressing need to address these challenges to unleash the full potential of these tools.

One noteworthy limitation in the research landscape is the contextual focus, with most studies concentrating on instructional learning analytics within educational rather than corporate settings. This suggests that most businesses might be utilizing existing Learning Management Systems (LMS) designed for educational institutions. Practical application and scalability of such instruments remain elusive due to the lack of standardized models and adaptability across varied contexts. Not all organizations readily embrace e-Learning technologies due to a lack of the appropriate mindset and understanding of their benefits.

Despite the extensive research on the subject, further exploration is warranted to confront evolving challenges in Learning Analytics. There remains a wealth of knowledge to uncover and improvements to implement for optimal integration of this learning technology. The complete potential of these tools is yet to be fully harnessed and actualized. To enhance the depth of potential Learning Analytics frameworks, integrating additional analytical layers or techniques is essential to gain profound insights that can significantly enhance learners' data comprehension and their learning trajectories.

Artificial Intelligence and data mining will undoubtedly play pivotal roles in data analysis and extraction, aiding in the assessment of various Key Performance Indicators (KPIs) outlined by the Learning Analytic frameworks. These technologies will facilitate trainers in accurately manipulating and managing data. Moreover, a behavioural and cultural mindset must accompany the technical aspects, as the perceived value of this technology can dictate organizational success and market positioning.

Another important concern to consider is the Ethical issue. Incorporating learning analytics within a company necessitates a careful consideration of data privacy, security, and ethical utilization. Adhering to best practices and ethical guidelines during this integration is vital to safeguard student privacy, uphold data security, and ensure responsible and ethical data usage. By following these principles, organizations can instil trust and use learning analytics in a manner that enhances student outcomes responsibly and ethically.

Future research efforts should explore emerging technologies like the metaverse and virtual reality, analysing their potential synergies with analytical and e-Learning tools. Additionally, specialized training and the establishment of dedicated business departments are imperative to equip organizations with the necessary knowledge for leveraging these tools effectively.

In conclusion, the validation of existing Learning Analytics frameworks through extensive testing within diverse organizations is paramount. This testing phase will yield crucial information, instrumental in refining the existing models, overcoming its limitations, and enhancing its applicability in real-world contexts. The effective and accurate implementation of a Learning Analytics framework will undeniably influence the success of the digital transformation within any business, fostering the creation of a unique Learning Organization.

REFERENCES

Agarkar, S. C. (2019). Influence of Learning Theories on Science Education. *Resonance*, *24*(8), 847–859. doi:10.100712045-019-0848-7

Bradley, V. M. (2021). Learning Management System (LMS) Use with Online Instruction. *International Journal of Technology in Education*, *4*(1), 68–92. doi:10.46328/ijte.36

Deho, O. B., Zhan, C., Li, J., Liu, J., Liu, L., & Duy Le, T. (2022). How do the existing fairness metrics and unfairness mitigation algorithms contribute to ethical learning analytics? *British Journal of Educational Technology*, *53*(4), 822–843. doi:10.1111/bjet.13217

Dias, J., & Santos, A. (2022). Learning Analytics Framework Applied to Training Context. In A. Reis, J. Barroso, P. Martins, A. Jimoyiannis, R. Y.-M. Huang, & R. Henriques (Eds.), *Technology and Innovation in Learning, Teaching and Education* (pp. 110–130). Springer Nature Switzerland., doi:10.1007/978-3-031-22918-3_9

Ewing, L.-A., & Cooper, H. B. (2021). Technology-enabled remote learning during Covid-19: Perspectives of Australian teachers, students and parents. *Technology, Pedagogy and Education*, *30*(1), 41–57. doi:10.1080/1475939X.2020.1868562

Greller, W., & Drachsler, H. (2012). Translating Learning into Numbers: A Generic Framework for Learning Analytics. *Journal of Educational Technology & Society*, *15*(3), 42–57.

Ifenthaler, D., & Yau, J. Y.-K. (2020). Utilising learning analytics to support study success in higher education: A systematic review. *Educational Technology Research and Development*, *68*(4), 1961–1990. doi:10.100711423-020-09788-z

Kew, S. N., & Tasir, Z. (2021). Analysing students' cognitive engagement in e-learning discussion forums through content analysis. *Knowledge Management and E-Learning*, *13*(1), 39–57. *Scopus*. doi:10.34105/j.kmel.2021.13.003

Kleimola, R., & Leppisaari, I. (2022). Learning analytics to develop future competences in higher education: A case study. *International Journal of Educational Technology in Higher Education, 19*(1), 17. doi:10.118641239-022-00318-w

LinkIt. (2010). https://www.linkit.com/

Lodge, J. M., Horvath, J. C., & Corrin, L. (2018). *Learning Analytics in the Classroom: Translating Learning Analytics Research for Teachers.* Routledge. doi:10.4324/9781351113038

Macfadyen, L. P. (2022). Institutional Analytics. Em C. Lang, G. Siemens, & A. F. Wise (Eds.), The Handbook of Learning Analytics (2.a ed., pp. 173–186). SOLAR. doi:10.18608/hla22.017

McCarthy, A. M., Maor, D., McConney, A., & Cavanaugh, C. (2023). Digital transformation in education: Critical components for leaders of system change. *Social Sciences & Humanities Open, 8*(1), 100479. doi:10.1016/j.ssaho.2023.100479

Rienties, B., Nguyen, Q., Holmes, W., & Reedy, K. (2017). A review of ten years of implementation and research in aligning learning design with learning analytics at the Open University UK. [s]. *Interaction Design and Architecture, 33*(33), 134–154. doi:10.55612-5002-033-007

Schwartz, M. J., & Rist, R. C. (2017). Organizational Learning, the Learning Organization, and Independent Evaluation. In *The International Monetary Fund and the Learning Organization.* International Monetary Fund., https://www.elibrary.imf.org/display/book/9781475546675/ch007.xml

Suswanto, B., Sulaiman, A. I., Sugito, T., Weningsih, S., Sabiq, A., & Kuncoro, B. (2021). Designing Online Learning Evaluation in Times of Covid-19 Pandemic. *International Educational Research, 4*(1). *Artigo, 1*(1), p18. doi:10.30560/ier.v4n1p18

Tsai, Y.-S., Rates, D., Moreno-Marcos, P. M., Muñoz-Merino, P. J., Jivet, I., Scheffel, M., Drachsler, H., Delgado Kloos, C., & Gašević, D. (2020). Learning analytics in European higher education—Trends and barriers. *Computers & Education, 155*, 103933. doi:10.1016/j.compedu.2020.103933

Tsai, Y.-S., Whitelock-Wainwright, A., & Gašević, D. (2021). More Than Figures on Your Laptop: (Dis)trustful Implementation of Learning Analytics. *Journal of Learning Analytics, 3*(3), 81–100. doi:10.18608/jla.2021.7379

Chapter 7
Designing Digital Learning Content to Support a Corporate Digital Learning Strategy

Lúcia Moreira
https://orcid.org/0009-0002-5384-0305
Human Architects, Portugal

ABSTRACT

In a global context of digital transformation, organisations have been challenged to embrace innovation and new technology and reviewed methodological approaches to enhance their digital learning ecosystems, including a systematic review of the internal value proposition of how people learn, share, and build new knowledge. The relationship between a learning organization, digital transformation, and digital learning is intertwined, as they are all interconnected and mutually reinforcing. Digital learning allows for integrating immersive learning experiences, personalized learning paths, and data-driven insights, which can drive performance improvements and foster innovation within the organization. This chapter aims to resume the main components an organization, and could promote an assessment and apply when designing digital learning content to support a broader digital learning strategy.

1. INTRODUCTION

In a global context of digital transformation, organisations have been challenged to embrace innovation and new technology and reviewed methodological approaches to

DOI: 10.4018/979-8-3693-0556-0.ch007

enhance their digital learning ecosystems (Leso et al., 2022), including a systematic review of the internal value proposition of how people learn, share, and build new knowledge, which are operational concepts for acting as a Learning Organisation (Senge, 2006).

The relationship between a Learning Organisation (LO), Digital Transformation (DT), and Digital Learning (DL) is intertwined, as they are all interconnected and mutually reinforcing (Helbis et al., 2021).

A Learning Organisation provides the foundation for embracing digital transformation initiatives. This, in turn, facilitates the development of a digital learning ecosystem within the organisation (Ifenthaler et al., 2020).

Digital learning plays a significant role in supporting digital transformation and the development of a learning organisation, as it encompasses using digital technologies and resources to facilitate and enhance learning experiences (Helbig et al., 2021). It may involve creating and delivering educational content through digital platforms, online courses, multimedia resources, and interactive learning materials (Alessi & Trollip, 2000). It leverages technology to provide flexible, personalised, and engaging learning opportunities.

Digital learning allows for integrating immersive learning experiences, personalised learning paths, and data-driven insights, which can drive performance improvements and foster innovation within the organisation (Helbig et al., 2021; Leso et al., 2022).

One of the core components of digital learning is digital content. They provide the necessary resources, tools, and learning experiences to adapt to digital technologies, enable access to digital skills, enhance flexibility and scalability, foster personalisation, and encourage collaboration and connectivity. They are integral components of the digital transformation journey in organisations (Seufert et al., 2016).

Digital content is any information or media created, stored, or distributed in a digital format. It may include articles, videos, images, audio files, and social media posts (Wiley D. et al., 2004).

Digital Learning Content (DLC), on the other hand, is specifically designed and developed to facilitate learning and educational experiences (Koedinger et al., 2012). It is intended to support instructional objectives, provide structured learning experiences, and enhance learners' knowledge, skills, or competencies (Majumdar, S., 2003; Seufert, S., & Meier, C., 2016).

Although digital content and digital learning content may seem similar, the latter prioritises learning objectives, instructional design principles and creating meaningful learning experiences (Jahnke, I., 2022).

According to Seufert, S., & Meier, C. (2016): "Digital transformation requires not only general skills and attitudes. These skills and attitudes must be applied and used in the specific functions and professional domains that constitute the organisation (…). Digital transformation emerges when usage enables innovation and creativity, leading to significant change – at the individual or organisational level."

Digital transformation and digital learning contents are closely intertwined. Digital learning content plays a vital role in supporting digital transformation as an enabler in educational institutions and organisations.

As institutions adopt digital technologies and strategies to transform their processes, systems, and learning environments, DLC provides the necessary resources and tools for delivering effective and engaging online education that is flexible and scalable (Egloffstein, M., and Ifenthaler, D. (2016). DLC facilitates the transition from traditional classroom-based learning to digital and online learning experiences, which can be personalised and adaptive to cater to individual learners' needs and preferences (Ifenthaler et al., 2020).

Furthermore, DLC generates valuable data to guide and drive digital transformation efforts. Learning analytics and data from digital learning platforms provide insights into learner behaviour, performance, and engagement. These insights can help optimise learning experiences, identify areas for improvement, and inform decision-making related to digital transformation initiatives (Wise, A., 2019). Additionally, DLC promotes access to knowledge and skills through online courses, tutorials, and other interactive resources, enabling the achievement of digital literacy and fluency. These resources can be easily updated, revised, and shared across multiple platforms.

In summary, DLC supports and facilitates digital transformation by providing the necessary resources, tools, and learning experiences to adapt to digital technologies, enable access to digital skills, enhance flexibility and scalability, foster personalisation and adaptability, encourage collaboration and connectivity, and generate valuable data-driven insights. They are an integral part of the digital transformation journey in educational institutions and organisations (Ifenthaler, D., 2018).

The process and strategy adopted for managing digital learning differ from organisation to organisation and are highly influenced by its culture, type of company and process maturity, among other criteria (Seufert, S., & Meier, C., 2016).

Many models, methodologies, principles, and standards support different digital learning strategies and policies associated with ROI and ROE. This plurality of approaches and ways of being a learning organisation plays a crucial role in tailoring the best learning experience in each organisation. However, following and adopting the best practices and reference model as a standard is critical to guarantee the criteria and integrity of the concept of a learning organisation (Visser et al., 2019).

A multidisciplinary team usually supports the entire lifecycle of digital learning content design and implementation (Santos et al., 2014). Digital transformation has also promoted a shift in this model from a team-based role design to a skill-based model design. With this reference, nowadays, multidisciplinary is focused on the core competencies required for each step in the process. This is particularly relevant not just for building a skill-based plan associated with the digital learning strategy of the organisation but also for defining the requirements related to the profile of the teams, which supports the design and implementation of the digital content (Seufert & Meier, 2016).

The European Union advocates for a paradigm shift by promoting 2023 as the "European Year of Skills" (European Commission, 2022). This initiative emphasises the importance of lifelong learning, empowering individuals, and encouraging organisations to contribute to green and digital transitions. It also supports innovation and competitiveness, which is a crucial component in the design and implementation of the DLC (European Commission, 2019).

This article aims to resume the main components an organisation could promote an assessment and apply when designing digital learning content to support a broader digital learning strategy through a five-level framework proposal (Figure 1).

The main components are associated with instructional design models and frameworks; standards and interoperability criteria for DL; DL Chunk reference model, which includes types of DL contents such as pedagogical requirements, instructional and multimedia principles for DL; Learning attributes and learner path personalisation and skills-based reference model to support the design and implementation of the DLC lifecycle.

Figure 1. Proposal of a Framework for DLC

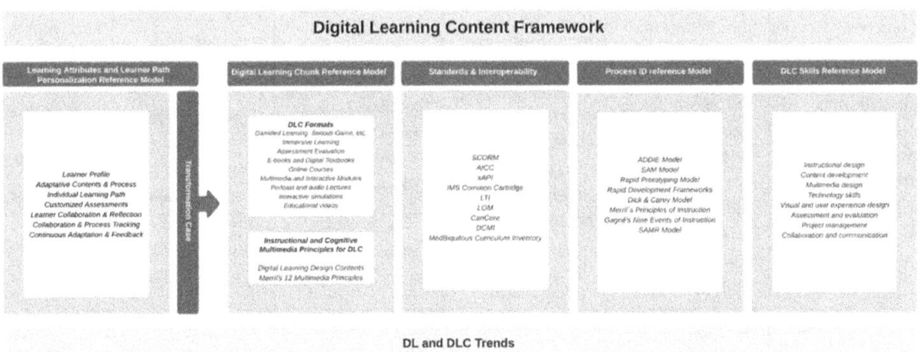

2. UNDERSTANDING THE DIGITAL LEARNING DESIGN MODEL CONCEPT

2.1 Overview of the Digital Learning Design Models

A digital learning design model is a structured framework or approach educators, instructional designers, and trainers use to plan, develop, and deliver practical learning experiences (Bower, M., 2017) in the digital ecosystem. It provides a systematic way to design educational activities, content, assessments, and interactions that align with specific learning objectives and strategies (Kulgemeyer, C., 2018).

According to Jogan, S. N. (2020), learning design models help to ensure the learning experience is coherent and engaging and promotes effective learning outcomes connected with the organisation's strategy.

Different models emphasise various aspects of the design process, such as learner engagement, content delivery, assessment strategies, and technology integration. Some common elements in learning content design models typically include guidelines organised by the following building blocks and associated activities: Analysis, Design, Development, Implementation, Evaluation, and Iteration (Jogan et al., 2020):

Several authors have contributed significantly to the field of digital learning design models with frameworks, theories, and principles that guide the design of

Table 1. Instructional Design Model´s Building Blocks and Activities

Analysis	Design	Development	Implementation	Evaluation	Iteration
Identifying the learners' needs, objectives, characteristics, and learning environment context is essential for effective learning.	When designing a learning experience, it is crucial to create a structured plan that includes decisions about content, activities, assessments, and interactions. This often involves storyboarding, outlining content, evaluation strategy design, and determining the sequence of activities.	Educational content creation can take many forms, including presentations, videos, quizzes, and interactive simulations. It also typically involves normalisation activities.	Configuring, parameterising, and testing the DLC and other materials are necessary to deliver a complete virtual learning experience.	Assessing the effectiveness of the learning experience by measuring whether the learning objectives were met. This phase involves collecting user feedback and possibly adjusting for improvement.	Revise and improve future learning experiences based on evaluation results.

Table 2. Main Contributors to the Digital Learning Ecosystem Models

George Siemens	Gilly Salmon	David Merril
George Siemens is recognised for his contributions to connectivism, a learning theory highlighting the significance of networks and connections in learning. His concepts have impacted the development of digital learning experiences that leverage social and networked learning environments.	Gilly Salmon's "Five-Stage Model," also known as the "e-tivities" model, offers a structured approach to creating and leading online learning experiences. The stages cover access, motivation, development, and reflection.	David Merrill developed the "First Principles of Instruction," which provides a framework for creating effective learning experiences. The model emphasises problem-centred learning, activating prior experience, demonstrating skills, applying skills, and integrating learning into real-world contexts.
Ruth Clark	**Richard Mayer**	**Michael Allen**
Ruth Clark is widely recognised for her contributions to evidence-based instructional design. She stresses the significance of matching instructional methods with how the brain perceives and retains information. Through her publications, including "e-Learning and the Science of Instruction," she offers practical advice on crafting impactful e-learning encounters.	Richard Mayer is a well-known researcher in multimedia learning and the cognitive theory that supports it. His work offers valuable insights into the best practices for designing multimedia elements in digital learning, including text, images, and animations, to achieve optimal learning outcomes.	The "CADDIE" model was developed by Michael Allen, an author known for emphasising creating meaningful and engaging learning experiences. In his book "Leaving ADDIE for SAM", he introduces the SAM (Successive Approximation Model) approach, which offers a more iterative and refined design and development process.
Karl Kapp	**Connie Malamed**	**Clark Quinn**
Karl Kaap emphasises using game elements to enhance engagement and motivation in digital learning experiences. His book, "The Gamification of Learning and Instruction," is a significant contribution to the field of gamification.	Connie Malamed, also known as "The eLearning Coach," offers practical advice and insights on instructional design for digital learning. Her resources, including books and blog, cover topics from visual design to user experience in e-learning.	Clark Quinn advocates designing learning experiences that align with cognitive science principles. His work emphasises considering cognitive aspects when designing digital learning materials.

compelling digital learning experiences, namely Ruth Clark, Michael Allen, David Merrill, George Siemens, Gilly Salmon, Richard Mayer, Karl Kapp, Connie Malamed, and Clark Quinn, among others (Allen, M. W., 2016; Clark, R. C., & Mayer, R. E., 2016, Merrill, M. D., 2020, Quinn, C., 2021, Mayer, R. E., 2009, Salmon, G., 2003, West, R., 2018, Malamed, C., 2011 and Kapp, K. M., 2012). The main contributors and their associated stream area are introduced in Table 2.

Examples of learning design models include the ADDIE model (Analysis, Design, Development, Implementation, Evaluation), the SAM model (Successive Approximation Model), Merrill's First Principles of Instruction, and the 5E Model (Engage, Explore, Explain, Elaborate, Evaluate).

Other initiatives like SCALA can be described as a "student-centred *active learning approach to deliver high-quality research-based education in a hybrid mode, as part of a supportive, enriching and community-focused experience"*[1] have also been adding enrichment perspectives on creating a systematic approach to designing, implementing, and evaluating learning experiences while fostering a culture of continuous improvement.

By integrating instructional design into their process management, learning organisations ensure that learning initiatives are strategic, evidence-based, and aligned with their overall success. This integration supports employee development, enhances skills, and improves organisational performance (Visser, M. & Tosey; P., 2019).

In resume, a learning content design model offers a flexible approach tailored to diverse learning objectives and environments rather than being a rigid blueprint. To make an informed decision on the most suitable model, it is crucial to conduct a comprehensive evaluation of the learners' needs, subject matter, available resources, and the overall organisational strategy.

2.2 Explore Instructional Design as A Strategic Asset Component of Project and Process Management in DLC In Organisations

Learning organisations integrate learning design models, such as instructional design, into their process and project management to ensure that learning initiatives are aligned with organisational goals, effectively designed, and consistently executed (Ifenthaler et al., 2020). To effectively accomplish their objectives, organisations typically engage in a set of activities that can be described into specific clusters:

a) **Alignment with Organisational Goals:** The team headed for the DLC, including the instructional designers, works closely with key stakeholders to understand the organisation's needs, challenges, and goals. They ensure that the learning experiences they design address specific performance gaps or skill development requirements that align with the organisation's overall mission.
b) **Needs Analysis**: Before implementing any learning initiative, learning organisations conduct thorough needs assessments to identify skill gaps, knowledge deficiencies, and performance issues. The team headed for the DLC uses the results of these assessments to create targeted learning objectives and design learning experiences that directly address the identified needs. If the DLC is being developed to a broader multi-context learning ecosystem, this stage mainly focuses on the primary objectives defined by the LO/Digital course/Digital Content.

c) **Process Integration**: Learning design models are integrated into the organisation's process management framework. This might involve incorporating instructional design phases into project management or process improvement cycles. This ensures that learning initiatives are systematically planned, executed, and assessed like any other business process.

d) **Continuous Improvement:** Learning organisations embrace a culture of continuous improvement. They collect data on the effectiveness of learning initiatives through assessments, learner feedback, and performance metrics. This data is used to refine and enhance future learning experiences. The iterative nature of many learning design models aligns well with this continuous improvement mindset.

e) **Technology Integration:** Many modern learning designs integrate technology to enhance learning experiences. Learning organisations incorporate learning management systems (LMS), e-learning platforms, virtual classrooms, and other technologies to effectively deliver and manage learning content.

f) **Monitoring and Evaluation**: Learning organisations establish mechanisms for monitoring and evaluating the success of learning initiatives. This might involve regular reviews of learner outcomes, participant feedback, and assessments of how well learning objectives were achieved. Based on this evaluation, adjustments can be made to the instructional design and delivery methods.

Learning Organisations prioritise the professional development of their instructional designers and trainers to ensure their teams know the latest trends, methodologies, and tools in instructional design. This focus on staying current enables them to create contemporary and practical learning experiences. They also often develop standardised processes for instructional design and documentation. This contributes to consistency in learning experiences across different projects and initiatives (Leso B. et al., 2022; Visser, M., & Tosey, P., 2019).

3. DIGITAL LEARNING CONTENT FRAMEWORK

3.1 Introduction to the Main Components and Definition of the Reference Model

The framework outlines the key components and attributes evaluated during the implementation of a digital learning strategy in an organisation.

The main components are associated with instructional design models and frameworks; standards and interoperability criteria for DL; DL Chunk reference model, which includes types of DL contents such as pedagogical requirements,

Figure 2. Proposal of a Framework for DLC

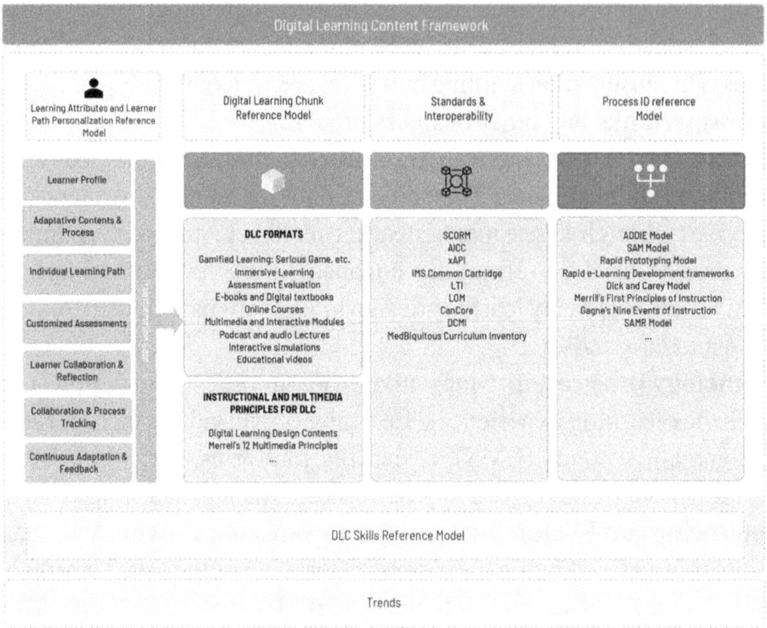

instructional and multimedia principles for DL; Learning attributes and learner path personalisation and skills-based reference model to support the design and implementation of the DLC lifecycle. Each component will be described in the following sections.

3.2 Instructional Design Models and Frameworks

Several instructional design models are commonly used in e-learning and digital content design. Some of the most common (Nazarova, O.B. et al., 2020) are described in Table 3.

These frameworks offer systematic approaches to guide the design process of digital content, ensuring that it meets user needs, aligns with business goals, and incorporates best practices in design and usability (Nazarova, O.B. et al., 2020). Instructional designers can adapt and combine these frameworks based on their project requirements and the specific needs of their target audience.

Table 3. Instructional Design Models and Frameworks

ADDIE Model: Analysis, Design, Development, Implementation, Evaluation	The ADDIE model is a widely accepted instructional design framework that provides a systematic approach to developing effective e-learning programs. This approach involves analysing the requirements and objectives, designing the content and activities, developing the materials, implementing the program, and evaluating its effectiveness.
SAM Model: SAM (Successive Approximation Model)	SAM is a model for instructional design that focuses on collaboration and iterative development. It is designed specifically for agile e-learning development and consists of three main phases: preparation, iterative design, and iterative development. SAM promotes rapid prototyping, frequent feedback, and collaboration among designers, subject matter experts, and stakeholders. It provides a framework for creating high-quality digital content through iterative cycles.
Rapid Prototyping Model	This model involves a cyclical process of designing, prototyping, testing, and refining the e-learning content until it meets desired objectives and quality standards, focusing on gathering feedback for improvements.
Rapid e-Learning Development frameworks	Frameworks such as the 5D framework (Define, Design, Develop, Deploy, and Deliver) are used for rapidly creating e-learning content. These frameworks prioritise efficient content development through templates, pre-built components, and rapid authoring tools. They aim to streamline the design and development process while maintaining high-quality content.
Dick and Carey Model	The Dick and Carey model is a systematic approach to instructional design, emphasising a hierarchical flow of tasks. It involves analysing instructional goals, identifying strategies, developing and selecting materials, and evaluating instructional effectiveness.
Merrill's First Principles of Instruction	Merrill's model emphasises real-world problem-solving, learner engagement, and application of knowledge and skills. It is based on five principles: activation, demonstration, application, integration, and evaluation.
Gagne's Nine Events of Instruction	According to Gagne's model, nine instructional events can promote successful learning. These events involve capturing the learner's attention, communicating the learning objectives, triggering the recollection of previous knowledge, presenting the material, offering direction for learning, encouraging the learner to perform, providing feedback, evaluating performance, and improving retention and transfer.
SAMR Model: The SAMR (Substitution, Augmentation, Modification, Redefinition)	SAMR's model is specifically focused on the integration of technology into education. It categorises the levels of technology integration, ranging from simple substitution to transformative redefinition of teaching and learning practices. These instructional design models provide frameworks and guidelines for designing effective e-learning and digital content. Designers can choose the model that best aligns with their project requirements, goals, and the target audience's needs. Adapting and customising these models to suit specific contexts and incorporating emerging technologies and trends is important.

3.3 Standards and Interoperability Criteria for DLC

The e-learning and digital content ecosystem has different standards that help ensure compatibility, interoperability, and quality across different platforms. Some of the most relevant and adopted standards for digital learning content are SCORM, AICC, xAPI, and LTI. Additionally, there are standard frameworks for learning objects, such as IEEE LOM.

A Learning Object Reference Model (LOM) is a standard that provides a structured approach to describing and organising digital learning resources or learning objects.

Table 4. Learning Object Reference Models

SCORM (Sharable Content Object Reference Model) https://scorm.com	The SCORM standard is widely utilised for e-learning content interoperability. It establishes technical specifications that enable e-learning content to be created and transmitted across various Learning Management Systems (LMS). SCORM ensures that content can be tracked, launched, and navigated consistently across different platforms.
AICC (Aviation Industry CBT Committee) https://www.aicc.org	AICC is a standard that focuses on the communication between learning content and learning management systems. It specifies how e-learning content should communicate with the LMS, including data exchange, launching content, and tracking learner progress.
xAPI (Experience API) https://xapi.com	Formerly known as Tin Can API, xAPI is a modern e-learning standard that allows more robust tracking and reporting of learner experiences. It enables data collection from various learning activities and devices, including simulations, mobile learning, and social learning. xAPI provides a more comprehensive view of learner interactions beyond traditional LMS boundaries.
IMS Common Cartridge https://www.imsglobal.org	Common Cartridge is a standard developed by the IMS Global Learning Consortium. It defines a format for packaging and exchanging e-learning content between different systems. Common Cartridge allows seamless content transfer across different platforms and LMS, including assessments, quizzes, and multimedia.
LTI (Learning Tools Interoperability) https://www.1edtech.org/standards	LTI is a standard that enables integration and interoperability between learning tools and learning platforms. It allows learning tools like simulations, virtual labs, and interactive content to be easily embedded and launched within an LMS without requiring complex integration efforts.
IEEE Learning Object Metadata (LOM) https://ieeexplore.ieee.org/document/9262118	LOM is a widely adopted standard that provides a comprehensive set of metadata elements for describing learning objects, covering aspects such as educational context, instructional methods, technical requirements, and intellectual property rights.
CanCore https://ieeexplore.ieee.org/document/1602137	CanCore is a Canadian initiative that provides a customised version of the IEEE LOM for describing learning objects. It includes additional metadata elements and guidelines specific to the Canadian educational context.
Dublin Core Metadata Initiative (DCMI) https://www.dublincore.org	While not specifically designed for learning objects, the Dublin Core Metadata Initiative provides a simple set of metadata elements that can be applied to various resources, including learning objects. It offers basic properties such as title, description, creator, subject, and date.
MedBiquitous Curriculum Inventory https://www.medbiq.org/standards/curriculum-data-exchange	The MedBiquitous Curriculum Inventory is a reference model for documenting medical education curricula and learning resources. It includes a comprehensive framework for learning objectives, competencies, activities, and assessment methods.

It defines a set of metadata elements and guidelines for describing learning objects' characteristics, properties, and instructional attributes (Allert H. et al., 2002).

A Learning Object Reference Model aims to promote the interoperability and reusability of learning objects across different systems and platforms (Lockyer L. et al., 2008). Educators, instructional designers, and content developers can create, share, and find learning objects more effectively (Allert H. et al., 2002). Some widely used Reference Models are shown in Table 4.

These standards play a crucial role in ensuring the compatibility, reusability, and portability of e-learning digital content. Adhering to these standards helps learners deliver, track, and access the content across various systems and devices (Allert, H. et al., 2002).

3.4 DLC Chunk Reference, Formats, and Instructional and Multimedia Principles For DL

3.4.1 Distance Learning Content

Digital learning content refers to educational materials and resources available in digital format, typically accessed through computers, tablets, or smartphones (Mayer, R. E., 2009). These resources can be used for self-paced learning, online courses, or blended learning approaches that combine digital and traditional classroom instruction. Digital learning content can include various forms of media, such as text, images, videos, interactive simulations, quizzes, and assessments (Clark, R. C., & Mayer, R. E. (2016). The main differences between digital content and digital learning content lie in their purpose and intended use, as described in Table 5.

Digital learning content encompasses various resources and materials that facilitate online learning experiences. The combination of those media types and interactive and pedagogical strategies is usually published in different types of DLC (Clark, R. C., & Mayer, R. E., 2016).

3.4.2 DLC Chunk Reference

eLearning content chunking refers to breaking down large amounts of information into smaller, more manageable chunks or modules. This strategy helps learners process and retain information more effectively (Clark, R. C., & Mayer, R. E., 2016). According to Merril, M. D. (2020), Mayer, R. (2009), Quinn, C. (2021) and Allen, M. W. (2016), some shared eLearning content chunking strategies are:

Table 5. Digital content vs. digital learning content

	Digital Content	Digital Learning Content
Purpose	Digital content encompasses all information and media produced, stored, or shared in digital formats. This can include a broad spectrum of materials, such as articles, videos, images, audio files, and social media posts. The main aim of digital content is to inform, entertain, or engage users without necessarily having a specific educational focus.	Digital learning content is created to facilitate education by supporting instructional objectives, providing structured learning experiences, and enhancing learners' knowledge, skills, or competencies.
Learning Objectives	Rather than explicit learning objectives, digital content is usually created for entertainment, inspiration, or engagement. Although users may gain knowledge or insights from it, learning outcomes are not the primary focus.	The creation of digital learning content is based on clear learning objectives. Its purpose is to aid learners in acquiring targeted knowledge, skill development, and learning outcomes. The content is aligned with instructional goals and structured to encourage active learning and meaningful engagement.
Instructional Design	Digital content may be created without following systematic instructional design processes or using pedagogical principles or evidence-based learning strategies.	Digital learning content is created systematically by analysing learning needs, setting clear objectives, designing learning activities, and assessing outcomes using instructional design principles and strategies. Pedagogical considerations are an integral part of developing digital learning content.
Interactivity and Engagement	Some digital content allows for interaction, such as quizzes, polls, and comment sections. However, the interactivity and engagement levels differ greatly and may not be intentionally designed to encourage active participation or facilitate in-depth learning.	Digital learning content is crafted to facilitate interactive and engaging educational experiences. It features interactive elements, simulations, games, collaborative activities, and assessments that encourage active participation and deeper understanding and application of knowledge.
Assessment and Feedback	Digital content typically does not include formal assessments or feedback mechanisms. While users may provide comments or feedback, it is not structured to assess learning outcomes systematically.	Digital learning content often includes assessments and feedback mechanisms to measure learners' progress, knowledge acquisition, or skill development. It includes quizzes, tests, assignments, or other assessments that provide feedback and enable learners to track their performance and learning progress.

Figure 3. Types of DLC

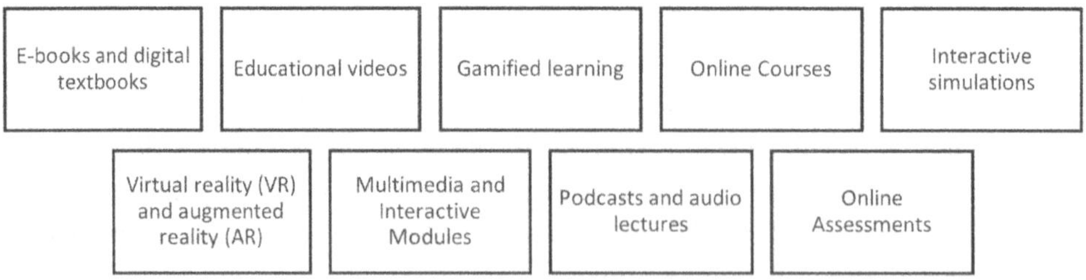

a) **Organisation by topic**: The content is organised into specific topics or sub-topics, with each section focusing on a single concept or idea to avoid cognitive overload.

b) **Sequential Learning**: The content is presented logically, starting with foundational concepts and progressing to more complex ideas. This helps learners build a solid understanding before moving on to advanced topics.

c) **Visual and Multimedia Elements**: Incorporating visual aids, such as images, infographics, or videos, helps enhance comprehension and engagement. Multimedia elements can also supplement textual information and make the content more interactive.

d) **Chunking with Progression**: The content is split into smaller chunks, and as learners progress through each chunk, they gradually build upon their knowledge. This creates a sense of accomplishment and motivates learners to continue.

e) **Microlearning or Nano learning**: The content is delivered in a small burst of information. Microlearning modules are typically 3 to 5 minutes long and address a specific learning objective. This approach is efficient for the industry and is known as just-in-time training.

f) **Interactive Assessments**: Including interactive assessments, quizzes, or knowledge validates within each chunk. This helps reinforce learning, allows learners to gauge their understanding, and provides immediate feedback.

g) **Learning Pathways**: Offer learners the flexibility to choose their learning path. Divide the content into modules or chunks and allow learners to navigate through them based on their needs and preferences.

h) **Clear Navigation**: Provide straightforward and intuitive navigation within the eLearning course. Use headings, subheadings, menus, and progress indicators to help learners understand the structure of the content and easily navigate between chunks.

i) **Mobile-Friendly Design**: Optimise the eLearning content for mobile devices. Chunking is particularly beneficial for mobile learning as it aligns with learners' shorter attention spans and on-the-go nature.

3.4.3 Instructional and Cognitive Multimedia Principles for DLC Design

In order to create engaging and effective digital learning content, it is essential to include multimedia principles and prioritise a positive user experience. This requires considering the user's cognitive capacity and designing content to maximise learning. The guidelines associated with this process have been reflecting multidisciplinary field efforts involving contributions from various authors and experts in instructional design, human-computer interaction, and cognitive psychology, where one of the most known is the 12 principles of Mayer.

According to Mayer, R. E. (2009), the design of DLC should follow a set of multimedia principles, namely:

a) **Redundancy**: When designing a DLC, avoid redundant presentation of information across multiple modalities. Multimedia should be used to complement and reinforce key concepts.
b) **Modality**: Integrate appropriate visuals, animations, videos, and audio to enhance learning.
c) **Coherence**: Multimedia content should be coherent and logically organised. Avoiding unnecessary or unrelated material that may divert learners' attention is essential to ensure effective learning.
d) **Signalling**: Use cues, prompts, or explicit instructions to guide learners' attention to important information within multimedia content.
e) **Spatial Contiguity**: The proximity of words and pictures on a page or screen has a noteworthy impact on learning outcomes. Adhering to this approach can optimise one's ability to learn.
f) **Temporal Contiguity**: Research shows that users tend to retain information more effectively when words and images are displayed simultaneously rather than one after the other.
g) **Segmenting**: Users retain information better through segmented multimedia lessons that are user-controlled, as opposed to continuous units.
h) **Pre-training**: Knowing the names and characteristics of the main concepts in a DLC helps users learn better. For example, using universally recognised iconography and standardised definitions facilitates the acquisition of essential knowledge in a DLC information chunk reference.
i) **Multimedia**: Research has indicated that the retention of information by individuals is significantly improved when it is conveyed through a combination of visual aids and spoken explanations rather than relying solely on animations and text displayed on a screen.
j) **Voice**: Studies show that people retain information better with a friendly human voice for narration in multimedia lessons than with machine voices. This is due to the personal touch of a human voice, leading to better understanding and retention.
k) **Image**: Adding the speaker's image to a multimedia lesson does not necessarily improve learning.
l) **Personalisation**: Adapt multimedia content to learners' preferences, prior knowledge, and needs. Offer control over pace, order, and detail.

3.5 Learning Attributes and Learner Path Personalisation

Personalised learning in the digital learning content development process refers to tailoring the learning experience to meet learners' needs, preferences, and abilities (Short, C., & Shemshack, A., 2023). It involves leveraging technology and instructional strategies to provide customised learning paths, content, and activities catering to each learner's requirements.

There are different strategies the DLC instructional design team can use to incorporate personalised learning in the digital learning content development process.

Personalised learning begins with creating learner profiles that capture individual characteristics, such as prior knowledge, learning style, interests, and goals. These profiles can be developed through pre-assessments, surveys, or learner analytics. Learner profiling helps understand each learner's unique needs and abilities (Bhutoria, A., 2022).

Adaptive technologies are also a strategy to deliver content and resources that match the individual learner's level of knowledge and learning pace. This may involve providing additional explanations, scaffolding, or advanced content based on the learner's progress.

Nowadays, adaptive learning platforms and intelligent tutoring systems can dynamically adjust the content to optimise learning and deliver individualised learning paths (Crittenden et al., 2018). DLC can be designed to offer multiple pathways or modules, giving learners choices in the sequence and depth of their learning. This strategy is usually connected with assessments designed to evaluate mastery of specific learning objectives or identify areas requiring further attention.

The results of assessments can inform content adaptation and provide learners with targeted feedback and recommendations. This feedback and recommendations (ongoing feedback and progress-tracking mechanisms) may encourage learners to reflect on their learning progress and collaborate with peers. It can foster a sense of community and provide opportunities for peer learning and support.

The learning path personalisation demands an iterative process based on learner feedback and changing needs (Bhutoria, A., 2022). Digital learning content development should allow continuous adaptation and improvement based on learner data and feedback. Regular analysis of learner interactions and outcomes helps identify areas where further personalisation or modifications are needed (Groff J., 2017).

3.6 Skills-Based Reference Model to Support the Design and Implementation of the DLC Lifecycle

To create engaging and effective learning experiences, it is essential to have a versatile set of skills that includes instructional design, content creation, technology proficiency, and pedagogical expertise. This is especially important for developing high-quality DLC.

Digital transformation has been promoting a shift in this model from a team-based role design to a skill-based model design (Mackenstein, L., & Santosa, K. (2019). With this reference, nowadays, multidisciplinary is focused on the core competencies required for each step in the process. This is particularly relevant not just for building a skill-based plan associated with the digital learning strategy of the organisation but also for defining the requirements associated with the profile of the teams, which supports the design and implementation of the digital content.

According to Tudor, S.L. (2016), this skill-based plan should reflect abilities in the following competencies: instructional design, content development, multimedia design, technology skills, visual and user experience design, assessment and evaluation, project management, collaboration and communication.

Instructional solid design skills are the foundation for creating effective DLC. This includes understanding learning theories, conducting needs assessments, setting learning objectives, designing learning activities, and assessing learning outcomes. Proficiency in content development is essential for creating engaging and informative DLC materials. This includes skills in researching, organising, and structuring content, writing clear and concise instructional text, and creating visually appealing multimedia elements.

Knowledge of multimedia design principles is essential to develop engaging and interactive digital learning content. Skills in graphic design, video production, audio editing, and animation enable the creation of visually appealing and compelling multimedia elements. Multimedia digital implementation requires proficiency in various digital tools and technologies.

Given the rapidly evolving nature of technology and digital learning, having adaptability and a willingness to learn new tools and techniques is crucial. This may include familiarity with e-learning authoring tools, learning management systems (LMS), multimedia editing software, and content delivery platforms. Additionally, knowledge of HTML, CSS, and other web technologies can be beneficial for customising and enhancing DLC.

Understanding visual design and user experience techniques creates engaging and user-friendly digital learning experiences. This includes layout, usability, and interaction design principles.

Skills in designing assessments and evaluation strategies are essential for measuring learning outcomes and providing feedback to learners. This includes creating effective quizzes, assignments, performance-based assessments and analysing and interpreting assessment data.

Effective project management requires strong skills in planning, organising, and executing DLC development projects. It includes time management, task prioritisation, collaboration, and communication to ensure projects are completed on time, within budget, and aligned with objectives. Developing DLC also requires strong collaboration and communication skills to work effectively with subject matter experts, instructional designers, multimedia specialists, and other stakeholders involved in content development. Clear and effective communication is crucial to understanding requirements, gathering feedback, and ensuring the content meets the intended objectives.

4. TRENDS IN DLC

Digital learning has significantly increased in popularity due to the ongoing COVID-19 pandemic. Due to the growing demand for remote learning, educational institutions and companies have embraced eLearning as a vital tool for consistent education and training (Hamdan M. et al.,2020). The approach of learning "*anytime, anywhere*" has become more popular as an increasing number of people value the ease and flexibility eLearning provides. This trend is being reinforced by introducing different technologies like the increased use of artificial intelligence (AI) in Digital Learning.

Artificial intelligence technologies like natural language processing and machine learning are being integrated into digital learning content development. AI-powered chatbots provide personalised support, answer learner queries, and deliver adaptive feedback, enhancing the learning experience and providing immediate assistance (Baz, 2018). When introducing these technologies, it is vital to consider instructional design principles and other DL ecosystem trends, such as microlearning, game-based learning, virtual and augmented reality, and data-driven analytics.

4.1 Trends in Digital Learning Contents Design

The Digital Learning industry constantly evolves, demanding high upskilling and retraining from the learning and design teams shaping how DLC is being designed and developed.

Artificial Intelligence (AI) tools have the potential to impact and enhance DLC in various ways, namely in areas like Personalization and Adaptive Learning, Intelligent Tutoring Systems, Natural Language Processing, Automated Content Creation, Content Recommendation and Curation, Learning Analytics and Insights, Automated Language Translation, Intelligent Content Tagging and Organization.

According to de Campos, A.D., & Cazella, S.C. (2019), personalisation and adaptive Learning can be described as the ability to analyse learners' data, such as their performance, preferences, and learning styles, to deliver personalised learning experiences. AI tools can optimise engagement, motivation, and learning outcomes by adapting the content, pace, and difficulty level to individual learners' needs.

Groff J. (2017) highlights that personalisation and adaptive learning have been identified as the most promising emerging tools for promoting efficiency in the learning process and success.

Another potential area of impact is in the generation of training plans. Although they are still far mature, IA systems can auto-generate courses and DLC chunks based on prompts and attributes from the user, and this could represent a high impact on the timeline and instructional design strategies of DLC development.

Intelligent tutoring Systems can provide individualised guidance and feedback to learners. These systems can analyse learner responses, identify misconceptions, and offer targeted explanations, resulting in more effective and personalised learning experiences (St-Hilaire et al., 2022).

AI-powered Natural Language processing enables chatbots and virtual assistants to interact with learners conversationally (Gonda, D.E., & Chu, B. (2019). Learners can ask questions, receive immediate responses, and engage in dialogue, creating a more interactive and dynamic learning environment (Alm, A., & Nkomo, L.M. (2020). Another field of application is the language translation tools that can facilitate multilingual learning experiences, translating learning content into different languages and making digital learning more accessible to learners worldwide (Kabanov A. et al., 2022).

AI tools can assist in generating digital learning content by automating certain aspects of content creation. For example, AI algorithms can automatically generate quizzes, assessments, or practice exercises based on learning objectives or existing content, saving time and effort for instructional designers (Rocha, O.R., & Zucker, C.F. (2017). Also, according to (Denny et al., 2023), Large language models (LLMs) are being tested as a solution to the rapid creation of DLC at scale, reducing instructors' workload.

AI algorithms can leverage learner data to make personalised recommendations for learning resources (Herath et al., 2018). Doing so empowers learners to explore novel topics that align with their interests and objectives, leading to a more engaging and fulfilling learning experience. This process demands a structured analysis of large volumes of learner data to provide valuable insights and analytics. This data-driven approach helps educators and instructional designers gain a deeper understanding of learner progress, engagement patterns, and areas of improvement, enabling them to make data-informed decisions and optimise learning experiences (Wise, A. (2019).

Microlearning or Nano learning involves delivering learning content in bite-sized, focused modules that can be consumed quickly (Susilana, R.,2022). It caters to learners' preference for short, targeted bursts of information and aligns with the average human attention span decreasing. Microlearning also increases engagement by breaking down information into smaller, more manageable chunks (Díaz Redondo, 2021; Kossen, C., & Ooi, C., 2021).

With the proliferation of smartphones and tablets, Mobile Learning is still growing. Mobile learning content is designed to be responsive and accessible in an omnichannel perspective, allowing learners to access digital learning resources anytime, anywhere (Uther, M. (2019). Recent research has been focused on adding a context-aware strategy to mobile learning to reach different levels of immersion (Curum, B. et al. 2016).

Gamification is increasingly applied in learning environments to increase engagement, interaction, motivation and learning outcomes (Smiderle, R, 2020). It incorporates game elements and mechanics into the learning process to increase engagement, interaction, and motivation (Legaki et al., 2020). Game-based learning uses actual games as the primary learning platform. These approaches leverage competition, rewards, challenges, and progression to enhance learning experiences and promote knowledge retention. Recent studies (Pithan, 2023) indicate that gamification can improve the completion rate in adaptative learning courses due to students' better behavioural responses and attitudes. It can also be particularly effective for adaptive learning personalisation surveys. On the other hand, according to Koivisto and Hamari (2019), there is still a lack of practical design guidelines and empirical data on the combination or integration of these gamification features in the context of educational information systems.

Personalised learning aims to tailor learning experiences to individual learners' needs, preferences, and abilities. Adaptive learning goes beyond personalisation by dynamically adjusting the content and learning path based on learners' progress and performance (Short, C., & Shemshack, A., 2023) and, according to Florence et al. (2020), has a direct connection with learner learning style, adaptive feedback, and adaptive navigation. These approaches may utilise learner analytics, algorithms, and artificial intelligence to provide customised learning experiences and optimise learning outcomes (Buthoria, 2022).

Augmented Reality (AR) and Virtual Reality (VR) technologies offer immersive and interactive learning experiences. AR overlays digital information in the real world, enhancing learners' understanding and engagement. VR creates simulated environments that allow learners to experience realistic scenarios and practice skills (Alzahrani, N. M., 2020; Yuliono, 2018). These technologies are used for virtual labs, field trips, simulations, and training that can stimulate the students' senses, involving them in learning activities. (Sala, N., 2021). According to Akcayir, M., & Akcayir, G. (2017), one of the main reasons AR and VR are being widely used is that they no longer require expensive hardware and sophisticated equipment, and this is a fact that can profoundly change the massification of the use of this technology. According to Dunleavy, Dede, and Mitchell (2009, p. 20), cited in

Akcayir, M., & Akcayir, G. (2017), "*AR's most significant advantage is its unique ability to create immersive hybrid learning environments that combine digital and physical objects, thereby facilitating the development of processing skills such as critical thinking, problem-solving, and communicating through interdependent collaborative exercises.*"

According to Menedez et al. (2022) and Wise, A. (2019), Learning Analytics is one of the areas of Technology-Enhanced Learning research that is growing fast and is a "*field that measures, analyses, and reports data about students and their contexts to understand/improve learning and the place in which it occurs*". It is also used as a diagnosis and prediction tool mainly focused on student retention, performance, engagement, employability, progression, attainment, and assessment (Ifenthaler, D., & Yau, J.Y. 2020). Data-Driven Learning Analytics leverages data collection, analysis, and visualisation to gain insights into learners' progress, behaviour, and performance. It helps identify learning gaps, optimise content delivery, personalise learning experiences, and make data-informed instructional decisions (Hernández de Menéndez, M. et al., 2022).

Video-based learning continues to be a popular and effective medium for delivering digital learning. Multiple definitions describe videos used in learning and instruction: instructional videos (Fiorella & Mayer, 2018), demonstration videos, Kahn Academy videos, classroom videos or video explanations (Köse et al., 2021). According to Bétrancourt, M., & Benetos, K. (2018), the future of video-based learning lies in three main areas: representational, cognitive-perceptual, and instructional. High-quality instructional videos, lectures, tutorials, and demonstrations engage learners visually and facilitate better understanding and retention of complex concepts. According to Brame's research (Brame, C., 2016), video content can effectively deliver DLC, regardless of the chosen methodology. However, it depends on the use by the LD team of three elements: how to manage the cognitive load of the video, how to maximise student engagement with the video, and how to promote active learning from the video (Chen, Y.-C., et al., 2021).

Developing digital content for e-learning involves using various software tools that cater to different aspects of content creation, including instructional design, multimedia development, assessment creation, and learning management. The choice of these software tools depends on the project's specific needs, budget, and the instructional designers' and e-learning developers' preferences (Jain, R., & Singh, A.K. (2020). For example, Articulate Storyline, Adobe eLearning Suite, H5P, Camtasia, Elucidat, Smart Sparrow; Knweton, Podomatic, Loom Movie Maker, Animoto (Dewanti, P., & Rusli, M., 2019). It is common for e-learning professionals to use a combination of these tools to create comprehensive and engaging digital learning experiences.

5. CONCLUSION

Digital transformation, digital learning, and digital learning contents in a learning organisation ecosystem are complex, organic, and intertwined processes as they are all interconnected and mutually reinforcing.

Those processes represent a significant challenge in the corporate learning and learning organisation ecosystem, encompassing digital technologies and resources to facilitate and enhance learning experiences.

The process and strategy adopted for managing digital learning differ from organisation to organisation and are highly influenced by its culture, type of company and process maturity, among other criteria.

By leveraging digital learning methodologies and technologies, organisations can enhance training programs, onboarding processes, and skill development initiatives.

Digital learning content provides the necessary resources, tools, and learning experiences to adapt to digital technologies, enable access to digital skills, enhance flexibility and scalability, foster personalisation, and encourage collaboration and connectivity.

This article described the main components an organization could promote an assessment and apply when designing digital learning content to support a broader digital learning strategy.

This proposal outlines a five-level framework, which includes an overview of the Digital Learning Design Models, standards and interoperability criteria for DL, DL Chunk reference model, learning personalization and skills-based reference model to support the design and implementation of the DLC lifecycle.

These components should be addressed considering the main trends in DLC. These trends may include the progress of Artificial Intelligence systems, virtual reality, and learning analytics. The main impact of AI tools in digital learning content is the ability to provide personalised, adaptive, and interactive learning experiences. AI enhances content delivery, assessment, and learner support, improving engagement, individualisation, and learning outcomes. Although there is high potential for AI-powered personalised learning, certain obstacles must be overcome, such as data privacy, affordability, and accessibility.

This transition requires a deliberate change in curriculum planning to cater to every student's distinct learning requirement and capability.

Technological advancements that should be reflected in DLC design strategy, including gamification, augmented educational content, virtual reality, video-based learning, and learning analytics, have transformed the education paradigm. This can create a more interactive, engaging, and motivation for students and should always be designed from an integrated pedagogical and digital perspective.

REFERENCES

Akcayir, M., & Akcayir, G. (2017). Advantages and challenges associated with augmented reality for education: A systematic literature review. *Educational Research Review*, *20*, 1–11. doi:10.1016/j.edurev.2016.11.002

Alessi, S. M., & Trollip, S. R. (2000). *Multimedia for Learning: Methods and Development* (3rd ed.). Pearson.

Allen, M. (2016). *Michael Allen's Guide to e-Learning: Building Interactive, Fun, and Effective Learning Programs for Any Company*. 389–408. . doi:10.1002/9781119176268.index

Allert, H., Dhraief, H., & Nejdl, W. (2002). *How are Learning Objects Used in Learning Processes?* Instructional Roles of Learning Objects in LOM.

Alm, A., & Nkomo, L. (2020). Chatbot Experiences of Informal Language Learners: A Sentiment Analysis. *International Journal of Computer-Assisted Language Learning and Teaching*, *10*(4), 51–65. doi:10.4018/IJCALLT.2020100104

Alzahrani, N. (2020). Augmented Reality: A Systematic Review of Its Benefits and Challenges in E-Learning Contexts. *Applied Sciences (Basel, Switzerland)*, *10*(16), 5660. Advance online publication. doi:10.3390/app10165660

Bétrancourt, M., & Benetos, K. (2018). Why and when does instructional video facilitate learning? A commentary to the special issue "Developments and trends in learning with instructional video.". *Computers in Human Behavior*, *89*, 471–475. doi:10.1016/j.chb.2018.08.035

Bhutoria, A. (2022). Personalised education and Artificial Intelligence in the United States, China, and India: A systematic review using a Human-In-The-Loop model. *Computers & Education: Artificial Intelligence*, *3*, 100068. doi:10.1016/j.caeai.2022.100068

Bower, M. (2017). *Design of Technology-Enhanced Learning - Integrating Research and Practice*. Emerald. . doi:10.1108/9781787141827

Brame, C. (2016). Effective Educational Videos: Principles and Guidelines for Maximising Student Learning from Video Content. *Cell Biology Education*, *15*(4), es6–es6. doi:10.1187/cbe.16-03-0125 PMID:27789532

Chen, Y.-C., Lu, Y.-L., & Lien, C.-J. (2021). Learning environments with different levels of technological engagement: A comparison of game-based, video-based, and traditional instruction on students' learning. *Interactive Learning Environments*, *29*(8), 1363–1379. doi:10.1080/10494820.2019.1628781

Clark, R. C., & Mayer, R. E. (2016). *E-Learning and the science of instruction.* John Wiley & Sons, Inc. eBooks. doi:10.1002/9781119239086

Crittenden, W., Biel, I. K., & Lovely, W. A. III. (2018). Embracing Digitalisation: Student Learning and New Technologies. *Journal of Marketing Education, 41*(1), 027347531882089. doi:10.1177/0273475318820895

de Campos, A., & Cazella, S. (2019)... *Learning Analytics and Cognitive Computing to Support Personalised Learning Experiences, 389-391*, 389–391. doi:10.1109/ICALT.2019.00120

Dewanti, P., & Muhammad, R. (2019). Implementing Adobe Captivate in Designing E-Learning's Digital Content. *International Journal of Computer Applications, 177*(16), 25–30. doi:10.5120/ijca2019919552

Egloffstein, M., & Ifenthaler, D. (2016). Employee Perspectives on MOOCs for Workplace Learning. *TechTrends, 61*(1), 65–70. doi:10.100711528-016-0127-3

European Commission. (2019). *Key competencies for lifelong learning*. Publications Office. https://data.europa.eu/doi/10.2766/569540

European Commission. (2022, October 12). *Commission kick-starts work on the European Year of Skills.* European Commission. https://ec.europa.eu/commission/presscorner/detail/en/ip_22_
6086

Fiorella, L., & Mayer, R. E. (2018). What works and doesn't work with instructional video. *Computers in Human Behavior, 89*, 465470. doi:10.1016/j.chb.2018.07.015

Gonda, D. & Chu, B. (2019). *Chatbot as a learning resource? Creating conversational bots as a supplement for teaching assistant training courses.* IEEE. . doi:10.1109/TALE48000.2019.9225974

Groff, J. (2017). *Personalised learning: the state of the field & future directions.* Center for Curriculum Redesign.

Hamdan, M., Jaidin, J., Fithriyah, M., & Anshari, M. (2020). E-Learning in Time of Covid-19 Pandemic. *Challenges & Experiences, 12-16*, 12–16. doi:10.1109/econf51404.2020.9385507

Helbig, C., Hofhues, S., Egloffstein, M., & Ifenthaler, D. (2021). Digital transformation in learning organisations. Springer eBooks. doi:10.1007/978-3-030-55878-9_14

Herath, D. & Jayarathne, L. (2018). Intelligent Recommendations for e-Learning Personalisation Based on Learner's Learning Activities and Performances. *International Journal of Computer Science and Software Engineering, 7.*

Hernández-de-Menéndez, M., Morales-Menendez, R., Escobar, C. A., & Ramírez Mendoza, R. A. (2022). Learning analytics: State of the art. [IJIDeM]. *International Journal on Interactive Design and Manufacturing, 16*(3), 1209–1230. doi:10.100712008-022-00930-0

Ifenthaler, D. (2018). *How We Learn at the Digital Workplace.* . doi:10.1007/978-3-319-46215-8_1

Ifenthaler, Dirk & Hofhues, Sandra & Egloffstein, Marc & Helbig, Christian. (2020). *Digital Transformation of Learning Organizations.* . doi:10.1007/978-3-030-55878-9

Ifenthaler, D., & Yau, J. Y. (2020). Utilising learning analytics to support study success in higher education: A systematic review. *Educational Technology Research and Development, 68*(4), 1961–1990. doi:10.100711423-020-09788-z

Jahnke, I. (2022). Quality of digital learning experiences – effective, efficient, and appealing designs? *The International Journal of Information and Learning Technology., 40*(1), 17–30. doi:10.1108/IJILT-05-2022-0105

Jain, R., & Singh, A. (2020). Technological Approaches for E-Content Development and Deployment: A Qualitative Analysis From Experts' Perspective. *International Journal of Information and Communication Technology Education, 16*(3), 92–112. doi:10.4018/IJICTE.2020070107

Jogan, S.N. (2020). *A Review on Developing Instructional Design Models For Effective Learning.*

Kabanov, A., Nevraeva, N., Pyrkova, T., Savelyeva, N., Oleynik, I., & Gurskaya, T. V. (2022). *Digital translation tools in the process of teaching foreign languages. SHS Web of Conferences, 141*, 03007. 10.1051hsconf/202214103007

Kapp, K. (2012). *The gamification of learning and instruction: Game-based methods and strategies for training and education.* Pfeiffer.

Koedinger, K. R., Corbett, A. T., & Perfetti, C. A. (2012). The Knowledge-Learning-Instruction Framework: Bridging the Science-Practice chasm to enhance robust student learning. *Cognitive Science, 36*(5), 757–798. doi:10.1111/j.1551-6709.2012.01245.x PMID:22486653

Koivisto, J., & Hamari, J. (2019). The rise of motivational information systems: A review of gamification research. *International Journal of Information Management*, *45*, 191–210. doi:10.1016/j.ijinfomgt.2018.10.013

Köse, E., Taşlıbeyaz, E., & Karaman, S. (2021). Classification of instructional videos. *Technology, Knowledge, and Learning*, *26*(4), 1079–1109. doi:10.100710758-021-09530-5

Kossen, C., & Chia-Yi, O. (2021). Trialling micro-learning design to increase engagement in online courses. *AAOU Journal*, *16*(3), 299–310. doi:10.1108/AAOUJ-09-2021-0107

Kulgemeyer, C. (2018). Towards a framework for effective instructional explanations in science teaching. *Studies in Science Education*, *54*(2), 109–139. doi:10.1080/03057267.2018.1598054

Legaki, N. Z., Xi, N., Hamari, J., Karpouzis, K., & Assimakopoulos, V. (2020). The effect of challenge-based gamification on learning: An experiment in the context of statistics education. *International Journal of Human-Computer Studies*, *144*, 102496. doi:10.1016/j.ijhcs.2020.102496 PMID:32565668

Leso, B. H., Cortimiglia, M. N., & Ghezzi, A. (2022). The contribution of organisational culture, structure, and leadership factors in the digital transformation of SMEs: A mixed-methods approach. *Cognition Technology and Work*, *25*(1), 151–179. doi:10.100710111-022-00714-2 PMID:36118918

Lockyer, L., & Bennett, S. Agostinho, S. & Harper, B. (2008). Handbook of research on learning design and learning objects: Issues, applications and technologies. IGI Global.

Mackenstein, L., & Santosa, K. (2019). *Exploring how Digital Transformation affects Job Design : A Multiple-Case Study based on the Job Characteristics Model* (Dissertation). Retrieved from https://urn.kb.se/resolve?urn=urn:nbn:se:hj:diva-43897

Majumdar, S. & Training, E. (2003). *Pedagogical framework for online learning*. IIEP. http://lst-iiep.iiep-unesco.org/cgi-bin/wwwi32.exe/[in=epidoc1.in]/?t2000=018954/(100)

Malamed, C. (2011). *Visual language for designers: Principles for Creating Graphics that People Understand*. Rockport Pub.

Martin, F., Chen, Y., Moore, R. L., & Westine, C. D. (2020). Systematic review of adaptive learning research designs, context, strategies, and technologies from 2009 to 2018. *Educational Technology Research and Development*, *68*(4), 1903–1929. doi:10.100711423-020-09793-2 PMID:32837122

Mayer, R. E. (2009). *Multimedia learning*. Cambridge University Press., doi:10.1017/CBO9780511811678

Merrill, M. D. (2020). *First Principles of Instruction* (Revised Edition).

Nazarova, O., Pulekha, I., Maslennikova, O. Y., & Osipov, Y. V. (2020). Rationale for choosing the model and tool for developing an e-learning course. *Journal of Physics: Conference Series*, *1661*(1), 012184. doi:10.1088/1742-6596/1661/1/012184

PitthanF.De WitteK. (2023). *Game Over or Continue? How Gamification Can Improve Completion Rate in Adaptive Learning*. doi:10.2139/ssrn.4507734

Quinn, C. (2021). *Learning Science for Instructional Designers: From Cognition to Application.*

Redondo, D. (2021). Integrating micro-learning content in traditional e-learning platforms. *Multimedia Tools and Applications*, *80*(2), 1–31. doi:10.100711042-020-09523-z

Rocha, O. & Faron-Zucker, R. (2017). *Automatic generation of educational quizzes from domain ontologies*. 4024-4030. . doi:10.21125/edulearn.2017.1866

Sala, N. (2021). Virtual Reality, Augmented Reality, and Mixed Reality in Education: A Brief Overview. In D. Choi, A. Dailey-Hebert, & J. Estes (Eds.), *Current and Prospective Applications of Virtual Reality in Higher Education* (pp. 48–73). IGI Global. doi:10.4018/978-1-7998-4960-5.ch003

Salmon, G. (2003). E-tivities: The Key to Active Online Learning. *Education + Training*, *45*(6). doi:10.1108/et.2003.00445fad.002

Santos, A., Peixinho, F., Moreira, L. (2014). *Projetos de e-Learning: Inovação, Implementação e Gestão*. FCA, Lidel

Senge, P. M. (2006). The Fifth Discipline: The Art and Practice of the Learning Organization. Doubleday (A Division of Random House), New York, 7.

Seufert, S., & Meier, C. (2016). From eLearning to Digital Transformation: A Framework and Implications for L&D. [iJAC]. *International Journal of Advanced Corporate Learning*, *9*(2), 27–33. doi:10.3991/ijac.v9i2.6003

Short, C. R., & Shemshack, A. (2023). *Personalised learning*. EdTechnica: The Open Encyclopedia of Educational Technology. https://edtechbooks.org/encyclopedia/personalized_learning

Smiderle, R., Rigo, S. J., Marques, L. B., De Miranda Coelho, J. P., & Jaques, P. A. (2020). The impact of gamification on students' learning, engagement and behavior based on their personality traits. *Smart Learning Environments*, *7*(1), 3. Advance online publication. doi:10.118640561-019-0098-x

St-Hilaire, F., Vu, D.D., Frau, A., Burns, N., Faraji, F., Potochny, J., Robert, S., Roussel, A., Zheng, S., Glazier, T., Romano, J.V., Belfer, R., Shayan, M., Smofsky, A., Delarosbil, T., Ahn, S., Eden-Walker, S., Sony, K., Ching, A.O., Elkins, S., Stepanyan, A.Z., Matajová, A., Chen, V., Sahraei, H., Larson, R., Markova, N., Barkett, A., Charlin, L., Bengio, Y., Serban, I., & Kochmar, E. (2022). *A New Era: Intelligent Tutoring Systems Will Transform Online Learning for Millions.* https://doi.org/10.48550/arXiv.2203.03724.

Susilana, R., Dewi, L., Rullyana, G., Hadiapurwa, A., & Khaerunnisa, N. (2022). Can microlearning strategy assist students' online learning? *Jurnal Cakrawala Pendidikan.*, *41*(2), 437–451. doi:10.21831/cp.v41i2.43387

Tudor, S. L. (2016). Skills-centered design - a model design centered on skills of training activities/ development of communicative skill in Integrated perspective. *Journal Plus Education.*

Uther, M. (2019). Mobile Learning—Trends and Practices. *Education Sciences*, *9*(1), 33. doi:10.3390/educsci9010033

Visser, Max & Tosey, Paul. (2019*). Learning in the learning organisation: Concepts and antecedents.*

West, R. E. (2018). *Foundations of Learning and Instructional Design Technology*. EdTech Books., doi:10.59668/3

Wiley, D., Waters, S., & Lambert, B. & Dawson, Deonne & Barclay, M. & Wade, D. & Nelson, L. (2004). Overcoming the limitations of learning objects. *Journal of Educational Multimedia and Hypermedia*, 13.

Wise, A. (2019). *Learning Analytics: Using Data-Informed Decision-Making to Improve Teaching and Learning: Maximising Student Engagement, Motivation, and Learning*. Contemporary Technologies in Education., doi:10.1007/978-3-319-89680-9_7

Yuliono, T. Sarwanto, & Rintayati, P. (2018). *The Promising Roles of Augmented Reality in Educational Setting: A Review of the Literature. International Journal of Educational Methodology*. doi:10.12973/ijem.4.3.125e

ENDNOTE

1 https://digitalpractice.leeds.ac.uk/scala/

Chapter 8
The Potential of Gamification in the Multigenerational Learning Organizations

Iolanda Bernardino
https://orcid.org/0000-0002-3956-4554
Escola Superior de Tecnologia e Gestão, Instituto Politécnico de Leiria, Portugal

ABSTRACT

This study is concerned with learning organizations' multigenerational workforce and how gamification is essential for digital transformation and digital learning, once learning organizations understand how knowledge growth can affect the organization's long-term success and its culture and innovation. As an essential development and competitiveness, learning organizations are expanding to the digital learning in its culture, for employees develop their own interpersonal and soft skills, through collaborative work and better communication. The main aim of this study is to analyze through a literature review to understand how gamification is a potential problem solver for the multigenerational workforce in its digital learning and development. After a research background and literature review, the analysis shows that organizations with a multigenerational workforce have several benefits—while young employees share their digital skills, older employees share their experience and knowledge. Through gamification, employees increase their motivation, digital skills, and productivity.

DOI: 10.4018/979-8-3693-0556-0.ch008

1. INTRODUCTION

Peter Senge (Silva & Santos, 2015) emphasized the organizations' success through the learning and leadership process for a continuous ability to respond to the world's needs. The concept of learning organizations was born, and its multiple benefits and challenges are seen as a means of educating employees and teams.

In a cycle, employees and teams seeking continuous professional qualification and generating knowledge for themselves and their peers can allow the organization to expand its economic results and adapt to constant market challenges.

In 2020, global organizations face the COVID-19 pandemic, which led to the lockdown; the people were working remotely from home, and consequently, both organizations and employees face a digital transformation and education challenge.

Digital transformation, according to Roth (2019), is a transition process from an analog to a digital period. It is the key change and renewal to organizations, in their business operations, processes, and structures. But it's not clear how it impacts the organizations' internal processes, design, and employees (Kretschmer & Khashabi, 2020).

As a strong influence on world organizations, digital transformation is seen as a new investment for organizations, where the focus leans toward improving the capacity of adaptation and leadership for digital development. Due to the COVID-19 pandemic, organizations realize how digital transformation is trending and can ease their crisis-affected. When facing a radical change, organizational leaders must adapt and adopt their minds and perceptions on digital transformation for their organizational culture and employees (Hai et al., 2021).

Hai et al. (2021) pointed out that organizational leaders should focus on changing education and vocational policies, contents, and methods to improve human resources' capacity to accept digital transformation trends and learning with the practice of the use of digital technology. The authors also refer that young employees must master digital transformation, in which organizations must empower the young generation to become more proactive, and creative and shape the organization's digital transition, but overall organizations have multigenerational employees.

An appropriate digital transformation requires employees with digital competencies and qualifications, where the workforce can use the information to analyze and critically evaluate the digital information to solve work-related problems and collaborative develop knowledge to empower the organizational practices. These digital skills do not only affect the organization's context but also the employees' professional life, education needs, and career expectations (Jedynak et al.,2021).

Accordingly, with Sousa & Rocha (2019), digital learning is a daily self-working process, where employees learn and work collaboratively and spontaneously regarding the learning outcomes, but digital learning is also a planned process, when the organization proposes specific courses that combine with other learning activities, like the searching of information for better understanding of the issues and help solving work-related problems. The authors' findings explained that the primary methods of learning are collaborative communities and learning, cooperative learning, and network participation with learning processes like open educational practice, technology-integrated teaching methods, educational games, webinars, i.e., and one of the main techniques is gamification (Sousa & Rocha, 2019).

As a new tool, gamification improves and increases learning outcomes and learner motivation, which is associated with employees' desire to keep learning, changing behaviors, and encouraging knowledge sharing (Nair & Mathew, 2022). The gamified approach increases the employees' learning capacity and processes by applying it to their professional training. The gamification contexts, that are being applied in higher education learning space, can be easily recognized by organizations, once gamification makes the educational process motivating by having internal competition and innovating. Therefore, gamification increases the active action of employees, makes learning more meaningful, and allows practical skills consolidation easier (Sadovets et al. (2022). In organizations, adult learning with gamified training has multiple effects on cognition, behavior, and performance changes and drives into increasing employees' satisfaction and enjoyment. Compared with conventional training, gamified training also improves interactive problem-solving and enhances knowledge acquisition and retention (Thomas et al., 2022).

Realizing that gamification is a key success for the digital transformation that can change the organization's multigenerational workforce, this chapter proposal aims to do a literature review to better understand the following research questions: What are the challenges of a multigenerational workforce in digital learning and consequently in organizational digital transformation culture. And is the learning technique gamification a potential problem solver for digital learning of a multigenerational workforce. And concerning the digital competencies of multigenerational employees, how gamified training can increase digital learning between peers.

This chapter is divided into three more sections, the research background, the literature review, and conclusions.

2. RESEARCH BACKGROUND

2.1 Learning Organizations

As the world becomes more interconnected and business becomes more complex and dynamic, work must become more "learningful." - Peter Senge, 1990.

A learning organization is focused on personal and professional knowledge growth, which encourages the learning culture as an essential part of the organization's long-term success (Senge, 1990). While organizational learning is a learning process and capacity of any organization, developed by people's knowledge and experience that improves the organizational capacities (Peschl, 2023; Örtenblad, 2001); the learning organization allows people to continuously improve their competencies and skills, in a common vision for the organization's performance benefit (Marsick & Watkins, 1999; Örtenblad, 2001). The learning organization has multiple within and outside partners that work collaboratively toward long-term success and the organization's innovation (Marsick & Watkins, 1999).

In this complex innovation system, the learning organization has four subsystems of (1) organization, (2) people, (3) knowledge, and (4) technology, that support each other in the learning process. The organizational environment inspires a collaborative and supportive learning culture that communicates how learning is crucial for long-term success. Leaders encourage emergent learning by promoting opportunities for sharing knowledge and experience. The workforce is encouraged to be reflective practitioners, by reflecting on their experience and sharing their knowledge in the learning and collaborative process, where the workforce team is seen as a learning community. The environment in networks of individuals creates opportunities for developing important knowledge and making it available to others, with documentation and collaborative working practices. Therefore, is crucial for a learning organization to understand the value of information and communication technology that manages the knowledge and learning communities (Serrat, 2017; Thomsen & Hoest, 2001).

Nowadays, classroom training is not the most efficient training method, where the standard training programs do not motivate and engage the participation of individuals in the learning process. As technologies enter people's routines, the learning process also benefits from digital content and information. With this, the new learning paradigm – digital learning, increases self-responsible and organized learning with a flexible and personalized learning method and individual and team-oriented collaborative learning methods (Serrat, 2017).

Accordingly, to Kumar Basak et al. (2018), digital learning is supported through digital tools and online content, and it is related to the use of information and communication technology (ICT) in distance, interactive, and collaborative learning and teaching. Digital technologies can promote collaborative tasks, enhance communication, and develop collaborative knowledge and learning (Redecker & Punie, 2017).

Organizations choose digital learning to help people to develop their interpersonal and soft skills on their own time and collaboratively, including management, human resource skills, ICT competencies, leadership, and communication (Derouin et al.,

2005) and help to develop critical thinking and solve complex problems (Rocha & Sousa, 2019). Seen the potential of digital learning in skills development for digital transformation, organizations tend to plan and organize learning activities to promote knowledge sharing, social learning, and developing digital and user-generated content. Digital technologies brought internal and external change to organizations and people. The external environment, such as the global marketplace, emerging customer segments, cultural diversity, and the raised customer expectation, shows how the Internet impacts the core business of organizations. While the internal environment urges new digital skills for great management and problem-solving skills, and consequently people gain a competitive advantage with the digital transformation (Rocha & Sousa, 2019; Jones et al., 2021; Zhang et al., 2021). On the other hand, Adnan & Anwar (2020) questioned the effectiveness of digital learning in less digitally developed countries and somehow in smaller or older organizations, in which the lack of access to digital technologies can increase digital marginalization and therefore the digital transformation and education marginalization.

So, digital transformation comes from the consolidation of digital technology with the digital economy process and the ability of innovation to improve the operational capacity of an organization. From a business perspective, digital transformation enhances the customer experience and also influences the internal perspective, like the business goal, structural leadership, and organizational culture, improving labor efficiency and people's work and social life. But, due to the Covid-19 pandemic, organizations had to reshape their business models, labor activities, and manage people's health, education, and online communication, due to the lockdown (Hai et al., 2021).

According to Martín et al, 2021, the confinement by Covid-19 required a rethink of the education model, where the online education model was the answer to the adaptation process. This repeated educational disruption improved the development of digital transformation and education. The integration of digital technologies in education strengthens digital competencies, where people are digitally dynamic by offering and getting immediate feedback, having more documentation and information, and the learning experience increases by the focus on understanding, motivation, and participation from a constructivist perspective.

To Schwarzmüller et al. (2018), digital transformation influences work design, leadership, and organizational communication. Employees can benefit from working at home by increasing work-life balance, but on the other hand, employees may feel they have to be available 24/7 and have a shorter reaction time for work-related tasks. Digital transformation can force the organization to be disruptive and increase the pressure for innovation, stress, and over-workload for employees. So, there is a need for a work balance, between, managing employees' health, availability, and delivery of job demands and organization production and success. The matter of information and communication technology, also changes communication and collaboration in organizations, once teamwork, interconnections, and relocations increase via digital technologies.

Bennett & McWhorter (2021) considered the Covid-19 pandemic as a fourth industrial revolution or the second information age, once it was seen as a reshaping and disruption of some economies, jobs, and educational models, where social isolation brought a unique and greater use of technologies and therefore the development of digital skills and competencies. The organization's future faces resilience to recovery and planning with technologies, like Artificial Intelligence, automatization, big data, cloud computing, and the Internet of Things. Those are seen as usable benefits for digital transformation and for a need to learn agility and developed the knowledge for the organization's success. Learning agility comes from the rapid advancement of technology and large data volume that need a quickly respond, orientation, and capacity to use the gained experience to a successful outcome. The capacity to learn shapes leadership and the adjustment of the organization in the technological environment.

According to Bennett & McWhorter (2021), participating in virtual human resource development builds up an organization's social and cultural work, which creates a sense of belonging and sharing learning that overrides the Covid-19 pos-pandemic anxiety. As a critical bonding for organizations, culture, communication, and collaborative learning through virtual environments kept the organization's economy and business moving.

Organizations are built on multiple people that work complementary and interdependent to reach a common goal, in which decision-makers and managers organize by groups the tasks for that goal. With digital transformation, available information increases and creates the need to establish new digital tasks and people comfortable with those, that are essential for successful market performance and competitiveness (Kretschmer & Khashabi, 2020). So, for better performance in the actual digital market, organizations have to increase people's digital knowledge and know-how. Organizations face multidimensional challenges due to the different age workforce, which have different skills, behaviors, and perceptions and influence the organization's performance (Bashir et al., 2021).

The overall population is aging and living longer, people over 50 years old are healthier and more educated, and this changes the organization's workplace dynamics with multigenerational experience and skills (OECD, 2020).

Organizations benefit from employees with both age groups (old and young), once older employees have a long and extensive experience and work knowledge; while younger employees give more importance to knowledge gaining, jog security, advancement opportunities, and new skills and ideas for a better organization's innovative performance. So, organizations need to value aged employees and their suitable knowledge and share it with them at the right time (Bashir et al., 2021; Taylor & Bisson, 2020; OECD, 2020; Pinto et al., 2014).

2.2 Gamification and E-Learning

Gamification is a valuable learning instrument applicable to changing organizational environments – Sehoon Kim, 2021

Gamification consists of the use of elements from game design, mechanics dynamics, and frameworks applied in non-gaming contexts, such as an application, to motivate a desired behavior and make learning more active (Saleem et al., 2022; Monterrat et al., 2014; Barata et al., 2013; Muntean, 2011).

To encourage players and improve goal-oriented behavior, the game mechanics focus on rewards, progress or levels, challenges, leaderboards, social calls, self-assessment, participation, communication, feedback, and the freedom to fail. By having a social connection, autonomy, and competence, gamification offers the essential motivation for learners to improve their capacities and directly increases the learners' dedication to educational activities. The motivation from gamification has two forms, extrinsic, in which the learner plays for social recognition and winning rewards, and intrinsic, where the learner plays for pleasure (Saleem et al., 2022; Barata et al., 2013; Strmecki et al., 2015).

According to Strmecki (2015), for a successfully gamified e-learning system, learners are motivated to do tasks to achieve a goal, by being challenged with significant effort, engaged, and rewarded with badges and leaderboards displayed publicly, but the system must not be too competitive once people used these learning moments also to socialize. Another gamified e-learning system mechanic is feedback, where learners have a return of their performance and information about their progress, allowing learners the freedom to fail and understand their mistakes, once experiences and positive instruction are a powerful learning tool.

E-learning allows the dynamisms of gamification online and with both resources, learners are more collaborative, interactive between peers, and efficient in learning, with entertaining technics, such as leaderboards, levels, challenges, and badges, e-learning with gamification has a positive impact on the involvement of learners and peers plays for pleasure (Saleem et al., 2022).

Gamification is a digital tool that engages the user's internal motivation and makes the learning process and daily work more fun, interesting, and unique experience, involving and motivating teams, in which an organization can combine competition between coworkers and teams, and public recognition for achieving a business goal as an award (Barata et al., 2013; Díaz, 2019; Kim, 2021). By uniting gamification with learning, an organization can grow digitally and change its culture, once digital transformation is more about people learning with technology and approaches the multigenerational employees since the main focus is developing digital skills with gamification (Avagyan & Brightwell, 2020; Kim, 2021).

Nowadays, an organization promotes innovative learning, replacing traditional methods in business with adaptations and using proper technologies for corporate learning and well-being. To Kim (2021), a gamification strategy that immerses employees in continuous and cooperative learning, transforming informal methods into corporate learning, is essential to an organization's sustainability and it will maximize the effectiveness by reinforcing learning with gamification.

This strengthening work engagement is created through digital engagement and gamification, once the technology was the tool that encourages engagement between work and personal life in the organization, boosting employees' productivity, since employees see the organization's dedication through gamification as a tool for their well-being (Kim, 2021; Nurkhori et al., 2021).

In the next section, we will see a literature review, to understand the challenges of a workforce in digital learning and how gamification is a potential problem solver in digital competencies of multigenerational employees.

3. LITERATURE REVIEW

To have a better analysis of what the literature can give as an answer to the research questions, a literature review is made.

Kitchenham (2004) refers to the literature review as a method of identifying, evaluating, and interpreting available and relevant studies to a specific research question. The author divided the review into three review phases: (1) Planning; (2) Conducting; (3) Reporting.

Newman & Gough (2020) describes that there are different review types, but the majority share a common process. This process is divided into different stages, but all of them are interconnected: (1) Develop research question; (2) Design conceptual framework; (3) Construct selection criteria; (4) Coding studies; (5) Select studies using selection criteria; (6) Develop search strategy; (7) Assess the quality of studies; (8) Synthesis results of individual studies to answer the review research question; (9) Report findings.

In the planning phase, is developed a review protocol where several components are defined, such as the research question, the criteria, the quality assessment tools, and extraction data methods.

This literature review was developed in the Parsif.al platform (https://parsif.al/). Firstly, was established the protocol with the following research questions:

Table 1. PICOC method of the research questions

PICOC element	Description
Population	Older employees; Age-Diverse Workforce.
Intervention	Gamified training; gamification; online learning; online collaborative learning.
Comparison	Conventional training.
Outcome	Gamification is a potential problem solver for the digital learning of a multigenerational workforce.
Context	Learning organizations.

- What are the challenges of a multigenerational workforce in digital learning and consequently in organizational digital transformation culture?
- Is the learning technique Gamification a potential problem solver for digital learning of a multigenerational workforce?
- Concerning the digital competencies of multigenerational employees, how gamified training can increase digital learning between peers?

To develop a solution for the research questions, the PICOC method was used, which describes five elements of a research question (table 1 - PICOC method of the research questions). Then, was outlined the keywords and their synonyms (table 2 - Keywords and synonyms for the search string.).

With those elements categorized, the primary search string was written:

("Older employees" **OR** "Middle Age Person" **OR** "Older workforce")

AND

Table 2. Keywords and synonyms for the search string

Keywords	Synonyms
Older employees	Middle Age Person Old Age Person Older Workforce Baby boomers
Gamified training	Games Games' content Gamification
Online learning	Digital learning Collaborative learning Collaborative training Online collaborative learning Online training
Conventional training	Traditional learning Traditional training

Table 3. Selection criteria of the search string

Inclusion	Exclusion
Date of publication between 2020 and 2023 Age-diverse workforce Employees over thirty-five Gamification contents Learning with gamification	Date of publication before 2020 Employees under thirty-five

("Gamified training" **OR** "Games" **OR** "Games' content" **OR** "Gamification")
AND
("Conventional training" **OR** "Traditional learning" **OR** "Traditional training")
AND
("Online learning" **OR** "Collaborative learning" **OR** "Collaborative training" **OR** "Digital learning" **OR** "Online collaborative learning" **OR** "Online collaborative training").

Afterward, the search string was applied to the sources: ACM Digital Library, Google Scholar, IEEE Digital Library, Science@Direct, and Scopus. Secondly, the selection criteria were defined to help analyze the studies with the terms of inclusion and exclusion (table 3 - Selection criteria of the search string.):

Lastly, was defined the quality assessment checklist with the following questions and score answers.

- Is the workforce over thirty-five years old?
- Are the gamified contents used?
- Does the organization have a cultural learning mechanism?
- Is Gamification seen as a learning technique for digital learning?
- Is the organization in a digital transformation?

The score answers aim to quantify, with a maximum of 5 points for each study found, and establish a quality assessment for the research. For each question, there is a punctuation of 1, 0.5, and 1 points, in which 1 refers to 100% of importance.

In the conduction phase, it gathered 453 imported studies of which only 66 studies were accepted to be analyzed and scored in the quality and relevant score for the findings, as seen in Table 4 - Source and imported studies.

The source Science@Direct almost had the majority of the imported studies at 41,1%, followed by ACM Digital Library, then Scopus, Google Scholar, and IEEE Digital Library (Figure 1. Imported studies by source.).

Table 4. Source and imported studies

Source	Imported Studies	Accepted Studies
ACM Digital Library	142	21
Google Scholar	50	12
IEEE Digital Library	21	0
Science@Direct	186	27
Scopus	54	6
Total	453	66

Figure 1. Imported studies by source

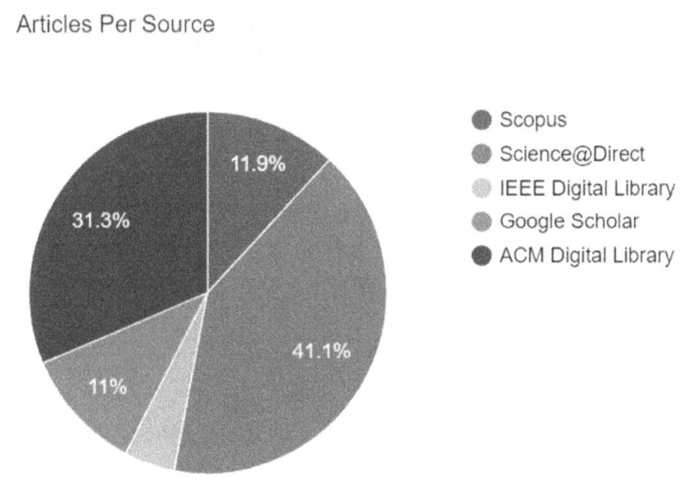

Figure 2. Accepted studies by source

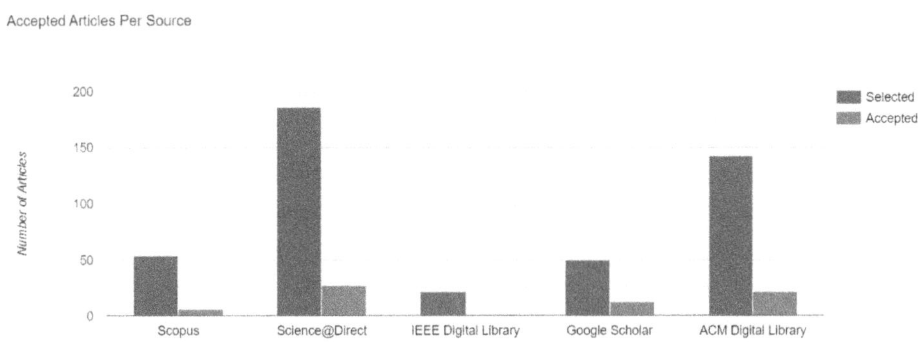

Table 5. Title of accepted studies and quality score

Title of accepted studies	Quality Score
The effect of gamification on the learning-the example of vendors' brand awareness	4.5
Fair play? Sex-, age-, and job-related correlates of performance in a computer-based simulation game	4.0
An experimental study on the effects of gamification on task performance	4.0
A Design for Gamified On-the-job Training	4.0
Unexplored Gamification Elements in Learning Environments	3.5
Role of digital simulation in employee training	3.5
Training Generations X Y Z in Human Resource Management	3.0
Gamification as a Driver of Motivation in the Organizations: A Bibliometric Literature Review	3.0

Once more, the source Science@Direct had 27 studies that were accepted, followed by ACM Digital Library, Google Scholar, and Scopus (Figure 2 Accepted studies by source).

From the 66 accepted studies, only 18 studies with over 2.5 quality scores were rigorously analyzed. Of those 18 studies, 8 were considered the most relevant for the findings (table 5 - Title of accepted studies and quality score.).

3.1 Findings

Organizations are built with people, from different generations, with different values, life priorities, self-recognition, and different ways to face work - attitude, workspace, communication, and obtaining information. So, organizations need to understand how different generations deal with the use of information technologies in the learning process. Authors Evseeva et al. (2020) gather information about the four generations (table 6 - Generations and characteristics (adopted from Evseeva et al., 2020).).

Between generations, there are differences in motivational and practice levels, while Generation X is focused on making money and has less patience with promotions. The millennials prefer a balance between work and life, challenging work, and want to contribute to society, but are self-centered and unmotivated, which could affect the organization and peers. Still, millennials are team workers, open and frequent communicators. Since this generation is the first generation born with technologies, it has a better sense of the new interactive and online media, than older generations (Evseeva et al., 2020).

Table 6. Generations and characteristics (adopted from Evseeva et al., 2020)

Generation	Characteristics
The Baby Boomer	Born between 1945 and 1964. Work for the sake of career and personal and social growth. Closed work zone, team spirit, and assigned people, with personal communication, printed documents, and calls. Technologies have minimal impact on their learning style.
Generation X	Born between 1964 and 1984. Have a sense of individualism, interest in acquiring practical skills, and focused on obtaining results. Prefer private and personalized areas for communications and use electronic communications. Prefer to plan their learning process, with deadlines, goals, and achievements.
Generation Y/Millennials	Born between 1984 and 2003. Grew with the rapid development of the information technology era, becoming a part of their daily routine. A group with a greater sense of responsibility and adaptability and prefers to take freedom of choice. Work for pleasure/fun, experience, and obtaining skills, focused on results and immediate rewards. Prefer remote work and interaction formats – multifunctional spaces/coworking, google information for themselves, and prefer spontaneous communication. Choose a learning process with gamification and edutainment style and collaborative learning.
Generation Z	Born between 2003 and the present. New in the labor market and are considered to be savvy, individualists, who appreciate personal security, recognition, and social equality. Have a sense of entrepreneurship, team worker and are focused on self-development, communicating in social networks, and always online and value the content in the stream. The learning process must have modern information technologies, with the originality of contents and presentation.

To Silva (2021), young and older employees have different attitudes in the workspace, while younger employees are more collaborative, are accustomed to teamwork, and deal better with technologies; older employees are less technologically skilled. The employees, young or older, who are less digitally skilled can seize the opportunities of peers who are better skilled technologically, once organizations are investing in digital learning, for digital transformation and training.

For older employees, a blended approach to learning methods, between traditional and online learning, gives more balance and a sense of overcoming the problems and discomfort with online learning. Digital learning is seen as an effective and flexible method of learning since employees can easily control their learning process. Organizations that embraced online learning have fewer costs associated with traveling costs and venues for the traditional learning method. But due to the multigenerational employees, a mixed-learning method offers inclusion between younger and older generations and sharing experience of the online learning and elements applied, such as gamification elements (Kulkarni et al., 2022; Dooley', 2022; Bend, 2023).

Gamification has become a popular tool in learning methods, easily adopted by organizations to increase workers' both extrinsic and intrinsic motivation, obtain rewards and recognition, and achieve personal and productivity goals. Gamification elements, like leaderboards, time pressure, and test report increases a competitive environment, in which employees try harder to obtain the best scores consequently, the learning process was improved and it motivated employees to learn in a dynamic and integrated and less tedious environment (Encarnação et al., 2021; Silva, 2021; Hosseini et al., 2022; Bend, 2023). Younger employees have a better performance with gamified online learning, than older employees, such as between genders, women have less performance than men, due to computer anxiety and less interest and experience with computer games (Melchers & Basch, 2022).

4. CONCLUSION

From the research background and literature review, the research questions are answered, in which are: what are the challenges of a multigenerational workforce in digital learning and consequently in organizational digital transformation culture; is the learning technique Gamification a potential problem solver for digital learning of a multigenerational workforce; and concerning the digital competencies of multigenerational employees, how gamified training can increase digital learning between peers. It can be concluded that as Bashir et al. (2021), Taylor & Bisson (2020), OECD (2020), and Pinto et al. (2014) said organizations can benefit from multigenerational employees, once older employees share their experience and work knowledge, while younger employees share their skills and ideas for the well-being of organization's innovative performance. Sharing knowledge, know-how, skills, and ideas, lead to the organization's digital transformation, success, and performance, so these values that come from multigenerational employees are essential to organizations. Dooley (2022) demonstrates that digital illiteracy is a common obstacle for organizations, so younger employees that are more comfortable with technologies, share their digital skills with employees that are more anxious about technologies.

Therefore, organizations need to invest in digital learning processes for the well-being and balance of the organizational ecosystem. A popular learning mechanism, such as gamification is gaining interest from originations, since is a powerful mechanism for multigenerational employee dynamics, while young employees help technologically, older employees help by sharing knowledge. But organizations must tailor gamification, while personalization refers to the process of adaption of gamification systems to the needs and interests of its users, customization is referred to as the process that allows users to control and modify the gamification elements by themselves (El-Shorbagy et al., 2020; Encarnação et al., 2021). This allows organizations to have a unique and best model for their ecosystem, once employees are motivated and focused on reaching their goals, success, and performance grow organically.

Gamification is a popular learning mechanism with great potential in learning organizations, that are focused on their employee's knowledge and empowerment. All studies analyzed reported that gamification increases motivation and softens the organization's environment, balancing the employees' inner competition and fun and digital learning, where young and older employees work together and consequently improve the organizational market performance.

REFERENCES

Adnan, M., & Anwar, K. (2020). Online Learning amid the COVID-19 Pandemic: Students' Perspectives. *Online Submission, 2*(1), 45–51. doi:10.33902/JPSP.2020261309

Avagyan, A., & Brightwell, S. (2020). *Learning gamification: using game design and fun to build digital transformation skills*. UN Volunteers. https://www.unv.org/Success-stories/learning-gamification-using-game-design-and-fun-build-digital-transformation-skills

Barata, G., Gama, S., Jorge, J., & Gonçalves, D. (2013, October). Improving participation and learning with gamification. In *Proceedings of the First International Conference on gameful design, research, and applications* (pp. 10-17). ACM. 10.1145/2583008.2583010

Bashir, M., Hameed, A., Bari, M. W., & Ullah, R. (2021). The impact of age-diverse workforce on organization performance: Mediating role of job crafting. *SAGE Open, 11*(1), 2158244021999058. doi:10.1177/2158244021999058

Bend, J. (2023). A Design for Gamified On-the-job Training. *International Journal of Advanced Corporate Learning, 16*(3), 4–20. doi:10.3991/ijac.v16i3.37771

Bennett, E. E., & McWhorter, R. R. (2021). Virtual HRD's role in crisis and the post Covid-19 professional lifeworld: Accelerating skills for digital transformation. *Advances in Developing Human Resources*, *23*(1), 5–25. doi:10.1177/1523422320973288

Derouin, R. E., Fritzsche, B. A., & Salas, E. (2005). E-learning in organizations. *Journal of Management*, *31*(6), 920–940. doi:10.1177/0149206305279815

Díaz, B. (2019). Gamification: when digital transformation makes work fun. In *The New Barcelona Post*. https://www.thenewbarcelonapost.com/en/gamification-when-digital-transformation-makes-work-fun/

El-Shorbagy, S. A., Sherief, N., & Abdelmoez, W. (2020, November). Unexplored Gamification Elements in Learning Environments. In *Proceedings of the 9th International Conference on Software and Information Engineering* (pp. 102-107). ACM.10.1145/3436829.3436852

Encarnação, R., Reuter, J., Ferreira Dias, M., & Amorim, M. (2021, October). Gamification as a driver of motivation in the organizations: A Bibliometric Literature Review. In *Ninth International Conference on Technological Ecosystems for Enhancing Multiculturality (TEEM'21)* (pp. 167-172). ACM. 10.1145/3486011.3486440

Evseeva, S., Rasskazova, O., Kalchenko, O., & Evseeva, O. (2020, November). Training generations xyz in human resource management. In *Proceedings of the International Scientific Conference-Digital Transformation on Manufacturing, Infrastructure and Service* (pp. 1-6).

Hai, T. N., Van, Q. N., & Thi Tuyet, M. N. (2021). Digital transformation: Opportunities and challenges for leaders in the emerging countries in response to COVID-19 pandemic. *Emerging Science Journal*, *5*(1), 21–36. doi:10.28991/esj-2021-SPER-03

Hosseini, C., Humlung, O., Fagerstrøm, A., & Haddara, M. (2022). An experimental study on the effects of gamification on task performance. *Procedia Computer Science*, *196*, 999–1006. doi:10.1016/j.procs.2021.12.102

Jedynak, M., Czakon, W., Kuźniarska, A., & Mania, K. (2021). Digital transformation of organizations: What do we know and where to go next? *Journal of Organizational Change Management*, *34*(3), 629–652. doi:10.1108/JOCM-10-2020-0336

Jones, M. D., Hutcheson, S., & Camba, J. D. (2021). Past, present, and future barriers to digital transformation in manufacturing: A review. *Journal of Manufacturing Systems*, *60*, 936–948. doi:10.1016/j.jmsy.2021.03.006

Kim, S. (2021). How a company's gamification strategy influences corporate learning: A study based on gamified MSLP (Mobile social learning platform). *Telematics and Informatics*, *57*, 101505. doi:10.1016/j.tele.2020.101505

Kitchenham, B. (2004). Procedures for performing systematic reviews. Keele, UK, Keele University.

Kretschmer, T., & Khashabi, P. (2020). Digital transformation and organization design: An integrated approach. *California Management Review*, *62*(4), 86–104. doi:10.1177/0008125620940296

Kulkarni, P. M., Appasaba, L. V., Gokhale, P., & Tigadi, B. (2022). Role of digital simulation in employee training. *Global Transitions Proceedings*, *3*(1), 149–156. doi:10.1016/j.gltp.2022.04.014

Kumar Basak, S., Wotto, M., & Belanger, P. (2018). E-learning, M-learning and D-learning: Conceptual definition and comparative analysis. *E-Learning and Digital Media*, *15*(4), 191–216. doi:10.1177/2042753018785180

Marsick, V. J., & Watkins, K. E. (1999). *Facilitating learning organizations: Making learning count*. Gower Publishing, Ltd.

Melchers, K. G., & Basch, J. M. (2022). Fair play? Sex-, age-, and job-related correlates of performance in a computer-based simulation game. *International Journal of Selection and Assessment*, *30*(1), 48–61. doi:10.1111/ijsa.12337

Monterrat, B., Lavoué, É., & George, S. (2014, April). Motivation for learning: Adaptive gamification for web-based learning environments. *In 6th international conference on computer supported education (CSEDU 2014)* (pp. 117-125). IEEE.

Muntean, C. I. (2011, October). Raising engagement in e-learning through gamification. *In Proc. 6th international conference on virtual learning ICVL* (Vol. 1, pp. 323-329). ACM.

Nair, S., & Mathew, J. (2022). Learning through Play: Gamification of Learning, A Systematic Review of Studies on Gamified Learning. *Journal of Information Technology Management*, *14*(1), 113–126.

Newman, M., & Gough, D. (2020). Systematic reviews in educational research: Methodology, perspectives and application. *Systematic reviews in educational research: Methodology, perspectives and application,* 3-22.

Nurkhori, A., Rahmatia, A., Wahyuningsih, S. H., & Surwanti, A. (2021). Strengthening work engagement through digital engagement, gamification and psychosocial safety climate in digital transformation. *Journal of Innovation in Business and Economics*, *5*(01), 35–48. doi:10.22219/jibe.v5i01.17477

Organisation for Economic Co-operation and Development (OECD). (2020). *Promoting an age-inclusive workforce: Living, learning and earning longer*. OECD.

Örtenblad, A. (2001). On differences between organizational learning and learning organization. *The Learning Organization*, *8*(3), 125–133. doi:10.1108/09696470110391211

Peschl, M. F. (2023). Learning from the future as a novel paradigm for integrating organizational learning and innovation. *The Learning Organization*, *30*(1), 6–22. doi:10.1108/TLO-01-2021-0018

Pinto, A. M. G. L. R. S., da Silva Ramos, S. C. M., & Nunes, S. M. M. D. (2014). Managing an aging workforce: What is the value of human resource management practices for different age groups of workers? *Tékhne (Instituto Politécnico do Cávado e do Ave)*, *12*, 58–68. doi:10.1016/j.tekhne.2015.01.007

Redecker, C., & Punie, Y. (2017). Digital Competence of Educators. Yves Punie.

Roth, S. (2019). Digital transformation of social theory. A research update. *Technological Forecasting and Social Change*, *146*, 88–93. doi:10.1016/j.techfore.2019.05.016

Sadovets, O., Martynyuk, O., Orlovska, O., Lysak, H., Korol, S., & Zembytska, M. (2022). Gamification in the informal learning space of higher education (in the context of the digital transformation of education). *Postmodern Openings*, *13*(1), 330–350. doi:10.18662/po/13.1/399

Saleem, A. N., Noori, N. M., & Ozdamli, F. (2022). Gamification applications in E-learning: A literature review. *Technology. Knowledge and Learning*, *27*(1), 139–159. doi:10.100710758-020-09487-x

Schwarzmüller, T., Brosi, P., Duman, D., & Welpe, I. M. (2018). How does the digital transformation affect organizations? Key themes of change in work design and leadership. *Management Review*, *29*(2), 114–138.

Schwarzmüller, T., Brosi, P., Duman, D., & Welpe, I. M. (2018). How does the digital transformation affect organizations? Key themes of change in work design and leadership. *Management Review*, *29*(2), 114–138.

Senge, P. (1990). *The Fifth Discipline*. Bantam.

Serrat, O. (2017). *Knowledge solutions: Tools, methods, and approaches to drive organizational performance*. Springer Nature. doi:10.1007/978-981-10-0983-9

Silva, A. & Santos, L. (2015). A quinta disciplina e o enfoque a qualificação profissional do administrador. *XII SEGeT – Simpósio de Excelência em Gestão e Tecnologia.*

Silva Puente Arnao, M. A. (2021). *The effect of gamification on learning-the example of vendors brand awareness/Author Maria Angelica Silva* [Doctoral dissertation, Universität Linz].

Sousa, M. J., & Rocha, Á. (2019). Digital learning: Developing skills for digital transformation of organizations. *Future Generation Computer Systems*, *91*, 327–334. doi:10.1016/j.future.2018.08.048

Strmecki, D., Bernik, A., & Radosevic, D. (2015). Gamification in E-Learning: Introducing Gamified Design Elements into E-Learning Systems. *Journal of Computational Science*, *11*(12), 1108–1117. doi:10.3844/jcssp.2015.1108.1117

Taylor, M. A., & Bisson, J. B. (2020). Changes in cognitive function: Practical and theoretical considerations for training the aging workforce. *Human Resource Management Review*, *30*(2), 100684. doi:10.1016/j.hrmr.2019.02.001

Thomas, N. J., Baral, R., & Crocco, O. S. (2022). Gamification for HRD: Systematic review and future research directions. *Human Resource Development Review*, *21*(2), 198–224. doi:10.1177/15344843221074859

Thomsen, H. K., & Hoest, V. (2001). Employees' perception of the learning organization. *Management Learning*, *32*(4), 469–491. doi:10.1177/1350507601324004

Torres Martín, C., Acal, C., El Homrani, M., & Mingorance Estrada, Á. C. (2021). Impact on the virtual learning environment due to COVID-19. *Sustainability (Basel)*, *13*(2), 582. doi:10.3390u13020582

Zhang, J., Long, J., & von Schaewen, A. M. E. (2021). How does digital transformation improve organizational resilience?—Findings from PLS-SEM and fsQCA. *Sustainability (Basel)*, *13*(20), 11487. doi:10.3390u132011487

Chapter 9
Improving Learning and Engagement in Professional Training Using Serious Games

Alvaro Marcos Antonio de Araujo Pistono
Universidade de Trás-os-Montes e Alto Douro, Portugal

ABSTRACT

In the ever-changing world of professional training, organizations constantly seek innovative methods to boost learning outcomes. A prominent approach gaining traction involves serious games, which merge play and education. Serious games offer immersive learning, encouraging active participation, problem-solving, and skill growth. Unlike conventional methods, they provide a safe space to practice real-world scenarios, fostering decision-making and consequence awareness. Serious games find applications in healthcare, military, engineering, and business. Despite benefits, evaluating and adapting serious games remains challenging. Effective assessment measures are needed, catering to diverse learners. The framework for adaptive serious games (F_4ASG) aims to tackle these issues. Based on literature amd expert standpoints, the F_4ASG is detailed, outlining dimensions and aspects. It's exemplified shedding light on improvements. An experiment demonstrates F_4ASG's efficacy in real-world training. Design, participants, data collection, and analysis are explained, followed by result discussions.

1. INTRODUCTION

In the dynamic and rapidly evolving professional training landscape, organisations constantly seek innovative and engaging approaches to enhance learning outcomes.

DOI: 10.4018/979-8-3693-0556-0.ch009

One such approach that has gained significant attention is utilising Serious Games, which combines the elements of play and entertainment with educational content. Serious Games offer a unique and immersive learning experience that promotes active participation, problem-solving, and skill development.

Serious Games can be defined as interactive digital applications designed with the specific purpose of imparting knowledge, skills, or attitudes to users while also entertaining and engaging them. Unlike traditional training methods, Serious Games create a safe and simulated environment where learners can practice real-life scenarios, make decisions, and experience the consequences of their actions. By incorporating game elements such as challenges, rewards, and competition, Serious Games have proven to be highly effective in capturing learners' attention and fostering motivation.

Many are studies about Serious Games in several areas. One of the areas in which they are widely used is science education, as described in the systematic literature review conducted by Kara (2021), which points out that these games have been used since elementary school.

The applications of Serious Games in professional training are diverse and wide-ranging. They have been employed in various domains, including healthcare, military, engineering, and business, to name a few. Serious Games have demonstrated their effectiveness in areas such as medical simulations, leadership development, team building, and technical skills training. These games offer a unique advantage by enabling learners to acquire knowledge and skills hands-on, interactively, leading to enhanced learning retention and transfer to real-world contexts.

Despite the potential benefits, evaluating and adapting Serious Games for professional training remain significant challenges. Evaluating the effectiveness of Serious Games requires establishing valid and reliable assessment measures that can capture the desired learning outcomes. Additionally, adapting Serious Games to cater to learners' diverse needs and preferences is crucial to ensure maximum engagement and learning efficacy. Addressing these challenges is essential to unlock the full potential of Serious Games as a powerful tool in professional training.

These challenges are compounded by other barriers to the use of Serious Games in organisations, such as the lack of adequate resources to develop effective solutions that provide an appropriate balance between game features and learning outcomes.

This chapter aims to contribute to the field of Serious Games in professional training by presenting a Framework for Adaptive Serious Games – F_4ASG.

Based on the findings from the literature review, experts and users' standpoints, the Framework for Adaptive Serious Games – F_4ASG is described in detail, outlining its dimensions, aspects and items. Furthermore, the application of the Framework for Adaptive Serious Games – F_4ASG is demonstrated through the development and evaluation of a specific Serious Game called "*Encontrando Tempo*". The evaluation results shed light on what can be improved for better learning outcomes and greater engagement.

Finally, an experiment using the Serious Game "*Encontrando Tempo*" is presented, providing insights into the practical application and efficacy of the F_4ASG in a real-world professional training context. The experiment's design, participants, data collection, and analysis methods are described, followed by a discussion of the results and their implications.

In conclusion, this chapter seeks to contribute to the advancement of using Serious Games in professional training by introducing the Framework for Adaptive Serious Games – F_4ASG. The framework offers a systematic approach to address the challenges of evaluation and adaptation, ultimately enhancing learning outcomes and engagement. The subsequent sections of this chapter delve into the details of the F_4ASG, its application in the development and evaluation of the Serious Game "*Encontrando Tempo*," and an experiment conducted to assess its effectiveness.

This chapter is organised into sections to develop its theme, starting with a section on the application of Serious Games in professional training, followed by a section describing the Framework for Adaptive Serious Games - F_4ASG.

After the presentation of this framework, there are two sections describing its application for developing and evaluating a Serious Game and a section aimed at applying this game to end users.

Finally, this chapter presents the concluding section, suggesting the application of the proposed framework to facilitate and improve the application of Serious Games in organisations with specific learning objectives.

The next section describes how Serious Games have been used, especially in professional training. It presents the analysis of the main results obtained in the systematic literature review on the application of Serious Games in organisations (Pistono, Santos, & Baptista, 2021).

2. SERIOUS GAMES IN PROFESSIONAL TRAINING

Although sometimes playing and learning seem contradictory, as cited by Huynh-Kim-Bang, Wisdom, and Labat (2010), these two activities can be brought together in Serious Games by exploiting the individual characteristics of each (game and instruction) for the best results. For example, taking advantage of the engagement potential of games to increase students' hours of dedication to study subjects and linking the challenges of games to those of problem-solving learning.

The effectiveness of games in learning is very much related to engagement, which O'Brien and Toms (2008) define as an experience composed of factors such as, among others, challenge, sensory appeal, attention, feedback, interactivity, and user control.

These engagement factors indicate that games are inherently engaging, which can be considered justification for their application to education.

Other facts cited by O'Brien and Toms (2008) are the similarities between the learning process and the act of playing. Both are generally long, complex and difficult, besides the fact that games are associated with learning (the player needs to learn how to play). The same authors complement this finding with the observation that, like games, learning is an interactive process that challenges learners and has rules for acquiring new knowledge and skills.

When observing these comparisons between games and learning, applying Serious Games in the teaching-learning process seems almost natural. However, this does not mean that the application of Serious Games ensures learning or knowledge and skills transfer to real-life scenarios. There is still much research to be done on these aspects.

In the literature review by Boyle et al. (2016), it is pointed out that Serious Games can be used with satisfactory results not only for knowledge acquisition but also for obtaining/improving skills, such as in health care, planning, behaviour change, and behavioural skills. In this same review, simulation is noted as the most popular genre of Serious Games.

Sousa, Antunes, Pinto, & Zagalo (2022, p. 127) highlight that "*games are useful for planners as supporting planning tools, but using games demands specific approaches*".

Another example of an application is the Serious Game developed by Yamin, Katt and Nowostawski (2021), used as a tool to model attack and defence in cyber security.

Serious Games are present in various fields, such as defence, manufacturing, education, and medicine (Wattanasoontorn, Hernández, & Sbert, 2014).

They are cited as a useful learning methodology for imparting skills on complex tasks by inserting pedagogical principles into their design and structure (Azadegan, Riedel, & Hauge, 2012).

Wouters, van der Spek and van Oostendorp (2009) analysed the results presented in the literature on the application of Serious Games and their learning outcomes. These authors observed positive effects in the learning outcomes of Serious Games compared to media and concluded in their research that these artefacts when compared to text, guided investigation, game without hypertext interactions, traditional investigative reporter instruction and traditional instruction, present better learning outcomes.

In professional training, although it is more common to apply games developed specifically for needs identified in each target audience and scenario, the so-called COTS (Commercial Off The Shelf) games are also used.

According to Larson (2020), in a gamified environment, there is a tendency for people to engage in repetitive tasks and take risks in their attempts.

Engagement in Serious Games has been investigated from a few perspectives, such as in (Nye, Core, & Ghosal, 2021) where it was examined from the science of learning and game design.

One very prominent application area is healthcare, with many examples of Serious Games, including, for example, augmented reality and virtual reality.

Regarding application in healthcare, Wattanasoontorn, Hernández, & Sbert (2014) classify Serious Games into:

- Games for physical exercises.
- Games for skill training or content transfer.
- Simulations, e.g. security awareness or positioning.

Wattanasoontorn, Hernández, & Sbert (2014) also classify Serious Games, in healthcare, as:

- Player roles: Patient or non-patient, exploring aspects such as treatment and rehabilitation for patient players and health and wellness for non-patients. Also, training and simulations for the non-patient players, whether they are healthcare professionals or not.
- Disease stages: Serious Games have specific purposes at each disease stage.
- Monitoring in the susceptibility stage.
- Detection in the presymptomatic stage.
- Treatment and therapy in the clinical disease stage.
- Rehabilitation, follow-up and screening at the stage of disability.
- Functionalities: Both concerning the application domain (thematic), technological resources, and user interaction forms.

Although applications of Serious Games in the health and military fields are the most common, they are not the only areas where Serious Games can be significant for training. Several authors have documented, in recent decades, the use of Serious Games in professional training, in companies of various areas in training related to knowledge acquisition, skills practice and attitude change, in contexts such as the Military (Hays, 2005; Greitzer, Kuchar, & Huston, 2007; Engberg-Pedersen, 2017); Telecommunications (Almeida et al., 2011); General businesses (Donovan & Lead, 2012; Kapp, 2013; Uskov & Sekar, 2014; Boller & Kapp, 2017); Healthcare (Wattanasoontorn, Hernández, & Sbert, 2014); Manufacturing companies (Riedel, Feng, Hauge, Hansen, & Tasuya, 2015); Hospitality (Pabon, 2016); Finance (Larson, 2020).

To offer game situations, such as problem-solving challenges, aligned to the players' knowledge and skills and apply Serious Games broadly and flexibly, adapting these games to each player's appropriate evolution is important to provide better learning results.

Lopes & Bidarra (2011) analysed the existing challenges in adapting games and simulations. These authors emphasise that the lack of adaptability in these media may result in the loss of efficiency in learning when users perceive the dynamics of the game and evolve even without reaching the learning objectives and in the impossibility of applying the game again for the same users (because they already know its content).

In this same article, it is concluded that games need to be adaptable to motivate users to play them, given the differences between users.

The challenges to the adaptability of games, according to the research conducted by Lopes & Bidarra (2011), are related to the treatment of the data captured from users and how they influence the adaptation both offline (during the design) and online (during the game), to accomplish to the players' expectations (such as difficulty level to motivate and not to discourage when too difficult, for example) and to the learning preferences of each user.

Artificial intelligence techniques, such as those applied by Beal, Beck, Westbrook, Atkin, & Cohen (2002) in intelligent tutoring, could be used in Serious Games research, adaptable to players, to increase their motivation and engagement, as well as to obtain better results. Also, instructional elements of Serious Games could be adapted according to some characteristics of players and their behaviour in the game.

Models such as those used by Pedersen, Togelius, & Yannakakis (2010), which use MLP - Multi-layer perceptron optimisation - and the performance of derived MLPs, could help predict the need and adaptation of Serious Games according to the evolution and actions of players.

Games can be adapted from the initial parameterisation of difficulty or other characteristics of the environment, such as sound and audio-visual resources, to dynamic changes during the game to adapt to the player's conditions or needs. It is possible, for example, to identify a player's learning characteristics and, during the game, present situations and resources that are more conducive to them achieving better learning outcomes. Another example of adaptation would be the use of Artificial Intelligence to create NPCs (non-player characters) to guide the player according to their evolutionary needs.

Therefore, adaptation in Serious Games is possible and should be planned so that the players achieve the expected learning outcomes and increase their engagement, motivating them to spend more time in the game.

Sousa et al. (2016) point out that one of the biggest challenges in getting Serious Games accepted in education is measuring their actual effects on learning.

According to Emmerich and Bockholt (2016), the design of a Serious Game should be based on the learning objectives. These authors emphasise that the evaluation of the results of Serious Games represents a challenge, i.e., how to measure that the learning objectives have been achieved.

Concerning the Serious Games' evaluation, Calderón & Ruiz (2015) have identified learning outcomes, usability and user experience as characteristics to assess the quality of these artefacts.

To amplify the range of Serious Games' evaluation beyond the four levels of evaluation described by Kirkpatrick and Kirkpatrick (2016), namely reaction, learning, behaviour, and outcomes, Emmerich and Bockholt (2016) suggest that they also be evaluated against the six components of the framework proposed by Mitgutsch and Alvarado (2012): purpose, content, game mechanic, narrative, aesthetics, and framing.

It is very important that the evaluation of Serious Games applied to professional training has as a reference a matrix of professional competencies, such as the European Qualifications Framework - EQF (Description of the eight EQF levels., n.d.), where the learning outcomes are organised in a hierarchical manner of knowledge, skills and responsibility and autonomy.

In addition to the aforementioned challenges of adapting and evaluating Serious Games, these artefacts encounter other barriers to their use in organisations, such as high development costs and time, as well as the complexity of designing an effective and attractive solution that balances game features and learning goals, which comes up against a lack of human and technical resources for its development, implementation, management and evaluation. Added to these barriers is the very acceptance of a game as a training solution, both by managers and trainees.

To address these challenges and use Serious Games as effective learning tools in organisations, the next section will present the Framework for Adaptive Serious Games – F_4ASG, which provides for the adaptation of game elements to enhance learning outcomes, as well as participant engagement. This framework is intended to be useful both for developing adaptive Serious Games and for assessing the suitability of this type of artefact in relation to the expected learning outcomes.

3. FRAMEWORK FOR ADAPTIVE SERIOUS GAMES: F_4ASG

In order to develop a framework for adaptive Serious Games applied to professional training, a broad approach is proposed to encompass all variables found in the literature review and add a focus on their adaptation related to learning outcomes and engagement measures.

Initially, the purposes of the framework and its dimensions were defined. These dimensions were defined from the theoretical references found in the systematic literature review, focus groups and experts' interviews, and were grouped into two sets: Learning and game.

The systematic literature review contributed to the theoretical basis and perspective of the investigation, while the focus groups and interviews complemented it with the experiences of professionals who use Serious Games in professional training.

In each of these sets, two dimensions were determined that would encompass all the aspects found in the literature and two more dimensions, one concerning results and one regarding adaptation.

Combining these dimensions and their dependencies is essential for a balanced Serious Game in terms of learning and game aspects to achieve better learning outcomes and higher engagement.

The proposed framework purposes are:

- Include learning outcomes as dimensions of the framework.
- Group the dimensions into learning and game.
- Consider the forms of adaptation in these two groups of dimensions.
- Be used for both the development and evaluation of adaptive Serious Games.
- Be used to improve Serious Games by comparing the application of the framework at the development stage (development team) and the evaluation stage (players).

The learning dimensions are those related to the elements of Serious Games that concern instruction and learning. They are related to the instructional treatment given to the content, appropriate to the target audience of the game, observing characteristics such as the participants' level of knowledge and the interesting and necessary audio-visual resources to promote learning.

Regarding learning, they must be observed:

- Instructional theories.
- Learning theories.
- Learning outcomes.
- Evaluation types.
- Adaptation types.

The game dimensions comprise all the game mechanics and game elements that a Serious Game may present, such as challenges, points, leaderboards, badges, game narrative, audio, and scenarios. The dimensions of this field should be considered as the ones responsible for the entertainment and engagement of the participants in Serious Games.

Regarding the game, the following must be observed:

Figure 1. Framework for adaptive serious games – F_4ASG version

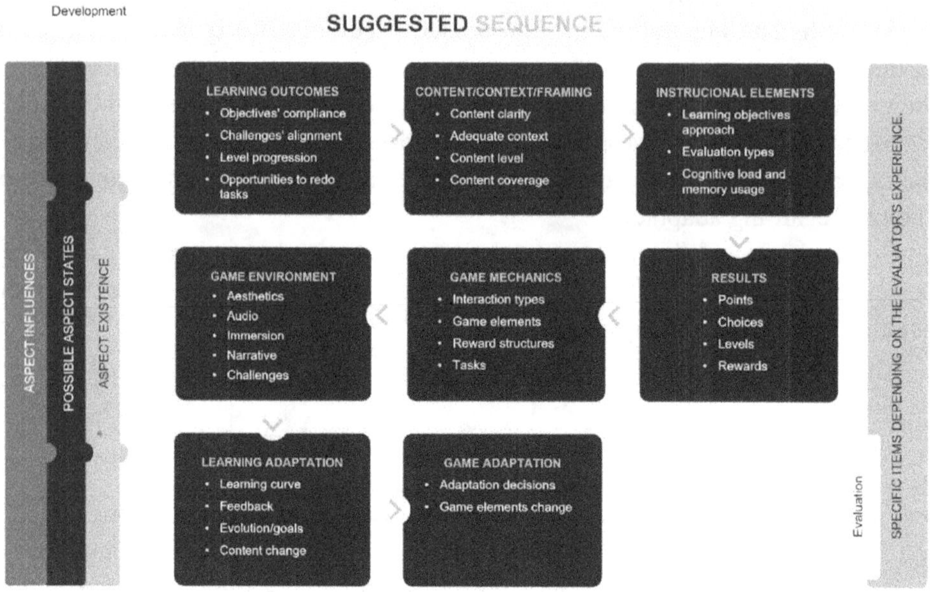

- Serious Games types (or genres).
- Serious Games in professional training.
- Frequently game elements and gamification.
- Motivation theories.
- Engagement.
- Flow.
- Adaptation types.
- Serious Games' frameworks.

Figure 1 shows the final Framework for Adaptive Serious Games – F_4ASG. This figure incorporates the suggested sequence of development and the flexibility to add items to the evaluation criteria.

It should be noted that this figure shows the first two levels of detail of the framework, and the more detailed level, i.e., the items, are described in the following sections section.

Following each dimension, its aspects, and items of the Framework for Adaptive Serious Games – F_4ASG are detailed.

3.1 L1: Content / Context / Framing

This dimension refers to the content contained in the Serious Game, which needs to be appropriate to the Serious Game objectives and offers real opportunities for understanding and deepening the content.

It should be appropriate to the target audience concerning the students/players' professional context and their level of knowledge and skills.

Special attention must be paid to the relevance of the topics covered and focus on the results expected from students, according to the purpose of its application, whether for motivation, training or assessment.

Table 1 shows the aspects and the respective items of the L1 dimension.

Table 1. L1: Content / context / framing dimension of the F_4ASG

Aspect	Item
Content clarity **L1.1**	The terms and expressions are used clear and familiar (or have they been defined previously).
	The flow of the content is direct and unambiguous.
	When necessary, because the language is very specific, there is a glossary of terms.
Adequate context **L1.2**	The situations presented or exemplified are possible situations in the reality of the student's work.
	The most common situations are present.
	The most important situations are highlighted.
	Exceptional situations are presented as such.
Content level **L1.3**	The necessary explanations are given for the student to absorb the content at each stage of the Serious Game.
	Throughout the content, the student can relate previous content to new content being presented.
Content coverage **L1.4**	The content reflects all the knowledge and/or skills the student will need in their day-to-day work in the specific context of its application.
	To facilitate understanding of the content, connections are made to other important topics that have the potential to facilitate understanding of the content under study.
	The content covers topics not related to the student's work only to relate them to the content, to provide external connections, highlighting them as non-essential.

3.2 L2: Instructional Elements

As an instructional artefact, the instructional elements present in a Serious Game should be appropriate to the audience, the content and the application context, with special attention to the approach to the learning objectives, the types of evaluation and the forms of access and interaction.

L2 aspects and items are listed in Table 2. In this table, this framework version presents a new item for L2.2 – Evaluation types, corresponding to a suggestion from the experimental evaluation of this artefact.

This item is related to behavioural evaluation, which should be realised whenever resources allow because it is a way to measure the transfer of knowledge and skills acquired or practised in the game to the work routine. Table 2 highlights this item in bold.

Table 2. L2: Instructional elements dimension of the F_4ASG

Aspect	Item
Learning objectives approach **L2.1**	All learning objectives are addressed.
	There are clear instructions on how students should demonstrate achievement of each objective.
	The objectives are ordered in increasing complexity concerning the knowledge and skills associated with them.
Evaluation types **L2.2**	Evaluations cover all the learning objectives of the Serious Game.
	The evaluations clearly indicate the learning outcomes.
	If possible, a behavioural evaluation, such as a survey, is applied to assess the effects of Serious Game on player behaviour sometime after the application of this artefact.
Cognitive load and memory usage **L2.3**	The game scenarios and situations present audio-visual resources that do not overload the players' cognitive load.
	The focus of the presented content is the working memory.
	There are situations that present previous experiences of the players, allowing these to be related to the other situations of the game.

3.3 L3: Learning Outcomes

Every Serious Game should have a set of expected learning outcomes. These outcomes should be aligned with the challenges and situations of the game and should be measurable throughout the game and also in pre and post-tests.

In Table 3, the aspects and items of the L3 dimension are listed.

Table 3. L3: Learning outcomes dimension of the F_4ASG

Aspect	Item
Objectives' compliance **L3.1**	All the enabling objectives for a learning outcome are clearly described and sequenced in a way that facilitates their achievement.
	The learning objectives have a clear relationship to the expected learning outcomes.
	There is a relationship between the objectives and outcomes with the goals of the daily work.
	The evaluation of the results is appropriate to the expected results according to their level (Reaction, Learning, Behavior, Results).
Challenges' alignment **L3.2**	The situations/challenges are presented to the players related to the expected results.
	It is possible to transfer a situation from the game to the work routine and link learning to everyday tasks.
Level progression **L3.3**	The game predicts incremental learning outcomes.
	Learning outcomes can be built on previous experiences in the game.
	The game makes it possible to relate learning outcomes to each other, enabling a holistic view of the topics covered.
Opportunities to redo tasks **L3.4**	There is a possibility to redo tasks.
	The tasks are redone with some kind of help/feedback.
	Some kind of adaptation is foreseen when redoing the tasks.
	All the attempts to execute a task are displayed to the player so they can see its evolution.

3.4 L4: Learning Adaptation

Learning dimensions can be adapted to deliver better learning outcomes.

Serious Games can be adapted to improve learning outcomes according to the student's interactions, the learning curve, the feedback (immediate and delayed), and the student's evolution in the game.

Also, the game's content can be changed to give each player better learning opportunities.

Table 4 shows the aspects and respective items of the L4 dimension.

3.5 G1: Game Mechanics

The mechanics of a Serious Game can be characterised as its general operation, including its rules and relations between the game elements. That is, it comprises all audio-visual elements of the game, the way they interact with each other forming

Table 4. L4: Learning adaptation dimension of the F_4ASG

Aspect	Item
Learning curve **L4.1**	The pace of the game changes when a player makes a mistake.
	The number of tasks is changed according to the learning outcomes.
	The type of task is changed according to the learning outcomes.
Feedback **L4.2**	The feedback is adapted based on the player's characteristics.
	The feedback is adapted according to the player's evolution in the game.
	The feedback is adapted to motivate the player's evolution.
Evolution/goals **L4.3**	The game situations are changed according to the player's evolution.
	The sequence of presentation of the situations/challenges is variable according to the results obtained throughout the game.
Content change **L4.4**	The content is adapted to provide better learning outcomes.

Table 5. G1: Game mechanics dimension of the F_4ASG

Aspect	Item
Interaction types **G1.1**	The forms of interaction are appropriate for the players.
	The forms of interaction are initially explained to players.
	There are sufficient instructions to interact and progress through the game (such as opportunities to practice before the game).
	If the Serious Game is applied to a varied audience, there are different ways of access, suitable for different groups of players, such as different age groups or with different familiarity with games.
Game elements **G1.2**	The game components characterise the artefact as a game.
	The game components are harmonious with each other.
	The game elements represent the context correctly.
	Similarities can be identified between game elements and the players' real-life context (activities, people or environments).
	The elements of the Serious Game were rebalanced after application to at least one pilot group of players.
Reward structures **G1.3**	There are reward structures in the game.
	The reward structures are clear to players.
	The reward structures are appropriate to the players' progression.
	The reward structures motivate players to continue playing and evolving.
Tasks **G1.4**	The tasks that the player must complete are linked to the learning objectives.
	The tasks are adapted according to the outcomes of the game.
	The tasks cover all learning objectives.

the game scenarios, besides the ways of interaction of the players with the game elements and with other players, as Table 5 shows.

This table highlights, in bold, two new items related to aspects G1.1 and G1.2 from the experimental evaluation suggestions.

3.6 G2: Game Environment

A Serious Game comprises several elements that together should compose a harmonious environment conducive to learning and player engagement.

The aspects and items of this dimension, listed in Table 6, make up the overall aspect of the artefact and correspond to a holistic view of the elements of the Serious Game.

This dimension is strongly related to the players' perception of the Serious Game.

Table 6. G2: Game environment dimension of the F_4ASG

Aspect	Item
Aesthetics **G2.1**	The aesthetics are appropriate to the theme.
	The aesthetics are appropriate to the application context.
	The aesthetics are appropriate to the audience.
Audio **G2.2**	The sound effects correctly reflect the game states.
	The sound effects complement the environment, adding useful sensory information.
	The sound effects do not distract the player when they should be focusing on some information.
Immersion **G2.3**	The game elements and mechanics provide the necessary degree of immersion to engage the player during the important moments of the game.
	The forms of interaction assist the player's immersion in the game context.
Narrative **G2.4**	The narrative enriches the other elements of the game.
	The narrative is appropriate to the game's context.
	The narrative is appropriate for the audience.
Challenges **G2.5**	At each level, the challenges are appropriate to the knowledge and skills of the players.
	The challenges highlight the learning objectives.
	The challenges present environments that motivate their solution.

3.7 G3: Results

Game results are measures of what happens during the game and can be used to adapt the game to, for example, keep the player in the flow state by balancing the challenges and the player's skills and knowledge.

Some examples of game results are the score achieved by a player, the amounts of collected items, the levels completed, and the time to overcome some challenges.

How the proposed framework handles the results is shown in Table 7.

Table 7. G3: Results dimension of the F_4ASG

Aspect	Item
Points **G3.1**	Points are recorded and displayed for players.
	The scoring criteria are variable, e.g. according to the player's performance and level.
	Points influence player performance or progress, for example by awarding bonuses or onus.
Choices **G3.2**	Players can make choices during the game.
	The choices clearly show changes in direction in the game.
	The choices are variable, according to the player's level or score, for example.
	The choices available, at each point in the game, are adapted to maintain the player's flow state.
	The available choices are optimised to bring learning outcomes closer to expected values.
Levels **G3.3**	The game is organised into levels according to the learning objectives.
	The levels are adaptable according to player performance.
	The sequence of levels can be changed according to the player's performance.
Rewards **G3.4**	There are rewards for players' actions.
	Player rewards can alter game states.
	The rewards are adapted, according to the student's actions history, for example.

3.8 G4: Game Adaptation

Adaptation of a game can be both offline, planned during game design and development, and online, during gameplay. It can be characterised as adaptability,

Table 8. G4: Game adaptation dimension of the F_4ASG

Aspect	Item
Adaptation decisions **G4.1**	It is possible to adjust the difficulty of the game.
	The game provides for interpretation and adaptation from player interactions, such as an intelligent tutoring system.
	Game elements' changes are intended to facilitate learning.
	Game elements' changes are conducive to engagement.
Game elements change **G4.2**	Game elements adapt based on information such as the player's activity history (such as changes to the player's avatar or accumulation of collectables).
	Game elements adapt as the player progresses in the game.

through player choices and parameterisations, or as adaptivity, through dynamic changes during gameplay (Streicher & Smeddinck, 2016).

When planning the adaptation of a Serious Game, one should identify if there are mandatory contents or activities that all players must attend.

Design patterns can facilitate the adaptation of Serious Games when using a repository of templates (ludemes), for example.

The framework reflects how a Serious Game can be adapted, as shown in Table 8.

4. APPLICATION OF THE F_4ASG TO DEVELOP A SERIOUS GAME

For the application of the Framework for Adaptive Serious Games – F_4ASG, the topic of time management, which is transversal in professional training, was chosen.

In the design and development of this game, all the guidelines were followed, and the existing alternatives for the game elements were observed, considering the most detailed level provided in the framework.

The game design was conducted by first detailing the aspects of each dimension of the framework, followed by defining the game elements at the next level of detail (items).

Then the resulting Serious Game "*Encontrando Tempo*" is evaluated with the framework.

4.1 Learning Outcomes: L3

The EQF (The European Qualifications Framework (EQF), n.d.) was used as a reference for determining the desired learning outcomes at levels 1 and 2, corresponding to individual knowledge, skills, initiative, and responsibility, with no teamwork or leadership characteristics.

4.2 Content/Context/Framing: L1

The content used in this Serious Game will be extracted from the Time Management Course provided by Fábrica de Cursos. (2022). This course is intended for the professional training general public, as it addresses basic concepts of time management in daily activities in the work environment.

4.3 Instructional Elements: L2

Regarding this dimension, the relevant aspects were considered, as shown in Table 9.

4.4 Results: G3

The recorded game results are described in Table 10, where the relevant aspects of this dimension are described.

Table 9. Serious Game's instructional elements approaches

Reference	Aspect	Approach
L2.1	Learning objectives approach	• How players will achieve the learning objectives must be clear. • Players should receive feedback on their actions to know if they are correct or not concerning the learning objectives. • Players' performance should be shown throughout the game, according to the learning objectives achieved. • Each learning objective should present the relationship between the game situation and the players' actual activities.
L2.2	Evaluation types	• Reaction evaluation (Kirkpatrick & Kirkpatrick (2016) reaction level). • Learning evaluation (Kirkpatrick & Kirkpatrick (2016) learning level).
L2.3	Cognitive load and memory usage	• The audio-visual elements should be used to compose the game environment and allow integration with the content without exaggeration or unnecessary distractions. • The contents should be relative to the game situations, without the need to memorise other situations, favouring the players' working memory. • Content other than that present in each situation can be included in the situations as long as it refers to the situations in which it appears to allow the players to use their long-term memory.

Table 10. Recorded game results

Reference	Aspect	Approach
G3.1	Points	• The player's points should always be shown in a highlighted screen area during the game. • Points should be given as the player progresses in the game and achieves learning objectives. • When the player satisfies a desired learning outcome, he should earn more points. That is, he should earn points by achieving learning objectives (enabling and final) and more points by demonstrating an expected learning outcome. • If the player's point accumulation is fast, he should have a bonus associated with time
G3.2	Choices	• Throughout the Serious Game, there should be choices of paths or activities to take. • The choices should clearly show that there are pros and cons of each decision, such as increasing points, discounting points, accumulating objects, etc.
G3.3	Levels	• The Serious Game must have levels which can be reached according to the player's performance. For this theme, time management, applied to professional training, levels are suggested that are aligned with the knowledge, skills, initiatives, and responsibilities foreseen in the EQF.
G3.4	Rewards	• Throughout the Serious Game, the player can be rewarded with the following: • Points according to their advancement in the game. • Points for reaching a game/learning objective. • Points for changing levels. • Bonus points. • Additional time to do or redo an activity. • Badges for progress in the game. • Badges for completing activities. • Badges for completing levels; • Desired items directly related to the game's theme, the issues addressed in each situation, and the learning objectives. • Compound rewards, such as reaching a certain level and possessing certain collectable items, you get another special item, for example.

4.5 Game Mechanics: G1

In this dimension, the game begins to be characterised, with important considerations about how players interact with the game, the elements of the game itself, what kinds of tasks players will be subjected to, and how players' performance is rewarded, i.e., what reward structures are envisaged.

4.6 Game Environment: G2

As a complement to the game mechanics, the game environment should be balanced to facilitate learning and engagement.

4.7 Learning Adaptation: L4

As one of the purposes of the proposed framework, adaptation of both learning and game should be seen as a transversal dimension regarding all other dimensions and their aspects.

4.8 Game Adaptation: G4

Also, as a transversal dimension, the relevant aspects of game adaptation are shown in Table 11.

To determine the elements of the Serious Game, corresponding to the third level of detail of the proposed framework, the considerations shown in Table 12 were made for each aspect previously defined.

Below are the specifications of the "*Encontrando Tempo*" game elements, according to the detailed items provided in the framework.

Table 11. Game adaptation aspects

Reference	Aspect	Approach
G4.1	Adaptation decisions	• The game should allow the change of game difficulty. This can be characterised by changing parameters in the game activities such as time available, number of points per hit, hints and feedback alternatives. These changes alter the player's path and, consequently, the learning curve. • Adaptation of the game should aim to facilitate learning or foster engagement.
G4.2	Game elements change	• The game elements should reflect the current state of the player. They should show, for example, the player's state in the game, his achievements, acquired objects, etc. • The game elements should be changed as the player progresses so that the game environment is coherent with the activity proposed at each moment.

Table 12. Items considerations for each Serious Game aspect

Item	Considerations
Existence	Is the aspect present in the game?
Possible configurations	What are the possible states of the aspect in the game?
Influences on the game, the player and other aspects	Do the different forms of the aspect influence the game, provide any reaction in the players, or alter other aspects of the game?

Figure 2. "Encontrando Tempo" game introduction

4.9 Narrative

The general narrative of the game is that the player has to retrieve some time capsules that have gone missing. As a new employee in the organisation, in the position of Time Hunter, the player has to accomplish some missions to help the Time Hunters succeed, as Figure 2 exemplifies.

4.10 Interaction Types

The central element of the game is a board that must all be covered for the player to win the game. At each point of this board, the player will face different missions and challenges one by one until the end of the game.

The types of interaction in the game are simple, like dragging and dropping elements across the screen.

The missions and challenges consist of simple games, such as matching items, hangman, word search, crosswords, puzzles and quizzes.

Figure 3 shows a sample mission where the player must drag items by type and drop them into the corresponding deposit.

Figure 3. "Encontrando Tempo" game interaction sample

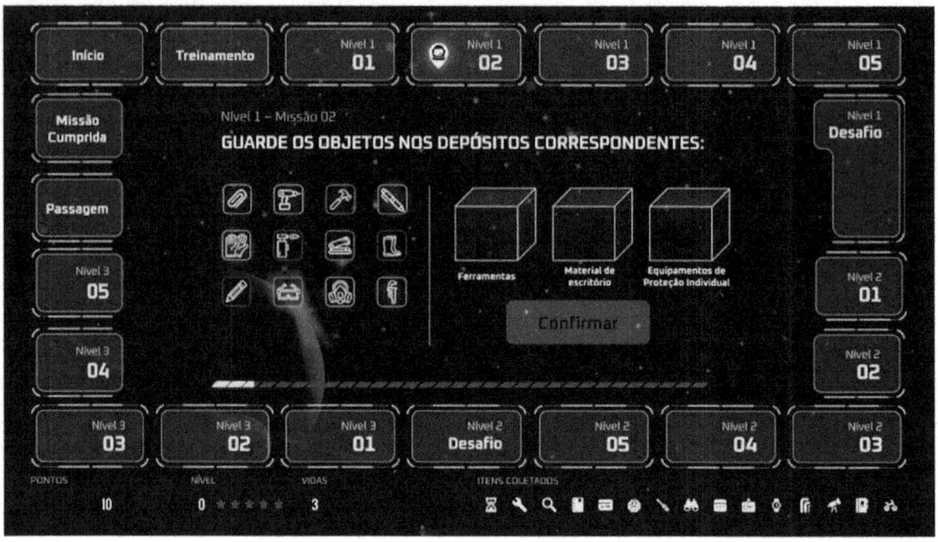

4.11 Content Coverage

As a generic time management game that can be applied to a diverse audience in professional training, the content covers basic concepts such as goals, priorities, wasting time and simple planning.

Figure 4 has an example of the content coverage. In this example, the player participates in a hangman game and should correctly answer the challenge to gain bonuses.

4.12 Level Objectives

To achieve the learning outcomes, derived from the EQF, and to facilitate learning with gradually increasing complexity, the learning objectives are organised into the game's levels.

The level objectives are presented to the player at the beginning of each level, as Figure 5 exemplifies.

4.13 Points

Points are the main reward element in the game. Players earn points for missions completed or in level-crossing challenges.

Figure 4. "Encontrando Tempo" game content sample

Figure 5. "Encontrando Tempo" game-level objective sample

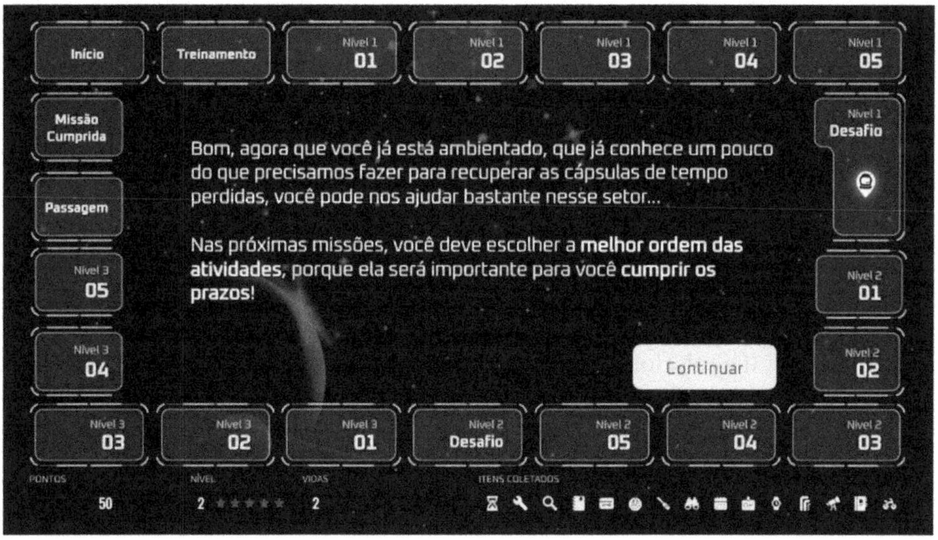

Players earn more or fewer points depending on the difficulty level of the successful mission. If a player successfully completes a mission that has a high difficulty level, the amount of points earned is higher than if the difficulty level was medium and even more if it was easy.

They also earn points per object collected as a bonus on each level challenge.

4.14 Achievements

In addition to points earned during the game for successfully completing missions, players can earn bonuses on level-crossing challenges.

Throughout the game, players can conquer and collect objects by successfully completing activities with the highest difficulty level. These objects can be:

- Used for measuring time.
- Tools for maintaining or repairing objects.
- Instruments used for investigation or to explore some scenarios.
- Items used for planning.
- Used to access some environments or to facilitate locomotion.
- Both the player's points and achievements are always on screen in a lower bar, as shown in Figure 6.

Figure 6. Bottom game bar with indicators

4.15 Preparatory Practice

Before starting the missions, the player must know his objective in the game, how he can reach it, and how to interact with the game elements.

He should also know the elements of the game environment, which can help him perform better in the missions.

The Serious Game "*Encontrando Tempo*" presents a level 0 before the first actual game level, where the player can practice how they will interact during the game, as Figure 7 shows.

Figure 7. "Encontrando Tempo" game practice level

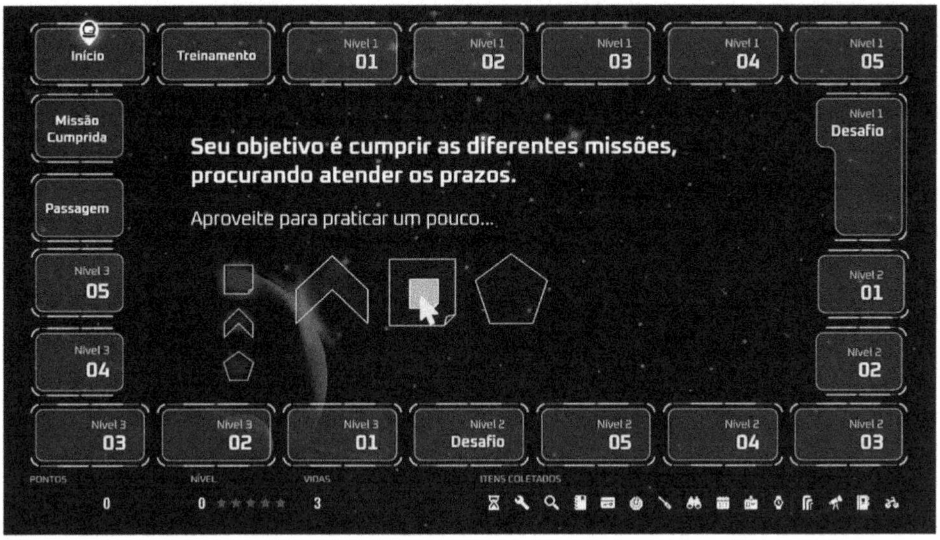

4.16 Difficulty Level Changes

During the game, according to the player's result in each mission, the difficulty level will be adjusted to motivate the player to continue the game and achieve the proposed objectives, balancing their degree of knowledge/skill with the challenges presented in each stage.

Each player starts the game with the highest difficulty level and, if he fulfils the mission in the determined period, evolves to the next mission with the same level of difficulty. If he does not complete the mission satisfactorily, either by completing the mission incorrectly or by having exceeded the determined deadline, he repeats the mission with a lower difficulty level.

Lowering the level of difficulty means:

- More time for mission completion.
- Tips for completing the mission, more detailed as the lower the difficulty level.

However, as the difficulty decreases, the points associated with the mission also decrease as an onus.

The difficulty level increases again when the player successfully completes two missions in a row.

4.17 Navigation

Navigation throughout the game depends on several factors, such as level progression and opportunities for the player to redo missions.

The learning curve and feedback are also associated with the player's navigation, adapting according to their performance.

Besides the rewards associated with the results obtained by the players, in each mission, the navigation is also adapted to provide better game evolution conditions.

4.18 Missions

The game missions correspond to the tasks that players must accomplish to evolve in the game.

They join almost every framework aspect and focus on the content level and feedback to guide the player.

Missions always require known and simple interactive forms, prioritising working memory.

An example of a mission is shown in Figure 8.

Figure 8. Mission example

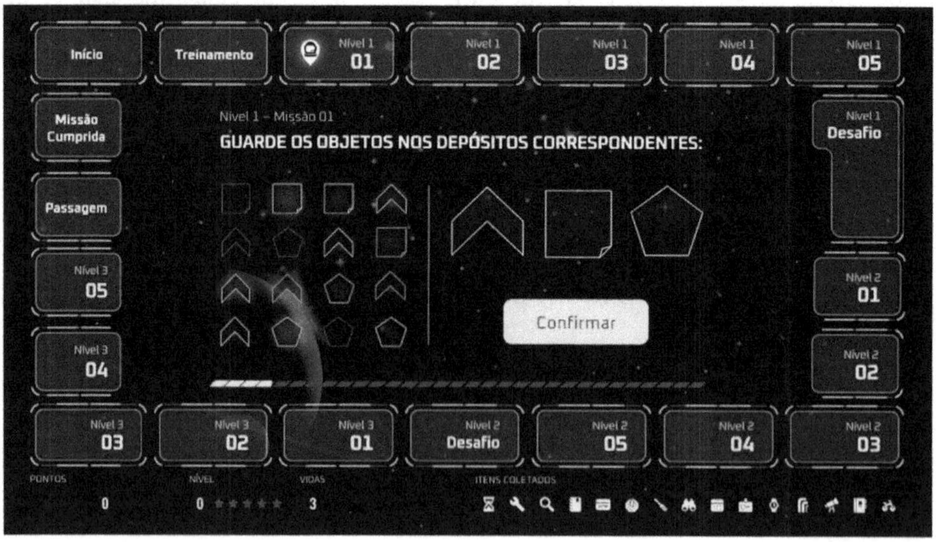

Table 13. Types of challenge per level

Level	Learning objectives	Challenge
1	• To carry out tasks on time. • Value attending the deadlines.	Hangman
2	• Focus on urgent and important tasks to meet their deadlines.	Crossword
3	• Prioritise simple tasks. • Organise daily tasks, avoiding distractions.	Word search

4.19 Challenges

After the missions of each level, there is a challenge when the player can receive bonuses.

The level challenges, corresponding to learning checkpoints, are related to the learning objectives and usual games, such as Hangman, to explore the contents and make some concepts explicit, as shown in Table 13.

Figure 9 exemplifies a challenge that the player faces during the game.

Figure 9. Challenge example

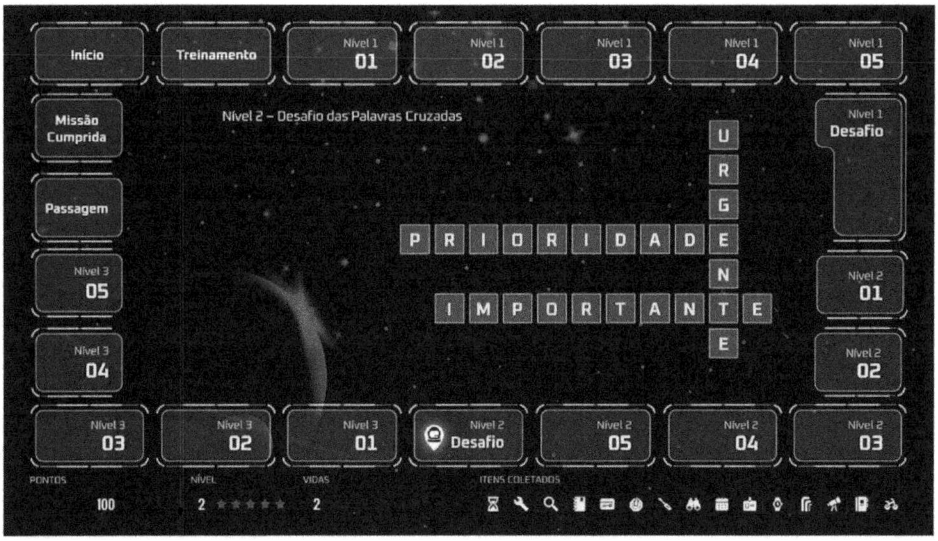

4.20 "*Encontrando Tempo*" Game Specifications

Using the previously described Serious Game design, the game "*Encontrando Tempo*" was developed, and its general specifications are shown in Table 14.

Table 14. "Encontrando Tempo" game specifications

Characteristic	Description
Content	Basics of time management
Delivery format	Web
Technologies	HTML5 and xAPI
Narrative	The general narrative of the game is that the player must retrieve some time capsules that have gone missing. As a new employee in the organisation, in the position of Time Hunter, the player has to accomplish some missions to help the Time Hunters succeed.
Main game mechanic	Board game with challenges.
Other game mechanics	Drag and drop matching items, hangman game, word search, and crosswords.
Adaptations	According to the player's performance in each mission, the difficulty level is altered, up or down. It is reflected in the feedback format, the visual clues, and the time available for completing the missions.
Rewards	Points, collectable items, bonus points for mission performance and stars for success in challenges.
Game results	Points achieved, missions performed on each difficulty level, levels completed, challenges succeeded, items accumulated and time spent playing the game.
Learning outcomes	Learning objectives successfully demonstrated in the missions and challenges (pedagogical milestones).
Data logs	Start and end time of each activity, performance in each mission, number of attempts and earned items (points, collectables and stars).

5. APPLICATION OF THE F_4ASG TO EVALUATE A SERIOUS GAME

In order to evaluate the developed Serious Game, a spreadsheet was prepared with all the dimensions, aspects and items of the **Framework for Adaptive Serious Games – F_4ASG**.

This spreadsheet has a 5-level scale, equivalent to a score described in Table 15.

It also calculates the weighted average of the points of each dimension, using the values of the evaluation scale as the weights used in this average.

In the evaluation spreadsheet developed, each dimension can be evaluated in the three levels of detail of the framework. One can, for instance, evaluate a dimension

Table 15. Evaluation scale

Scale item	Score
Suitable in its entirety	4
Suitable in most parts	3
Suitable in some parts	2
Unsuitable in many parts	1
Totally unsuitable	0

as a whole if one does not have much information to detail this dimension. It is also possible to evaluate each aspect of a dimension or even each item of an aspect.

For each dimension, the weighted average was compared with the maximum possible average for this dimension, according to the number of aspects and items. Thus, the dimension potential was defined as the division of the weighted average of the dimension in this evaluation with the maximum possible, ranging from 0 to 1.

The evaluation of the "*Encontrando Tempo*" game resulted in the potential for each dimension of the **Framework for Adaptive Serious Games – F_4ASG**, as listed in Table 16.

Figure 10 shows these potentials ordered, where it is possible to verify which elements are more or less adequate to the greater efficiency of the Serious Game, according to the **Framework for Adaptive Serious Games – F_4ASG**.

Based on these potentials, it is possible, for instance, to decide which improvements can be planned for new versions of the Serious Game.

Table 16. Potentials of the "Encontrando Tempo" game dimensions, according to the F_4ASG evaluation

Dimension	Potential
Content/context/framing – L1	0,90
Instructional elements – L2	0,97
Learning outcomes – L3	0,87
Learning adaptation – L4	0,72
Game mechanics – G1	0,89
Game environment – G2	0,82
Results – G3	0,77
Game adaptation – G4	0,79

Figure 10. Potentials of the "Encontrando Tempo" game dimensions, according to the F_4ASG evaluation

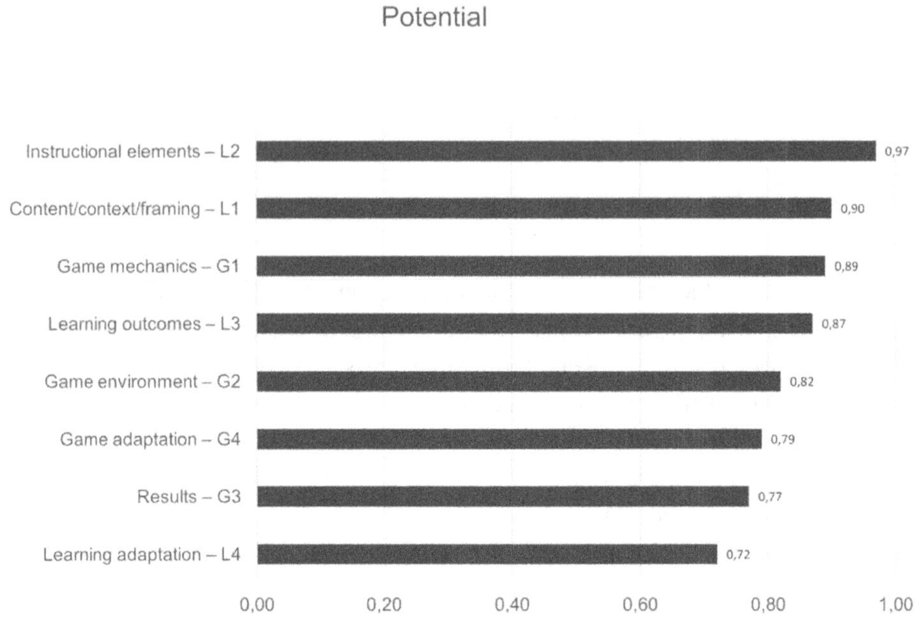

6. APPLICATION OF AN ADAPTIVE SERIOUS GAME CREATED WITH F_4ASG

This section describes the application of the game "*Encontrando Tempo*", developed using the Framework for Adaptive Serious Games – F_4ASG.

The results of the application of this game were used to evaluate the framework itself.

A within-subjects experiment design was applied to a sample with 51 participants who interacted in a gamified online environment with five activities, among which the Serious Game "*Encontrando Tempo*" was the main activity.

Before accessing the game, participants followed a predetermined pathway, identifying themselves and then answering a pre-test.

After playing the Serious Game "*Encontrando Tempo*", they underwent a post-test and a reaction assessment. This assessment was used in the quantitative and qualitative analysis that enabled the relation of the users' experience to the proposed framework dimensions.

Table 17. Players' responses related to the framework dimensions

Framework dimension	Question	Agreement %	
L1 and L2	The game content was adequately covered	Agree	53,1
		Strongly agree	40,8
G1, G4 and L4	The game has interesting and motivating mechanics.	Agree	44,9
		Strongly agree	44,9
G1, G4 and L4	The ways of interacting with the game facilitate its playability.	Agree	42,9
		Strongly agree	40,8
G2	The game provides an enjoyable and enriching experience.	Agree	51,0
		Strongly agree	36,7
G2	The audio-visual elements of the game are appropriate.	Agree	38,8
		Strongly agree	42,9

Following the five operations of classification and description of qualitative data stated by Spiggle (1994), the comments in the reaction assessment were analysed as follows:

- Categorization: The comments were labelled as learning, game and general.
- Abstraction: Comments were grouped according to the F_4ASG dimensions.
- Comparison: The similarities between each group's comments were identified.
- Dimensionalization: The highlights and strengths positioning of each comment were listed.
- Integration: In this analysis stage, the framework dimensions were identified in each comment.

In this analysis, it was possible to identify that most of the users' comments are related to the game mechanics since they consider that the game elements and the gameplay are the same. Moreover, it was observed that, for users' perception, the elements of Serious Games, both game and learning elements, are integrated.

The quantitative analysis highlighted the players' agreement with the framework dimensions proposals, as shown in Table 17.

This table shows the perceived dimensions of the players and, in some cases, group dimensions as the players perceive the Serious Game as an integrated set of elements, either of learning or game types.

Two dimensions, L3 and G3, are not listed in this table as they are related to the Serious Games results and were present in the qualitative analysis. Comments related to these two dimensions are shown in Table 18.

Table 18. Players' comments related to learning outcomes and game results

Dimension	Highlights
L3	• It's super interesting and instigating for continuous improvement.
	• I found it interesting how we lost more time the first time because we did not know how to execute the task, but the second time, we managed to do it within the time limit because we understood what had to be done.
G3	• It's super interesting and instigating for continuous improvement.
	• I noticed that the score reflects no difference in whether you do it on time.
	• This leads to the reinforcement of Learning by repeating some of the correct steps and managing to face the still-difficult step.
	• I also thought about the person who uses the trackpad if there is no difference in performance.
	• I found it interesting how we lost more time the first time because we did not know how to execute the task, but the second time, we managed to do it within the time limit because we understood what had to be done.
	• According to task performance, the dynamic of changing and adapting to the difficulty is an important incentive to keep trying.

Comments such as those in Table 18 reaffirm the relevance of dimension L3 - Learning Outcomes, highlighting the importance of the game for learning outcomes, i.e., it provides learning opportunities. It motivates the continuation of the learning process.

Thus, players' comments on learning outcomes show their perception of the evolution of Learning while playing the game. This perception reinforces the importance of learning outcomes as the focus of Serious Game, advocated by the L3 dimension of the framework.

The players' comments show that they are paying attention to the results, thus justifying the G3 dimension as one of the main focuses in a Serious Game.

The analysis of the results of this experiment highlighted the players' involvement, and the enthusiasm for participating in learning initiatives like this was shown in the reaction assessment.

7. CONCLUSION

Serious Games are a powerful tool to enhance learning and engagement in professional training and have been used for decades.

With the evolution of information and communication technologies (ICT), it is now possible to use varied and increasingly interesting resources to enhance the player's involvement and immersion, such as augmented and virtual realities, or even immersive environments like the metaverse. Allied with these technologies, artificial intelligence can be used to create adaptive Serious Games that personalize each player's experience and increase their learning results.

The technologies currently available at increasingly affordable costs, the experience of using Serious Games in organisations and research into their effectiveness for learning are proving to be opportunities for applying this type of methodology to training, especially in Learning Organisations, i.e. environments that value this type of activity.

It is well known that the application of Serious Games must face several challenges, as described in this chapter, but it is hoped that Framework for Adaptive Serious Games – F_4ASG will be a valuable tool for both the development and the evaluation of Serious Games, as the concepts it addresses constitute a set formed by the union between the existing theoretical bases and practical experiences of Serious Games experts, developers and users.

It is hoped that this framework will help the acceptance of Serious Games as learning objects in corporate training programmes consistently, where their results can be related to the learning and engagement of participants.

In each application of this framework, development and evaluation, the framework presents a useful tool for users:

- Content with a theoretical basis and the list of dimensions, aspects, and items to be considered in the design and development of adaptable Serious Games.
- List of all the dimensions, aspects and items of the framework that could be used in a spreadsheet to evaluate a Serious Game and that could calculate the potential of each dimension of adaptive Serious Games, as was done in the examples used to develop and apply the framework, where flexibility was also provided to allow three levels of detail to assess each dimension.

It can also be considered a contribution, the approach of adapting Serious Games to optimise the learning outcomes and the players' potential engagement.

REFERENCES

Almeida, P., Pedro, L., Moita, M., Magalhães, R., Santos, A., & Moreira, L. (2011). Serious Games as an onboarding organizational tool for new employees. *6th Iberian Conference on Information Systems and Technologies (CISTI 2011)*. IEEE, Chaves, Portugal. https://ieeexplore.ieee.org/abstract/document/5974334/

Azadegan, A., Riedel, J. C. K. H., & Baalsrud Hauge, J. (2012). Serious Games Adoption in Corporate Training. *Serious Games Development and Applications*, 74–85. doi:10.1007/978-3-642-33687-4_6

Beal, C., Beck, J., Westbrook, D., Atkin, M., & Cohen, P. (2002). Intelligent modeling of the user in interactive entertainment. *AAAI Stanford Spring Symposium*, Stanford CA. https://www.aaai.org/Papers/Symposia/Spring/2002/SS-02-01/SS 02-01-002.pdf

Boller, S., & Kapp, K. (2017). *Play to learn*. ATD Press.

Boyle, E. A., Hainey, T., Connolly, T. M., Gray, G., Earp, J., Ott, M., Lim, T., Ninaus, M., Ribeiro, C., & Pereira, J. (2016). An update to the systematic literature review of empirical evidence of the impacts and outcomes of computer games and Serious Games. *Computers & Education, 94*, 178–192. doi:10.1016/j.compedu.2015.11.003

Calderón, A., & Ruiz, M. (2015). A systematic literature review on Serious Games evaluation: An application to software project management. *Computers & Education, 87*, 396–422. doi:10.1016/j.compedu.2015.07.011

Donovan, L., & Lead, P. (2012). *The use of Serious Games in the corporate sector*. A State of the Art Report. Learnovate Center. https://www.learnovatecentre.org/wpcontent/uploads/2013/06/U se_of_Serious_Games_in_the_Corporate_Sector_PRINT_FINAL.pdf

Emmerich, K., & Bockholt, M. (2016). Serious Games Evaluation: Processes, Models, and Concepts. In R. Dörner, S. Göbel, M. Kickmeier-Rust, M. Masuch, & K. Zweig (Eds.), *Entertainment Computing and Serious Games: International GI-Dagstuhl Seminar 15283*, (pp. 265–283). Springer International Publishing. 10.1007/978-3-319-46152-6_11

Engberg-Pedersen, A. (2017). Technologies of Experience: Harun Farocki's Serious Games and Military Aesthetics. *Boundary 2, 44*(4), 155–178. https://read.dukeupress.edu/boundary-2/article-abstract/44/4 /155/130459. doi:10.1215/01903659-4206373

Greitzer, F. L., Kuchar, O. A., & Huston, K. (2007). Cognitive science implications for enhancing training effectiveness in a serious gaming context. *ACM Journal on Educational Resources in Computing, 7*(3), 2 - es. doi:10.1145/1281320.1281322

Hays, R. T. (2005). *The effectiveness of instructional games: A literature review and discussion*. MIL. https://apps.dtic.mil/sti/citations/ADA441935

Huynh-Kim-Bang, B., Wisdom, J., & Labat, J.-M. (2010). Design patterns in Serious Games: A blue print for combining fun and learning. *Project SE-SG,* 1–18. https://seriousgames.lip6.fr/DesignPatterns/designPatternsForSeriousGames.pdf

Kapp, K. M. (2013). *The gamification of learning and instruction Fieldbook: Ideas into practice*. John Wiley&Sons. https://books.google.com/books?hl=pt-BR&lr=&id=cdtnAQAAQBAJ&oi=fnd&pg=PR25&dq=%22The+gamification+of+learning+and+ins

Kara, N. (2021). A Systematic Review of the Use of Serious Games in Science Education. *Contemporary Educational Technology*, *13*(2), ep295. https://www.cedtech.net/article/a-systematic-review-of-the-use-of-serious-games-in-science-education-9608. doi:10.30935/cedtech/9608

Kirkpatrick, J. D., & Kirkpatrick, W. K. (2016). *Kirkpatrick's four levels of training evaluation*. Association for Talent Development. https://www.google.com/books?hl=pt-BR&lr=&id=mo--DAAAQBAJ&oi=fnd&pg=PT10&dq=kirkpatrick+2016&ots=LNG9XSkiQw&sig=p2r8Cc-W6dneqD7pTJHyyGSPs-Y

Larson, K. (2020). Serious Games and Gamification in the Corporate Training Environment: A Literature Review. *TechTrends*, *64*(2), 319–328. doi:10.100711528-019-00446-7

Lopes, R., & Bidarra, R. (2011). Adaptivity Challenges in Games and Simulations: A Survey. *IEEE Transactions on Computational Intelligence and AI in Games*, *3*(2), 85–99. doi:10.1109/TCIAIG.2011.2152841

Mitgutsch, K., & Alvarado, N. (2012). Purposeful by design? A Serious Game design assessment framework. *FDG '12: Proceedings of the International Conference on the Foundations of Digital Games,* (pp. 121-28). IEEE. 10.1145/2282338.2282364

Nye, Core, & Ghosal. (2021). *Metrics for Engagement in Games and Simulations for Learning And Affective Metrics*. Springer. https://doi.org/doi:10.4324/9780429282201-5/metrics-engagement-games-simulations-learning-benjamin-nye-mark-core-aviroop-ghosal-peter-walker

O'Brien, H. L., & Toms, E. G. (2008). What is user engagement? A conceptual framework for defining user engagement with technology. Journal of the American Society for Information Science. *Journal of the American Society for Information Science and Technology*, *59*(6), 938–955. doi:10.1002/asi.20801

Pabon, L. C. (2016). Training Through Serious Games: The Relationship Between Travel Agent Engagement, Knowledge of Cruise Products and Cruise Sales. [Theses and Dissertations, FIU]. doi:10.25148/etd.FIDC000713

Pedersen, C., Togelius, J., & Yannakakis, G. N. (2010). Modeling Player Experience for Content Creation. *IEEE Transactions on Computational Intelligence and AI in Games*, *2*(1), 54–67. doi:10.1109/TCIAIG.2010.2043950

Pistono, A. M. A. A., Santos, A. M. P., & Baptista, R. J. V. (2021). A Review of Adaptable Serious Games Applied to Professional Training. *Journal of Digital Media & Interaction*, *4*(11), 60–85. doi:10.34624/jdmi.v4i11.26419

Riedel, J. C., Feng, Y., Hauge, J. M. B., Hansen, P. K., & Tasuya, S. (2015). The adoption and application of Serious Games in corporate training-The case of manufacturing. *2015 IEEE International Conference on Engineering, Technology and Innovation/International Technology Management Conference (ICE/ITMC),* (pp. 1-9). IEEE. https://ieeexplore.ieee.org/abstract/document/7438684/

Sousa, L., Figueiredo, M., Monteiro, J., Bidarra, J., Rodrigues, J., & Cardoso, P. (2016). Developments of Serious Games in Education. In Handbook of Research on Human-Computer Interfaces, Developments, and Applications (pp. 392–419). IGI Global. doi:10.4018/978-1-5225-0435-1.ch016

Sousa, M., Antunes, A. P., Pinto, N., & Zagalo, N. (2022). Serious Games in Spatial Planning: Strengths, Limitations and Support Frameworks. *International Journal of Serious Games*, *9*(2), 115–133. doi:10.17083/ijsg.v9i2.510

Spiggle, S. (1994). Analysis and Interpretation of Qualitative Data in Consumer Research. *The Journal of Consumer Research*, *21*(3), 491–503. doi:10.1086/209413

Streicher, A., & Smeddinck, J. D. (2016). Personalized and Adaptive Serious Games. In R. Dörner, S. Göbel, M. Kickmeier-Rust, M. Masuch, & K. Zweig (Eds.), *Entertainment Computing and Serious Games: International GI-Dagstuhl Seminar 15283*, (pp. 332-377). Springer International Publishing. 10.1007/978-3-319-46152-6_14

The European Qualifications Framework (EQF). (n.d.). *Qualifications.* Europea. https://europa.eu/europass/en/european-qualifications-framework-eqf

Uskov, A., & Sekar, B. (2014). Serious Games, gamification and game engines to support framework activities in engineering: Case studies, analysis, classifications and outcomes. *IEEE International Conference on Electro/Information Technology,* (pp. 618–623). IEEE. 10.1109/EIT.2014.6871836

Wattanasoontorn, V., Hernández, R. J. G., & Sbert, M. (2014). Serious Games for e-Health Care. In Y. Cai & S. L. Goei (Eds.), *Simulations, Serious Games and Their Applications* (pp. 127–146). Springer Singapore. doi:10.1007/978-981-4560-32-0_9

Wouters, P., van der Spek, E. D., & van Oostendorp, H. (2009). Current Practices in Serious Game Research: A Review from a Learning Outcomes Perspective. In Games-Based Learning Advancements for Multi-Sensory Human-Computer Interfaces: Techniques and Effective Practices (pp. 232–250). IGI Global. doi:10.4018/978-1-60566-360-9.ch014

Yamin, M. M., Katt, B., & Nowostawski, M. (2021). Serious games as a tool to model attack and defence scenarios for cyber-security exercises. *Computers & Security*, *110*, 102450. doi:10.1016/j.cose.2021.102450

Chapter 10
Organizational Communication:
The Impact of Social Media as a Mode of Communication on Learning Organizations

Divya Suresh
https://orcid.org/0009-0007-2644-0214
Jain University (Deemed), India

Ujjal Mukherjee
https://orcid.org/0000-0002-5205-4604
Institute of Public Enterprise, Hyderabad, India

ABSTRACT

To gain a competitive advantage in dynamic and complex environments, organizations are continuously seeking strategies. One such strategy is the emergence of learning organizations, which foster collective and collaborative learning. Effective communication plays a vital role within learning organizations as it facilitates the efficient exchange of knowledge and information. Moreover, with the advent of digitization, social media has become a widespread mode of communication even within the workplace. This chapter analyzes the impact of social media on intra-organizational communication in learning organizations. It explores how managers can choose appropriate communication platforms and discusses the potential positive and negative implications of social media on various aspects of learning organizations such as organizational effectiveness, structure, pattern, and content of communication. The researchers have proposed a model to assist managers in selecting suitable social media platforms based on situational demands. Furthermore, the chapter highlights areas for future research.

DOI: 10.4018/979-8-3693-0556-0.ch010

1. INTRODUCTION

Organizations are constantly in search of strategies that give them a competitive edge in changing and uncertain environments (Vrontis et al., 2022). To facilitate this, organizations must create a learning environment that enables efficient knowledge and information sharing (Belinski et al., 2019). "Organizations where people continually expand their capacity to create the result they truly desire" are known as learning organizations (LOs) (Senge 1990). Dirani et al., (2021) emphasize the importance of collection and collaboration for learning to take place at all levels of the organization. Therefore, communication is an integral part of a LO, it may be viewed as a means to achieve collective and collaborated learning in organizations. As a result, managers are regularly in pursuit of efficient methods of communication to fulfil this objective (Turaga, 2019).

Given the rapid pace of technological advancement, digitization has entered nearly every domain of an organization in turn transforming the traditional medium of communication. This transformation has also altered the way in which people interact with each other (Grover et al., 2022). Within the context of organizational communication, social media (SM) platforms are some of the most widely used and accepted media of communication (Borah et al., 2022). Consequently, it is increasingly adopted for organizational communication (Brain, 2021).

Managers are often left to interpret and implement theoretical information and academic knowledge without understanding whether these practices are suitable to the organization's structure and culture (Alerasoul et al., 2021). This challenge paves the way for further literature that focuses on the impact of SM on intra-organizational communication in LOs. This chapter conducts a comprehensive review of existing literature to gain insights into the integration of SM into intra-organizational communication within LOs. Based on the Media Richness Model and the Social Information Processing Model, the chapter specifically focuses on how managers may select suitable media for intra-organizational communication. This chapter proposes a model to aid managers in selecting appropriate SM for intra-organizational communication. It also analyses the positive and negative implications of SM on organizational effectiveness, structure as well as the content and pattern of communication. Literature in relation to SM utilization in the organizational setting is scarce (Baxter & Connolly, 2014; Pandey et al., 2020). Moreover, there is a lack of research associating SM and collaborative learning in organizations (Breunig, 2016; Sobko, 2019). Research in the recent years bridging this gap has tended to focus more on organizational learning rather than LOs.

Communication is indispensable to the formation and sustenance of a successful LO. It is the foundation of everyday organizational tasks such as decision-making, providing instructions on tasks and roles, collecting feedback, monitoring progress and most importantly, learning. In other words, it is through communication that individuals establish their roles in an organization and fulfil their functions (Santra & Giri, 2009). Organizational communication can be defined as "the process of creating, exchanging, interpreting (correctly or incorrectly), and storing messages within a system of human interrelationships" (Modaff et al; 2007). Additionally, Santra and Giri (2009) perceive organizational communication to facilitate more than just the exchange of information, stating that it also aims to influence certain behaviours. Previous research (Mintzberg 1973) suggests that a few decades ago, organizational communication was mostly verbal (meetings, phone calls, etc). However, today managers have more options regarding their medium of communication as a result of digitization leading to easy availability of such media. As organizational processes become increasingly time bound and competitive, there is a growing need for efficient modes of communication that allow for receiving, interpreting and sharing knowledge and information to produce desirable outcomes (Sinkula, 1994).

The rapid pace of digital evolution has created a plethora of new technology which have been adopted by organizations with the aim to integrate new media and strategies to accelerate their growth. Digitization implies the adoption of digital technology and human-centric practices that are channelled toward more agile organizational processes (Følstad & Kvale, 2018; Dörner & Edelman, 2015). With regard to communication, the most notable advancement was the emergence of Web 2.0.

Contrary to Web 1.0, known as the 'read-only' web, Web 2.0 enables both the creation and exchange of user-generated content (Kaplan & Haenlein, 2010; Briciu & Briciu, 2021). This principle has established the foundation for several SM which operate largely based on the creation and exchange of user-generated content. SM can be defined as "web-based internet networks where users can share information and communicate with other users in a collective manner" (Venezia, 2012; p.24). Within the context of LOs, it may be incorporated into activities that require "producing user-generated content, developing and maintaining social relationships, or enabling other computer-mediated interactions and collaborations in the context of a specific organization and its environment" (Coursaris & van Osch, 2013).

The current chapter provides clarity to managers regarding the management of SM usage for organizational communication. This chapter proposes a model that enables managers so select SM for intra-organizational communication based on situational demands. Additionally, it explores the positive and negative implications of using such platforms for intra-organizational communication in LOs. In addition to this, it consolidates existing literature within the domain of communication in LOs along with exploring the influence of digitization on communication. Considering the rapid pace of digitization and the increasing number of LOs, the chapter also suggests scope for further research to enhance the practical understanding of industry practitioners and researchers alike regarding the impact of using SM for intra-organizational communication on various aspects of LOs.

The chapter is divided into six sections. Section one introduces concepts such as LOs, organizational communication, digitization and SM. This section also substantiates the relationship between these concepts. Following this, section two is a review of literature within the context of SM and LOs. Section three discusses the methodology employed to identify relevant resources for this chapter. Section four entails the analysis comprising of five major themes. It analyses the effectiveness of SM for organizational communication. This section also substantiates how SM influence organizational structure and aims to understand how this mode of communication may positively or negatively alter the content communicated between employees. Additionally, it examines how SM have changed the pattern of information flow within organizations. Based on these insights, this section consists of a model to assist managers to choose suitable SM platforms. Section five discusses the scope for further research within the domain of digitization in LOs. Section six substantiates the implications of this chapter and section seven concludes the chapter by summarizing its major findings.

2. REVIEW OF LITERATURE

The review of literature has been classified into two sub-sections based on the focus of this chapter. Each sub-section comprises of the evolution of the concept, the definition of the term as well as its subsequent research developments.

2.1. Social Media (SM)

Digitization has transformed traditional organizational practices (Fernandez-Vidal et al., 2022). This transformation has led to organizational communication in the twenty-first century to have few similarities with the same a hundred years back. For instance, handwriting and typing have evolved into word processing and using high-speed copying machines to create simple documents. The storage of those documents has progressed from boxes to file cabinets and presently to hard drives, CDs, and flash drives. Advancements from stagecoaches and telegrams to airmails, emails, and mobile phones, currently help in communication across the globe. Video conferences and online chat rooms instead of physical conference rooms are often used for meetings. Presentations are now made using PowerPoint as opposed to the traditional paper flipchart (Miller, 2016 p.237; Ortiz-Ospina, 2019). Having said that, the most significant digital advancement revolutionizing organizational communication was that of Web 2.0. Web 2.0 which is also known as the 'user-generated web' allows the exchange of information between users. SM have emerged out of Web 2.0 and operates largely on this principle (Balaji & Murthy, 2019). Further digital transformation has led to the emergence of the Semantic Web and Web 3.0. With the growth of Web 3.0, SM are expected to continue becoming more interactive thereby improving knowledge sharing and creativity among users (Joshi, 2023).

SM can be defined as "a group of Internet-based applications that build on the ideological and technological foundations of Web 2.0, and that allow the creation and exchange of User Generated Content" (Kaplan & Haenlein, 2010). Further, Obar and Wildman (2015), and Ortiz-Ospina (2019) have identified the same four criteria to define SM;

i. SM currently operate based on Web 2.0
ii. User-generated content is the essence of SM
iii. User profiles for websites or apps are maintained by SM services
iv. SM services enable networking by connecting different user profiles

SM have become increasingly common in everyday communication over the last decade due to its easy availability and the new, user-friendly technology that it offers. This ubiquity has led scholars and researchers across a multitude of disciplines to study the impactful existence of such widespread global platforms. SM have gained immense recognition in the context of research. 78% of research related to SM has been published in communication journals (Khang et al., 2012). Research related to communication technology used in organizations is said to have progressed from "technological determinism" to "social determinism" and has evolved to a phase where the focus lies on both these aspects and their correlation (Rice & Aydin, 1991). Nevertheless, the impact of digitization (especially SM) within the context of LOs has yet to be explored significantly (Hoe, 2019).

Apart from everyday casual communication, a significant area in which SM have played an impactful role is organizational communication (Leonardi et al., 2013). Compared to traditional communication media, SM enable faster and easier flow of information between organizational actors, thereby improving the communication process, encouraging creativity, and enhancing organizational culture (Badea, 2014). Research also suggests a relationship between SM use and learning however, there lacks a unified consensus on whether its impacts are positive or negative. One perspective argues that SM enhances collaborative learning by facilitating resource sharing and interaction (e.g., Ansari & Khan, 2020). On the contrary, the use of SM has been found to be a distraction and thereby may be considered counterproductive in LOs (e.g., Kolhar et al., 2021). Hence, there is a need to analyse the impact of using SM as a mode of communication in LOs. Moreover, this chapter aims to analyse the positive and negative implications of SM in LOs.

2.2. Learning Organizations (LOs)

Firstly, it is important to understand that LOs and organizational learning are not synonymous. Primarily, organizational learning is a process whereas LOs describe the nature of an organization (Ortenblad, 2001). This distinction did not exist before the term LO was coined. Hence, early literature regarding learning in the organizational context cannot be easily distinguished between. The concept of LOs was first defined by Peter Senge in his book titled "The Fifth Discipline". The book has specified five dimensions or "component technologies" that build LOs (Senge, 1990);

i. Systems Thinking - This is a conceptual framework that enables change by adopting a comprehensive view of the situation at hand. Senge argues that organizations are often unable to solve problems because each individual problem is viewed as an independent phenomenon.
ii. Personal Mastery - Here, mastery implies a high level of proficiency rather than superiority. This drive to mastery commits people to lifelong learning. According to Senge, this quality is fundamental to LOs implying that personal commitment to learning translates to organizational learning.
iii. Mental Models - Mental models refer to one's way of thinking and their interpretation of the world which in turn influences their behaviour. Senge states that the key to modifying mental models is introspection and openness.
iv. Building a Shared Vision - According to Senge, a vision to achieve a shared goal is essential to ensure success for an organization. Instilling this shared vision is executed through strong leadership by fostering shared "pictures of the future".
v. Team Learning - Team learning enhances individual learning at a pace much faster than individual learning. This is achieved through the art of dialogue to recognize the patterns of interaction that facilitate group learning. Here the emphasis lies on the group rather than the individual as teams are "fundamental learning units".

Senge's philosophical take on business has been criticized but is yet to be replaced (Hansen et al., 2020). The fundamental definition of LOs has only recently been expanded further by exploring the influence of factors such as ethics and morality on learning in LOs (Smith et al., 2014; Verbos et al., 2007). Further, the rise of LOs today can be attributed to the discovery of a successful path to growth by leveraging intellectual resources to achieve desired organizational goals (Morgan, 2003).

Considering that teams in organizations are created in order to fulfil a certain function or to achieve a task, recent research is focused on understanding the relationship between learning and team effectiveness (Mathieu et al., 2017). Currently, research is centred on determining the factors that accelerate or hinder learning in LOs with a particular emphasis on gathering empirical evidence (Rebelo et al., 2019). With SM increasingly being used for organizational communication, it is important to understand the impact of SM as a mode of communication in LOs.

3. METHODOLOGY

The initial search for literature was widespread in order to estimate the nature of existing research. Later, search terms such as "learning organizations", "social media" and "communication" were frequently used to narrow down to literature relevant to the research objective. The researchers have used Google Scholar to acquire resources. Eighty-one research papers, ten books, and six internet articles published between 1934 and 2022 written in English or translated into English were analyzed. This chapter comprises findings from qualitative and quantitative secondary data.

4. ANALYSIS

After analyzing ninety-seven published research in the relevant domain, the researchers have decided to study the impact of SM as a mode of communication on five aspects of LOs as illustrated in *figure 1*. In the subsequent sections, the researchers have analyzed the selection of communication media and its impacts on various aspects of LOs. The findings are drawn from models and theories applied to the context of LOs. The rationale behind these particular themes is to provide a holistic analysis by studying modifications that may occur to various aspects of LOs. It is also driven by the existing research gaps and is additionally based on the sufficient availability of literature that can be used to fulfil the research objective.

4. 1. Effectiveness of Social Media in Intra Organizational Communication

Organizational effectiveness is "dependent on how well an organization's members are able to communicate and use relevant information" (Kreps 1985). Any medium on its own does not guarantee any particular outcome rather, the effectiveness of the medium depends largely on the manner in which it is utilized (Scott & DeSanctis, 1992). Past research has had conflicting views on the effectiveness of such media in organizational communication, with some researchers suggesting that SM improve information flow of knowledge and information within organizations and contributes to building organizational culture and the feeling of belongingness (Badea,

2014, Ewing et al., 2019), with others suggesting that the absence of an organized framework (as in SM) could also result in counterproductivity (Miller, 2016). In the following section, the researchers have employed the "Systems Theory" to analyze the effectiveness of using SM as a mode of communication in LOs.

4. 1. 1. The Systems Theory

The Systems Theory (Bertalanffy, 1968) objectifies the operations of an organization as an evolving process that includes plenty of interaction, internal and external to the organization. Emphasizing that these interactions play a vital role in the success and sustenance of the organization (Almaney, 1974), Hickson III (1973) studied how organizations adapt to environmental needs by modifying their operation, this adaptation translates into several aspects of the organization. In other words, the theory signifies the interconnectedness of the various elements of a whole. Applying this theory to the organizational context, it talks about communication as the force that holds together various elements and makes goals like collaborative learning, organizational growth, and stability achievable (Almaney, 1974).

Figure 1. Diagrammatic representation of the flow of the analysis section

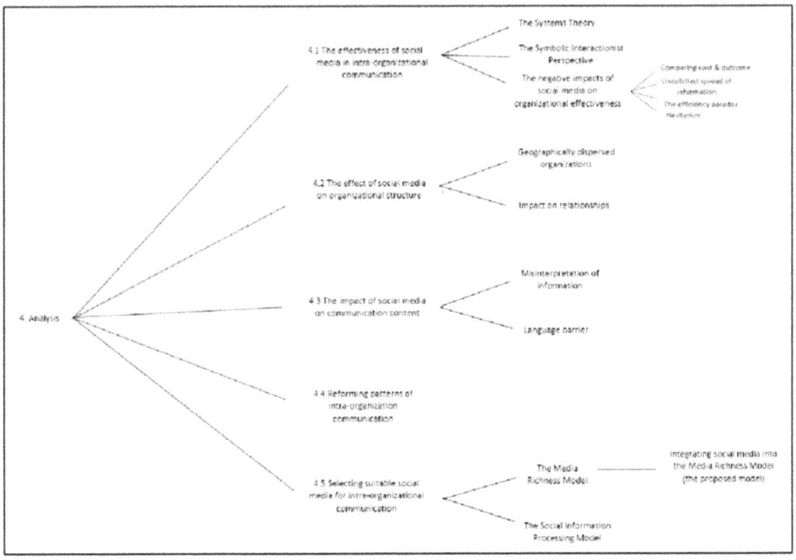

4. 1. 2. The Symbolic Interactionist Perspective

Symbolic interactionism (Blumer, 1969; Mead, 1934) is a micro-level theory that aims to explain sociological and social psychological phenomena. The theory views society as a "web of communication" thus considering the existence of society on its own to be 'interaction' through which people assign meanings to things. This theory can be used to understand organizational communication further by looking at an organization as a society. In this way, we can consider an organization to also be a web of interactions. Through interaction, the members of an organization create a shared understanding of situations in the absence of well-defined situations (Weick, 1979, Daft & Weick, 1984).

It is through discussion, feedback, and negotiation that they come to a common consensus thereby clearly defining their situation. Hence, through interaction, the members of an organization create their shared reality together. Further interaction takes place between the manager and the other employees and together they integrate their varied interpretations and come to a joint consensus. This newly established interpretation is further used to make decisions (Trevino et al., 1990). Simultaneously, this interaction enhances collaborative learning through employee engagement (Simon & Zhou, 2017). There exists further research that substantiates the relationship between employee engagement and collective learning (Song et al., 2014). However, the direction of the relationship between these two variables has yet to be established conclusively.

This perspective entails the idea that symbols change over time and eventually take on a more definitive meaning after being negotiated over extensively (Chen et al., 2020). Symbols that are already established are then transmitted and easily accepted. With SM enabling synchronous or real-time communication that is easily available, organizational actors are able to discuss and negotiate to establish a common interpretation. This is helpful in reducing conflicts in organizations by clearly defining the roles and functions to be undertaken by each employee thereby eliminating the possibility of role ambiguity (Weaver & Agle, 2002). When every employee is aware of their own and other employees' roles, it creates an environment where interactions can be oriented towards collective and collaborative learning.

4. 1. 3. The Negative Impacts of Social Media on Organizational Effectiveness

In order to select a suitable communication medium, organizations must consider that not all media are appropriate for all types of communication. With organizations having varied goals, the strategies employed and functions of communication are relative to that entity. Therefore, organizations may face the following challenges that can affect the 'effectiveness' of SM in organizational communication:

i. **Comparing cost and outcome** –Botezatu (2012) suggests that the cost of adopting SM into organizational communication is typically larger than estimated. The reason for this is that, although physical costs are lower than with other channels, the human resources costs are high. These costs are not quite reducible because organizations have confidential data that is vulnerable to security risks and thereby require technology-savvy professionals to protect the organization's privacy and maintain discretion (Soukup, 2003). However, it must also be considered that this estimate is not absolute because the cost incurred by organizations is also dependent on their strategy and efficiency (Botezatu, 2012). Therefore, organizations must weigh the input cost and outcome of SM as a communication medium to analyze its effectiveness with respect to their specific organizational goals.
ii. **Unsolicited spread of information** - The increasing use of SM and technology comes at a price. Users are asked to give personal information about themselves to be able to use an application and often don't have much knowledge or control over how this information is used or spread over the internet. The same goes for organizations, for instance, if the name of an organization is typed into Google search, there is abundant information about the organization, however, not all of it was consciously uploaded by the organization themselves (Thomas & Dittman, 2016). This could affect their reputation, cause internal conflict, or sabotage future plans and deals. In order to manage this problem, organizations must establish a clearly defined parameter with regard to what information can be shared on SM.
iii. **The efficiency paradox** - Employees and supervisors may choose communication media such as direct messaging or phone calls as opposed to video conferencing for the sake of speed and efficiency. In such cases, the message communicated may be misinterpreted or difficult to inhabit due to ambiguity caused by the lack of social cues. In order to avoid this, managers must strategically select SM platforms that are suited to the current task/goal. The ambiguity of messages communicated through SM in turn threatens the added advantage of speed due to the risk of misinterpretation of information. Moreover, the reception of unsolicited information reduces employee efficiency as employees are constantly receiving excessive information and experience the feeling of "drowning in data" which reduces productivity by up to 60% (Tanaka, 1997). Therefore, it is essential that managers select communication media that does not provoke unsolicited communication by enabling more interaction than what is required.

iv. **Hesitation** – Often, employees hesitate to embrace such changes in an organization. This is because, individuals who are not technology-savvy may be required to be a part of the communication process despite being unfamiliar with the functioning of the medium used (Ciochina, 2013). Moreover, they are unable to accurately estimate the potential of the medium and hence underestimate it while simultaneously overestimating previously existing technology (Gourville, 2003). Research suggests that less than 20% of employees processed some amount of self-efficacy in relation to using SM for organizational communication (Pekkala & Van Zoonen, 2022). In order to maximize employees' self-efficacy, managers may conduct training programs and encourage all employees to improve their skills through collective and collaborative learning.

v. **Spread of fake news –** SM is inundated with an overwhelming amount of information, making it practically impossible for users to sift through it all manually. To address this challenge, SM platforms employ algorithms that tailor content to individuals based on their interests, creating what is commonly referred to as 'filter bubbles.' These filter bubbles limit a user's access to diversified information, thereby constricting shared knowledge among people (Ekström et al., 2022).

Moreover, research by Kitchens et al. (2020) suggests that these personalized algorithms may inadvertently foster extremist beliefs and opinions. This is because users are constantly provided information that corresponds with their existing beliefs, and minimizes access to information that contradicts their views. Some of the most drastic effects of filter bubbles are evident in the role it played in 2016 Brexit Referendum and the Presidential US Elections (Difranzo & Gloria-Garcia, 2017).

Translating the understanding to the organizational context, filter bubbles can have a similar and possibly augmented influence within LOs. This is because, the spread of fake news can be faster in organizations since employees interact with each other on a regular basis. The unsolicited spread of fake news can hinder the goals of co-operative learning by creating conflicts and a hostile work environment for employees.

4. 2. The Effect of Social Media on Organizational Structure

SM have been tremendously impactful with regard to altering a traditional workspace. These alterations have also translated into other areas affecting employee diversity, demographic dispersion, etc, and have both positive as well as adverse implications. The subsequent sections discuss how SM have led to the rise of geographically dispersed organizations as well as the negative impacts of this practice on organizational processes. Additionally, it also highlights how SM have altered the nature of relationships that employees establish with one another.

4. 2. 1. Geographically Dispersed Organization

The integration of SM into organizational communication has brought about more portability of work (Miller, 2016 p. 250). This is because, SM enable both synchronous and asynchronous communication (Trittin-Ulbrich et al., 2020). Synchronous communication can be defined as 'real-time' or simultaneous communication and can take place over platforms such as Zoom, FaceTime, etc. Asynchronous communication can be defined as communication in which the involved individuals need not engage in communication at the same time and can reciprocate when required. Recently, SM such as Instagram and X (formerly Twitter) have gained immense attention due to their features that enable synchronous communication (Waters & Williams, 2011). Therefore, individuals simultaneously working on one organizational task may be geographically dispersed. This expands the organization's range of communication and enables collaboration between diverse professionals to form a "powerful global discourse" (Berger, 2008). Hence, organizations need not limit their human resources to those who can be physically present at the workplace.

On the downside, managers/supervisors feel that they must constantly track work progress, schedules, and meetings as it is impossible for discussion to arise at the workplace by chance (Pearlson & Saunders, 2001). Furthermore, employees who are not physically present at the workplace feared missing out on opportunities such as being considered for bonuses and new projects as well as not being given their due credit simply because they are out of sight (Hylmo & Buzzanell, 2002). Therefore, the use of SM in intra-organizational communication may be perceived as a double-edged sword (Zoonen et al., 2022). In other words, it is important for organizations to correctly identify SM platforms for intra-organizational communication for it to be truly effective.

4. 2. 2. Impact on Relationships

SM have provided a platform for the creation and exchange of information, ideas and experiences, through which individuals establish their own way of defining relationships (Langer, 2014). Employee interaction on SM is said to be reinforced when employees combine their personal and professional identities on SM (Oksa et al., 2021). Past research (Langer, 2014) suggests that employees found that establishing out-of-work relationships with their fellow employees through SM allows for better understanding and cooperation between them. However, a few of the interviewed employees chose to demarcate between personal and professional relationships because they preferred to maintain personal space and avoid obtruding into their employees' personal lives.

In the latter case, some employees who maintain out-of-work relationships could build close relationships and may consciously or unconsciously establish certain norms, this can lead to 'groupism' at the workplace where the individuals who conform to those norms receive security or extra power in exchange for their conformity. The same applies to employees that are geographically dispersed. The members of a team that are not physically present at the organization may feel left out amongst those who interact in proximity on a daily basis.

The rise of virtual organizations today increases the need for further research to clarify whether out of work relationships between employees are beneficial. Further, there is a need to understand whether these relationships have the ability to overcome the lack of face-to-face contact between employees of virtual organization.

4. 3. The Impact of Social Media on Communication Content

As stated previously, the most basic transformation brought about by SM is that it permits the creation and exchange of user-generated content. This enhances two-way communication between organizational actors through which mutual understanding is established and disagreement is limited. In addition to this, SM have also largely benefitted organizations by providing the means for collaboration through which organizations are able to connect with diverse professionals and are able to use their expertise and learn about various cultures. This in turn helps organizations improve their marketing strategies and product customization (Nisar et al., 2019). Nevertheless, past research is mostly contradictory and has recorded numerous ways in which SM have negatively impacted communication content.

4. 3. 1. The Negative Impacts of Social Media on Communication Content

As discussed previously, SM in the organizational context is not undeniably efficacious (Akram & Kumar, 2017). A review of literate within this domain suggests communication content is the most negatively impacted as compared to other aspects of organizational communication.

i. **Misinterpretation of messages** – Misinterpretation of information may be caused by the lack of social cues, the medium of communication itself or mistakes such as typographical and autocorrect errors. For instance, the level of formality that is required to be maintained between professionals may not be appropriately transmitted by that medium and can thus result in misinterpreting the message leading to misunderstandings. Furthermore, accidental typographical and autocorrect errors which are of common occurrence and are often unconsciously overlooked in direct messaging and could shift the receiver's attention or reduce the impact of the message. The possibility of misinterpretation also becomes particularly problematic during instances of 'socio-emotional' messages. Research proposes that computer-mediated communication could include many instances of 'flaming' (sarcasm, irony, emotional outburst, etc). In certain cases, 'flaming' can escalate and lead to emotional abuse and targeting through cyberbullying (Sproull & Kiesler, 1986). Moreover, one of the biggest challenges organizations face regarding SM is related to employees posting inappropriate content and controversial personal opinions which can harm the organization's reputation and cause conflict. (Langer, 2014).

ii. **Language barrier** - Most of the information present online is in English, this puts non-English speakers at a disadvantage as they will be unable to neither comprehend the information nor contribute their expertise (Bertot et al., 2010). Additionally, the problem of mistranslation and misinterpretation originating from varied cultural contexts could change the meaning of the content communicated.

4. 4. Reforming Patterns of Intra-Organizational Communication

Organizations traditionally follow a pattern of information flow that is in accordance with its hierarchy or formal chain of command. The point of dispersion of information is dependent on the pattern of communication which can be categorized into three; vertical, horizontal, and diagonal communication (Berger, 2008). Vertical communication indicates the flow of information across various levels of hierarchy as opposed to horizontal communication in which the flow of information takes place between individuals who belong to the same hierarchical level. Lastly, diagonal communication follows a web-like pattern of communication across hierarchical levels and departments.

In the organizational context, the pattern of information flow can be characterised as vertical communication. In this type of communication, there exists a hierarchical order in which information flows, and can further be classified into two; downward and upward communication. Downward communication is when the flow of information begins at the top of the hierarchy and flows downward whereas, upward communication is where the flow of information begins at the bottom of the hierarchy and flows upward. Traditionally, organizational communication is constituted mostly of downward communication. However, SM have altered the pattern of dispersion of information from only downward communication to a dialogue pattern, thereby diminishing the idea of a central point from where information is dispersed by transforming managers/supervisors into 'primary communicators' (Berger 2008).

In terms of employee satisfaction regarding patterns of communication, past research is mostly unanimous, suggesting a general discontent with either vertical communication or with the lack of two-way communication. For instance, a study conducted by Opinion Research Corporation over the span of 50 years, discovered that employees were generally dissatisfied with vertical communication (Cutlip et al., 2006). Another study by Gibson and Hodgetts (1991) concluded that one of the root causes of employee dissatisfaction stems from the fact that management strategies often lack two-way communication. As stated previously, SM enable two-way communication which allows both managers/supervisors to disperse information as well as employees to seek clarification and give feedback. This in turn boosts employee satisfaction which correlates with organizational commitment, productivity, and performance (Gray & Laidlaw, 2004). Through this, organizations have the potential to overcome the shortcomings brought about by media while simultaneously benefitting from its easy availability and efficiency (Wiesenfeld et al., 1998). However, it must be ensured that such dialogue must arise as and when the situation demands it. In other words, the ability to converse back and forth must not pave the way for excessive or unnecessary communication.

4. 5. Selecting Suitable Social Media for Intra-Organizational Communication

Every organization includes both intra-organizational as well as extra-organizational communication and actors who partake in these processes (Valiyeva & Thomas, 2022). In each of these scenarios, SM undertake different functions. Nevertheless, previous research has mostly viewed SM as marketing tools and emphasized on its role in extra-organizational communication such as promotion and advertising, with limited research studying only a few aspects of SM in the context of intra-organizational communication. In order to understand how organizational actors choose suitable SM for intra-organizational communication, the focus must be on communication between internal actors such as managers, supervisors, employees, subordinates, etc. The following section explains Media Richness Model. This model substantiates the parameters based on which organizations adopt technology for communication.

4. 5. 1. The Media Richness Model

This model was proposed by Daft and Lengel (1984, 1986) as a framework to understand the choices that organizations make regarding the technology used in organizational communication. To explain these choices, the theorists suggest that there exists a range of interpretations and contradicting aspects to a communication task in organizations. Daft, Lengel, and Trevino (1987) further argue that the selection of suitable communication technology depends on a task's intricacy and equivocality (Trevino et al., 1990).

Equivocality refers to how ambiguous a piece of information is, when a message can have multiple interpretations, it is said to be highly equivocal and vice versa (Lee & Lee, 2020). High ambiguity suggests that one's interpretation of a message can be deeply influenced by their environment, distinctive needs, approach and past experience (Trevino et al., 1990). Consequently, there is more room for conflicting interpretations and confusion. To avoid this, managers preferred to communicate using media that captured more social cues (such as body language, facial expression, tone etc. in order to make messages more precise (Trevino et al., 1990). Additionally, their study also found that the managers who appropriately corresponded media richness to equivocality were also generally better performing managers and were termed as "media sensitive" whereas those who failed to correctly do so were termed as "media insensitive". Furthermore, low equivocality and high message transparency are said to be key determinants of manager and employee work efficiency (Yang et al., 2021).

The model categorizes communication media into two – rich media; which are more precise and likely to have one common interpretation, and lean media; which are more ambiguous and likely to have multiple interpretations. These categories were established on the following parameters; whether the medium can facilitate instant feedback, its capacity to include social cues, the use of "natural language" and the significant ways in which the medium itself conveys messages. The model lists communication media in the following hierarchy – face-to-face communication, telephone, electronic mail, letter, note, memo, special report and flier/bulletin.

Integrating social media into the Media Richness Model

In order to choose suitable SM for organizational communication, intra-organizational actors must strategically implement the previously mentioned parameters to correspond contemporary SM that embody the required specificity, with the level of equivocality of the message to find suitable SM for a specific task. Managers must also consider factors such as formality between intra-organizational actors as well as the regulations of the organization and how they correlate with the choice of SM adopted for organizational communication.

Even so, the traditional nature of a communication medium may be altered with the adoption of SM. For example, 'face-to-face communication' no longer holds its literal meaning as SM facilitate face-to-face communication even between individuals who are not in proximity. However, SM platforms such as Instagram, WhatsApp, Zoom, etc. do comprise all the characteristics that face-to-face communication would traditionally offer. Media like these also allow for group interaction which is a means to gather multiple perspectives on one idea or issue and negotiate to establish a common interpretation, thereby reducing its equivocality (Fulk et al., 1990). Similarly, other dated technology mentioned in the model can also be substituted with contemporary SM. For instance, managers may choose to form a WhatsApp group to convey important information to other employees rather than using bulletins, or a subordinate may prefer sending a direct message to their boss about an important message that was taken for them in their absence instead of leaving them a note. Additionally, these platforms may also be utilised for information and knowledge sharing to facilitate collective learning. In these ways, SM prove to be a tool that can potentially substitute traditional communication media for more efficient learning. Nevertheless, over the years, researchers continue to search for ways to refine this model to be able to understand more accurately an organization's choice of communication media.

Research has addressed the need to improve the effectiveness of communication media by evaluating the practical medium richness of various media. This is because, the employees' perception of the quality of supervision they receive is dependent on this (Park & Cho, 2020). The proposed model was developed in order to facilitate the selection of a SM platform for intra-organizational communication. The model was developed after a thorough analysis of the positive and negative implications of using SM for intra-organizational communication in LOs. The purpose of the

Table 1. The model proposed for managers to select suitable social media for intra-organizational communication

Situation	Components of nonverbal/ paraverbal communication required				Synchronous	Asynchronous	Features required	Equivocality
	Body language	Tone	Facial expression & eye contact	Proximity				
1. Task allocation						✓	Text only	
2. Giving instructions						✓	Text and picture/document attachment	
3. Providing feedback								
• Positive feedback						✓		
• Negative feedback		✓			✓		Text, picture/document attachment and voice call/recording	
4. Resolving employees' queries		✓			✓			
5. Performance appraisal		✓	✓		✓		Text, picture/document attachment, voice calls/recordings and group/personal video conferencing	
6. Team meetings		✓	✓	✓	✓			
7. Job interview	✓	✓	✓	✓	✓			

model developed in this study is to assist managers in selecting an appropriate SM platform for intra-organizational communication. The importance of using an adequate medium of communication is highlighted by its ability to enhance liking and trust by conveying nonverbal cues (Aburumman et al., 2022). Trust and liking amongst employees are crucial to enable collective and collaborative learning.

In *table 1*, situation refers to the various job-related events that occur in organizations. Further, the model includes four broad components of nonverbal/ paraverbal communication namely; body language, tone, facial expressions & eye contact, and proximity. The term synchronous implies real time communication which may be required in certain situations, whereas asynchronous does not require simultaneous interaction. Additionally, the model addresses the different features that must be present in a SM platform to convey the required nonverbal/paraverbal cues. In correspondence with the Media Richness Model, the equivocality of any mode of communication is shown to reduce as more nonverbal/ paraverbal cues are conveyed and if it possesses the ability to enable synchronous communication. The researchers have proposed a model that aids managers select SM platforms for intra-organizational communication based on the current task/goal.

4. 5. 2. The Social Information Processing Model

The Media Richness model would choose a communication medium by corresponding the ambiguity of the message and the ability of the medium to minimize ambiguity as required by the task. On the other hand, this model (Fulk, et al, 1990, Fulk, et al., 1987) theorizes that the adoption of communication media can be explained in terms of the organization's observation of the usage of a particular medium in their social environment either through individual-level interaction with organizational actors such as supervisors, co-workers, customers, etc. or by observing the use of that medium in other organizations and evaluating its dissemination. This theory also addresses the previously discussed media richness model (Daft & Lengel, 1984, 1986). In addition, this model also considers the influence of interaction and feedback on decision-making regarding the 'right medium' of communication and thus can be seen as an augmentation to the media richness model.

Organizations are constantly analysing their competitors to improve their existing strategies. Therefore, organizations often rely on their counterparts by evaluating their success or failure with a particular mode of communication before deeming it as the 'right choice' (Zhou et al., 2006).

5. SCOPE FOR FURTHER RESEARCH

The current landscape of organizational communication is heavily influenced by the pervasive use of social media, making further research in this area imperative. Considering the inevitability of SM in workplace communication, future studies could explore enhancing organizational effectiveness and learning within the context of improving knowledge and information sharing in Learning Organizations. Investigating the nuances of how SM can be strategically employed to foster collaboration, innovation, and efficient communication channels within LOs would be valuable. Moreover, scrutinizing the intricate relationship between SM usage and employee wellbeing is crucial, as employee wellbeing significantly impacts productivity and, consequently, organizational effectiveness. This avenue of research could shed light on the potential positive or adverse effects of prolonged SM engagement on the mental health and job satisfaction of employees.

In light of the rapidly advancing technological landscape, it is essential to probe into learning strategies that empower employees to adeptly navigate the challenges posed by accelerating digitization, including the integration of artificial intelligence (AI) and the emergence of virtual organizations. Research in this area could focus on identifying and developing effective training programs that equip employees with the necessary skills to harness the benefits of digitization, ensuring that they are not hindered but rather empowered by these technological advancements. Understanding how employees can adapt and thrive in a digitally transformed organizational environment is pivotal for both individual career development and overall organizational success.

Furthermore, exploring the evolving dynamics of communication content in the era of SM would be beneficial. Investigating ways to mitigate challenges such as language barriers and information misinterpretation on SM platforms could contribute to enhancing the overall quality and effectiveness of communication within LOs. Additionally, examining strategies to prevent the potential pitfalls associated with the exchange of unprecedented information, which may lead to distraction and conflict, is essential for maintaining a positive and focused organizational communication environment.

In conclusion, the scope for further research in the realm of SM's impact on organizational communication and learning is vast and multidimensional. Future studies can contribute significantly to our understanding of how organizations can harness the potential of SM for positive outcomes while addressing the challenges posed by these communication platforms in contemporary work environments.

5.1 Additional Research Propositions

Objective 1: *To gain a competitive advantage in dynamic and complex environments, organizations are continuously seeking strategies. One such strategy is the emergence of LOs, which foster collective and collaborative learning.*

1. *Dynamic Adaptation Strategies:* Investigate how LOs can adapt their strategies in real-time to respond effectively to rapidly changing environments, considering factors such as technology advancements, market disruptions, and regulatory changes.
2. *Cultural Alignment:* Explore how LOs can align their internal cultures with their strategies to ensure that employees' values and behaviours are consistent with the organization's learning-oriented goals.
3. *Cross-Industry Learning:* Examine the potential benefits of cross-industry learning within LOs, investigating how knowledge and practices from different sectors can be integrated to foster innovation and competitive advantage.

Objective 2: *Effective communication plays a vital role within LOs as it facilitates the efficient exchange of knowledge and information, thereby enhancing the learning process.*

1. *Multimodal Communication*: Research how LOs can effectively leverage various communication modes (verbal, written, visual, etc.) to cater to different learning preferences and improve knowledge sharing and retention.
2. *Cognitive Load and Communication*: Study how different communication strategies impact cognitive load within LOs, and explore methods to optimize information delivery to enhance learning without overwhelming employees.
3. *Psychological Safety:* Investigate how creating a psychologically safe communication environment can encourage open sharing of ideas and knowledge, promoting a culture of continuous learning and improvement.

Objective 3: *With the advent of digitization, SM has become a widespread mode of communication even within the workplace. This chapter aims to examine the impact of SM on intra-organizational communication within the context of LOs.*

1. *Digital Literacy and Adoption:* Research the challenges and strategies associated with promoting digital literacy among employees to ensure effective and responsible use of SM for intra-organizational communication.

2. *Privacy and Security Concerns*: Explore the potential risks and concerns related to using SM platforms within LOs, such as data breaches, privacy violations, and strategies to mitigate these risks.
3. *Network Analysis and Communication Patterns*: Analyze communication patterns on SM platforms within LOs using network analysis techniques, uncovering influential nodes and identifying potential bottlenecks in information flow.

Objective 4: *The researchers have proposed a model to assist managers in selecting suitable SM for intra-organizational communication based on situational demands.*

1. *Model Validation*: Conduct empirical studies to validate the proposed model's effectiveness across various industries, organizational sizes, and cultural contexts, assessing its practical applicability and adaptability.
2. *Dynamic Model*: Develop an adaptive version of the proposed model that can evolve based on changing organizational contexts, technological advancements, and user preferences, providing real-time recommendations for SM platform selection.
3. *Comparative Analysis*: Compare the effectiveness of the proposed model with alternative decision-making frameworks in terms of SM platform selection for intra-organizational communication, considering factors such as accuracy, usability, and impact on learning outcomes.

Objective 5: *Furthermore, the chapter highlights areas for future research in this domain.*

1. *Long-Term Effects of SM Usage:* Investigate the long-term effects of incorporating SM into LOs' communication strategies, examining how it impacts employee engagement, retention, and organizational culture over time.
2. *Cognitive and Behavioural Effects*: Study how SM usage affects employees' cognitive processes, such as attention, memory, and information retention, and explore potential behavioural changes stemming from increased digital communication.
3. *Ethical Considerations*: Explore the ethical implications of using SM for intra-organizational communication, particularly concerning data privacy, surveillance, and potential biases introduced by algorithmic content curation.
4. *Hybrid Communication Strategies*: Examine the potential benefits and challenges of hybrid communication strategies that integrate both traditional and digital communication methods within LOs, balancing the advantages of each approach.

5. *Impact on Innovation:* Investigate how the use of SM for intra-organizational communication influences innovation processes, idea generation, and the development of new products or services within LOs.

These future research agenda points can provide a comprehensive roadmap for further exploration and advancement within the realm of SM's impact on intra-organizational communication within LOs.

6. IMPLICATIONS

6. 1. Academic Implications

This chapter adds to the existing literature within the domains of SM and LOs. Additionally, it explains the relationship between SM as a mode of communication and LOs by assessing the influence of SM on various aspects of LOs.

6. 2. Practical Implications

Managers often come across studies and theories that can be beneficial to the organization. However, they are left confused about what strategies to implement for specific functions and how to implement them. This chapter proposes a model to facilitate the adoption of SM for organizational communication thereby bridging the gap between theory and industry.

6. 3. Social Implications

This chapter has highlighted the use of SM for collaborative and collective learning through knowledge and information sharing. The ability of SM to enhance collective and collaborative learning may in turn promote social interdependence which focuses on collective achievement (Johnson & Johnson, 2009).

7. CONCLUSION

This chapter constitutes a comprehensive literature review spanning 88 years (1934-2022) that synthesizes extant research within the context of organizational communication, specifically focusing on the influence of social media (SM) as a communication mode on various facets of Learning Organizations (LOs). The examination of pertinent literature reveals a nuanced understanding of the positive and negative implications associated with the incorporation of SM in intra-organizational communication within LOs. Notably, the chapter introduces a managerial decision-making model aimed at aiding organizational leaders in the judicious selection of SM platforms for effective communication.

The major findings derived from the review are delineated as follows: the efficacy of a communication medium is primarily contingent upon its capacity to interconnect diverse organizational components, and secondarily, on its facilitation of interaction to foster collaborative learning among employees. Regarding organizational structure, SM serve as an enabler for geographically dispersed or virtual organizations. However, the success of such entities hinges upon their adept management of integrating dispersed personnel into a cohesive team, compensating for the absence of personal association and face-to-face interactions. Importantly, SM demonstrate a predilection for exerting a negative impact on communication content due to impediments such as language barriers and information misinterpretation. The ready accessibility of SM may induce employees to engage in the exchange of unprecedented information, thereby potentially instigating distraction and conflict within organizational settings.

Furthermore, a noteworthy observation emerges concerning the modification of information flow patterns, transitioning from a traditional 'downward communication' model with managers/supervisors as the primary information source to a more dialogic pattern between employees of different hierarchical levels. This shift has been empirically associated with heightened levels of employee satisfaction and organizational commitment. Finally, the chapter underscores the significance of selecting communication media judiciously, positing that platforms characterized by low equivocality and ambiguity are more effective. Such platforms are deemed conducive to collective learning, as they are likely to engender a common interpretation among organizational members.

REFERENCES

Akram, W., & Kumar, R. (2017). A Study on Positive and Negative Effects of Social Media on Society. *International Journal on Computer Science and Engineering*, *5*(10), 351–354. doi:10.26438/ijcse/v5i10.351354

Alerasoul, S. A., Afeltra, G., Hakala, H., Minelli, E., & Strozzi, F. (2021). Organisational learning, learning organisation, and learning orientation: An integrative review and framework. *Human Resource Management Review*, *32*(3), 100854. doi:10.1016/j.hrmr.2021.100854

Almaney, A. (1974). Communication and the Systems Theory of Organization. *Journal of Business Communication*, *12*(1), 35–43. doi:10.1177/002194367401200106

Ansari, J. A., & Khan, N. A. (2020). Exploring the role of social media in collaborative learning the new domain of learning. *Smart Learning Environments*, *7*(1), 9. doi:10.118640561-020-00118-7

Badea, M. (2014). Social Media and Organizational Communication. *Procedia: Social and Behavioral Sciences*, *149*, 70–75. doi:10.1016/j.sbspro.2014.08.192

Balaji, P., & Murthy, S. S. (2019). Web 2.0: An Evaluation of Social Media Networking Sites. *International Journal of Innovative Technology and Exploring Engineering*, *8*(10), 752–759. doi:10.35940/ijitee.J8892.0881019

Barker, R., & Camarata, M. M. (1998). The Role of Communication in Creating and Maintaining a Learning Organization: Preconditions, Indicators, and Disciplines. *Journal of Business Communication*, *35*(4), 443–467. doi:10.1177/002194369803500402

Baxter, G., & Connolly, T. (2014). Implementing Web 2.0 tools in organisations: Feasibility of a systematic approach. *The Learning Organization*, *21*(1), 6–25. doi:10.1108/TLO-11-2012-0069

Belinski, R., Peixe, A., Frederico, G., & Garza-Reyes, J. (2020). Organizational learning and Industry 4.0: findings from a systematic literature review and research agenda. *Benchmarking: An International Journal*. https://www.emerald.com/insight/content/doi/10.1108/BIJ-04-2020-0158/full/html?skipTracking=true

Berger, B. (2015, June 9). *Employee / Organizational Communications*. Institute for Public Relations. https://instituteforpr.org/employee-organizational-communications/

Bertot, J. C., Jaeger, P. T., Munson, S., & Glaisyer, T. (2010). Engaging the Public in Open Government: Social Media Technology and Policy for Government Transparency. *Computer*, *43*(11), 53–59. doi:10.1109/MC.2010.325

Borah, P. S., Iqbal, S., & Akhtar, S. (2022). Linking social media usage and SME's sustainable performance: The role of digital leadership and innovation capabilities. *Technology in Society*, *68*, 101900. doi:10.1016/j.techsoc.2022.101900

Botezatu, A. (2012). *Cum sa iti faci strategia de social media*. Startups.ro. http://www.startups.ro/tutoriale/cum-sa-iti-facistrategia-de-social-media

Breunig, K. J. (n.d.). *Limitless Learning: Assessing Social Media Use for Global Workplace Learning*. https://eric.ed.gov/?id=EJ1106943

Briciu, V., & Briciu, A. (2021). Social Media and Organizational Communication. *Advances in Logistics, Operations, and Management Science Book Series*, 2609–2624. doi:10.4018/978-1-7998-3473-1.ch180

Chen, R. R., Davison, R. M., & Ou, C. X. (2020). A symbolic interactionism perspective of using social media for personal and business communication. *International Journal of Information Management*, *51*, 102022. doi:10.1016/j.ijinfomgt.2019.10.007

Ciochina, R. (2015, April 5). Social media şi comunicarea internă: paşi mărunţi, nesiguri. *Organizational Learning RO*. https://organizationslearning.wordpress.com/2013/12/21/social-media-si-comunicarea-interna-pasi-marunti-nesiguri/

Daft, R. L., & Lengel, R. (1984). *Information Richness A New Approach to Managerial Behavior and Organizational Design.* Greenwich, CT JAI Press. https://www.scirp.org/(S(vtj3fa45qm1ean45vvffcz55))/reference/ReferencesPapers.aspx?ReferenceID=1199991

Daft, R. L., & Lengel, R. H. (1986). Organizational Information Requirements, Media Richness and Structural Design. *Management Science*, *32*(5), 554–571. doi:10.1287/mnsc.32.5.554

Daft, R. L., & Weick, K. E. (1984). Toward a Model of Organizations as Interpretation Systems. *Academy of Management Review*, *9*(2), 284–295. doi:10.2307/258441

DiFranzo, D., & Gloria-Garcia, K. (2017). Filter bubbles and fake news. *Crossroads*, *23*(3), 32–35. doi:10.1145/3055153

Dirani, K., Medina-Cetina, Z., Wowk, K., Herzka, S., Bolio, R., Martinez, V., & Ubando, L. (2021). Learning organization as a framework for networks' learning and collaboration. *In The Learning Organization* (ISSN- 0969–6474). https://www.emerald.com/insight/content/doi/10.1108/TLO-05-2020-0089/full/html

Dörner, K., & Edelman, D. (2015). *What 'digital' really means*. McKinsey. www.mckinsey.com/industries/technology-media-and-telecommunications/our-insights/what-digital-really-means

Ekström, A. G., Niehorster, D. C., & Olsson, E. J. (2022). Self-imposed filter bubbles: Selective attention and exposure in online search. *Computers in Human Behavior Reports*, *7*, 100226. doi:10.1016/j.chbr.2022.100226

Ewing, M., Men, L. R., & O'Neil, J. (2019). Using Social Media to Engage Employees: Insights from Internal Communication Managers. *International Journal of Strategic Communication*, *13*(2), 110–132. doi:10.1080/1553118X.2019.1575830

Fernandez-Vidal, J., Gonzalez, R., Gascó, J. L., & Llopis, J. (2022). Digitalization and corporate transformation: The case of European oil & gas firms. *Technological Forecasting and Social Change, 174*, 121293. doi:10.1016/j.techfore.2021.121293

Følstad, A., & Kvale, K. (2018). Customer journeys: A systematic literature review. *Journal of Service Theory and Practice, 28*(2), 196–227. doi:10.1108/JSTP-11-2014-0261

Fulk, J., Schmitz, J., & Steinfield, C. (1990). A Social Influence Model of Technology use. *Organizations and Communication Technology*, 117–140. doi:10.4135/9781483325385.n6

Fulk, J., Steinfield, C. W., Schmitz, J., & Power, J. G. (1987). A Social Information Processing Model of Media Use in Organizations. *Communication Research, 14*(5), 529–552. doi:10.1177/009365087014005005

Gibson, J. W., & Hodgetts, R. M. (1991). *Organizational Communication – A Managerial Perspective* (2nd ed.). HarperCollins Publishers.

Gourville, J. T. (2004). Why Consumers Don't Buy: The Psychology of New Product Adoption. *Harvard Business School Background Note 504-056.*

Gray, J., & Laidlaw, H. (2004). Improving the Measurement of Communication Satisfaction. *Management Communication Quarterly, 17*(3), 425–448. doi:10.1177/0893318903257980

Hansen, J. Ø., Jensen, A., & Nguyen, N. (2020). The responsible learning organization: Can Senge (1990) teach organizations how to become responsible innovators? *The Learning Organization, 27*(1), 65–74. doi:10.1108/TLO-11-2019-0164

Hickson, M. III. (1973). The open systems model: Auditing the effectiveness of organizational communication. *Journal of Business Communication, 10*(3), 7–14.

Hoe, S. L. (2019). *Digitalization in practice: the fifth discipline advantage*. The Learning Organization. https://www.emerald.com/insight/content/doi/10.1108/TLO-09-2019-0137/full/html http://pqm-online.com/assets/files/lib/books/senge.pdf https://www.scirp.org/(S(czeh2tfqw2orz553k1w0r45))/reference/referencespapers.aspx?referenceid=2993386

Hylmö, A., & Buzzanell, P. (2002). Telecommuting as viewed through cultural lenses: An empirical investigation of the discourses of utopia, identity, and mystery. *Communication Monographs, 69*(4), 329–356. doi:10.1080/03637750216547

Johnson, D. W., & Johnson, R. T. (2009). An Educational Psychology Success Story: Social Interdependence Theory and Cooperative Learning. *Educational Researcher*, *38*(5), 365–379. doi:10.3102/0013189X09339057

Joshi, N. (2023, August 18). *How Web 3.0 will transform social Media*. Linkedin. https://www.linkedin.com/pulse/how-web-30-transform-social-media-naveen-joshi/

Kaplan, A. M., & Haenlein, M. (2010). Users of the world, unite! The challenges and opportunities of Social Media. *Business Horizons*, *53*(1), 59–68. doi:10.1016/j.bushor.2009.09.003

Khang, H., Ki, E. J., & Ye, L. (2012). Social Media Research in Advertising, Communication, Marketing, and Public Relations, 1997–2010. *Journalism & Mass Communication Quarterly*, *89*(2), 279–298. doi:10.1177/1077699012439853

Kitchens, B., Johnson, S. L., & Gray, P. B. (2020). Understanding echo chambers and filter bubbles: The impact of social media on diversification and partisan shifts in news consumption. *Management Information Systems Quarterly*, *44*(4), 1619–1649. doi:10.25300/MISQ/2020/16371

Kolhar, M., Kazi, R. N., & Alameen, A. (2021). Effect of social media use on learning, social interactions, and sleep duration among university students. *Saudi Journal of Biological Sciences*, *28*(4), 2216–2222. doi:10.1016/j.sjbs.2021.01.010 PMID:33911938

Kreps, G. L. (1985). Organizational communication and organizational effectiveness. *World Communication*, *14*(2), 109–119.

Langer, E. (2014). What's Trending? Social Media and its Effects on Organizational Communication. *UW-L Journal of Undergraduate Research XVII (2014)*. https://www.uwlax.edu/globalassets/offices-services/urc/jur-online/pdf/2014/langer.emily.cst.pdf

Lee, S. H., & Lee, S. Y. (2020). Social Media Use and Job Performance in the Workplace: The Effects of Facebook and KakaoTalk Use on Job Performance in South Korea. *Sustainability (Basel)*, *12*(10), 4052. doi:10.3390u12104052

Lee, Y., & Li, J. C. (2021). The role of communication transparency and organizational trust in publics' perceptions, attitudes and social distancing behaviour: A case study of the COVID-19 outbreak. *Journal of Contingencies and Crisis Management*, *29*(4), 368–384. doi:10.1111/1468-5973.12354

Lengel, R. H., & Daft, R. L. (1984). *An Exploratory Analysis of the Relationship between Media Richness and Managerial Information Processing. An Exploratory Analysis of the Relationship between Media Richness and Managerial Information Processing*. Research Gate. https://www.researchgate.net/publication/235157580_An_Exploratory_Analysis_of_the_Relationship_between_Media_Richness_and_Managerial_Information_Processing

Leonardi, P. M., Huysman, M., & Steinfield, C. (2013). Enterprise Social Media: Definition, History, and Prospects for the Study of Social Technologies in Organizations. *Journal of Computer-Mediated Communication, 19*(1), 1–19. doi:10.1111/jcc4.12029

Mathieu, J. E., Hollenbeck, J. R., van Knippenberg, D., & Ilgen, D. R. (2017). A century of work teams in the Journal of Applied Psychology. *The Journal of Applied Psychology, 102*(3), 452–467. doi:10.1037/apl0000128 PMID:28150984

Mead, G. H. (1934). *Mind, Self, and Society from the Standpoint of a Social Behaviorist*. University of Chicago Press.

Miller, K. (2016). *Organizational Communication: Approaches and Processes* (6th ed.). Cengage.

Mintzberg, H. (2015). Henry MINTZBERG, The Nature of Managerial Work (1973) & Simply Managing: What Manager Do - And Can Do Better (2013). *M@n@gement, 18*(2), 186. doi:10.3917/mana.182.0186

Modaff, D. P., & DeWine, S. (2002). *Organizational Communication: Foundations.* Challenges, Misunderstandings.

Morgan, R. (2003). *Market-Based Organizational Learning: Business Performance Gains in Financial Services Organizations*. Semantic Scholar. https://www.semanticscholar.org/paper/market-based-organizational-learning-%3a-business-in-Morgan-Turnell/a5774abcda480167a8bb1a486f2a11742b2c79bc

Nisar, T. M., Prabhakar, P., & Strakova, L. (2019). Social media information benefits, knowledge management and smart organizations. *Journal of Business Research, 94*, 264–272. doi:10.1016/j.jbusres.2018.05.005

ObarJ. A.WildmanS. S. (2015). Social Media Definition and the Governance Challenge - An Introduction to the Special Issue. *Social Science Research Network.* doi:10.2139/ssrn.2663153

Oksa, R., Kaakinen, M., Savela, N., Ellonen, N., & Oksanen, A. (2021). Professional social media usage: Work engagement perspective. *New Media & Society*, *23*(8), 2303–2326. doi:10.1177/1461444820921938

Örtenblad, A. (2001). On Differences between Organizational Learning and Learning Organization. [Scientific Research Publishing] [n.d.]. *The Learning Organization*, *8*(3), 125–133. doi:10.1108/09696470110391211

Ortiz-Ospina, E. (2023, May 25). The rise of social media. *Our World in Data*. https://ourworldindata.org/rise-of-social-media?ref=tms

Pandey, N., Nayal, P., & Rathore, A. S. (2020). Digital marketing for B2B organizations: Structured literature review and future research directions. *Journal of Business and Industrial Marketing*, *35*(7), 1191–1204. doi:10.1108/JBIM-06-2019-0283

Pearlson, K. E., & Saunders, C. S. (2001). There's no place like home: Managing telecommuting paradoxes. *The Academy of Management Perspectives*, *15*(2), 117–128. doi:10.5465/ame.2001.4615008

Pekkala, K., & Van Zoonen, W. (2021). Work-related social media use: The mediating role of social media communication self-efficacy. *European Management Journal*, *40*(1), 67–76. doi:10.1016/j.emj.2021.03.004

Rebelo, T., Lourenço, P. B., & Dimas, I. D. (2019). The journey of team learning since "The Fifth Discipline.". *The Learning Organization*, *27*(1), 42–53. doi:10.1108/TLO-10-2019-0144

Rice, R. E., & Aydin, C. (1991). Attitudes Toward New Organizational Technology: Network Proximity as a Mechanism for Social Information Processing. *Administrative Science Quarterly*, *36*(2), 219. doi:10.2307/2393354

Santra, T., & Giri, V. N. (2009). Analyzing Computer-Mediated Communication and Organizational Effectiveness. *The Review of Communication*, *9*(1), 100–109. doi:10.1080/15358590701772259

Scott, M., & DeSANCTIS, P. G. (1992). Microlevel Structuration in Computer-Supported Group Decision Making. *Human Communication Research*, *19*(1), 5–49. doi:10.1111/j.1468-2958.1992.tb00294.x

Simon, G. R., & Zhou, I. (2017). Harmonizing Modern Day Employee Engagement with the Sociological Theory of Symbolic Interactionism. *American Journal of Business and Management*, *6*(2), 52. doi:10.11634/216796061706894

Sinkula, J. M. (1994). Market Information Processing and Organizational Learning. *Journal of Marketing*, *58*(1), 35–45. doi:10.1177/002224299405800103

Smith, G., Barnes, K. C., & Harris, C. R. (2014). A learning approach to the ethical organization. *The Learning Organization*. doi:10.1108/TLO-07-2011-0043

Sobko, S., Unadkat, D., Adams, J., & Hull, G. (2019). Learning through collaboration: A networked approach to online pedagogy. *E-Learning and Digital Media*, *17*(1), 36–55. doi:10.1177/2042753019882562

Song, J. H., Lim, D. H., Kang, I., & Kim, W. (2014). Team performance in learning organizations: Mediating effect of employee engagement. *The Learning Organization*, *21*(5), 290–309. doi:10.1108/TLO-07-2012-0049

Soukup, E. (2003, September 22). CEOs: That's What That Is. *Newsweek*.

Sproull, L., & Kiesler, S. (1986). Reducing Social Context Cues: Electronic Mail in Organizational Communication. *Management Science*, *32*(11), 1492–1512. doi:10.1287/mnsc.32.11.1492

Tanaka, J. (1997, April 28). Drowning in Data. *Newsweek*.

The College of New Jersey. (n.d.) *Creating a Social Media Presence*. TCNJ. https://communications.tcnj.edu/about/media-relations-and-marketing/use-social-media/

Thomas, P. J., & Dittman, K. C. (2016). Social Media and its Impact on Quality of Communication Management. *Proceedings of the 2016 IAJC-ISAM Joint International Conference*. IEEE.

Trevino, L. K., Daft, R. L., & Lengel, R. H. (1990). Understanding managers' media choices: A symbolic interactionist perspective. In J. Fulk & C. W. Steinfield (Eds.), *Organizations and communication technology* (pp. 71–94). Sage Publications, Inc. doi:10.4135/9781483325385.n4

Trevino, L. K., Lengal, R. H., & Daft, R. L. (1987). Media Symbolism, Media Richness, and Media Choice in Organizations. *Communication Research*, *14*(5), 553–574. doi:10.1177/009365087014005006

Trittin-Ulbrich, H., Scherer, A. G., Munro, I., & Whelan, G. (2020). Exploring the dark and unexpected sides of digitalization: Toward a critical agenda. *Organization*, *28*(1), 8–25. doi:10.1177/1350508420968184

Turaga, R. (2019). Effective Communication in Organizations - ProQuest. IUP Journal of Soft Skills: Vol. 13. (*Iss. 1,*). University of California Press., https://www.proquest.com/openview/f66811fddb041d7db2b3a5a94688c20e/1?pq-origsite=gscholar&cbl=2029989

Valiyeva, A., & Thomas, B. J. (2022). Successful Organizational Business Communication and its Impact on Business Performance: An Intra- and Inter-Organizational Perspective. *Journal of Accounting. Business and Finance Research, 15*(2), 83–91. doi:10.55217/102.v15i2.586

Van Osch, W., & Coursaris, C. K. (2013). Organizational Social Media: A Comprehensive Framework and Research Agenda. 2013 *46th Hawaii International Conference on System Sciences*. IEEE. https://doi.org/10.1109/hicss.2013.439Van

Venezia, A. S. J (2012). *The interaction of social media and the law and how to survive the social media revolution.*

Verbos, A. K., Gerard, J. G., Forshey, P. R., Harding, C. J., & Miller, J. M. (2007). The Positive Ethical Organization: Enacting a Living Code of Ethics and Ethical Organizational Identity. *Journal of Business Ethics, 76*(1), 17–33. doi:10.100710551-006-9275-2

Von Bertalanffy, L. (1968). General Systems Theory as Integrating Factor in Contemporary Science. In *Akten des XIV* (pp. 335–340). Internationalen Kongresses für Philosophie. doi:10.5840/wcp1419682120

Vrontis, D., Belás, J., Thrassou, A., Santoro, G., & Christofi, M. (2022). Strategic agility, openness and performance: A mixed method comparative analysis of firms operating in developed and emerging markets. *Review of Managerial Science, 17*(4), 1365–1398. doi:10.100711846-022-00562-4

Waters, R. D., & Williams, J. M. (2011). Squawking, tweeting, cooing, and hooting: Analyzing the communication patterns of government agencies on Twitter. *Journal of Public Affairs, 11*(4), 353–363. doi:10.1002/pa.385

Weaver, R., & Agle, R. (n.d.). Religiosity and Ethical Behavior in Organizations: A Symbolic Interactionist Perspective on JSTOR. *The Academy of Management Review*. https://www.jstor.org/stable/4134370

Welch, M., & Jackson, P. R. (2007). Rethinking internal communication: A stakeholder approach. *Corporate Communications, 12*(2), 177–198. doi:10.1108/13563280710744847

Wiesenfeld, B. M., Raghuram, S., & Garud, R. (1998). Communication Patterns as Determinants of Organizational Identification in a Virtual Organization. *Journal of Computer-Mediated Communication, 3*(4). doi:10.1111/j.1083-6101.1998.tb00081.x

Yang, X., Ye, H., & Wang, X. (2021). Social media use and work efficiency: Insights from the theory of communication visibility. *Information & Management, 58*(4), 103462. doi:10.1016/j.im.2021.103462

Zhou, K. Z., Brown, J. H., Dev, C. S., & Agarwal, S. (2006). The effects of customer and competitor orientations on performance in global markets: A contingency analysis. *Journal of International Business Studies, 38*(2), 303–319. doi:10.1057/palgrave.jibs.8400259

Zoonen, W., Treem, J. W., & Ter Hoeven, C. L. (2022). A tool and a tyrant: Social media and well-being in organizational contexts. *Current Opinion in Psychology, 45*, 101300. doi:10.1016/j.copsyc.2022.101300 PMID:35231788

Chapter 11
Didactic Knowledge (DK) eLearning Optimizing Digital Strategies for the Continuous Pedagogical Training of Trainers

Daniela Melare Vieira Barros
Universidade Aberta, Portugal

Ana Maria de Jesus Ferreira Nobre
https://orcid.org/0000-0002-9902-1850
Universidade Aberta, Portugal

Antonio Chenoll Mora
https://orcid.org/0000-0001-8802-5293
Universidade Católica Portuguesa, Portugal

Paula Alexandra Valente da Silva
IEFP, Portugal

ABSTRACT

Although some research on optimising digital strategies is already known in higher education, in the context of vocational training, more specifically in the continuous pedagogical training of trainers, there have been few studies to date in Portugal. There is a call for new digital strategies that enable innovation and change. However, in vocational training, change occurs when the actors want to "change their identity." It is against this backdrop of a desire to change paradigms that this chapter aims to bring this topic, and its importance, into the discussion. This work is the result of analysing online courses in the continuous pedagogical training of trainers based on criteria that have already been validated in terms of the pedagogical design of learning in an e-learning context. The methodological procedures involve a qualitative, interpretative approach that is applied in a vocational training context.

DOI: 10.4018/979-8-3693-0556-0.ch011

1. INTRODUCTION

The term "digital skills" used to mean knowing how to send emails or write in a word processing programme. But this expression has evolved considerably. Digital literacy now means knowing the skills needed to succeed in a society where communication and access to information are increasingly dependent on digital technologies. As this concept encompasses a broad understanding of a range of digital tools, digital technology has become an essential component of society, triggering cultural, social, economic and societal paradigm shifts. The characteristics of this digital shift in society and the economy are such that it has had a direct impact on education and vocational training.

Digital technologies have brought about a new way of (re)thinking vocational training. In the midst of the 21st century, global crises have forced training organisations to discover new ways of working, using digital tools, software, applications and platforms to continue their pedagogical activity, which until then was mostly face-to-face (Dias & Rocha, 2018, p. 5).

Many studies produced in recent years (OECD, 2015, 2016) Arntz & Zierah (2016) World Economic Forum (2015, 2016, 2017, 2018, 2021) even point out that the digital transformation is changing the profile of employment, with profound changes expected in the labour market in the short and medium term, which will eliminate many professions and create others. In this context, the professional competences required of trainers today are related to the use of digital educational technologies, with pedagogically appropriate digital strategies (European Commission, 2022). In light of these recommendations, we note that traditional learning models, both in the school system and in vocational training, are no longer adapted to the methods or needs of our knowledge and information economies.

The limitations of the traditional system, especially its dependence on face-to-face training, emphasise the need for alternative solutions based on digital models. The recent COVID-19 pandemic has reinforced a pre-existing need for digital skills and new teaching models.

Vocational training is an essential link in a country's skills development architecture, so the need to rethink vocational training is particularly important.

Analyses and discussions on the subject have led to advances in the area of training, especially with pedagogies and didactics for online intervention in the teaching and learning process (Nobre et al, 2019). Reflection on learning how to learn has changed paradigms in practice and encouraged a new perspective on valuing knowledge and the need to be in interaction and contact with it. Continuous pedagogical training and in-service training are based on this perspective, between knowledge and individuals who recognise the challenges of digital culture and the need to learn how to learn (Trilla, 2019; Aramburuzabala, 2015).

Continuous online training, particularly that which takes place in the context of the pedagogical training of trainers, meets the needs of using digital for teaching and learning and should therefore be a solution for differentiated professional training, capable of (re)orientating, (re)training and (re)integrating the individual so that they are able to assert themselves, differentiate themselves and act in an increasingly digital, global and competitive world.

The connected and analytical world we live in makes it possible to create new and powerful online teaching models in which trainers must play an active role. This could take the form of attending continuing training courses online, in e-learning format, so that in the course of this experience, trainers deepen their knowledge, acquire new skills, such as emancipatory skills, social and emotional skills, humanistic and artistic skills, and can apply them when delivering training (Figueiredo, 2019).

Although some research on optimising digital strategies is already known in higher education, in the context of vocational training, more specifically in the continuous pedagogical training of trainers, there have been few studies to date in Portugal. There is a call for new digital strategies that enable innovation and change. However, in vocational training, change occurs when the actors want to "change their identity" (Machado & Formosinho, 2009, p.302). Thus, it is against a backdrop of a desire to change paradigms that this chapter aims to bring this topic, and its importance, into the discussion (Ordinance no. 214/2011 of 30 May, art. 6).

The methodology used assumes a qualitative, interpretative approach that will be applied in a vocational training context. It will use an instrument that has already been validated and built by researchers at the Universidade Aberta. This instrument, called the DK e-learning-TPCK Observation Table, was theoretically underpinned by the didactic-pedagogical framework, encompassing the elements of the TPCK Amador et al. (2016), the pedagogical model of the Universidade Aberta. Pereira et al. (2007) and other fundamentals that underpin professional training, 2007) and other foundations that support the pedagogical aspects of distance education such as: Rudestan and Read-Schoenholt (2010), Garrison (1989), Aretio et al. (2007), Anderson (2005; 2008); Garrison and Anderson (2003); Downes (2007) and Peters (2001).

The dimensions of the table were: didactic knowledge; pedagogical knowledge; technological knowledge and content knowledge. The DK-eLearning table was created in Excel and automatically calculates the stipulated values on a scale of 1 to 5, with 1 being the minimum and 5 the maximum for each of the points observed. There are some items that have multiplier values because they are considered more important in the evaluation process. The results of their values added together at the end and represented in percentages show a graph, a tetrahedron that highlights the final results of each dimension.

Table 1. Initial structure of the DK Learning tool (Nobre et al., 2019)

Degree	*Name of the degree*
Subject	*Name of the curriculum unit*
Aim	**To observe the dynamics of the process of didactic transposition in the virtual classroom**

Dimensions	Points to observe
Didactic Knowledge (DK)	**Contents**
	Are they all the same? Do they all have the same relevance?
	Does the content provide the minimum necessary for the construction of knowledge?
	What are the contents of a subject?
	Give an example.
	Objectives
	What are the objectives of a content and/or a theme and/or a topic?
	Are the objectives relevant to the intended knowledge?
	Give an example.
	Are objectives and contents interconnected?
	Skills
	What are the developed skills of a theme and/or topic?
	Are they relevant to the intended knowledge?
	Give an example of the skills.
	Are skills and objectives connected?
	Strategies
	Which strategies are used?
	Are there main strategies and secondary strategies?
	How are they structured? Are they individual or collective?
	Are they relevant to the intended knowledge?
	Give an example of a strategy.
	Are strategies, competences and objectives interconnected?
	Tasks / Exercises / Activities
	How many tasks, exercises or activities are there per content and/or theme and/or topic?
	How are they organised for acquiring knowledge? From the simplest to the most complex?
	Is there guidance on how to carry out tasks, exercises or activities?
	How many tasks, exercises or activities does the learner need to complete for the acquisition of the skills, objectives or content?
	Do the exercises prepare for evaluation?
	What are the proposed tasks, exercises, activities? Give an example.

The following image makes it easier to understand and illustrates the appearance of the Excel tool, highlighting the introduction of the tool and the initial dimension "Didactic Knowledge".

The tool was applied at the *Instituto do Emprego e Formação Profissional*, IP (IEFP). This institute is "part of the indirect administration of the State, and is endowed with administrative and financial autonomy and its own assets, pursuing the attributions of the Ministry of Labour, Solidarity and Social Security, under the superintendence and tutelage of the respective minister (...) it operates throughout the continental territory and its main objective is to combat unemployment through active employment policies, of which vocational training stands out" (Decree-Law no. 143/2012). Its mission is to:

promote information, guidance, qualification and professional rehabilitation, with a view to the placement and professional progression of workers in the labour market, the educational and professional qualification of young people and adults, through the provision of dual certification training and certified professional training, respectively, adjusted to individual paths and relevant to the modernisation of the economy and the implementation, by itself or in collaboration with other entities, of professional training actions appropriate to the needs of people and the modernisation and development of the economic fabric [...]. Encouraging the professional integration of different groups of people through specific measures, particularly for those most at risk of exclusion from the job market and participating in the coordination of technical cooperation activities developed with national and international organisations and foreign countries in the fields of employment, training and professional rehabilitation (Decree-Law no. 213/07 of 29/05, p. 3483).

In order to fulfil the aim of this research and use the proposed DK e-Learning-TPCK Observation Table, thirty participants were chosen from two e-Learning Continuing Pedagogical Training courses "Specialisation in Digital Content for Self-Learning (*e-Conteúdos*)" given in 2022 by the IEFP. These courses aim, above all, to respond to the growing need for training to learn how to build digital content for vocational training (Santos, Moreira, Valente & Vieira, 2022).

The impact of this research has triggered important contributions to the optimisation of digital strategies in the context of vocational training, more specifically in the continuous pedagogical training of trainers, since the DK e-learning-TPCK Observation Table in this specific context has enabled the development of learning and new proposals for pedagogical strategies and structures that meet the needs of trainees.

2. VOCATIONAL TRAINING

Work-related training and non-formal and informal learning in the workplace, i.e. vocational training in school and professional contexts, is now recognised as a key to teaching and learning and the development of lifelong skills. Globalisation, technological changes (digital), along with demographic changes and climate change are transforming the world of work. These impact on the development of new skills and the ways in which work is organised (ILO/OECD, 2018). Organisations such as the Organisation for Economic Co-operation and Development (OECD), the International Labour Organisation (ILO) and the European Union (EU) have developed strategies (e.g. the OECD Skills Strategy and the EU's New Skills Agenda for Europe) for skills development and the future of work. As pointed out in the report Global Skills Trends, Training Needs and Lifelong Learning Strategies for the Future of Work (2018), the world of work is changing and poses a huge challenge to traditional education and training systems and calls for new approaches in education and training and learning.

According to CEDEFOP (2021), Portugal's current education and training system comprises compulsory education lasting 12 years (or until the age of 18) with the updating of the Basic Law of the Education System - LBSE in 2009. Compulsory education covers all children over the age of 6 and includes the completion of the three cycles of basic education (four years for the first cycle, two years for the second cycle and three years for the third cycle), and secondary education (three-year cycle of studies).

Vocational training in Portugal is governed by the LBSE, which is supervised by the Ministry of Education, and by Decree-Law no. 401/91 and Decree-Law no. 405/91, which are supervised by the Ministry of Labour and Social Security, differentiating between vocational training within the education system and vocational training within the employment market. The legal regulations governing vocational training are currently based on Decree-Law no. 396/2007, amended and republished by Decree-Law no. 14/2017, which regulates the National Qualifications System (SNQ) and the structuring elements that guarantee its operation. The National Qualifications Catalogue (CNQ) has emerged as an instrument for managing non-higher education qualifications with a view to better articulating the skills considered necessary for the country's development and promoting qualification offers promoted by the education and training system (Azevedo & Capucha, 2021).

The National Qualifications Framework (NQF) refers to and classifies qualifications in the Portuguese education and training system, structured into 8 qualification levels. The qualification levels and respective descriptors of the NQF correspond to the qualification systems of the European Qualifications Framework (EQF), which aims to unify, as a single reference framework, the qualification levels of different countries (Ministerial Order no. 782/2009).

According to CEDEFOP (2021), basic education corresponds to levels 1 and 2 of the EQF, secondary education to levels 3 and 4 of the EQF, non-tertiary post-secondary education to level 5 of the EQF and tertiary education to levels 6, 7 and 8 of the EQF.

Ministerial Order no. 474/2010 defines certified training within the scope of the National Qualifications System (SNQ) as training carried out by a certified training entity, or by an educational establishment recognised by the competent ministries, as well as in-house training for workers.

On vocational education:

More than just a different type of school, vocational education is an innovative education and training paradigm, governed by a new relationship between the state, schools and local social actors, based on trust between all those involved and on the co-operation and creative initiative of civil society, based on the freedom, autonomy and responsibility of education and training professionals and all the local actors involved, a pedagogy that effectively promotes the real success of all young people, built on hard, daily work and hope for the future, and that overcomes the old, stifling hegemony of the "high school and academic" model that prevails at secondary level and, finally, a type of school that approaches each context and each student as a person in full and progressive development. (Azevedo, 2014, p. 17).

With a view to standardising an international classification in the area of initial and continuing training, based on the International Standard Classification of Education (ISCED) drawn up by UNESCO, a technical instrument for statistical coordination in the area of education and training was defined under the supervision of the Statistical Office of the European Communities (EUROSTAT) and CEDEFOP: the National Classification of Areas of Education and Training (CNAEF).

According to Canário (2000), today's society and its subsequent evolution have highlighted the increasingly pressing need to rethink the value acquired through professional experience, and the concept of work experience is essentially based on professional training contexts. Finally, Fernandéz (2006) states that the current recognition of the workplace as a space for learning comes from the performance of the act itself.

3. CONTINUOUS PEDAGOGICAL TRAINING FOR TRAINERS

The digital transformation is one of the factors responsible for global social, economic and cultural changes (Digital Decade in Europe, 2023). The world has become a global village - the Knowledge Society - where digital technologies play an important role in the dissemination of information. The processing time for information and learning is happening at a dizzying pace, leading to the constant need for learning, metamorphosing formative events into continuous educational processes.

In the 21st century, it has become clear that vocational training needs to be (re) invented, using Distance Education (DE) to enable trainees to obtain competences of a "transversal, multidimensional nature, incorporating knowledge, skills, attitudes and values that support higher-order behaviour when applied to complex or highly uncertain situations". (Figueiredo, 2019, p. 2)

In the current economic, political and social climate, the greatest capacity for influence is in the hands of those with the most continuous skills.

Investment in education and training for skills development is essential to boost growth and competitiveness: skills determine Europe's capacity to increase productivity (...) European education and training systems continue to fall short in providing the right skills for employability and are not working adequately with business or employers to bring the learning experience closer to the reality of the working environment. These skills mismatches are a growing concern for European industry's competitiveness. (Commission, 2012, p. 2)

Continuous Pedagogical Training for Trainers is not only a need that is recognised as a right and duty for all trainers, given the numerous roles and functions they have to play in the training context, but also a requirement that arises from the growing, rapid and constant mutation of society, especially digital society. It is therefore argued that this plays a fundamental role in updating and improving trainers' skills, enabling them to keep up with the changes and demands of vocational training and the constantly evolving labour market.

In Portugal, the legal framework for the continuous training of trainers states, in Article 6 of Ministerial Order no. 214/2011 of 30 May, that

Continuous pedagogical training is based on various competency benchmarks, is organised in modularly structured courses of varying duration and includes, from a lifelong learning perspective, one or more of the following dimensions: a) Pedagogical, which includes modules aimed at improving, deepening or diversifying the competences provided for in the trainer profile, depending on their context of intervention, and may also include critical reflection and reinforcement of the competences acquired in the organisational, practical, deontological and ethical dimensions of the initial pedagogical training course; b) Scientific and/or technological, which includes modules aimed at ensuring that trainers are constantly updated in their specific area of intervention, taking into account the constant technical and organisational changes observed in the labour market; c) Study or operational research, which includes modules aimed at analysing, researching and optimising references, models, processes and training methods, ensuring their transferability or application in different situations, with a special focus on learning in a work context (Ministerial Order no. 214/2011 of 30 May 2011). º 214/2011 de 30 de Mayo, Art. 6, p. 2960).

It is therefore understood that the Continuous Pedagogical Training of Trainers plays a fundamental role in the area of pedagogy, contributing to the updating and improvement of trainers' educational practices. Through continuous pedagogical training, trainers have the opportunity to acquire new knowledge, develop skills and pedagogical resources that can be applied in their training activities, using reflection on pedagogical practice, which is essential for professional development and improving the quality of professional training. In addition, the continuous training of trainers promotes the exchange of experiences and good practices between training professionals, through courses, workshops and other training activities, enabling trainers to interact with their peers, share experiences, overcome challenges and find joint solutions. This co-operative and at the same time collaborative interaction strengthens the community of trainers and contributes to the collective improvement of teaching practice.

However, the Continuous Pedagogical Training of Trainers also plays an important role in promoting heutagogy, the model for describing the learning process proposed by Stewart Hase and Chris Kenyon in the 2000s, and the personalisation of learning. On the one hand, heutagogy emphasises the learner's ability to lead their own learning process, taking responsibility for their development and defining their learning objectives. It is a descriptive model of learning in which the role of the trainer is a facilitator of the educational process, the individual who seeks knowledge, being responsible for searching for the content to be learnt and designing their own methodology (Blaschke, 2012; Oliveira, 2018).

On the other hand, through the personalisation of learning, trainers acquire new knowledge, skills and didactic strategies to create training environments that meet learners' individual needs. David Hargreaves (2006) was one of the first authors to defend the idea of personalising learning, rather than personalised learning, thus emphasising that it is a process rather than a product. To support his theory, he presents nine access doors for personalising learning, namely: the voice of the learner; learning assessment; learning to learn; technologies; curriculum plan; advice and guidance, mentoring and training; work capacity development and projection, design and organisation, as shown in Figure 2.

In this way, thinking about digital personalisation in the continuous pedagogical training of trainers requires certain elements such as inclusion and flexibility, through new scenarios, paths and experiences so that trainers can combine and complement didactic strategies in the work they do, enabling interaction and collaborative and cooperative learning (Valente, 2022).

According to the figure above, the personalisation of learning makes individualisation possible and encompasses configurations that take diversity into account and give options so that the trainee/trainer can make their own choices and feel included in the teaching and learning process, while at the same time becoming the author of it, guided by objectives and competences.

Continuing Pedagogical Training for Trainers, heutagogy and the personalisation of learning are closely linked. It is therefore essential to have adapted virtual learning environments, different from a simple virtual environment, so that the proposal to apply different assessments and deliver different content can be made feasible and constantly changed, considering the volatility of technologies.

Figure 1. Access doors for personalising learning in continuous pedagogical training
(adapted from Valente, 2022)

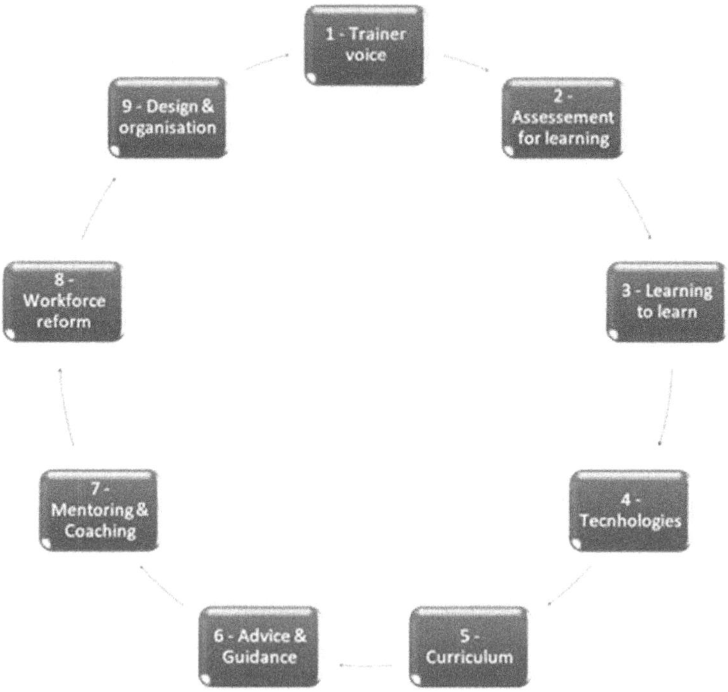

Figure 2. Digital personalisation
(adapted from Barros, 2020)

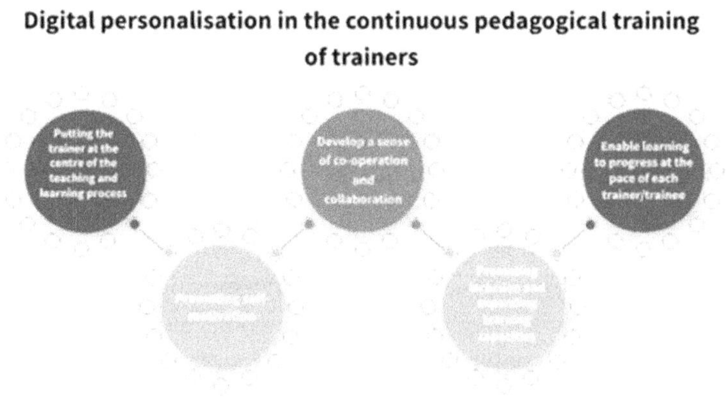

4. TRAINING TRAINERS USING DIGITAL TECHNOLOGIES

The term "didactic transposition" first appeared in the French-speaking scientific community (Chevallard, 1985; Joshua and Dupin, 2003; Clément, 2010), and was later appropriated and transformed by some Anglo-Saxon authors (Shulman, 1986, 1987; Mishra and Koehler, 2006).

Didactic transposition is a concept in which researcher Yves Chevallard, 1985, refers to the process by which scientific knowledge is transformed into school knowledge, in other words, it is adapted and recontextualised to be taught in schools. Didactic transposition recognises that scientific knowledge, such as that produced in academic research and studies, is not directly transferable to the school context. It needs to be organised, simplified and adapted to make it accessible to students and teachable by teachers.

This transposition process involves several stages, such as:

- Selection: scientific content is selected, identifying which aspects are most relevant and suitable to be taught;
- Simplification: scientific knowledge is often complex, and didactic transposition involves simplifying concepts, reducing the amount of information and making them more understandable;
- Organisation: content is organised in a logical and structured sequence to facilitate learning;
- Adaptation: the content is adapted to the school context, considering the characteristics of the students, the age group, the curriculum and the resources available;
- Creating learning situations: didactic transposition also involves creating teaching situations and activities that allow students to interact with knowledge, apply it and build their own understanding.

The aim of didactic transposition is to make scientific knowledge accessible and meaningful to students, considering their characteristics and needs. It is a fundamental process for teaching practice, as teachers are responsible for mediating the transposition of scientific knowledge into school knowledge, adapting it appropriately to the classroom context.

Amador et al. (2016) proposed a didactic transposition model for eLearning environments that reconciles various aspects of previous models. The model is based on a regular tetrahedron (a polyhedron made up of four faces - equilateral triangles). This three-dimensional shape allows us to move the model around and analyse the themes from different perspectives while at the same time unfolding it on each of the faces. In this proposal we have given a central role to Didactic Knowledge (DK),

Figure 3. Didactic transposition model, centered on eLearning didactics
(Amador et al., 2016)

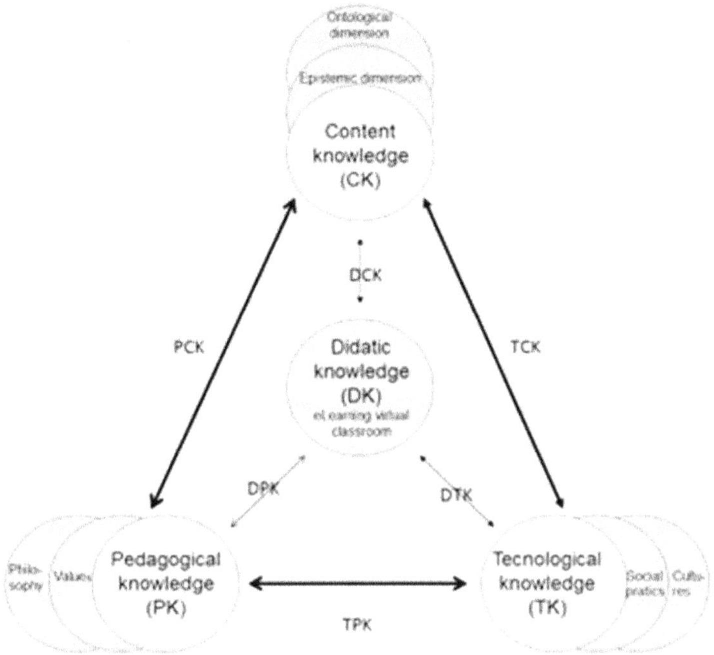

the point where the three edges converge, which we consider corresponding to the space of the virtual classroom.

Legend: PCK (pedagogical and content knowledge); TCK (technological and content knowledge); TPK (technological and pedagogical knowledge); DCK (didactic and content knowledge); DPK (didactic and pedagogical knowledge); DTK (didactic and technological knowledge).

Reflecting on didactics in eLearning environments is a process in which we try to deepen the relationships between the vertices of this model, because in each lesson and in each virtual space the teacher is creating situations in which these three aspects are in balance and is trying to motivate students who live with powerful data storage repositories in their daily lives to make an effort, to organise and classify them, in other words, to give them meaning.

In order to delve deeper into this didactic transposition, we used the theoretical model that describes the knowledge that teachers need to have in order to integrate technology effectively into their teaching practices. This knowledge is called

Technological Pedagogical Content Knowledge (TPACK), proposed by Punya Mishra and Matthew J. Koehler in 2006.

TPACK proposes that in order to effectively integrate technology into education, it is necessary to combine these three components into an integrated knowledge. This means that teachers need to understand how to use technology in a pedagogically appropriate way, taking into account the specific content they are teaching. The ultimate goal of the TPACK model is to enable teachers to design and implement teaching strategies that appropriately integrate technology in order to improve student learning and promote an enriched educational environment.

The TPACK model recognises that in order to use technology effectively in teaching, teachers need to combine three types of knowledge Mishra & Koehler (2006):

- Technology Knowledge (TK): Refers to knowledge about the tools and technologies available and how to use them appropriately in the educational context. This includes understanding the features and functionalities of the technologies, as well as their application in learning activities;
- Pedagogical Knowledge (PK): Involves knowledge about teaching practices, instructional strategies, methodologies, and how students learn. It is the knowledge of how to teach effectively, regardless of technology;
- Content Knowledge (CK): Refers to knowledge of the specific topics being taught. It is knowledge about the concepts, theories and principles of the academic content that teachers are teaching.

TPACK emphasises that when integrating technology effectively into teaching, teachers need to combine these three types of knowledge to a point where they overlap. This overlap is the area called TPACK, where technological, pedagogical and content knowledge merge to support the creation of meaningful and effective learning environments.

The image below makes this overlap clear:

The TPACK model is widely used in teacher training programmes and educational research to understand and improve the integration of technology into teaching and learning. It recognises the complexity of the teacher's task when using technology in the classroom and emphasises the importance of an appropriate balance between technological, pedagogical and content knowledge to promote student success.

In this sense, the use of technologies in the continuous pedagogical training of trainers has been expanded post-pandemic through the encouragement and viability of e-learning courses. These courses have used TPACK as the foundation for their organisation and development, in addition to other pedagogical theories.

Figure 4. The TPACK model
(Mishra & Koehler, 2006)

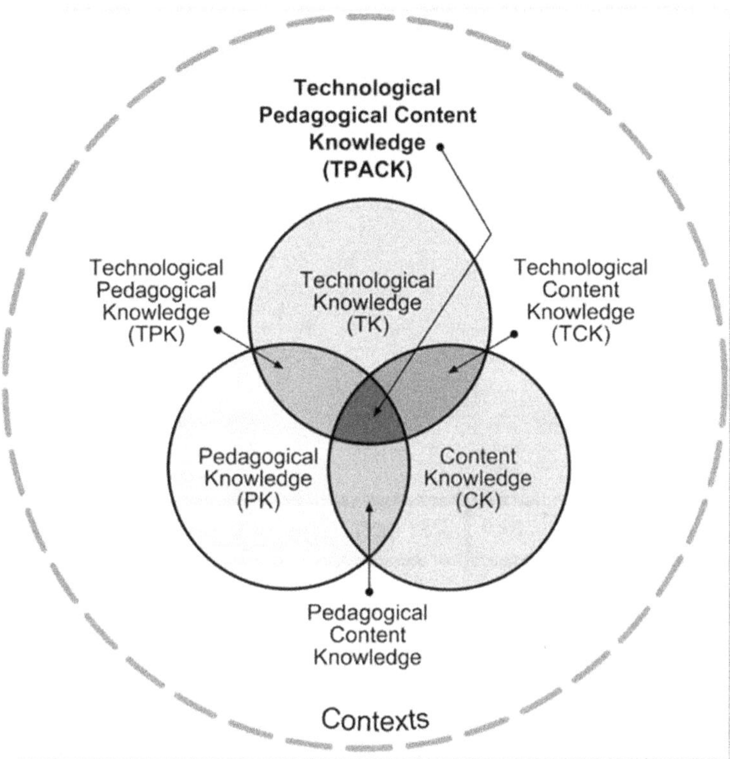

5. DK - E-LEARNING

The DK - e-Learning is the observation grid drawn up by the researchers Nobre et al. (2019) with the following elements as the objectives of the observation: to identify the pedagogical aspects of eLearning courses; to list the main didactic-pedagogical flaws in the course structures facilitating the improvement of these structures in an eLearning course.

The dimensions of the grid were: didactic knowledge, pedagogical knowledge, technological knowledge and content knowledge. These elements are common to the development of online courses as we can identify in Pereira et al. (2007) and other foundations that support the pedagogical aspects of eLearning such as: Rudestan & Read-Schoenholt (2010), Garrison (1989), Aretio & all. (2007), Anderson, (2005), Garrison & Anderson (2003), Downes (2007).

The DK - e-Learning grid prepared in Excel automatically calculates the stipulated values on a scale of 1 to 5, with 1 being the minimum and 5 the maximum for each

Figure 5. Excel image of the calculations of the observations made on the grid (Nobre et al., 2019)

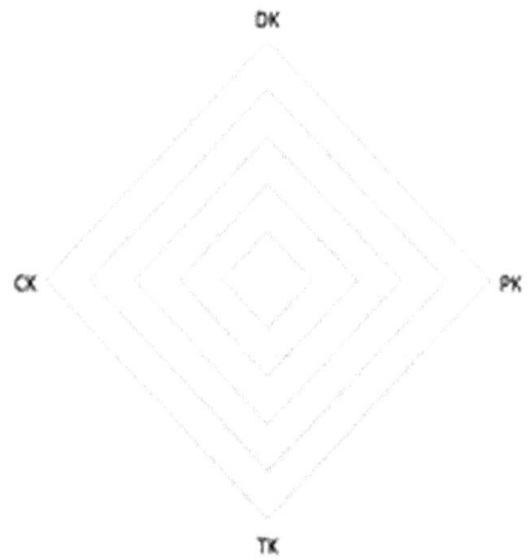

Type of knowledge	Percentage of types of knowledge
DK	0
PK	0
TK	0
CK	0

of the points observed. There are some items that have multiplier values because they are considered more important in the evaluation process. The results of their values added together at the end and represented in percentages represent a graph, a tetrahedron that highlights the final results for each dimension, as can be seen in Figure 5.

6. METHODOLOGY

The methodological options for this research were based on a variety of information-gathering strategies, favouring the use of qualitative methodologies, taking into account the object of the study in question.

Qualitative research methodology is a research approach that focuses on in-depth and detailed understanding of social, cultural, psychological or other phenomena through the collection and analysis of non-quantitative data. According to Marconi &

Lakatos (2012), Flick, (2005), Hill & Hill (2000), qualitative research is concerned with interpreting, analysing and understanding the complexities underlying the phenomena studied, rather than relying on numbers and statistics.

In this specific case, the qualitative research methodology presented focused on data collection and analysis methods, specifically non-participant observation, which has been gaining prominence, particularly when it comes to entering the specific world of the organisational studies context. In reality, the researcher can't always gain access to a particular field except through observation. In this sense, it was necessary to use the instrument called DK learning, already validated for analysing distance learning structures in higher education, available at: https://figshare.com/s/9dd5bf8d12f462cdb058 (Nobre, et al. 2019).

In this article, this tool was used to pedagogically analyse the structure of the Continuing Pedagogical Training Course Specialising in Digital Content for Self-Learning (e-Conteúdos), delivered through the CNQF, whose target audience is trainers. In this way, it was possible to adapt an already validated instrument to a new research context.

7. OBJECT OF INVESTIGATION, CONTEXTUALISATION OF THE PROBLEM

The *Instituto do Emprego e Formação Profissional,* IEFP is, as has already been mentioned, the national public employment service. Its mission is to promote the creation and quality of employment and combat unemployment by implementing active employment policies, namely vocational training. To this end, it has an e-learning platform to support the development of courses to be carried out within the scope of the directly managed and participated Vocational Training Centres, courses and actions developed by the National Centre for the Qualification of Trainers (CNQF), of which the Continuous Pedagogical Training of Trainers stands out for this research.

As already mentioned, the focus of this research was essentially on the Continuing Pedagogical Training course specialising in Digital Content for Self-Learning (e-Conteúdos), delivered through the CNQF.

What prompted reflection and encouraged this research was the experience and quality in distance training gained by the institute, in a short space of time, in the post-pandemic social context.

Based on its strategies and action plans, underpinned by the vision of the European Union's guiding documents and national legislation, the IEFP has highlighted trends in training people for the world of work.

Concerned with qualitative innovation, the IEFP has developed the necessary innovation with studies, internal working groups, documents and initiatives of great relevance that have introduced the institute to a constant culture of innovation in this area of training. Following on from these innovations, the IEFP, always with a view to training quality, intends to evaluate, expand and perfect the work already done. To this end, the teams have been supporting and adjusting initiatives in the area of distance learning throughout the process, both for the initial pedagogical training of trainers and for the ongoing pedagogical training of trainers.

In order to add to, encourage and provide improvements that are even more consistent with trends and studies in the area of distance learning, this research is particularly important. The aim is to deepen the quality of the strategies and formats of distance learning courses based on what has been identified in the analyses and discussions of the theoretical references and in constant dialogue with members of the IEFP itself.

7.1 Objectives

The aim of this study was to analyse the IEFP's Continuing Pedagogical Training course specialising in Digital Content for Self-Learning (e-Conteúdos) based on criteria that have already been validated for the pedagogical design of learning in an e-Learning context.

7.2 Research Design

After a thorough review and collaborative discussions between colleagues, conducted through course analysis meetings, and after obtaining the necessary authorisations and approvals from the IEFP, as well as guaranteeing the privacy and protection of personal data in strict compliance with the General Data Protection Regulation, we began to carry out the steps established in this study, which are set out in the following table:

Below we will present and discuss the results of the observation carried out by the researchers.

8. ANALYSING THE RESULTS

Analysing platforms with pedagogical intent, digital learning spaces, is constantly an element with many subjective variables, as it is greatly influenced by individual vision and beliefs. However, we believe that the construction of the grid indicated represents some variables to be considered, which may align more or less with the reality perceived by others involved in the process. This is why an instrument of objectivity in our practices should be considered an essential pillar in evaluation, seeking to achieve the desired impartiality.

Table 2. Steps taken in the development of the research (Organized by the authors)

Preparation stages	**Description of actions and aims**
Stage 1 - Bibliographical and documentary research	Survey of sources and bibliographical references using as a theoretical reference works by authors in line with the guidelines required by the topic. Specifically, the IEFP's Reference for Continuing Pedagogical Training for Specialisation in Digital Content for Self-Learning (e-Conteúdos), Portugal.
Stage 2 - Definition of actions to observe and analyse the course	Definition of the experts who analysed the course and preparation, adaptation of the DK e-learning observation grid (Nobre et al, 2019)
Stage 3 - Analysing the course using the DK e-learning grid	Discussion meetings between the researchers and IEFP management to request authorisation, access to the platform and analysis of the course in August 2023.
Stage 4 - analysing the results	Dialogue between the work team on the analysis carried out by the experts, discussion, synthesis and argumentation based on the results obtained. Construction of the results in accordance with the aim of the study.

It was also noted that the course offered was planned with specific goals and a target audience. In addition, the teams responsible for developing the course were influenced by various approaches and interpretations of how to implement e-learning, adjusting these influences according to the particular situations.

The structure of the instrument was analysed by the team's researchers and some of the questions had to be adapted to take account of the reality under investigation. There were no changes to the content, only to the type of question in relation to the content. This adaptation did not alter the structure or the validation of the instrument, thus maintaining its elements and evaluation indicators.

8.1 Researcher's Analysis (01)

The DK e-learning grid drawn up in Excel automatically calculates the stipulated values on a scale of 1 to 5, with 1 (-) and 5 (+) for each of the "points to be observed". The results of these values are then added together to form a graph, a tetrahedron that highlights the final results for each dimension. The researcher brought back the results shown in the graph below:

The outstanding result that we will analyse in greater depth is the result relating to pedagogical knowledge in the structure of the course (20 points) on a scale of 100. The rest are on average structured in the 60 to 65 point range. Pedagogical knowledge (PK), its meaning and importance, boils down to the pedagogical strategies employed by the teacher, based on learning theories, promoting access to knowledge for students. This includes recognising students' personal styles, tendencies and challenges through continuous checks, assessments and exercises. Pedagogical knowledge has a multidisciplinary and transdisciplinary nature in itself.

Figure 6. Didactic transposition
(organized by the authors)

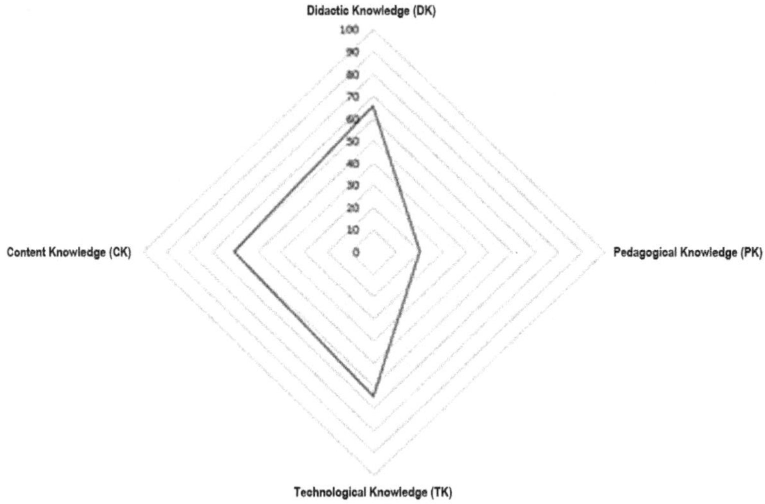

Percentage Results	
Didactic Knowledge (DK)	65.45455
Pedagogical Knowledge (PK)	20
Technological Knowledge (TK)	65
Content knowledge (CK)	60

This multidisciplinary nature implies that it is not restricted to a single discipline, but incorporates principles, theories and methodologies from various areas of knowledge, such as educational psychology, sociology of education, philosophy of education and cognitive neuroscience. Amador et al. (2016), Prado (2021), Valente (2022).

he pedagogical understanding of learning plays a fundamental role in Aretio's (2007) online courses. This perspective is built through instructions, guides, suggestions, feedback and progressive guidance to students throughout the different phases of the learning process. Interaction on the part of teachers should be a continuous, specific and indicator-based approach, ensuring that the learning process is aligned with the individual characteristics of the students Pereira et al. (2007). These phases can be facilitated through activities, exercises and tasks that fulfil these guidelines Barros, (2020).

Figure 7. Didactic transposition
(Organized by the authors)

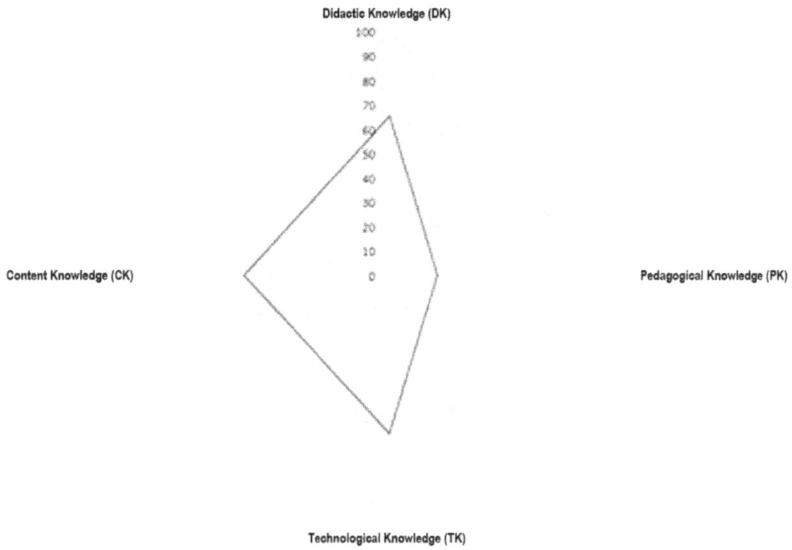

Percentage Results	
Didactic Knowledge (DK)	75
Pedagogical Knowledge (PK)	75
Technological Knowledge (TK)	75
Content Knowledge (CK)	55.55556

8.2 Researcher's Analysis (02)

The following are the results of researcher 2 filling in the DK e-learning grid.

The analysis of the Continuing Pedagogical Training course specialising in Digital Content for Self-Learning (e-Conteúdos) was based on the following indicators: Didactic Knowledge (DK), Pedagogical Knowledge (PK), Technological Knowledge (TK) and Content Knowledge (CK).

The Graph 02 and the percentage results shown show that the highest score, 75 on a scale of 0 to 100, is for Didactic Knowledge (DK) and Pedagogical Knowledge (PK) as well as Technological Knowledge (TK) Amador et al. (2016), allowing us to realise that didactic scenarios and strategies, virtual use styles and "the diversification of activities and tools in the training process take into account learning preferences and individualities" (Barros, 2020, p. 132).

Content Knowledge (CK) came in at 55.5. Although the degree of applicability of the content of this course to the context of vocational training is extremely relevant, there are aspects such as content ecology, interdisciplinarity, transdisciplinarity, communication with other content (language, origin/meta-culture, among others) that, although they are evident in some way, are not relevant to the objective of the course in question. Furthermore, the way the course is structured, i.e. the fact that it combines theory and practice as content, allows trainers to "open up emancipatory paths for the training of subjects who think about society in a coherent way" (Fortuna, 2015, p. 64).

Having presented the individual results of the two researchers, it is important to carry out a comparative analysis. According to Graph 01 and 02 we can see that the big discrepancy between the researchers' analyses lies in Pedagogical Knowledge (PK). The first analysis shows a score of 20 points, while the second gives us 75 points. This can be explained by the fact that researcher 1 is totally external to the context of the course in question and researcher 2 has already participated as a pedagogical supervisor in one of the courses and therefore has a more in-depth knowledge of how the whole teaching and learning process takes place and how the personalisation of learning is taken into account.

The results for the other indicators are similar. In this way, we can understand that in the analysis of researchers 1 and 2, the view of the course in general is > 50 points in all the indicators analysed. In some of the results = 75 points on a scale of 0 to 100. Considering the aspects that were analysed and evaluated using the DK e-learning grid.

Figure 8. Comparative didactic transposition
(Organized by the authors)

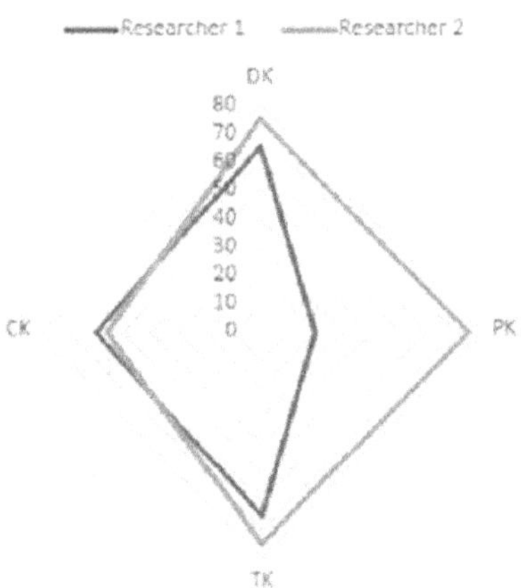

Level	Researcher 1	Researcher 2
DK	65.45454545	75
PK	20	75
TK	65	75
CK	60	55.55555556

In this way, it is understood that qualitative adjustments to the course can be made based on these indicators, thus enabling new experiences and didactic approaches according to the needs of the continuous pedagogical training of trainers.

The DK e-learning grid and the results were forwarded to the CNQF of the IEFP, IP, thus facilitating qualification, accessibility and innovation in the course indicated.

9. CONCLUSION

The research presented here on the subject of DK e-learning: optimising digital strategies for the continuous pedagogical training of trainers, has so far had few studies in Portugal.

Undoubtedly, online continuing education, especially in the context of the pedagogical training of trainers, plays a crucial role in adapting to the current needs of digital teaching and learning. This educational approach has the potential to offer a comprehensive solution to the demands of professional training in an increasingly digital and competitive world.

The main aim of this article was to interpret the results of analysing an online course specially structured for the continuous pedagogical training of trainers. Based on already validated criteria on the pedagogical design of learning in an e-learning context, the instrument used in the analysis was DK e-learning, (Nobre, et al. 2019). This analysis provided qualitative improvement indicators for the design of courses and didactic strategies used by trainers.

The instrument was applied at the *Instituto do Emprego e Formação Profissional*, IP (IEFP). The methodology used assumed a qualitative, interpretative approach and was applied in a vocational training context. As mentioned elsewhere, the dimensions of the table were: didactic knowledge; pedagogical knowledge; technological knowledge and content knowledge. The DK-eLearning table was created in Excel and automatically calculates the stipulated values on a scale of 1 to 5, with 1 being the minimum and 5 the maximum for each of the points observed. There are some items that have multiplier values because they are considered more important in the evaluation process. The results of the values totalled at the end and represented in percentages were presented in graphs, tetrahedrons that highlight the final results of each dimension.

In order to fulfil the aim of this research and use the proposed DK e-Learning-TPCK Observation Table, the "Specialisation in Digital Content for Self-Learning (e-Conteúdos)" Continuing Pedagogical Training course taught in 2022 by the IEFP was chosen.

The impact of this research has triggered important contributions to the optimisation of digital strategies in the context of vocational training, more specifically in the continuous pedagogical training of trainers, since the DK e-learning-TPCK Observation Table in this specific context has enabled indicators of innovation for learning with structuring reflections on didactic strategies that meet the needs of trainees.

The aim is to extend the application of the grid to other IEFP courses in order to contribute directly to the structuring, innovation and expansion of didactic strategies for teaching and learning among trainees. In addition, the grid provides information that directly helps trainers to build courses and content without jeopardising the Institute's mission and objectives.

REFERENCES

Amador, F., Nobre, A., & Barros, D. (2016). Towards a model of a didactic of eLearning: an application to education for sustainable development. In *Handbook of Research on Engaging Digital Natives in Higher Education Settings*. IGI GLOBAL. doi:10.4018/978-1-5225-0039-1.ch019

Anderson, T. (2005). Distance learning – Social software's killer ap? *17th Biennial Conference of the Open and Distance Learning*. Association of Australia (ODLAA).

Aramburuzabala, P., Cerrillo, R., & Tello, I. (2015). Aprendizaje-Servicio: una propuesta metodológica para la introducción de la sostenibilidad curricular en la Universidad In *Revista de curriculum y Formación del professorado*. UGR. http://www.ugr.es/local/recfpro/rev191ART5.pdf

Area, M., & Adell, J. (2021). Tecnologías digitales y cambio educativo. Una aproximación crítica. In *REICE. Revista Electrónica Iberoamericana sobre Calidad, Eficacia y Cambio en Educación, 19*(4), 83–96. doi:10.15366/reice2021.19.4.005

Aretio, L. G., Corbella, M. R., & Figaredo, D. D. (2007). *De la educación a distancia a la educación virtual*. Editorial Ariel.

Arntz, M. T. G., & Zierahn, U. (2016), The Risk Of Automation For Jobs In *Countries: A Comparative Analysis, OECD Social, Employment and Migration*. OECD Publishing, Paris.

Azevedo, J. (2014). O ensino profissional em Portugal, 1989-2014: viagem da periferia para o centro das políticas educativas. In Rodrigues, M. de L. (Org) - *40 anos de políticas de educação em Portugal*. Almedina. https://repositorio.ucp.pt/handle/10400.14/16362?mode=full

Azevedo, J., & Capucha, L. (2021). *Recomendação: Perspetivar o futuro do Ensino Profissional.* Conselho Nacional de Educação https://www.cnedu.pt/content/noticias/CNE/Recomendacao__Perspetivar_o_futuro_do_Ensino_Profissional.pdf

Barros, D. M. V. (2020). Didática e Estilos de uso do Virtual para a Educação a Distância. In Revista Diálogo Educacional, 20(64), 123-142. doi:10.7213/1981-416X.20.064.DS06

Blaschke, L. (2012). Heutagogy and lifelong learning: A review of heutagogical practice and selfdetermined learning. In *The International Review of Research in Open and Distance Learning, 13*, 56-71. https://www.researchgate.net/publication/241891015_Heutagogy_and_Lifelong_Learnin g_A_Review_of_Heutagogical_Practice_and_Self-Determined_Learning

CEDEFOP. (2021). *O sistema de educação e formação profissional em Portugal: descrição sumária.* Serviço das Publicações. https://data.europa.eu/doi/10.2801/359964

Chevallard, Y. (1985). *La Transposition didactique: Du savoir savant au savoir enseigné.* La Pensée Sauvage.

Dias, A., & Rocha, A. (2018). *Referencial de Formação Pedagógica Contínua do Formador a Distância* (e-Formador). Lisboa: IEFP Associação Universidade.

Downes, S. (2007). *e-Learning 2.0 in development.* Brandon Hall Research Innovations in Learning Conference, San Jose, California. https://www.downes.ca/presentation/149

Downes, S. (2012). *Connectivism and Connective Knowledge Essays on meaning and learning networks.* Creative Common License. https://bit.ly/3gfAQtL

Europeia, C. (2022). *Ensino e formação profissional Competências para hoje e para o futuro.* Serviço das Publicações da União Europeia., doi:10.2767/500117

Fernández, F. (2006). *As Raízes Históricas dos Modelos Actuais de Educação de Pessoas Adultas.* Disponível. https://repositorio.ul.pt/handle/10451/5762

Figueiredo, A. (2019). Compreender e desenvolver as competências digitais. In *RE@D - Revista de Educação a Distância e Elearning, 2*(1). https://revistas.rcaap.pt/lead_read/article/view/22051/16227

Flick, U. (2005). *Método qualitativos na investigação científica.* Monitor.

Fortuna, V. (2015). *A relação teoria e prática na educação em Freire.* REBES - Rev. Brasileira de Ensino Superior. doi:10.18256/2447-3944/rebes.v1n2p64-72

Garrison, D. Randy (1989). Understanding Distance Education - a framework for the future. Routledge: London and New York.

Garrison, R., & Anderson, T. (2003). eLearning in the 21st Century: A Framework for Research and Practice. London & New York: RoutledgeFalmer.

Hargreaves, D. (2006). *Personalising Learning-6. The Final Gateway: School Design and Organisation.* London: Association of School and College Leaders. https://aschofield.files.wordpress.com

Hill, M., & Hill, A. (2000). *Investigação por Questionário*. Edições Sílabo.

Hurtado Velit, A. L. (2017). Los procesos cognitivos: metacognición como proceso de aprendizaje. In Educación, (23), 19–24. doi:10.33539/educacion.2017.n23.1165

Machado, J., & Formosinho, J. (2009). Professores, escola e formação. Políticas e práticas de formação contínua. In *João Formosinho (org.) Formação de Professores. Aprendizagem profissional e acção docente* (pp. 287–302). Porto Editora.

Marconi, M., & Lakatos, E. (2012). *Técnicas de pesquisa* (7th ed.). Atlas.

OECD. (2015). *New Skills For The Digital Economy: Measuring The Demand And Supply Of Ict Skills At Work, Technical Report Prepared For The 2016 Ministerial Meeting On The Digital Economy, OECD Publishing, Paris. OECD (2015a), OECD Digital Economy Outlook 2015*. OECD Publishing. doi:10.1787/9789264239814-

OECD. (2016). New Forms Of Work. In *The Digital Economy, Technical Report Prepared For The 2016 Ministerial Meeting On The Digital Economy*. OECD Publishing.

OECD. (2018). Report On Pension Systems For The Self-Employed. In *Oecd And Eu Countries*. OECD Publishing.

Oliveira, I. (2018). Educação de Jovens e Adultos (EJA) - Século XXI: Diversas Formas de Aprender e Ensinar ao Longo da Vida (4 ed., Vol. 2). In Revista Científica Multidisciplinar Núcleo do Conhecimento.

Pereira, A., Quintas Mendes, A., Morgado, L., Amante, L., & Bidarra, J. (2007). *Modelo Pedagógico Virtual da Universidade Aberta*. Universidade Aberta.

Peters, O. (2001). *Didática do ensino a distância: experiências e estágio da discussão numa visão internacional. Tradução Ilson Kayser*. Unisinos.

Portaria n.º 214/2011 de 30 de maio. Diário da República, 1.ª série — N.º 104 — 30 de maio de 2011.

Prado, A. (2021). Conectivismo y diseño instruccional: Ecología de aprendizaje para la universidad del siglo XXI en México. *Márgenes Revista De Educación De La Universidad De Málaga*, *2*(1), 4–20. doi:10.24310/mgnmar.v2i1.9349

Rigney (1978). *Estrategias de aprendizaje: Una perspectiva teórica*. O'Neill, New York: Academia Press.

Rudestan, K. E., & Read-Schoenholtz, J. (2010). Handbook of online Learning. SAGE:Unites Estates of American.

Santos, A., Moreira, L., Valente da S., P., & Vieira, P. (2022). *Referencial de Formação Pedagógica Contínua de Formação em Conteúdos Digitais para Autoaprendizagem* (e-Conteúdos). Lisboa: IEFP – Instituto do Emprego e Formação Profissional, IP.

Siemens, G. (2004). *Conectivismo: Una teoría de aprendizaje para la era digital*. Traducción de Leal, D [Blog]. https://bit.ly/2BZUbPL

Sweller, J., van Merriënboer, J. J. G., & Paas, F. (2019). Cognitive Architecture and Instructional Design: 20 Years Later. *Educational Psychology Review*, *31*(2), 261–292. doi:10.100710648-019-09465-5

Thorndike, E. L. (1920). A constant error on psychological rating. *The Journal of Applied Psychology*, *IV*(1), 25–29. doi:10.1037/h0071663

Trilla, J. (2019). El aprendizaje servicio en la pedagogia Contemporânea. In J. M. Puig (Ed.), *Coord.): Aprendizagem Serviço: Educação e Compromisso Cívico*. Editorial Graó.

Valente, P. (2022). e-Learning e Formação Profissional: cenários e estratégias didáticas para o Ensino de Língua Inglesa (LE/L2). [Tese de Doutoramento, Universidade Aberta]. Faculdade de Ciências Sociais e Humanas-Universidade Nova de Lisboa, Portugal.

Weinert, F. E., & Kluwe, R. H. (1987). *Metacognición, motivación y comprensión*. N. J. LEA.

World Economic Forum. (2015). *The global competitiveness report 2015-2016*. Geneva: World Economic Forum. https://www3.weforum.org/docs/gcr/2015-2016/Global_Competitiveness_Report_2015- 2016.pdf

World Economic Forum. (2016). *New Vision for Education: Fostering Social and Emotional Learning*. W. E. Forum, Ed. https://www3.weforum.org/docs/WEF_New_Vision_for_Education.pdf

World Economic Forum. (2017). Promise or Peril: Decoding the Future of Work. https://www.weforum.org/agenda/2017/01/promise-or-perildecoding-the-future-of-work/

World Economic Forum. (2018). *The Future of Jobs Report*. WEF. https://www3.weforum.org/docs/WEF_Future_of_Jobs_2020.pdf

World Economic Forum. (2021). *Annual Report 2020-2021*. Geneva: World Economic Forum. https://www.weforum.org/reports/annual-report-2020- 2021/

Compilation of References

Adamopoulou, E., & Moussiades, L. (2020). An overview of chatbot technology. In I. Maglogiannis, L. Iliadis, & E. Pimenidis (Eds.), *Artificial intelligence applications and innovations. AIAI 2020. IFIP advances in information and communication technology* (Vol. 584, pp. 373–383). Springer. doi:10.1007/978-3-030-49186-4_31

Adnan, M., & Anwar, K. (2020). Online Learning amid the COVID-19 Pandemic: Students' Perspectives. *Online Submission, 2*(1), 45–51. doi:10.33902/JPSP.2020261309

Adner, R. (2012). *The Wide Lens – What Successful Innovators See That Others Miss*. Penguin.

Adner, R. (2017). Ecosystem as structure: An actionable construct for strategy. *Journal of Management, 43*(1), 39–58. doi:10.1177/0149206316678451

Agarkar, S. C. (2019). Influence of Learning Theories on Science Education. *Resonance, 24*(8), 847–859. doi:10.100712045-019-0848-7

Akcayir, M., & Akcayir, G. (2017). Advantages and challenges associated with augmented reality for education: A systematic literature review. *Educational Research Review, 20*, 1–11. doi:10.1016/j.edurev.2016.11.002

Akram, W., & Kumar, R. (2017). A Study on Positive and Negative Effects of Social Media on Society. *International Journal on Computer Science and Engineering, 5*(10), 351–354. doi:10.26438/ijcse/v5i10.351354

Alerasoul, S. A., Afeltra, G., Hakala, H., Minelli, E., & Strozzi, F. (2021). Organisational learning, learning organisation, and learning orientation: An integrative review and framework. *Human Resource Management Review, 32*(3), 100854. doi:10.1016/j.hrmr.2021.100854

Alessi, S. M., & Trollip, S. R. (2000). *Multimedia for Learning: Methods and Development* (3rd ed.). Pearson.

Allen, M. (2016). *Michael Allen's Guide to e-Learning: Building Interactive, Fun, and Effective Learning Programs for Any Company*. 389–408. . doi:10.1002/9781119176268.index

Allert, H., Dhraief, H., & Nejdl, W. (2002). *How are Learning Objects Used in Learning Processes?* Instructional Roles of Learning Objects in LOM.

Alm, A., & Nkomo, L. (2020). Chatbot Experiences of Informal Language Learners: A Sentiment Analysis. *International Journal of Computer-Assisted Language Learning and Teaching*, *10*(4), 51–65. doi:10.4018/IJCALLT.2020100104

Almaney, A. (1974). Communication and the Systems Theory of Organization. *Journal of Business Communication*, *12*(1), 35–43. doi:10.1177/002194367401200106

Almeida, P., Pedro, L., Moita, M., Magalhães, R., Santos, A., & Moreira, L. (2011). Serious Games as an onboarding organizational tool for new employees. *6th Iberian Conference on Information Systems and Technologies (CISTI 2011)*. IEEE, Chaves, Portugal. https://ieeexplore.ieee.org/abstract/document/5974334/

Alzahrani, N. (2020). Augmented Reality: A Systematic Review of Its Benefits and Challenges in E-Learning Contexts. *Applied Sciences (Basel, Switzerland)*, *10*(16), 5660. Advance online publication. doi:10.3390/app10165660

Amador, F., Nobre, A., & Barros, D. (2016). Towards a model of a didactic of eLearning: an application to education for sustainable development. In *Handbook of Research on Engaging Digital Natives in Higher Education Settings*. IGI GLOBAL. doi:10.4018/978-1-5225-0039-1.ch019

Anderson, T. (2005). Distance learning – Social software's killer ap? *17th Biennial Conference of the Open and Distance Learning*. Association of Australia (ODLAA).

Ansari, J. A., & Khan, N. A. (2020). Exploring the role of social media in collaborative learning the new domain of learning. *Smart Learning Environments*, *7*(1), 9. doi:10.118640561-020-00118-7

Anwar, M., & Greer, J. (2012). Facilitating trust in privacy-preserving E-learning environments. *IEEE Transactions on Learning Technologies*, *5*(1), 62–73. doi:10.1109/TLT.2011.23

Aramburuzabala, P., Cerrillo, R., & Tello, I. (2015). Aprendizaje-Servicio: una propuesta metodológica para la introducción de la sostenibilidad curricular en la Universidad In *Revista de curriculum y Formación del professorado*. UGR. http://www.ugr.es/local/recfpro/rev191ART5.pdf

Area, M., & Adell, J. (2021). Tecnologías digitales y cambio educativo. Una aproximación crítica. In *REICE. Revista Electrónica Iberoamericana sobre Calidad, Eficacia y Cambio en Educación*, *19*(4), 83–96. doi:10.15366/reice2021.19.4.005

Aretio, L. G., Corbella, M. R., & Figaredo, D. D. (2007). *De la educación a distancia a la educación virtual*. Editorial Ariel.

Argyris, C. (1990). *Overcoming organizational defences*. Allyn & Bacon.

Argyris, C. (1991). Teaching smart people how to learn. *Harvard Business Review*, *69*(3), 99–109.

Argyris, C., & Schon, D. (1978). *Organizational learning: A theory of action approach*. Addison-Wesley.

Arntz, M. T. G., & Zierahn, U. (2016), The Risk Of Automation For Jobs In *Countries: A Comparative Analysis, OECD Social, Employment and Migration*. OECD Publishing, Paris.

Avagyan, A., & Brightwell, S. (2020). *Learning gamification: using game design and fun to build digital transformation skills*. UN Volunteers. https://www.unv.org/Success-stories/learning-gamification-using-game-design-and-fun-build-digital-transformation-skills

Azadegan, A., Riedel, J. C. K. H., & Baalsrud Hauge, J. (2012). Serious Games Adoption in Corporate Training. *Serious Games Development and Applications*, 74–85. doi:10.1007/978-3-642-33687-4_6

Azevedo, J. (2014). O ensino profissional em Portugal, 1989-2014: viagem da periferia para o centro das políticas educativas. In Rodrigues, M. de L. (Org) - *40 anos de políticas de educação em Portugal.* Almedina. https://repositorio.ucp.pt/handle/10400.14/16362?mode=full

Azevedo, J., & Capucha, L. (2021). *Recomendação: Perspetivar o futuro do Ensino Profissional.* Conselho Nacional de Educação https://www.cnedu.pt/content/noticias/CNE/Recomendacao__Perspetivar_o_futuro_do_Ensino_Profissional.pdf

Badea, M. (2014). Social Media and Organizational Communication. *Procedia: Social and Behavioral Sciences*, *149*, 70–75. doi:10.1016/j.sbspro.2014.08.192

Bahja, M., Hammad, R., & Butt, G. (2020). A User-Centric Framework for Educational Chatbots Design and Development. In C. Stephanidis, M. Kurosu, H. Degen, & L. Reinerman-Jones (Eds.), Lecture Notes in Computer Science: Vol. 12424. *HCI International 2020 - Late Breaking Papers: Multimodality and Intelligence. HCII 2020.* Springer. doi:10.1007/978-3-030-60117-1_3

Baker, R., & Siemens, G. (2014). *Educational data mining and learning analytics.* Cambridge University Press., doi:10.1017/CBO9781139519526.016

Balaji, P., & Murthy, S. S. (2019). Web 2.0: An Evaluation of Social Media Networking Sites. *International Journal of Innovative Technology and Exploring Engineering*, *8*(10), 752–759. doi:10.35940/ijitee.J8892.0881019

Balavadze, T., & Zhgenti, T. (2018). The Bank of Georgia Learning Hub. *International Journal of Advanced Corporate Learning*, *11*(1), 5–9. doi:10.3991/ijac.v11i1.9367

Barata, G., Gama, S., Jorge, J., & Gonçalves, D. (2013, October). Improving participation and learning with gamification. In *Proceedings of the First International Conference on gameful design, research, and applications* (pp. 10-17). ACM. 10.1145/2583008.2583010

Barker, R., & Camarata, M. M. (1998). The Role of Communication in Creating and Maintaining a Learning Organization: Preconditions, Indicators, and Disciplines. *Journal of Business Communication*, *35*(4), 443–467. doi:10.1177/002194369803500402

Barros, D. M. V. (2020). Didática e Estilos de uso do Virtual para a Educação a Distância. In Revista Diálogo Educacional, 20(64), 123-142. doi:10.7213/1981-416X.20.064.DS06

Bashir, M., Hameed, A., Bari, M. W., & Ullah, R. (2021). The impact of age-diverse workforce on organization performance: Mediating role of job crafting. *SAGE Open*, *11*(1), 2158244021999058. doi:10.1177/2158244021999058

Baxter, G., & Connolly, T. (2014). Implementing Web 2.0 tools in organisations: Feasibility of a systematic approach. *The Learning Organization*, *21*(1), 6–25. doi:10.1108/TLO-11-2012-0069

Bazavan, L. C., Roibu, H., Petcu, F. B., Cismaru, S. I., & George, B. N. (2021). Virtual Reality and Augmented Reality in Education. *Proceedings of the 2021 30th Annual Conference of the European Association for Education in Electrical and Information Engineering, EAEEIE 2021.* IEEE. 10.1109/EAEEIE50507.2021.9531005

Beal, C., Beck, J., Westbrook, D., Atkin, M., & Cohen, P. (2002). Intelligent modeling of the user in interactive entertainment. *AAAI Stanford Spring Symposium*, Stanford CA. https://www.aaai.org/Papers/Symposia/Spring/2002/SS-02-01/SS02-01-002.pdf

Belinski, R., Peixe, A., Frederico, G., & Garza-Reyes, J. (2020). Organizational learning and Industry 4.0: findings from a systematic literature review and research agenda. *Benchmarking: An International Journal.* https://www.emerald.com/insight/content/doi/10.1108/BIJ-04-2020-0158/full/html?skipTracking=true

Bellegarda, J. R. (2004). Statistical language model adaptation: Review and perspectives. *Speech Communication*, *42*(1), 93–108. doi:10.1016/j.specom.2003.08.002

Bend, J. (2023). A Design for Gamified On-the-job Training. *International Journal of Advanced Corporate Learning*, *16*(3), 4–20. doi:10.3991/ijac.v16i3.37771

Bengio, Y., Ducharme, R., & Vincent, P. (2000). A neural probabilistic language model. *Advances in Neural Information Processing Systems*, *13*, 1–7.

Bennett, E. E., & McWhorter, R. R. (2021). Virtual HRD's role in crisis and the post Covid-19 professional lifeworld: Accelerating skills for digital transformation. *Advances in Developing Human Resources*, *23*(1), 5–25. doi:10.1177/1523422320973288

Benotti, L., Martnez, M. C., & Schapachnik, F. (2018). Atool for introducing computer science with automatic formative assessment. *IEEE Transactions on Learning Technologies*, *11*(2), 179–192. doi:10.1109/TLT.2017.2682084

Berger, B. (2015, June 9). *Employee / Organizational Communications.* Institute for Public Relations. https://instituteforpr.org/employee-organizational-communications/

Bernardini, S., Porayska-Pomsta, K., & Smith, T. J. (2014). ECHOES: An intelligent serious game for fostering social communication in children with autism. *Information Sciences*, *264*, 41–60. doi:10.1016/j.ins.2013.10.027

Bertot, J. C., Jaeger, P. T., Munson, S., & Glaisyer, T. (2010). Engaging the Public in Open Government: Social Media Technology and Policy for Government Transparency. *Computer*, *43*(11), 53–59. doi:10.1109/MC.2010.325

Bétrancourt, M., & Benetos, K. (2018). Why and when does instructional video facilitate learning? A commentary to the special issue "Developments and trends in learning with instructional video.". *Computers in Human Behavior*, *89*, 471–475. doi:10.1016/j.chb.2018.08.035

Betts, B. E. N. (2020). Are LXPs the Next Best Thing? *TD: Talent Development, 74*(1), 30–35. https://widgets.ebscohost.com/prod/customerspecific/ns000290/authentication/index.php?url=https%3a%2f%2fsearch.ebscohost.com%2flogin.aspx%3fdirect%3dtrue%26AuthType%3dip%2cshib%2cuid%26db%3da9h%26AN%3d140964999%26lang%3dpt-pt%26site%3deds-live%26scope%3dsite

Bhutoria, A. (2022). Personalised education and Artificial Intelligence in the United States, China, and India: A systematic review using a Human-In-The-Loop model. *Computers & Education: Artificial Intelligence, 3*, 100068. doi:10.1016/j.caeai.2022.100068

Binkis, M., Kubiliūnas, R., Sturienė, R., Dulinskienė, T., Blažauskas, T., & Jakštienė, V. (2021). Rule-Based Chatbot Integration into Software Engineering Course. In A. Lopata, D. Gudonienė, & R. Butkienė (Eds.), *Information and Software Technologies. ICIST 2021. Communications in Computer and Information Science* (Vol. 1486). Springer. doi:10.1007/978-3-030-88304-1_29

Blaschke, L. (2012). Heutagogy and lifelong learning: A review of heutagogical practice and selfdetermined learning. In *The International Review of Research in Open and Distance Learning, 13*, 56-71. https://www.researchgate.net/publication/241891015_Heutagogy_and_Lifelong_Learnin g_A_Review_of_Heutagogical_Practice_and_Self-Determined_Learning

Boddington, P. (2017). *Towards a code of ethics for artificial intelligence research.* Springer. doi:10.1007/978-3-319-60648-4

Boller, S., & Kapp, K. (2017). *Play to learn.* ATD Press.

Bonk, C. J., & Wiley, D. A. (2020). Preface: Reflections on the waves of emerging learning technologies. In Educational Technology Research and Development, 68(4). doi:10.100711423-020-09809-x

Borah, P. S., Iqbal, S., & Akhtar, S. (2022). Linking social media usage and SME's sustainable performance: The role of digital leadership and innovation capabilities. *Technology in Society, 68*, 101900. doi:10.1016/j.techsoc.2022.101900

Botezatu, A. (2012). *Cum sa iti faci strategia de social media.* Startups.ro. http://www.startups.ro/tutoriale/cum-sa-iti-facistrategia-de-social-media

Bower, M. (2017). *Design of Technology-Enhanced Learning - Integrating Research and Practice.* Emerald. . doi:10.1108/9781787141827

Boyle, E. A., Hainey, T., Connolly, T. M., Gray, G., Earp, J., Ott, M., Lim, T., Ninaus, M., Ribeiro, C., & Pereira, J. (2016). An update to the systematic literature review of empirical evidence of the impacts and outcomes of computer games and Serious Games. *Computers & Education, 94*, 178–192. doi:10.1016/j.compedu.2015.11.003

Bradley, V. M. (2021). Learning Management System (LMS) Use with Online Instruction. *International Journal of Technology in Education, 4*(1), 68–92. doi:10.46328/ijte.36

Brame, C. (2016). Effective Educational Videos: Principles and Guidelines for Maximising Student Learning from Video Content. *Cell Biology Education, 15*(4), es6–es6. doi:10.1187/cbe.16-03-0125 PMID:27789532

Breunig, K. J. (n.d.). *Limitless Learning: Assessing Social Media Use for Global Workplace Learning*. https://eric.ed.gov/?id=EJ1106943

Briciu, V., & Briciu, A. (2021). Social Media and Organizational Communication. *Advances in Logistics, Operations, and Management Science Book Series*, 2609–2624. doi:10.4018/978-1-7998-3473-1.ch180

Bughin, J. R., Kretschmer, T., & van Zeebroeck, N. (2019). Experimentation, Learning and Stress: The Role of Digital Technologies in Strategy Change (SSRN Scholarly Paper N.o 3328421). doi:10.2139/ssrn.3328421

Bughin, J., Hazan, E., Lund, S., Dahlström, P., Wiesinger, A., & Subramaniam, A. (2018). *Skill Shift: Automation and the Future of the Workforce*. McKinsey Global Institute.

Bulger, S. M., Bright, A. D., & Richards, A. (Eds.). (2020). *Building the Agile Business through Digital Transformation*. Kogan Page Publishers.

Cahn, J. (2017). *CHATBOT: Architecture, design, & development*. University of Pennsylvania School of Engineering and Applied Science Department of Computer and Information Science.

Calderón, A., & Ruiz, M. (2015). A systematic literature review on Serious Games evaluation: An application to software project management. *Computers & Education, 87*, 396–422. doi:10.1016/j.compedu.2015.07.011

CEDEFOP. (2021). *O sistema de educação e formação profissional em Portugal: descrição sumária*. Serviço das Publicações. https://data.europa.eu/doi/10.2801/359964

Chaves, A. P., & Gerosa, M. A. (2021). How should my chatbot interact? A survey on social characteristics in human–chatbot interaction design. *International Journal of Human-Computer Interaction, 37*(8), 729–758. doi:10.1080/10447318.2020.1841438

Chen, R. R., Davison, R. M., & Ou, C. X. (2020). A symbolic interactionism perspective of using social media for personal and business communication. *International Journal of Information Management, 51*, 102022. doi:10.1016/j.ijinfomgt.2019.10.007

Chen, Y.-C., Lu, Y.-L., & Lien, C.-J. (2021). Learning environments with different levels of technological engagement: A comparison of game-based, video-based, and traditional instruction on students' learning. *Interactive Learning Environments, 29*(8), 1363–1379. doi:10.1080/10494820.2019.1628781

Chevallard, Y. (1985). *La Transposition didactique: Du savoir savant au savoir enseigné*. La Pensée Sauvage.

Christensen, C. (2013). *The Innovator's Dilemma: When New Technologies Cause Great Firms to Fail*. Harvard Business Review Press.

Christensen, C. M., Horn, M. B., & Johnson, C. W. (2008). *Disrupting Class: How Disruptive Innovation Will Change the Way the World Learns*. McGraw-Hill.

Clark, R. C., & Mayer, R. E. (2016). *E-Learning and the science of instruction*. John Wiley & Sons, Inc. eBooks. doi:10.1002/9781119239086

Cline, M., & Williamson, D. (2020). Drivers of digital innovation and transformation in U.S. hospitals: A mixed methods study. *Health Care Management Review*, *45*(4), 309–316.

Crittenden, W., Biel, I. K., & Lovely, W. A. III. (2018). Embracing Digitalisation: Student Learning and New Technologies. *Journal of Marketing Education*, *41*(1), 027347531882089. doi:10.1177/0273475318820895

Daft, R. L., & Lengel, R. (1984). *Information Richness A New Approach to Managerial Behavior and Organizational Design*. Greenwich, CT JAI Press. https://www.scirp.org/(S(vtj3fa45qm1ean45vvffcz55))/reference/ReferencesPapers.aspx?ReferenceID=1199991

Daft, R. L., & Lengel, R. H. (1986). Organizational Information Requirements, Media Richness and Structural Design. *Management Science*, *32*(5), 554–571. doi:10.1287/mnsc.32.5.554

Daft, R. L., & Weick, K. E. (1984). Toward a Model of Organizations as Interpretation Systems. *Academy of Management Review*, *9*(2), 284–295. doi:10.2307/258441

Dahlander, L., & Wallin, M. (2020). Why now is the time for 'open innovation. *Harvard Business Review*. https://hbr.org/2020/06/why-now-is-the-time-for-open-innovation

de Campos, A., & Cazella, S. (2019).. . *Learning Analytics and Cognitive Computing to Support Personalised Learning Experiences*, *389-391*, 389–391. doi:10.1109/ICALT.2019.00120

DeepMind Ethics & Society. (2017). https://deepmind.com/about/ethics-and-society

Deho, O. B., Zhan, C., Li, J., Liu, J., Liu, L., & Duy Le, T. (2022). How do the existing fairness metrics and unfairness mitigation algorithms contribute to ethical learning analytics? *British Journal of Educational Technology*, *53*(4), 822–843. doi:10.1111/bjet.13217

Deloitte. (2023). 2023 Global Human Capital Trends. *Deloitte Insights*. https://www2.deloitte.com/us/en/insights/focus/human-capital-trends.html#get-connected

Derouin, R. E., Fritzsche, B. A., & Salas, E. (2005). E-learning in organizations. *Journal of Management*, *31*(6), 920–940. doi:10.1177/0149206305279815

Deshpande, K. V., Pan, S., & Foulds, J. R. (2020). Mitigating demographic Bias in AI-based resume filtering. Adjunct Publication of the *28th ACM Conference on User Modeling, Adaptation and Personalization*, (pp. 268–275). ACM. 10.1145/3386392.3399569

Dewanti, P., & Muhammad, R. (2019). Implementing Adobe Captivate in Designing E-Learning's Digital Content. *International Journal of Computer Applications*, *177*(16), 25–30. doi:10.5120/ijca2019919552

Di Battista, A., Zahidi, S., Rayner, M., Li, R., Leopold, T., Hasselaar, E., & Grayling, S. (2023, April 30). The Future of Jobs Report 2023. World Economic Forum. https://www.weforum.org/reports/the-future-of-jobs-report-2023/

Dias, A., & Rocha, A. (2018). *Referencial de Formação Pedagógica Contínua do Formador a Distância* (e-Formador). Lisboa: IEFP Associação Universidade.

Dias, J., & Santos, A. (2022). Learning Analytics Framework Applied to Training Context. In A. Reis, J. Barroso, P. Martins, A. Jimoyiannis, R. Y.-M. Huang, & R. Henriques (Eds.), *Technology and Innovation in Learning, Teaching and Education* (pp. 110–130). Springer Nature Switzerland., doi:10.1007/978-3-031-22918-3_9

Díaz, B. (2019). Gamification: when digital transformation makes work fun. In *The New Barcelona Post*. https://www.thenewbarcelonapost.com/en/gamification-when-digital-transformation-makes-work-fun/

Dickenson, M., Burgoyne, J., & Pedler, M. (2010). Virtual action learning: Practices and challenges. *Action Learning*, *7*(1), 59–72. doi:10.1080/14767330903576978

DiFranzo, D., & Gloria-Garcia, K. (2017). Filter bubbles and fake news. *Crossroads*, *23*(3), 32–35. doi:10.1145/3055153

Dirani, K., Medina-Cetina, Z., Wowk, K., Herzka, S., Bolio, R., Martinez, V., & Ubando, L. (2021). Learning organization as a framework for networks' learning and collaboration. *In The Learning Organization* (ISSN- 0969–6474). https://www.emerald.com/insight/content/doi/10.1108/TLO-05-2020-0089/full/html

Donovan, L., & Lead, P. (2012). *The use of Serious Games in the corporate sector*. A State of the Art Report. Learnovate Center. https://www.learnovatecentre.org/wpcontent/uploads/2013/06/Use_of_Serious_Games_in_the_Corporate_Sector_PRINT_FINAL.pdf

Doolani, S., Wessels, C., Kanal, V., Sevastopoulos, C., Jaiswal, A., Nambiappan, H., & Makedon, F. (2020). A Review of Extended Reality (XR) Technologies for Manufacturing Training. Technologies, 8(4). *Technologies*, *8*(4), 77. Advance online publication. doi:10.3390/technologies8040077

Dörner, K., & Edelman, D. (2015). *What 'digital' really means*. McKinsey. www.mckinsey.com/industries/technology-media-and-telecommunications/our-insights/what-digital-really-means

Downes, S. (2007). *e-Learning 2.0 in development*. Brandon Hall Research Innovations in Learning Conference, San Jose, California. https://www.downes.ca/presentation/149

Downes, S. (2012). *Connectivism and Connective Knowledge Essays on meaning and learning networks*. Creative Common License. https://bit.ly/3gfAQtL

Downes, L., & Mui, C. (2000). *Unleashing the Killer App: Digital Strategies for Market Dominance* (Revised Edition). Harvard Business Review Press.

Drucker, P. F. (1994). The Theory of the Business. *Harvard Business Review*, (Sept-Oct), 95104.

Duan, Y., Edwards, J. S., & Dwivedi, Y. K. (2019). Artificial intelligence for decision making in the era of Big Data – evolution, challenges and research agenda. *International Journal of Information Management, 48*, 63–71. doi:10.1016/j.ijinfomgt.2019.01.021

Egloffstein, M., & Ifenthaler, D. (2016). Employee Perspectives on MOOCs for Workplace Learning. *TechTrends, 61*(1), 65–70. doi:10.100711528-016-0127-3

Ekström, A. G., Niehorster, D. C., & Olsson, E. J. (2022). Self-imposed filter bubbles: Selective attention and exposure in online search. *Computers in Human Behavior Reports, 7*, 100226. doi:10.1016/j.chbr.2022.100226

Else, H. (2023). Abstracts written by ChatGPT fool scientists, 423-423. *Nature, 613*(7944), 423. doi:10.1038/d41586-023-00056-7 PMID:36635510

El-Shorbagy, S. A., Sherief, N., & Abdelmoez, W. (2020, November). Unexplored Gamification Elements in Learning Environments. In *Proceedings of the 9th International Conference on Software and Information Engineering* (pp. 102-107). ACM.10.1145/3436829.3436852

Emmerich, K., & Bockholt, M. (2016). Serious Games Evaluation: Processes, Models, and Concepts. In R. Dörner, S. Göbel, M. Kickmeier-Rust, M. Masuch, & K. Zweig (Eds.), *Entertainment Computing and Serious Games: International GI-Dagstuhl Seminar 15283*, (pp. 265–283). Springer International Publishing. 10.1007/978-3-319-46152-6_11

Encarnação, R., Reuter, J., Ferreira Dias, M., & Amorim, M. (2021, October). Gamification as a driver of motivation in the organizations: A Bibliometric Literature Review. In *Ninth International Conference on Technological Ecosystems for Enhancing Multiculturality (TEEM'21)* (pp. 167-172). ACM. 10.1145/3486011.3486440

Engberg-Pedersen, A. (2017). Technologies of Experience: Harun Farocki's Serious Games and Military Aesthetics. *Boundary 2, 44*(4), 155–178. https://read.dukeupress.edu/boundary-2/article-abstract/44/4/155/130459. doi:10.1215/01903659-4206373

European Commission. (2019). *Key competencies for lifelong learning*. Publications Office. https://data.europa.eu/doi/10.2766/569540

European Commission. (2022, October 12). *Commission kick-starts work on the European Year of Skills*. European Commission. https://ec.europa.eu/commission/presscorner/detail/en/ip_22_6086

European Union. (2019). *Ethics guidelines for trustworthy AI*. Independent High-Level Expert Group on Artificial Intelligence. European Union. https://ec.europa.eu/digital-single-market/en/news/ethics-guidelines-trustworthy-ai

Europeia, C. (2022). *Ensino e formação profissional Competências para hoje e para o futuro*. Serviço das Publicações da União Europeia., doi:10.2767/500117

Evseeva, S., Rasskazova, O., Kalchenko, O., & Evseeva, O. (2020, November). Training generations xyz in human resource management. In *Proceedings of the International Scientific Conference-Digital Transformation on Manufacturing, Infrastructure and Service* (pp. 1-6).

Ewing, L.-A., & Cooper, H. B. (2021). Technology-enabled remote learning during Covid-19: Perspectives of Australian teachers, students and parents. *Technology, Pedagogy and Education, 30*(1), 41–57. doi:10.1080/1475939X.2020.1868562

Ewing, M., Men, L. R., & O'Neil, J. (2019). Using Social Media to Engage Employees: Insights from Internal Communication Managers. *International Journal of Strategic Communication, 13*(2), 110–132. doi:10.1080/1553118X.2019.1575830

Extremera, J., Vergara, D., Rodriguez, S., & Davila, L. P. (2022). Reality-Virtuality Technologies in the Field of Materials Science and Engineering. *APPLIED SCIENCES-BASEL, 12*(10), 4968. doi:10.3390/app12104968

Fadel, C., Trilling, B., & Bialik, M. (2015). *Four-Dimensional Education: The Competencies Learners Need to Succeed.* Center for Curriculum Redesign.

Ferguson, R., Brasher, A., Clow, D., Cooper, A., Hillaire, G., Mittelmeier, J., Rienties, B., Ullmann, T., & Vuorikari, R. (2016). *Research evidence on the use of learning analytics: Implications for education policy.* ORO. http://oro.open.ac.uk/48173/

Fernández, F. (2006). *As Raízes Históricas dos Modelos Actuais de Educação de Pessoas Adultas.* Disponível. https://repositorio.ul.pt/handle/10451/5762

Fernandez-Vidal, J., Gonzalez, R., Gascó, J. L., & Llopis, J. (2022). Digitalization and corporate transformation: The case of European oil & gas firms. *Technological Forecasting and Social Change, 174*, 121293. doi:10.1016/j.techfore.2021.121293

Fernoagă, V., Stelea, G. A., Gavrilă, C., & Sandu, F. (2018). Intelligent Education Assistant Powered by Chatbots. *eLearning & Software for Education, 2.*

Figueiredo, A. (2019). Compreender e desenvolver as competências digitais. In *RE@D - Revista de Educação a Distância e Elearning, 2*(1). https://revistas.rcaap.pt/lead_read/article/view/22051/16227

Fiorella, L., & Mayer, R. E. (2018). What works and doesn't work with instructional video. *Computers in Human Behavior, 89*, 465470. doi:10.1016/j.chb.2018.07.015

Fissel, J. (2023). Taming the AI Beast: How Artificial Intelligence Can Optimize L&D. *Employee Learning & Development Excellence, 10*(7), 38–42.

Flick, U. (2005). *Método qualitativos na investigação científica.* Monitor.

Floridi, L. (2019). Translating principles into practices of digital Ethics: Five risks of being unethical. *Philosophy & Technology, 32*(2), 185–193. doi:10.100713347-019-00354-x

Følstad, A., & Kvale, K. (2018). Customer journeys: A systematic literature review. *Journal of Service Theory and Practice, 28*(2), 196–227. doi:10.1108/JSTP-11-2014-0261

Forbes. (2021). Digital Transformation Trends 2021: CEOs Prioritize Customers, But Speed Is Key. *Forbes.*

Fortuna, V. (2015). *A relação teoria e prática na educação em Freire*. REBES - Rev. Brasileira de Ensino Superior. doi:10.18256/2447-3944/rebes.v1n2p64-72

Fredberg, T., & Pregmark, J. E. (2018). Organization renewal through corporate entrepreneurship: When the seed changes the soil [Emerald, Bingley, UK.]. *Research in Organizational Change and Development*, *26*. doi:10.1108/S0897-301620180000026003

Fulk, J., Schmitz, J., & Steinfield, C. (1990). A Social Influence Model of Technology use. *Organizations and Communication Technology*, 117–140. doi:10.4135/9781483325385.n6

Fulk, J., Steinfield, C. W., Schmitz, J., & Power, J. G. (1987). A Social Information Processing Model of Media Use in Organizations. *Communication Research*, *14*(5), 529–552. doi:10.1177/009365087014005005

Fung, D. (2014). *Connected Curriculum: Transforming education at University College London.* UCL Academic Committee paper. UCL. https://www.ucl.ac.uk/teaching-learning/connected-curriculum/resources.

Galer, I. (2021). E-Learning in Education: Analysis of Advantages and Disadvantages. *Comparative Professional Pedagogy*, *11*, 41–44.

Garavan, T. N. (2020). The Current State of Research on Training Effectiveness. In *Learning and Development Effectiveness in Organisations*. Palgrave Macmillan. doi:10.1007/978-3-030-48900-7_5

Garrison, D. Randy (1989). Understanding Distance Education - a framework for the future. Routledge: London and New York.

Garrison, R., & Anderson, T. (2003). eLearning in the 21st Century: A Framework for Research and Practice. London & New York: RoutledgeFalmer.

Gartner. (2023). *Managers are cracking - and more training won't help*. Gartner. https://www.gartner.com/en/human-resources/trends/managers-are-cracking-and-more-training-wont-help

Gašević, D., Siemens, G., & Sadiq, S. (2023). Empowering learners for the age of artificial intelligence. *Computers and Education: Artificial Intelligence*, *4*, 100130.

Gates, B. (2023). The Age of AI has begun. *GatesNotes*. <gatesnotes.com/The-Age-of-AI-Has-Begun>

Gearhart, D. (2012). Lack of Ethics for eLearning: Two sides of the ethical coin. *International Journal of Technoethics*, *3*(4), 33–40. doi:10.4018/jte.2012100103

Gee, J. P. (2018). Affinity spaces: How young people live and learn on line and out of school. *Phi Delta Kappan*, *99*(6), 8–13. doi:10.1177/0031721718762416

Gibson, J. W., & Hodgetts, R. M. (1991). *Organizational Communication – A Managerial Perspective* (2nd ed.). HarperCollins Publishers.

Gillespie, N., Lockey, S., Curtis, C., Pool, J., & Akbari, A. (2023). *Trust in Artificial Intelligence: A Global Study*. The University of Queensland and KPMG Australia. doi:10.14264/00d3c94

Gonda, D. E., & Chu, B. (2019, December). Chatbot as a learning resource? Creating conversational bots as a supplement for teaching assistant training course. In *2019 IEEE International Conference on Engineering, Technology and education (TALE)* (pp. 1-5). IEEE. 10.1109/TALE48000.2019.9225974

Gourville, J. T. (2004). Why Consumers Don't Buy: The Psychology of New Product Adoption. *Harvard Business School Background Note 504-056.*

Graesser, A. C., VanLehn, K., Rosé, C. P., Jordan, P. W., & Harter, D. (2001). Intelligent tutoring systems with conversational dialogue. *AI Magazine*, *22*(4), 39.

Graham, J. (2018). *Meet the robots teaching Singapore's kids tech.* aPolitical. https://apolitical.co/solution_article/meet-the-robots-teaching-singapores-kids-tech/

Gray, J., & Laidlaw, H. (2004). Improving the Measurement of Communication Satisfaction. *Management Communication Quarterly*, *17*(3), 425–448. doi:10.1177/0893318903257980

Greitzer, F. L., Kuchar, O. A., & Huston, K. (2007). Cognitive science implications for enhancing training effectiveness in a serious gaming context. *ACM Journal on Educational Resources in Computing, 7*(3), 2 - es. doi:10.1145/1281320.1281322

Greller, W., & Drachsler, H. (2012). Translating Learning into Numbers: A Generic Framework for Learning Analytics. *Journal of Educational Technology & Society*, *15*(3), 42–57.

Groff, J. (2017). *Personalised learning: the state of the field & future directions.* Center for Curriculum Redesign.

Guan, C., Wang, X., Zhang, Q., Chen, R., & He, D. Xie, & X., M. (2019). Towards a deep and unified understanding of deep neural models in NLP. In *International conference on Machine Learning* (pp. 2454–2463). http://proceedings.mlr.press/v97/guan19a/guan19a.pdf.

Hai, T. N., Van, Q. N., & Thi Tuyet, M. N. (2021). Digital transformation: Opportunities and challenges for leaders in the emerging countries in response to COVID-19 pandemic. *Emerging Science Journal*, *5*(1), 21–36. doi:10.28991/esj-2021-SPER-03

Hamdan, M., Jaidin, J., Fithriyah, M., & Anshari, M. (2020). E-Learning in Time of Covid-19 Pandemic. *Challenges & Experiences*, *12-16*, 12–16. doi:10.1109/econf51404.2020.9385507

Hansen, J. Ø., Jensen, A., & Nguyen, N. (2020). The responsible learning organization: Can Senge (1990) teach organizations how to become responsible innovators? *The Learning Organization*, *27*(1), 65–74. doi:10.1108/TLO-11-2019-0164

Hargreaves, D. (2006). *Personalising Learning-6. The Final Gateway: School Design and Organisation.* London: Association of School and College Leaders. https://aschofield.files.wordpress.com

Hasal, M., Nowaková, J., Ahmed Saghair, K., Abdulla, H., Snášel, V., & Ogiela, L. (2021). Chatbots: Security, privacy, data protection, and social aspects. *Concurrency and Computation*, *33*(19), e6426. doi:10.1002/cpe.6426

Hays, R. T. (2005). *The effectiveness of instructional games: A literature review and discussion.* MIL. https://apps.dtic.mil/sti/citations/ADA441935

Helbig, C., Hofhues, S., Egloffstein, M., & Ifenthaler, D. (2021). Digital transformation in learning organisations. Springer eBooks. doi:10.1007/978-3-030-55878-9_14

Herath, D. & Jayarathne, L. (2018). Intelligent Recommendations for e-Learning Personalisation Based on Learner's Learning Activities and Performances. *International Journal of Computer Science and Software Engineering, 7.*

Hernández-de-Menéndez, M., Morales-Menendez, R., Escobar, C. A., & Ramírez Mendoza, R. A. (2022). Learning analytics: State of the art. [IJIDeM]. *International Journal on Interactive Design and Manufacturing*, *16*(3), 1209–1230. doi:10.100712008-022-00930-0

Hess, T., Matt, C., Benlian, A. & WiesböCk, F. (2016). Options for formulating a digital transformation strategy. *MIS Quarterly Exclusive, 15*(2).

Hickson, M. III. (1973). The open systems model: Auditing the effectiveness of organizational communication. *Journal of Business Communication, 10*(3), 7–14.

Hill, M., & Hill, A. (2000). *Investigação por Questionário*. Edições Sílabo.

Hillman, T., & Säljö, R. (2016). Learning, knowing and opportunities for participation: Technologies and communicative practices. *Learning, Media and Technology*, *41*(2), 306–309. doi:10.1080/17439884.2016.1167080

Hoe, S. L. (2019). *Digitalization in practice: the fifth discipline advantage*. The Learning Organization. https://www.emerald.com/insight/content/doi/10.1108/TLO-09-2019-0137/full/html http://pqm-online.com/assets/files/lib/books/senge.pdf https://www.scirp.org/(S(czeh2tfqw2orz553k1w0r45))/reference/referencespapers.aspx?referenceid=2993386

Holden, G. (2021). *The Enterprise Project What is digital transformation?* Enterprise Project. https://enterprisersproject.com/what-is-digital-transformation

Holmes, W., Bialik, M., & Fadel, C. (2019). *Artificial Intelligence in Education: Promises and implications for teaching and learning*. Center for Curriculum Redesign.

Holmes, W., Bialik, M., & Fadel, C. (2023). Artificial intelligence in education. In *Data ethics: building trust: how digital technologies can serve humanity* (pp. 621–653). Globethics Publications. doi:10.58863/20.500.12424/4276068

Holstein, K., McLaren, B. M., & Aleven, V. (2019). Designing for complementarity: Teacher and student needs for orchestration support in AI-enhanced classrooms. In S. Isotani, E. Millán, A. Ogan, P. Hastings, B. McLaren, & R. Luckin (Eds.), *Artificial Intelligence in Education* (Vol. 11625, pp. 157–171). Springer International Publishing AG. doi:10.1007/978-3-030-23204-7_14

Hosseini, C., Humlung, O., Fagerstrøm, A., & Haddara, M. (2022). An experimental study on the effects of gamification on task performance. *Procedia Computer Science*, *196*, 999–1006. doi:10.1016/j.procs.2021.12.102

House of Lords. (2018). *Ai in the UK: Ready, Willing and Able*. House of Lords. https://publications.parliament.uk/pa/ld201719/ldselect/ldai/100/100.pdf

Huang, R., Shang, K. C., & Yu, P. P. (2019). Opportunities and Challenges in Digital Transformation of Learning Environments. *Journal of Educational Technology & Society*, *22*(1), 37–51.

Hurtado Velit, A. L. (2017). Los procesos cognitivos: metacognición como proceso de aprendizaje. In Educación, (23), 19–24. doi:10.33539/educacion.2017.n23.1165

Huynh-Kim-Bang, B., Wisdom, J., & Labat, J.-M. (2010). Design patterns in Serious Games: A blue print for combining fun and learning. *Project SE-SG,* 1–18. https://seriousgames.lip6.fr/DesignPatterns/designPatternsForSeriousGames.pdf

Hylmö, A., & Buzzanell, P. (2002). Telecommuting as viewed through cultural lenses: An empirical investigation of the discourses of utopia, identity, and mystery. *Communication Monographs*, *69*(4), 329–356. doi:10.1080/03637750216547

Ifenthaler, D. (2018). *How We Learn at the Digital Workplace*. . doi:10.1007/978-3-319-46215-8_1

Ifenthaler, Dirk & Hofhues, Sandra & Egloffstein, Marc & Helbig, Christian. (2020). *Digital Transformation of Learning Organizations*. . doi:10.1007/978-3-030-55878-9

Ifenthaler, D., & Yau, J. Y.-K. (2020). Utilising learning analytics to support study success in higher education: A systematic review. *Educational Technology Research and Development*, *68*(4), 1961–1990. doi:10.100711423-020-09788-z

Iivari, N., Sharma, S., & Ventä-Olkkonen, L. (2020). Digital transformation of everyday life – how COVID-19 pandemic transformed the basic education of the young generation and why information management research should care. *International Journal of Information Management*, *55*, 102183. doi:10.1016/j.ijinfomgt.2020.102183 PMID:32836640

Jahnke, I. (2022). Quality of digital learning experiences – effective, efficient, and appealing designs? *The International Journal of Information and Learning Technology.*, *40*(1), 17–30. doi:10.1108/IJILT-05-2022-0105

Jain, R., & Singh, A. (2020). Technological Approaches for E-Content Development and Deployment: A Qualitative Analysis From Experts' Perspective. *International Journal of Information and Communication Technology Education*, *16*(3), 92–112. doi:10.4018/IJICTE.2020070107

Jedynak, M., Czakon, W., Kuźniarska, A., & Mania, K. (2021). Digital transformation of organizations: What do we know and where to go next? *Journal of Organizational Change Management*, *34*(3), 629–652. doi:10.1108/JOCM-10-2020-0336

Jobin, A., Ienca, M., & Vayena, E. (2019). Artificial intelligence: The global landscape of ethics guidelines. *Nature Machine Intelligence*, *1*(9), 389–399. doi:10.103842256-019-0088-2

Jogan, S.N. (2020). *A Review on Developing Instructional Design Models For Effective Learning*.

Johnson, D. W., & Johnson, R. T. (2009). An Educational Psychology Success Story: Social Interdependence Theory and Cooperative Learning. *Educational Researcher*, *38*(5), 365–379. doi:10.3102/0013189X09339057

Jones, M. D., Hutcheson, S., & Camba, J. D. (2021). Past, present, and future barriers to digital transformation in manufacturing: A review. *Journal of Manufacturing Systems*, *60*, 936–948. doi:10.1016/j.jmsy.2021.03.006

Joshi, N. (2023, August 18). *How Web 3.0 will transform social Media*. Linkedin. https://www.linkedin.com/pulse/how-web-30-transform-social-media-naveen-joshi/

Kabanov, A., Nevraeva, N., Pyrkova, T., Savelyeva, N., Oleynik, I., & Gurskaya, T. V. (2022). *Digital translation tools in the process of teaching foreign languages. SHS Web of Conferences, 141*, 03007. 10.1051hsconf/202214103007

Kalyuga, S., & Dörney, Z. (2021). Digital Transformation in Higher Education: Challenges and Opportunities for Implementation of AI and Data-Driven Analytics. *Computers in Human Behavior*, *118*, 106663.

Kaplan, A. M., & Haenlein, M. (2010). Users of the world, unite! The challenges and opportunities of Social Media. *Business Horizons*, *53*(1), 59–68. doi:10.1016/j.bushor.2009.09.003

Kapp, K. (2012). *The gamification of learning and instruction: Game-based methods and strategies for training and education*. Pfeiffer.

Kapp, K. M. (2013). *The gamification of learning and instruction Fieldbook: Ideas into practice*. John Wiley&Sons. https://books.google.com/books?hl=pt-BR&lr=&id=cdtnAQAAQBAJ&oi=fnd&pg=PR25&dq=%22The+gamification+of+learning+and+ins

Kar, A. K. (2016). Bio inspired computing–a review of algorithms and scope of applications. *Expert Systems with Applications*, *59*, 20–32. doi:10.1016/j.eswa.2016.04.018

Kara, N. (2021). A Systematic Review of the Use of Serious Games in Science Education. *Contemporary Educational Technology*, *13*(2), ep295. https://www.cedtech.net/article/a-systematic-review-of-the-use-of-serious-games-in-science-education-9608. doi:10.30935/cedtech/9608

Kaufman, I., & Horton, C. (2015). Digital transformation: Leveraging digital technology with core values to achieve sustainable business goals. *The European Financial Review*, (December–January), 63–66.

Kew, S. N., & Tasir, Z. (2021). Analysing students' cognitive engagement in e-learning discussion forums through content analysis. *Knowledge Management and E-Learning, 13*(1), 39–57. *Scopus*. doi:10.34105/j.kmel.2021.13.003

Khang, H., Ki, E. J., & Ye, L. (2012). Social Media Research in Advertising, Communication, Marketing, and Public Relations, 1997–2010. *Journalism & Mass Communication Quarterly*, *89*(2), 279–298. doi:10.1177/1077699012439853

Kim, S. (2021). How a company's gamification strategy influences corporate learning: A study based on gamified MSLP (Mobile social learning platform). *Telematics and Informatics*, *57*, 101505. doi:10.1016/j.tele.2020.101505

Kirkpatrick, J. D., & Kirkpatrick, W. K. (2016). *Kirkpatrick's four levels of training evaluation*. Association for Talent Development. https://www.google.com/books?hl=pt-BR&lr=&id=mo--DAAAQBAJ&oi=fnd&pg=PT10&dq=kirkpatrick+2016&ots=LNG9XSkiQw&sig=p2r8Cc-W6dneqD7pTJHyyGSPs-Y

Kirkpatrick, D. L. (1987). Evaluation of training. In R. L. Craig (Ed.), *Training and development handbook: A guide to human resource development* (pp. 301–319). McGraw-Hill.

Kitchenham, B. (2004). Procedures for performing systematic reviews. Keele, UK, Keele University.

Kitchens, B., Johnson, S. L., & Gray, P. B. (2020). Understanding echo chambers and filter bubbles: The impact of social media on diversification and partisan shifts in news consumption. *Management Information Systems Quarterly*, *44*(4), 1619–1649. doi:10.25300/MISQ/2020/16371

Kleimola, R., & Leppisaari, I. (2022). Learning analytics to develop future competences in higher education: A case study. *International Journal of Educational Technology in Higher Education*, *19*(1), 17. doi:10.118641239-022-00318-w

Kobsa, A. (2007). Privacy-enhanced web personalization. In P. Brusilovsky, A. Kobsa, & W. Nejdl (Eds.), *The Adaptive Web: Methods and Strategies of Web Personalization* (Vol. 4321, pp. 136–154). Springer. doi:10.1007/978-3-540-72079-9_4

Koedinger, K. R., Corbett, A. T., & Perfetti, C. A. (2012). The Knowledge-Learning-Instruction Framework: Bridging the Science-Practice chasm to enhance robust student learning. *Cognitive Science*, *36*(5), 757–798. doi:10.1111/j.1551-6709.2012.01245.x PMID:22486653

Kohli, R., & Melville, N. P. (2019). Digital Transformation and Information Systems Research: A Productivity Perspective. *Management Information Systems Quarterly*, *43*(1), 1–21.

Koivisto, J., & Hamari, J. (2019). The rise of motivational information systems: A review of gamification research. *International Journal of Information Management*, *45*, 191–210. doi:10.1016/j.ijinfomgt.2018.10.013

Kolb, D. A. (1984). *Experiential learning: Experience as the source of learning and development* (Vol. 1). Prentice-Hall.

Kolhar, M., Kazi, R. N., & Alameen, A. (2021). Effect of social media use on learning, social interactions, and sleep duration among university students. *Saudi Journal of Biological Sciences*, *28*(4), 2216–2222. doi:10.1016/j.sjbs.2021.01.010 PMID:33911938

Köse, E., Taşlıbeyaz, E., & Karaman, S. (2021). Classification of instructional videos. *Technology, Knowledge, and Learning*, *26*(4), 1079–1109. doi:10.100710758-021-09530-5

Kossen, C., & Chia-Yi, O. (2021). Trialling micro-learning design to increase engagement in online courses. *AAOU Journal*, *16*(3), 299–310. doi:10.1108/AAOUJ-09-2021-0107

Kreps, G. L. (1985). Organizational communication and organizational effectiveness. *World Communication*, *14*(2), 109–119.

Kretschmer, T., & Khashabi, P. (2020). Digital transformation and organization design: An integrated approach. *California Management Review*, *62*(4), 86–104. doi:10.1177/0008125620940296

Kronblad, C., & Pregmark, J. E. (2019). Beyond digital inventions – diffusion of technology and organizational capabilities to change. In M. Corrales, M. Fenwick, & H. Haapio (Eds.), *Legal Tech* (pp. 123–146). Smart Contracts and Blockchain.

Kronblad, C., & Pregmark, J. E. (2021). *How Covid-19 Has Changed the Digital Trajectory for Professional Advisory Firms, COVID-19 and the Future of the Service Industry Post-Pandemic: Insights and Resources*. Springer.

Kudyba, S. (2020). COVID-19 and the acceleration of digital transformation and the future of work. *Information Systems Management*, *37*(4), 284–287. doi:10.1080/10580530.2020.1818903

Kuhail, M. A., Alturki, N., Alramlawi, S., & Alhejori, K. (2023). Interacting with educational chatbots: A systematic review. *Education and Information Technologies*, *28*(1), 973–1018. doi:10.100710639-022-11177-3

Kulgemeyer, C. (2018). Towards a framework for effective instructional explanations in science teaching. *Studies in Science Education*, *54*(2), 109–139. doi:10.1080/03057267.2018.1598054

Kulkarni, P. M., Appasaba, L. V., Gokhale, P., & Tigadi, B. (2022). Role of digital simulation in employee training. *Global Transitions Proceedings*, *3*(1), 149–156. doi:10.1016/j.gltp.2022.04.014

Kumar Basak, S., Wotto, M., & Belanger, P. (2018). E-learning, M-learning and D-learning: Conceptual definition and comparative analysis. *E-Learning and Digital Media*, *15*(4), 191–216. doi:10.1177/2042753018785180

Kumar, J. A. (2021). Educational chatbots for project-based learning: Investigating learning outcomes for a team-based design course. *International Journal of Educational Technology in Higher Education*, *18*(1), 65. doi:10.118641239-021-00302-w PMID:34926790

Kushwaha, A. K., & Kar, A. K. (2021). MarkBot – A Language Model-Driven Chatbot for Interactive Marketing in Post-Modern World. *Information Systems Frontiers*. doi:10.100710796-021-10184-y

Kutzner, K., Schoormann, T., & Knackstedt, R. (2018). *Digital Transformation in Information Systems Research: A Taxonomy-Based Approach to Structure the field.*

Lacity, M., Khan, S. U., & Yan, A. (2020). The Digital Transformation of Business Process Services. *MIS Quarterly Executive, 19*(3).

Langer, E. (2014). What's Trending? Social Media and its Effects on Organizational Communication. *UW-L Journal of Undergraduate Research XVII (2014).* https://www.uwlax.edu/globalassets/offices-services/urc/jur-online/pdf/2014/langer.emily.cst.pdf

Larson, K. (2020). Serious Games and Gamification in the Corporate Training Environment: A Literature Review. *TechTrends, 64*(2), 319–328. doi:10.100711528-019-00446-7

Laurillard, D. (2002). *Rethinking university teaching: a conversational framework for the effective use of learning technologies* (2nd ed.). Routledge Falmer. doi:10.4324/9780203160329

Laurillard, D. (2012). *Teaching as a design science: building pedagogical patterns for learning and technology*. Routledge.

Lave, J., & Wenger, E. (1991). *Situated Learning: Legitimate Peripheral Participation.* Cambridge University Press. doi:10.1017/CBO9780511815355

Law, E. H., & Soh, P. C. (2019). Challenges and Opportunities of Digital Transformation: A Service Ecosystems Perspective. *Journal of the Association for Information Systems, 20*(1), 4.

LeCun, Y., Bengio, Y., & Hinton, G. (2015). Deep learning. *Nature, 521*(7553), 436–444. doi:10.1038/nature14539 PMID:26017442

Leelawong, K., & Biswas, G. (2008). Designing learning by teaching agents: The Betty's Brain system. *International Journal of Artificial Intelligence in Education, 18*(3), 181–208.

Lee, S. H., & Lee, S. Y. (2020). Social Media Use and Job Performance in the Workplace: The Effects of Facebook and KakaoTalk Use on Job Performance in South Korea. *Sustainability (Basel), 12*(10), 4052. doi:10.3390u12104052

Lee, Y., & Li, J. C. (2021). The role of communication transparency and organizational trust in publics' perceptions, attitudes and social distancing behaviour: A case study of the COVID-19 outbreak. *Journal of Contingencies and Crisis Management, 29*(4), 368–384. doi:10.1111/1468-5973.12354

Legaki, N. Z., Xi, N., Hamari, J., Karpouzis, K., & Assimakopoulos, V. (2020). The effect of challenge-based gamification on learning: An experiment in the context of statistics education. *International Journal of Human-Computer Studies, 144*, 102496. doi:10.1016/j.ijhcs.2020.102496 PMID:32565668

Lengel, R. H., & Daft, R. L. (1984). *An Exploratory Analysis of the Relationship between Media Richness and Managerial Information Processing. An Exploratory Analysis of the Relationship between Media Richness and Managerial Information Processing*. Research Gate. https://www.researchgate.net/publication/235157580_An_Exploratory_Analysis_of_the_Relationship_between_Media_Richness_and_Managerial_Information_Processing

Leonardi, P. M. (2020). COVID-19 and the new technologies of organizing: Digital exhaust, digital footprints, and artificial intelligence in the wake of remote work. *Journal of Management Studies*, *58*(1), 249–253. doi:10.1111/joms.12648

Leonardi, P. M., Huysman, M., & Steinfield, C. (2013). Enterprise Social Media: Definition, History, and Prospects for the Study of Social Technologies in Organizations. *Journal of Computer-Mediated Communication*, *19*(1), 1–19. doi:10.1111/jcc4.12029

Leso, B. H., Cortimiglia, M. N., & Ghezzi, A. (2022). The contribution of organisational culture, structure, and leadership factors in the digital transformation of SMEs: A mixed-methods approach. *Cognition Technology and Work*, *25*(1), 151–179. doi:10.100710111-022-00714-2 PMID:36118918

Li, C. H. J., Liang, V., Chow, Y. T. H., Ng, H.-Y., & Li, S.-P. (2022). A Mixed Reality-Based Platform towards Human-Cyber-Physical Systems with IoT Wearable Device for Occupational Safety and Health Training. *Applied Sciences (Basel, Switzerland)*, *12*(23), 23. doi:10.3390/app122312009

LinkIt. (2010). https://www.linkit.com/

Lockyer, L., & Bennett, S. Agostinho, S. & Harper, B. (2008). Handbook of research on learning design and learning objects: Issues, applications and technologies. IGI Global.

Lodge, J. M., Horvath, J. C., & Corrin, L. (2018). *Learning Analytics in the Classroom: Translating Learning Analytics Research for Teachers*. Routledge. doi:10.4324/9781351113038

Lokman, A. S., & Ameedeen, M. A. (2018). Modern chatbot systems: A technical review. *Proceedings of the Future Technologies Conference*. Springer, Cham. 10.1007/978-3-030-02683-7_75

Lopes, R., & Bidarra, R. (2011). Adaptivity Challenges in Games and Simulations: A Survey. *IEEE Transactions on Computational Intelligence and AI in Games*, *3*(2), 85–99. doi:10.1109/TCIAIG.2011.2152841

Luckin, R., Cukurova, M., Baines, E., Holmes, W., & Mann, M. (2017). *Solved! Making the case for collaborative problem- solving*, London, Nesta. https://www.nesta.org.uk/report/solved-making-the-case-for-collaborative-problem-solving/

Luo, B., Lau, R. Y., Li, C., & Si, Y. W. (2022). A critical review of state-of-the-art chatbot designs and applications. *Wiley Interdisciplinary Reviews. Data Mining and Knowledge Discovery*, *12*(1), e1434. doi:10.1002/widm.1434

Macfadyen, L. P. (2022). Institutional Analytics. Em C. Lang, G. Siemens, & A. F. Wise (Eds.), The Handbook of Learning Analytics (2.a ed., pp. 173–186). SOLAR. doi:10.18608/hla22.017

Machado, J., & Formosinho, J. (2009). Professores, escola e formação. Políticas e práticas de formação contínua. In *João Formosinho (org.) Formação de Professores. Aprendizagem profissional e acção docente* (pp. 287–302). Porto Editora.

Mackenstein, L., & Santosa, K. (2019). *Exploring how Digital Transformation affects Job Design : A Multiple-Case Study based on the Job Characteristics Model* (Dissertation). Retrieved from https://urn.kb.se/resolve?urn=urn:nbn:se:hj:diva-43897

Mafra, M., Nunes, K., Castro, A., Lopes, A., Oran, A. C., Braz, G. Junior, ... Rivero, L. (2022). Defining Requirements for the Development of Useful and Usable Chatbots: An Analysis of Quality Attributes from Academy and Industry. In *International Conference on Human-Computer Interaction* (pp. 479-493). Springer, Cham. 10.1007/978-3-031-05412-9_33

Majumdar, S. & Training, E. (2003). *Pedagogical framework for online learning*. IIEP. http://lst-iiep.iiep-unesco.org/cgi-bin/wwwi32.exe/[in=epidoc1.in]/?t2000=018954/(100)

Malafouris, L. (2013). *How Things Shape the Mind A Theory of Material Engagement* (1st ed.). The MIT Press Cambridge. doi:10.7551/mitpress/9476.001.0001

Malamed, C. (2011). *Visual language for designers: Principles for Creating Graphics that People Understand*. Rockport Pub.

Mandal, A., & Pal, S. (2015). Identifying the Reasons for Software Project Failure and Some of their Proposed Remedial through BRIDGE Process Models. *International Journal on Computer Science and Engineering*, *3*, 118–126.

Marconi, M., & Lakatos, E. (2012). *Técnicas de pesquisa* (7th ed.). Atlas.

Marr, B. (2021). *The Important Difference Between Augmented Reality And Mixed Reality*. Bernard Marr. https://bernardmarr.com/the-important-difference-between-augmented-reality-and-mixed-reality/

Marsick, V. J., & Watkins, K. E. (1999). *Facilitating learning organizations: Making learning count*. Gower Publishing, Ltd.

Martin, F., Chen, Y., Moore, R. L., & Westine, C. D. (2020). Systematic review of adaptive learning research designs, context, strategies, and technologies from 2009 to 2018. *Educational Technology Research and Development*, *68*(4), 1903–1929. doi:10.100711423-020-09793-2 PMID:32837122

Mathieu, J. E., Hollenbeck, J. R., van Knippenberg, D., & Ilgen, D. R. (2017). A century of work teams in the Journal of Applied Psychology. *The Journal of Applied Psychology*, *102*(3), 452–467. doi:10.1037/apl0000128 PMID:28150984

Mayer, R. (2022). Instructional media and instructional methods in digital language learning: Are we asking the right questions? *Bilingualism: Language and Cognition*, *25*(3), 396–397. doi:10.1017/S1366728921000559

Mayer, R. E. (2009). *Multimedia learning*. Cambridge University Press., doi:10.1017/CBO9780511811678

McCarthy, A. M., Maor, D., McConney, A., & Cavanaugh, C. (2023). Digital transformation in education: Critical components for leaders of system change. *Social Sciences & Humanities Open*, *8*(1), 100479. doi:10.1016/j.ssaho.2023.100479

McKinsey & Company. (2020). *Digital Transformation: Improving the Odds of Success*. McKinsey & Company.

Mead, G. H. (1934). *Mind, Self, and Society from the Standpoint of a Social Behaviorist*. University of Chicago Press.

Melchers, K. G., & Basch, J. M. (2022). Fair play? Sex-, age-, and job-related correlates of performance in a computer-based simulation game. *International Journal of Selection and Assessment*, *30*(1), 48–61. doi:10.1111/ijsa.12337

Melis, G., Dyer, C., & Blunsom, P. (2017). *On the state of the art of evaluation in neural language models*. arXiv preprint, arXiv:1707.05589.

Merrill, M. D. (2020). *First Principles of Instruction* (Revised Edition).

Metz, A. (2022). 6 exciting ways to use ChatGPT – from coding to poetry. *TechRadar*. https://www.techradar.com/features/6-exciting-ways-to-use-chatgpt-from-coding-to-poetry

Miller, S. (2014). *Why E-HR Projects Fail to Deliver Business Benefits*. Legal Island. https://www.legal-island.com/articles/uk/features/hr/2014/june/why-e-hr-projects-fail-to-deliver-business-benefits/

Miller, K. (2016). *Organizational Communication: Approaches and Processes* (6th ed.). Cengage.

Mintzberg, H. (2015). Henry MINTZBERG, The Nature of Managerial Work (1973) & Simply Managing: What Manager Do - And Can Do Better (2013). *M@n@gement*, *18*(2), 186. doi:10.3917/mana.182.0186

Mitgutsch, K., & Alvarado, N. (2012). Purposeful by design? A Serious Game design assessment framework. *FDG '12: Proceedings of the International Conference on the Foundations of Digital Games,* (pp. 121-28). IEEE. 10.1145/2282338.2282364

Mobasher, B., Kleanthous, S., Ekstrand, M., Berendt, B., Otterbacher, J., & Shulner Tal, A. (2020). FairUMAP 2020: The 3rd Workshop on Fairness in User Modeling, Adaptation and Personalization. Proceedings of the *28th ACM Conference on User Modeling, Adaptation and Personalization*, (pp. 404–405). ACM. 10.1145/3340631.3398671

Modaff, D. P., & DeWine, S. (2002). *Organizational Communication: Foundations*. Challenges, Misunderstandings.

Mondal, T., (2021). Three Strategies To Leverage Skills As The New Currency To Create Organizational Agility. *Forbes*. https://www.forbes.com/sites/forbeshumanresourcescouncil/2021/03/16/three-strategies-to-leverage-skills-as-the-new-currency-to-create-organizational-agility/?sh=1bd5662f28a1

Monterrat, B., Lavoué, É., & George, S. (2014, April). Motivation for learning: Adaptive gamification for web-based learning environments. *In 6th international conference on computer supported education (CSEDU 2014)* (pp. 117-125). IEEE.

Moore, M., & Tambini, D. (2018). *Digital Dominance: The Power of Google, Amazon, Facebook, and Apple*. Oxford University Press.

Morgan, R. (2003). *Market-Based Organizational Learning: Business Performance Gains in Financial Services Organizations*. Semantic Scholar. https://www.semanticscholar.org/paper/market-based-organizational-learning-%3a-business-in-Morgan-Turnell/a5774abcda480167a8bb1a486f2a11742b2c79bc

Mourtzis, D., Angelopoulos, J., & Panopoulos, N. (2022). Closed-Loop Robotic Arm Manipulation Based on Mixed Reality. Applied Sciences (Switzerland), 12(6). *Applied Sciences (Basel, Switzerland)*, *12*(6), 2972. doi:10.3390/app12062972

Muntean, C. I. (2011, October). Raising engagement in e-learning through gamification. *In Proc. 6th international conference on virtual learning ICVL* (Vol. 1, pp. 323-329). ACM.

Murtarelli, G., Gregory, A., & Romenti, S. (2020). A conversation-based perspective for shaping ethical human–machine interactions: The particular challenge of chatbots. *Journal of Business Research*. doi:10.1016/j.jbusres.2020.09.018

Nair, S., & Mathew, J. (2022). Learning through Play: Gamification of Learning, A Systematic Review of Studies on Gamified Learning. *Journal of Information Technology Management*, *14*(1), 113–126.

Nambisan, S., Lyytinen, K., Majchrzak, A., & Song, M. (2017). Digital innovation management: Reinventing innovation management research in a digital world. *Management Information Systems Quarterly*, *41*(1), 223–238. doi:10.25300/MISQ/2017/41:1.03

Nazarova, O., Pulekha, I., Maslennikova, O. Y., & Osipov, Y. V. (2020). Rationale for choosing the model and tool for developing an e-learning course. *Journal of Physics: Conference Series*, *1661*(1), 012184. doi:10.1088/1742-6596/1661/1/012184

Newman, M., & Gough, D. (2020). Systematic reviews in educational research: Methodology, perspectives and application. *Systematic reviews in educational research: Methodology, perspectives and application,* 3-22.

Nimavat, K., & Champaneria, T. (2017). Chatbots: An overview types, architecture, tools and future possibilities. *Int. J. Sci. Res. Dev.*, *5*, 1019–1024.

Nisar, T. M., Prabhakar, P., & Strakova, L. (2019). Social media information benefits, knowledge management and smart organizations. *Journal of Business Research*, *94*, 264–272. doi:10.1016/j.jbusres.2018.05.005

Nonaka, I. (1994). A dynamic theory of organizational knowledge creation. *Organization Science*, *5*(1), 14–37. doi:10.1287/orsc.5.1.14

Nurkhori, A., Rahmatia, A., Wahyuningsih, S. H., & Surwanti, A. (2021). Strengthening work engagement through digital engagement, gamification and psychosocial safety climate in digital transformation. *Journal of Innovation in Business and Economics*, *5*(01), 35–48. doi:10.22219/jibe.v5i01.17477

Nye, Core, & Ghosal. (2021). *Metrics for Engagement in Games and Simulations for Learning And Affective Metrics*. Springer. https://doi.org/ doi:10.4324/9780429282201-5/metrics-engagement-games-simulations-learning-benjamin-nye-mark-core-aviroop-ghosal-peter-walker

O'Brien, H. L., & Toms, E. G. (2008). What is user engagement? A conceptual framework for defining user engagement with technology. Journal of the American Society for Information Science. *Journal of the American Society for Information Science and Technology*, *59*(6), 938–955. doi:10.1002/asi.20801

ObarJ. A.WildmanS. S. (2015). Social Media Definition and the Governance Challenge - An Introduction to the Special Issue. *Social Science Research Network*. doi:10.2139/ssrn.2663153

OECD. (2015). *New Skills For The Digital Economy: Measuring The Demand And Supply Of Ict Skills At Work, Technical Report Prepared For The 2016 Ministerial Meeting On The Digital Economy, OECD Publishing, Paris. OECD (2015a), OECD Digital Economy Outlook 2015*. OECD Publishing. doi:10.1787/9789264239814-

OECD. (2016). New Forms Of Work. In *The Digital Economy, Technical Report Prepared For The 2016 Ministerial Meeting On The Digital Economy*. OECD Publishing.

OECD. (2018). Report On Pension Systems For The Self-Employed. In *Oecd And Eu Countries*. OECD Publishing.

Ogibowski, V. (2023). Learn Smarter with AI-Powered Learning. *Employee Learning & Development Excellence*, *10*(7), 29–32.

Okonkwo, C. W., & Ade-Ibijola, A. (2021). Chatbots applications in education: A systematic review. *Computers and Education: Artificial Intelligence*, *2*, 100033. doi:10.1016/j.caeai.2021.100033

Oksa, R., Kaakinen, M., Savela, N., Ellonen, N., & Oksanen, A. (2021). Professional social media usage: Work engagement perspective. *New Media & Society*, *23*(8), 2303–2326. doi:10.1177/1461444820921938

Oliveira, I. (2018). Educação de Jovens e Adultos (EJA) - Século XXI: Diversas Formas de Aprender e Ensinar ao Longo da Vida (4 ed., Vol. 2). In Revista Científica Multidisciplinar Núcleo do Conhecimento.

Organisation for Economic Co-operation and Development (OECD). (2020). *Promoting an age-inclusive workforce: Living, learning and earning longer*. OECD.

Örtenblad, A. (2001). On differences between organizational learning and learning organization. *The Learning Organization*, *8*(3), 125–133. doi:10.1108/09696470110391211

Ortiz-Ospina, E. (2023, May 25). The rise of social media. *Our World in Data.* https://ourworldindata.org/rise-of-social-media?ref=tms

Osterwalder, A. (2011). *Businessmodel generation.* Alex Oster Walder. https://alexosterwalder.com/books.html

Osterwalder, A., & Pigneur, Y. (2010). *Business Model Generation: A Handbook for Visionaries, Game Changers, and Challengers.* John Wiley & Sons, Inc.

Osterwalder, A., Pigneur, Y., Bernada, G., & Smith, A. (2014). *Value Proposition Canvas: How to create products and services customers want.* John Wiley & Sons, Inc.

Pabon, L. C. (2016). Training Through Serious Games: The Relationship Between Travel Agent Engagement, Knowledge of Cruise Products and Cruise Sales. [Theses and Dissertations, FIU]. doi:10.25148/etd.FIDC000713

Pandey, N., Nayal, P., & Rathore, A. S. (2020). Digital marketing for B2B organizations: Structured literature review and future research directions. *Journal of Business and Industrial Marketing, 35*(7), 1191–1204. doi:10.1108/JBIM-06-2019-0283

Pargman, C. T. (2019). Unpacking Emergent teaching Practices with Digital Technology. In C. T. Pargman & I. Jahnke (Eds.), *Emergent Practices and Material Conditions in Learning and Teaching with Technologies* (1st ed., pp. 33–51). Springer Netherlands. doi:10.1007/978-3-030-10764-2_3

Pasmore, W., Winby, S., Mohrman, S. A., & Vanasse, R. (2019). Reflections: Sociotechnical systems design and organization change. *Journal of Change Management, 19*(2), 67–85. doi:10.1080/14697017.2018.1553761

Pearlson, K. E., & Saunders, C. S. (2001). There's no place like home: Managing telecommuting paradoxes. *The Academy of Management Perspectives, 15*(2), 117–128. doi:10.5465/ame.2001.4615008

Pedersen, C., Togelius, J., & Yannakakis, G. N. (2010). Modeling Player Experience for Content Creation. *IEEE Transactions on Computational Intelligence and AI in Games, 2*(1), 54–67. doi:10.1109/TCIAIG.2010.2043950

Pekkala, K., & Van Zoonen, W. (2021). Work-related social media use: The mediating role of social media communication self-efficacy. *European Management Journal, 40*(1), 67–76. doi:10.1016/j.emj.2021.03.004

Pereira, A., Quintas Mendes, A., Morgado, L., Amante, L., & Bidarra, J. (2007). *Modelo Pedagógico Virtual da Universidade Aberta.* Universidade Aberta.

Pérez, J. Q., Daradoumis, T., & Puig, J. M. M. (2020). Rediscovering the use of chatbots in education: A systematic literature review. *Computer Applications in Engineering Education, 28*(6), 1549–1565. doi:10.1002/cae.22326

Perovic, N., & Young, C. (2015). Rapid and creative course design: as easy as ABC? In: Procedia - Social and Behavioral Sciences, 228, 390 – 395.

Peschl, M. F. (2023). Learning from the future as a novel paradigm for integrating organizational learning and innovation. *The Learning Organization*, *30*(1), 6–22. doi:10.1108/TLO-01-2021-0018

Peters, O. (2001). *Didática do ensino a distância: experiências e estágio da discussão numa visão internacional. Tradução Ilson Kayser*. Unisinos.

Pinto, A. M. G. L. R. S., da Silva Ramos, S. C. M., & Nunes, S. M. M. D. (2014). Managing an aging workforce: What is the value of human resource management practices for different age groups of workers? *Tékhne (Instituto Politécnico do Cávado e do Ave)*, *12*, 58–68. doi:10.1016/j.tekhne.2015.01.007

Pistono, A. M. A. A., Santos, A. M. P., & Baptista, R. J. V. (2021). A Review of Adaptable Serious Games Applied to Professional Training. *Journal of Digital Media & Interaction*, *4*(11), 60–85. doi:10.34624/jdmi.v4i11.26419

PitthanF.De WitteK. (2023). *Game Over or Continue? How Gamification Can Improve Completion Rate in Adaptive Learning*. doi:10.2139/ssrn.4507734

Portaria n.º 214/2011 de 30 de maio. Diário da República, 1.ª série — N.º 104 — 30 de maio de 2011.

Potgieter, I. (2020). Privacy concerns in educational data mining and learning analytics. *International Journal of Information Ethics*, *28*. https://informationethics.ca/index.php/irie/article/view/384. doi:10.29173/irie384

Prado, A. (2021). Conectivismo y diseño instruccional: Ecología de aprendizaje para la universidad del siglo XXI en México. *Márgenes Revista De Educación De La Universidad De Málaga*, *2*(1), 4–20. doi:10.24310/mgnmar.v2i1.9349

Prahalad, C. K., & Hamel, G. (1990). 'The Core Competence of the Corporation'. *Harvard Business Review*, (May/June), 79–91.

PricewaterhouseCoopers. (2023). *Generative AI tools push new boundaries for responsible AI*. PwC. https://www.pwc.com/us/en/tech-effect/ai-analytics/business-impacts-of-generative-aitools.html

Quinn, C. (2021). *Learning Science for Instructional Designers: From Cognition to Application.*

Radford, A., Narasimhan, K., Salimans, T., & Sutskever, I. (2018). *Improving language understanding by generative pre-training*. Preprint. https://paperswithcode.com/paper/improving-language-understanding-by

Rebelo, T., Lourenço, P. B., & Dimas, I. D. (2019). The journey of team learning since "The Fifth Discipline.". *The Learning Organization*, *27*(1), 42–53. doi:10.1108/TLO-10-2019-0144

Redecker, C., & Punie, Y. (2017). Digital Competence of Educators. Yves Punie.

Redondo, D. (2021). Integrating micro-learning content in traditional e-learning platforms. *Multimedia Tools and Applications*, *80*(2), 1–31. doi:10.100711042-020-09523-z

Reed, L. (2022). *ChatGPT for Automated Testing: From conversation to code.* Sauce Labs. https://saucelabs.com/blog/chatgpt-automated-testing-conversation-to-code

Reis, J., Amorim, M., Melão, N., & Matos, P. (2018). Digital transformation: a literature review and guidelines for future research. In Á. Rocha, H. Adeli, L. P. Reis, & S. Costanzo (Eds.), *Trends and Advances in Information Systems and Technologies. Advances in Intelligent Systems and Computing* (Vol. 745). Springer. doi:10.1007/978-3-319-77703-0_41

Revans, R. W. (1982). *The origin and growth of action learning*. Chartwell-Bratt.

Revans, R. W. (2011). *The ABC of Action Learning*. Gower Publishing.

Rice, R. E., & Aydin, C. (1991). Attitudes Toward New Organizational Technology: Network Proximity as a Mechanism for Social Information Processing. *Administrative Science Quarterly*, *36*(2), 219. doi:10.2307/2393354

Richards, D., & Dignum, V. (2019). Supporting and challenging learners through pedagogical agents: Addressing ethical issues through designing for value. *British Journal of Educational Technology*, *50*(6), 2885–2901. doi:10.1111/bjet.12863

Riedel, J. C., Feng, Y., Hauge, J. M. B., Hansen, P. K., & Tasuya, S. (2015). The adoption and application of Serious Games in corporate training-The case of manufacturing. *2015 IEEE International Conference on Engineering, Technology and Innovation/International Technology Management Conference (ICE/ITMC),* (pp. 1-9). IEEE. https://ieeexplore.ieee.org/abstract/document/7438684/

Rienties, B., Nguyen, Q., Holmes, W., & Reedy, K. (2017). A review of ten years of implementation and research in aligning learning design with learning analytics at the Open University UK. [s]. *Interaction Design and Architecture*, *33*(33), 134–154. doi:10.55612-5002-033-007

Rigney (1978). *Estrategias de aprendizaje: Una perspectiva teórica*. O'Neill, New York: Academia Press.

Rocha, O. & Faron-Zucker, R. (2017). *Automatic generation of educational quizzes from domain ontologies.* 4024-4030. . doi:10.21125/edulearn.2017.1866

Roschelle, J., Lester, J., & Fusco, J. (Eds.). (2020). AI and the future of learning: Expert panel report [Report]. *Digital Promise*. https://circls.org/reports/ai-report

Ross, J., Sebastian, I., & Beath, C. (2017). How to develop a great digital strategy. *MIT Sloan Management Review*, *58*(2), 7–9.

Roth, S. (2019). Digital transformation of social theory. A research update. *Technological Forecasting and Social Change*, *146*, 88–93. doi:10.1016/j.techfore.2019.05.016

Rudestan, K. E., & Read-Schoenholtz, J. (2010). Handbook of online Learning. SAGE:Unites Estates of American.

Rummel, N., Mavrikis, M., Wiedmann, M., Loibl, K., Mazziotti, C., Holmes, W., & Hansen, A. (2016). Combining exploratory learning with structured practice to foster conceptual and procedural fractions knowledge. C. K. Looi, J. Polman, U. Cress, and P. Reimann (eds.), *Transforming Learning, Empowering Learners: The International Conference of the Learning Sciences (ICLS) 2016*. Singapore, International Society of the Learning Sciences.

Saberi, S., Kouhizadeh, M., & Sarkis, J. (2020). Blockchain technology and its relationships to sustainable supply chain management. *International Journal of Production Research*, *58*(7), 2063–2085.

Sacharidis, D., Mukamakuza, C. P., & Werthner, H. (2020). Fairness and diversity in social-based recom- mender systems. Adjunct Publication of the *28th ACM Conference on User Modeling, Adaptation and Personalization*, (pp. 83–88). ACM. 10.1145/3386392.3397603

Sadovets, O., Martynyuk, O., Orlovska, O., Lysak, H., Korol, S., & Zembytska, M. (2022). Gamification in the informal learning space of higher education (in the context of the digital transformation of education). *Postmodern Openings*, *13*(1), 330–350. doi:10.18662/po/13.1/399

Saebi, T., & Foss, N. J. (2015). Business Models for Open Innovation: Matching Heterogeneous Open Innovation Strategies with Business Model Dimensions. *European Management Journal*, *33*(3), 201–213. doi:10.1016/j.emj.2014.11.002

Sahoo, N., & Dhir, A. (2021). Digital Transformation: Challenges, Opportunities, and Lessons Learned from COVID-19. *Journal of Enterprise Information Management*, *34*(4), 747–768.

Sala, N. (2021). Virtual Reality, Augmented Reality, and Mixed Reality in Education: A Brief Overview. In D. Choi, A. Dailey-Hebert, & J. Estes (Eds.), *Current and Prospective Applications of Virtual Reality in Higher Education* (pp. 48–73). IGI Global. doi:10.4018/978-1-7998-4960-5.ch003

Saleem, A. N., Noori, N. M., & Ozdamli, F. (2022). Gamification applications in E-learning: A literature review. *Technology. Knowledge and Learning*, *27*(1), 139–159. doi:10.100710758-020-09487-x

Säljö, R. (2019). Materiality, Learning, and Cognitive Practices: Artifacts as Instruments of Thinking. In C. T. Pargman & I. Jahnke (Eds.), *Emergent Practices and Material Conditions in Learning and Teaching with Technologies* (pp. 21–32). Springer. doi:10.1007/978-3-030-10764-2_2

Salmon, G. (2013). E-tivities - the key to active online learning. Routledge.

Salmon, G. (2003). E-tivities: The Key to Active Online Learning. *Education + Training*, *45*(6). doi:10.1108/et.2003.00445fad.002

Sandu, N., & Gide, E. (2019, September). Adoption of AI-Chatbots to enhance student learning experience in higher education in India. In *2019 18th International Conference on Information Technology Based Higher Education and Training (ITHET)* (pp. 1-5). IEEE.

Santos, A., Moreira, L., Valente da S., P., & Vieira, P. (2022). *Referencial de Formação Pedagógica Contínua de Formação em Conteúdos Digitais para Autoaprendizagem* (e-Conteúdos). Lisboa: IEFP – Instituto do Emprego e Formação Profissional, IP.

Santos, A., Peixinho, F., Moreira, L. (2014). *Projetos de e-Learning: Inovação, Implementação e Gestão*. FCA, Lidel

Santra, T., & Giri, V. N. (2009). Analyzing Computer-Mediated Communication and Organizational Effectiveness. *The Review of Communication*, *9*(1), 100–109. doi:10.1080/15358590701772259

Saunders, M. N. K., Lewis, P., & Thornhill, A. (2019). *Research Methods for Business Students* (8th ed.). Pearson.

Schelenz, L., Segal, A., & Gal, K. (2020). Best practices for transparency in machine generated personaliza- tion. Adjunct Publication of the *28th ACM Conference on User Modeling, Adaptation and Personalization*, (pp. 23–28). ACM. 10.1145/3386392.3397593

Schreck, J. (2003). *Security and Privacy in User Modeling* (Vol. 2). Springer. doi:10.1007/978-94-017-0377-2

Schwartz, M. J., & Rist, R. C. (2017). Organizational Learning, the Learning Organization, and Independent Evaluation. In *The International Monetary Fund and the Learning Organization*. International Monetary Fund., https://www.elibrary.imf.org/display/book/9781475546675/ch007.xml

Schwarzmüller, T., Brosi, P., Duman, D., & Welpe, I. M. (2018). How does the digital transformation affect organizations? Key themes of change in work design and leadership. *Management Review*, *29*(2), 114–138.

Scott, M., & DeSANCTIS, P. G. (1992). Microlevel Structuration in Computer-Supported Group Decision Making. *Human Communication Research*, *19*(1), 5–49. doi:10.1111/j.1468-2958.1992.tb00294.x

Selwyn, N. (2020). Approches critiques des technologies en éducation: Un aperçu. *Formation et Profession*, *27*(3), 6. doi:10.18162/fp.2019.579

Selwyn, N., Nemorin, S., Bulfin, S., & Johnson, N. (2020). The “obvious” stuff: Exploring the mundane realities of students’ digital technology use in school. *Digital Education Review*, *37*(37), 1–14. doi:10.1344/der.2020.37.1-14

Senge, P. M. (2006). The Fifth Discipline: The Art and Practice of the Learning Organization. Doubleday (A Division of Random House), New York, 7.

Senge, P. (1990). *The Fifth Discipline*. Bantam.

Senge, P. (1990). *The Fifth Discipline: The Art and Practice of the Learning Organization*. Doubleday.

Serrat, O. (2017). *Knowledge solutions: Tools, methods, and approaches to drive organizational performance*. Springer Nature. doi:10.1007/978-981-10-0983-9

Seufert, S., & Meier, C. (2016). From eLearning to Digital Transformation: A Framework and Implications for L&D. [iJAC]. *International Journal of Advanced Corporate Learning*, *9*(2), 27–33. doi:10.3991/ijac.v9i2.6003

Shiohira, K., & Holmes, W. (2023). Proceed with Caution: The Pitfalls and Potential of AI and Education. In D. Araya & P. Marber (Eds.), *Augmented Education in the Global Age*. Routledge.

Short, C. R., & Shemshack, A. **(2023).** *Personalised learning*. EdTechnica: The Open Encyclopedia of Educational Technology. https://edtechbooks.org/encyclopedia/personalized_learning

Siegel, E. (2013). *Predictive Analytics: The Power to Predict Who Will Click, Buy, Lie or Die*. John Wiley & Sons, Inc.

Siemens, G. (2004). *Conectivismo: Una teoría de aprendizaje para la era digital*. Traducción de Leal, D [Blog]. https://bit.ly/2BZUbPL

Siemens, G. (2005). Connectivism: A Learning Theory for the Digital Age. *International Journal of Instructional Technology and Distance Learning*, *2*. https://www.itdl.org/Journal/Jan_05/article01.htm

Silva Puente Arnao, M. A. (2021). *The effect of gamification on learning-the example of vendors brand awareness/Author Maria Angelica Silva* [Doctoral dissertation, Universität Linz].

Silva, A. & Santos, L. (2015). A quinta disciplina e o enfoque a qualificação profissional do administrador. *XII SEGeT – Simpósio de Excelência em Gestão e Tecnologia*.

Silva, L. L., Ribeiro, M. M., & Ferreira, C. F. (2020). Digital Transformation Leadership and Navigating the Digitalization Process. *Computers in Human Behavior*, *111*, 106414.

Simon, G. R., & Zhou, I. (2017). Harmonizing Modern Day Employee Engagement with the Sociological Theory of Symbolic Interactionism. *American Journal of Business and Management*, *6*(2), 52. doi:10.11634/216796061706894

Simonsen, H. K. (2019): From Ego-based to Eco-based Online Learning: Presentation of a Model for Eco-based Online Learning. At *Promoting Online Training Opportunities for the Workforce in Europe*. Europea. https://publications.europa.eu/en/publication-detail/-/publication/812aeaf7-dccd-11e8-afb3-01aa75ed71a1

Simonsen, H. K. (2020). *Forsøg med uddannelsesdigitalisering og uddannelsesformater* (H. K. Simonsen, Ed.). Samfundslitteratur.

Simonsen, H. K. (2021). *Forsøg med uddannelsesdigitalisering og hybride formater* (H. K. Simonsen, Ed.). Samfundslitteratur.

Simonsen, H. K., & Walther, L. R. (2021). Fleksible og skalerbare undervisningsmodeller. In H. K. Simonsen (Ed.), *Forsøg med uddannelsesdigitalisering og hybride formater* (pp. 145–160). Samfundslitteratur.

Singh, V., Chen, S. S., Singhania, M., Nanavati, B., & Gupta, A. (2022). How are reinforcement learning and deep learning algorithms used for big data-based decision making in financial industries - A review and research agenda. *International Journal of Information Management Data Insights*, *2*(2), 100094. https://www.sciencedirect.com/science/article/pii/S2667096822000374. doi:10.1016/j.jjimei.2022.100094

Singh, V., Nanavati, B., Kar, A. K., & Gupta, A. (2022). How to maximize clicks for display advertisement in digital marketing? A reinforcement learning approach. *Information Systems Frontiers*, 1–18. doi:10.100710796-022-10314-0

Sinkula, J. M. (1994). Market Information Processing and Organizational Learning. *Journal of Marketing*, *58*(1), 35–45. doi:10.1177/002224299405800103

Slade, S., & Prinsloo, P. (2013). Learning analytics ethical issues and dilemmas. *The American Behavioral Scientist*, *57*(10), 1510–1529. doi:10.1177/0002764213479366

Smiderle, R., Rigo, S. J., Marques, L. B., De Miranda Coelho, J. P., & Jaques, P. A. (2020). The impact of gamification on students' learning, engagement and behavior based on their personality traits. *Smart Learning Environments*, *7*(1), 3. Advance online publication. doi:10.118640561-019-0098-x

Smith, G., Barnes, K. C., & Harris, C. R. (2014). A learning approach to the ethical organization. *The Learning Organization*. doi:10.1108/TLO-07-2011-0043

Smith, J. (2022). Applications of artificial intelligence in educational management. *Educational Technology Research and Development*, *70*(2), 457–478. 10.100711423-022-09981-1

Sobko, S., Unadkat, D., Adams, J., & Hull, G. (2019). Learning through collaboration: A networked approach to online pedagogy. *E-Learning and Digital Media*, *17*(1), 36–55. doi:10.1177/2042753019882562

Song, J. H., Lim, D. H., Kang, I., & Kim, W. (2014). Team performance in learning organizations: Mediating effect of employee engagement. *The Learning Organization*, *21*(5), 290–309. doi:10.1108/TLO-07-2012-0049

Soukup, E. (2003, September 22). CEOs: That's What That Is. *Newsweek*.

Sousa, L., Figueiredo, M., Monteiro, J., Bidarra, J., Rodrigues, J., & Cardoso, P. (2016). Developments of Serious Games in Education. In Handbook of Research on Human-Computer Interfaces, Developments, and Applications (pp. 392–419). IGI Global. doi:10.4018/978-1-5225-0435-1.ch016

Sousa, M. J., & Rocha, Á. (2019). Digital learning: Developing skills for digital transformation of organizations. *Future Generation Computer Systems*, *91*, 327–334. doi:10.1016/j.future.2018.08.048

Sousa, M., Antunes, A. P., Pinto, N., & Zagalo, N. (2022). Serious Games in Spatial Planning: Strengths, Limitations and Support Frameworks. *International Journal of Serious Games*, *9*(2), 115–133. doi:10.17083/ijsg.v9i2.510

Spiggle, S. (1994). Analysis and Interpretation of Qualitative Data in Consumer Research. *The Journal of Consumer Research*, *21*(3), 491–503. doi:10.1086/209413

Sproull, L., & Kiesler, S. (1986). Reducing Social Context Cues: Electronic Mail in Organizational Communication. *Management Science*, *32*(11), 1492–1512. doi:10.1287/mnsc.32.11.1492

St-Hilaire, F., Vu, D.D., Frau, A., Burns, N., Faraji, F., Potochny, J., Robert, S., Roussel, A., Zheng, S., Glazier, T., Romano, J.V., Belfer, R., Shayan, M., Smofsky, A., Delarosbil, T., Ahn, S., Eden-Walker, S., Sony, K., Ching, A.O., Elkins, S., Stepanyan, A.Z., Matajová, A., Chen, V., Sahraei, H., Larson, R., Markova, N., Barkett, A., Charlin, L., Bengio, Y., Serban, I., & Kochmar, E. (2022). *A New Era: Intelligent Tutoring Systems Will Transform Online Learning for Millions*. https://doi.org/10.48550/arXiv.2203.03724.

Stokel-Walker, C. J. N. (2023). ChatGPT listed as author on research papers: Many scientists disapprove. *Nature*, *613*(7945), 620–621. doi:10.1038/d41586-023-00107-z PMID:36653617

Streicher, A., & Smeddinck, J. D. (2016). Personalized and Adaptive Serious Games. In R. Dörner, S. Göbel, M. Kickmeier-Rust, M. Masuch, & K. Zweig (Eds.), *Entertainment Computing and Serious Games: International GI-Dagstuhl Seminar 15283*, (pp. 332-377). Springer International Publishing. 10.1007/978-3-319-46152-6_14

Strmecki, D., Bernik, A., & Radosevic, D. (2015). Gamification in E-Learning: Introducing Gamified Design Elements into E-Learning Systems. *Journal of Computational Science*, *11*(12), 1108–1117. doi:10.3844/jcssp.2015.1108.1117

Susilana, R., Dewi, L., Rullyana, G., Hadiapurwa, A., & Khaerunnisa, N. (2022). Can microlearning strategy assist students' online learning? *Jurnal Cakrawala Pendidikan.*, *41*(2), 437–451. doi:10.21831/cp.v41i2.43387

Suswanto, B., Sulaiman, A. I., Sugito, T., Weningsih, S., Sabiq, A., & Kuncoro, B. (2021). Designing Online Learning Evaluation in Times of Covid-19 Pandemic. *International Educational Research*, *4*(1). *Artigo*, *1*(1), p18. doi:10.30560/ier.v4n1p18

Sweller, J., van Merriënboer, J. J. G., & Paas, F. (2019). Cognitive Architecture and Instructional Design: 20 Years Later. *Educational Psychology Review*, *31*(2), 261–292. doi:10.100710648-019-09465-5

Szabadi, A. (2023, janeiro 5). *ChatGPT Will Change Many Things—But It Won't Change Everything*. BCG Henderson Institute. https://bcghendersoninstitute.com/chatgpt-will-change-many-things-but-it-wont-change-everything

Tanaka, J. (1997, April 28). Drowning in Data. *Newsweek*.

Tarran, B. (2018). What can we learn from the Facebook—Cambridge Analytica scandal? *Significance*, *15*(3), 4–5. doi:10.1111/j.1740-9713.2018.01139.x PMID:32536948

Tassetto, J.-M. (2019). *The Rise of The Learning Experience Platform (LXP/LEP).* Credit Control, 40(3/4).

Tawse, A., & Tabesh, P. (2021). Strategy implementation: A review and an introductory framework. *European Management Journal*, *39*(1), 22–33. doi:10.1016/j.emj.2020.09.005

Taylor, M. A., & Bisson, J. B. (2020). Changes in cognitive function: Practical and theoretical considerations for training the aging workforce. *Human Resource Management Review*, *30*(2), 100684. doi:10.1016/j.hrmr.2019.02.001

Teece, D. J. (2007). Explicating dynamic capabilities: The nature and microfoundations of (sustainable) enterprise performance. *Strategic Management Journal*, *28*(13), 1319–1350. doi:10.1002mj.640

Teece, D. J., & Linden, G. (2017). Business models, value capture, and the digital enterprise. *Journal of Organization Design*, *6*(1), 8. doi:10.118641469-017-0018-x

The College of New Jersey. (n.d.) *Creating a Social Media Presence.* TCNJ. https://communications.tcnj.edu/about/media-relations-and-marketing/use-social-media/

The European Qualifications Framework (EQF). (n.d.). *Qualifications.* Europea. https://europa.eu/europass/en/european-qualifications-framework-eqf

Thomas, N. J., Baral, R., & Crocco, O. S. (2022). Gamification for HRD: Systematic review and future research directions. *Human Resource Development Review*, *21*(2), 198–224. doi:10.1177/15344843221074859

Thomas, P. J., & Dittman, K. C. (2016). Social Media and its Impact on Quality of Communication Management. *Proceedings of the 2016 IAJC-ISAM Joint International Conference.* IEEE.

Thomsen, H. K., & Hoest, V. (2001). Employees' perception of the learning organization. *Management Learning*, *32*(4), 469–491. doi:10.1177/1350507601324004

Thorndike, E. L. (1920). A constant error on psychological rating. *The Journal of Applied Psychology*, *IV*(1), 25–29. doi:10.1037/h0071663

Torres Martín, C., Acal, C., El Homrani, M., & Mingorance Estrada, Á. C. (2021). Impact on the virtual learning environment due to COVID-19. *Sustainability (Basel)*, *13*(2), 582. doi:10.3390u13020582

Training Magazine Network. (2022). Don't Get Left Behind: Understanding & Succeeding with Tomorrow's L&D Ecosystem. *Training Magazine Network.* https://www.trainingmagnetwork.com/events/3197?gref=calendar

Trenerry, B., Chng, S., Wang, Y., Suhaila, Z. S., Lim, S. S., Lu, H. Y., & Oh, P. H. (2021). Preparing Workplaces for Digital Transformation: An Integrative Review and Framework of MultiLevel Factors. *Frontiers in Psychology*, *12*, 620766. https://www.frontiersin.org/articles/10.3389/fpsyg.2021.620766. doi:10.3389/fpsyg.2021.620766 PMID:33833714

Trevino, L. K., Daft, R. L., & Lengel, R. H. (1990). Understanding managers' media choices: A symbolic interactionist perspective. In J. Fulk & C. W. Steinfield (Eds.), *Organizations and communication technology* (pp. 71–94). Sage Publications, Inc. doi:10.4135/9781483325385.n4

Trevino, L. K., Lengal, R. H., & Daft, R. L. (1987). Media Symbolism, Media Richness, and Media Choice in Organizations. *Communication Research*, *14*(5), 553–574. doi:10.1177/009365087014005006

Trilla, J. (2019). El aprendizaje servicio en la pedagogia Contemporânea. In J. M. Puig (Ed.), *Coord.): Aprendizagem Serviço: Educação e Compromisso Cívico*. Editorial Graó.

Trittin-Ulbrich, H., Scherer, A. G., Munro, I., & Whelan, G. (2020). Exploring the dark and unexpected sides of digitalization: Toward a critical agenda. *Organization*, *28*(1), 8–25. doi:10.1177/1350508420968184

Tsai, Y.-S., Rates, D., Moreno-Marcos, P. M., Muñoz-Merino, P. J., Jivet, I., Scheffel, M., Drachsler, H., Delgado Kloos, C., & Gašević, D. (2020). Learning analytics in European higher education—Trends and barriers. *Computers & Education*, *155*, 103933. doi:10.1016/j.compedu.2020.103933

Tsai, Y.-S., Whitelock-Wainwright, A., & Gašević, D. (2021). More Than Figures on Your Laptop: (Dis)trustful Implementation of Learning Analytics. *Journal of Learning Analytics*, *3*(3), 81–100. doi:10.18608/jla.2021.7379

Tudor, S. L. (2016). Skills-centered design - a model design centered on skills of training activities/ development of communicative skill in Integrated perspective. *Journal Plus Education*.

Tung, L. (2023). ChatGPT can write code. Now researchers say it's good at fixing bugs, too. *ZDNet*. https://www.zdnet.com/article/chatgpt-can-write-code-now-researchers-say-its-good-at-fixing-bugs-too/

Turaga, R. (2019). Effective Communication in Organizations - ProQuest. IUP Journal of Soft Skills: Vol. 13. (*Iss. 1,*). University of California Press., https://www.proquest.com/openview/f66811fddb041d7db2b3a5a94688c20e/1?pq-origsite=gscholar&cbl=2029989

Turner, M. E. (Ed.). (2001). Communities of Practice: Learning, Meaning, and Identity. Cambridge University Press.

Uc-Cetina, V., Navarro-Guerrero, N., Martin-Gonzalez, A., Weber, C., & Wermter, S. (2022). Survey on reinforcement learning for language processing. *Artificial Intelligence Review*, 1–33. doi:10.100710462-022-10205-5

UNESCO. (2019). *Artificial intelligence in education: Challenges and opportunities for sustainable development*. UNESCO. https://unesdoc.unesco.org/ark:/48223/pf0000366994

Université de Montréal. (2018). *Declaration of Montréal for a responsible development of AI*. Université de Montréal. https://www.montrealdeclaration-responsibleai.com

Uskov, A., & Sekar, B. (2014). Serious Games, gamification and game engines to support framework activities in engineering: Case studies, analysis, classifications and outcomes. *IEEE International Conference on Electro/Information Technology,* (pp. 618–623). IEEE. 10.1109/EIT.2014.6871836

Uther, M. (2019). Mobile Learning—Trends and Practices. *Education Sciences*, *9*(1), 33. doi:10.3390/educsci9010033

Valente, P. (2022). e-Learning e Formação Profissional: cenários e estratégias didáticas para o Ensino de Língua Inglesa (LE/L2). [Tese de Doutoramento, Universidade Aberta]. Faculdade de Ciências Sociais e Humanas-Universidade Nova de Lisboa, Portugal.

Valiyeva, A., & Thomas, B. J. (2022). Successful Organizational Business Communication and its Impact on Business Performance: An Intra- and Inter-Organizational Perspective. *Journal of Accounting. Business and Finance Research*, *15*(2), 83–91. doi:10.55217/102.v15i2.586

Van Osch, W., & Coursaris, C. K. (2013). Organizational Social Media: A Comprehensive Framework and Research Agenda. 2013 *46th Hawaii International Conference on System Sciences*. IEEE. https://doi.org/10.1109/hicss.2013.439Van

Vaswani, A., Shazeer, N., Parmar, N., Uszkoreit, J., Jones, L., Gomez, A. N., & Polosukhin, I. (2017). *Attention is all you need. 31st Conference on Neural Information Processing Systems*, Long Beach, CA, USA.

Venezia, A. S. J (2012). *The interaction of social media and the law and how to survive the social media revolution.*

Verbos, A. K., Gerard, J. G., Forshey, P. R., Harding, C. J., & Miller, J. M. (2007). The Positive Ethical Organization: Enacting a Living Code of Ethics and Ethical Organizational Identity. *Journal of Business Ethics*, *76*(1), 17–33. doi:10.100710551-006-9275-2

Vial, G. (2019). Understanding digital transformation: A review and a research Agenda. *The Journal of Strategic Information Systems*, *28*(2), 118–144. doi:10.1016/j.jsis.2019.01.003

Vial, G. (2020). Data-Driven Decision-Making and Management. *California Management Review*, *62*(1), 49–71.

Visser, Max & Tosey, Paul. (2019*). Learning in the learning organisation: Concepts and antecedents.*

Von Bertalanffy, L. (1968). General Systems Theory as Integrating Factor in Contemporary Science. In *Akten des XIV* (pp. 335–340). Internationalen Kongresses für Philosophie. doi:10.5840/wcp1419682120

Vrontis, D., Belás, J., Thrassou, A., Santoro, G., & Christofi, M. (2022). Strategic agility, openness and performance: A mixed method comparative analysis of firms operating in developed and emerging markets. *Review of Managerial Science*, *17*(4), 1365–1398. doi:10.100711846-022-00562-4

Waters, R. D., & Williams, J. M. (2011). Squawking, tweeting, cooing, and hooting: Analyzing the communication patterns of government agencies on Twitter. *Journal of Public Affairs*, *11*(4), 353–363. doi:10.1002/pa.385

Wattanasoontorn, V., Hernández, R. J. G., & Sbert, M. (2014). Serious Games for e-Health Care. In Y. Cai & S. L. Goei (Eds.), *Simulations, Serious Games and Their Applications* (pp. 127–146). Springer Singapore. doi:10.1007/978-981-4560-32-0_9

Weaver, R., & Agle, R. (n.d.). Religiosity and Ethical Behavior in Organizations: A Symbolic Interactionist Perspective on JSTOR. *The Academy of Management Review*. https://www.jstor.org/stable/4134370

Weill, P., & Woerner, S. (2018). *What's Your Digital Business Model? Six Questions to Help You Build the Next-Generation Enterprise*. Harvard Business Review Press.

Weinert, F. E., & Kluwe, R. H. (1987). *Metacognición, motivación y comprensión*. N. J. LEA.

Welch, M., & Jackson, P. R. (2007). Rethinking internal communication: A stakeholder approach. *Corporate Communications*, *12*(2), 177–198. doi:10.1108/13563280710744847

Westerman, G., Bonnet, D., & McAfee, A. (2014). Leading Digital: Turning Technology into Business Transformation. *Harvard Business Review Press*.

West, R. E. (2018). *Foundations of Learning and Instructional Design Technology*. EdTech Books., doi:10.59668/3

Whittaker, M., Crawford, K., Dobbe, R., Fried, G., Kaziunas, E., & Mathur, V. MyersWest, S., Richardson, R., Schultz, J., & Schwartz, O. (2018). AI now report 2018. AI Now Institute: New York University.

Wiesenfeld, B. M., Raghuram, S., & Garud, R. (1998). Communication Patterns as Determinants of Organizational Identification in a Virtual Organization. *Journal of Computer-Mediated Communication*, *3*(4). doi:10.1111/j.1083-6101.1998.tb00081.x

Wiley, D., Waters, S., & Lambert, B. & Dawson, Deonne & Barclay, M. & Wade, D. & Nelson, L. (2004). Overcoming the limitations of learning objects. *Journal of Educational Multimedia and Hypermedia*, 13.

Winfield, A. F. T., & Jirotka, M. (2018). Ethical governance is essential to building trust in robotics and artificial intelligence systems. *Philosophical Transactions. Series A, Mathematical, Physical, and Engineering Sciences*, *376*(2133), 20180085. doi:10.1098/rsta.2018.0085 PMID:30323000

Winkler, R., & Söllner, M. (2018). Unleashing the potential of chatbots in education: A state-of-the-art analysis. In *Academy of management annual meeting (AOM)*. AOM. 10.5465/AMBPP.2018.15903abstract

Wise, A. (2019). *Learning Analytics: Using Data-Informed Decision-Making to Improve Teaching and Learning: Maximising Student Engagement, Motivation, and Learning*. Contemporary Technologies in Education., doi:10.1007/978-3-319-89680-9_7

World Economic Forum. (2015). *The global competitiveness report 2015-2016*. Geneva: World Economic Forum. https://www3.weforum.org/docs/gcr/2015-2016/Global_Competitiveness_Report_2015- 2016.pdf

World Economic Forum. (2016). *New Vision for Education: Fostering Social and Emotional Learning*. W. E. Forum, Ed. https://www3.weforum.org/docs/WEF_New_Vision_for_Education.pdf

World Economic Forum. (2017). Promise or Peril: Decoding the Future of Work. https://www.weforum.org/agenda/2017/01/promise-or-perildecoding-the-future-of-work/

World Economic Forum. (2018). *The Future of Jobs Report*. WEF. https://www3.weforum.org/docs/WEF_Future_of_Jobs_2020.pdf

World Economic Forum. (2019). *Generation AI*. WEF. https://www3.weforum.org/docs/WEF_Generation_AI_%20May_2019_Workshop_Report.pdf

World Economic Forum. (2020). *Top 10 Emerging Technologies of 2020*. World Economic Forum.

World Economic Forum. (2021). *Annual Report 2020-2021*. Geneva: World Economic Forum. https://www.weforum.org/reports/annual-report-2020- 2021/

Wouters, P., van der Spek, E. D., & van Oostendorp, H. (2009). Current Practices in Serious Game Research: A Review from a Learning Outcomes Perspective. In Games-Based Learning Advancements for Multi-Sensory Human-Computer Interfaces: Techniques and Effective Practices (pp. 232–250). IGI Global. doi:10.4018/978-1-60566-360-9.ch014

Yamin, M. M., Katt, B., & Nowostawski, M. (2021). Serious games as a tool to model attack and defence scenarios for cyber-security exercises. *Computers & Security*, *110*, 102450. doi:10.1016/j.cose.2021.102450

Yang, X., Ye, H., & Wang, X. (2021). Social media use and work efficiency: Insights from the theory of communication visibility. *Information & Management*, *58*(4), 103462. doi:10.1016/j.im.2021.103462

Yoo, S. J., & Huang, W. D. (2016). Can E-Learning System Enhance Learning Culture in the Workplace? A Comparison among Companies in South Korea. *British Journal of Educational Technology*, *47*(4), 575–591. doi:10.1111/bjet.12240

Yuliono, T. Sarwanto, & Rintayati, P. (2018). *The Promising Roles of Augmented Reality in Educational Setting: A Review of the Literature. International Journal of Educational Methodology*. doi:10.12973/ijem.4.3.125e

Yusoff, M. S. B. M., & Rejab, M. R. M. (2021). Advantages and Challenges of E-learning During the Pandemic in Malaysia. *International Journal of Academic Research in Business & Social Sciences*, *11*(4), 51–59.

Zaoui, F., & Souissi, N. (2020). Roadmap for digital transformation: A literature review. *Procedia Computer Science*, *175*, 621–628. doi:10.1016/j.procs.2020.07.090

Zapata-Rivera, J.-D., & Greer, J. E. (2004). Interacting with inspectable bayesian student models. *International Journal of Artificial Intelligence in Education, 14*(2), 127–163.

Zawacki-Richter, O., Marín, V. I., Bond, M., & Gouverneur, F. (2019). Systematic review of research on artificial intelligence applications in higher education – where are the educators? *International Journal of Educational Technology in Higher Education, 16*(1), 1–27. doi:10.118641239-019-0171-0

Zhang, J., Long, J., & von Schaewen, A. M. E. (2021). How does digital transformation improve organizational resilience?—Findings from PLS-SEM and fsQCA. *Sustainability (Basel), 13*(20), 11487. doi:10.3390u132011487

Zhou, K. Z., Brown, J. H., Dev, C. S., & Agarwal, S. (2006). The effects of customer and competitor orientations on performance in global markets: A contingency analysis. *Journal of International Business Studies, 38*(2), 303–319. doi:10.1057/palgrave.jibs.8400259

Zhu, E., & Kaplan, A. (2020). Advantages and Disadvantages of Online Education During the COVID-19 Pandemic: Longitudinal Case Study. *Journal of Medical Internet Research, 22*(10), e20107.

Zhu, K., & Kraemer, K. L. (2015). Post-adoption Variations in Usage and Value of E-business by Organizations: Cross-country Evidence from the Retail Industry. *Information Systems Research, 26*(1), 173–192.

Zoonen, W., Treem, J. W., & Ter Hoeven, C. L. (2022). A tool and a tyrant: Social media and well-being in organizational contexts. *Current Opinion in Psychology, 45*, 101300. doi:10.1016/j.copsyc.2022.101300 PMID:35231788

About the Contributors

Henrique Mamede is an Assistant Professor at the Department of Science and Technology of the Open University. Coordinator of the Master in Information and Business Systems. He has his PhD in Information Systems and Technologies from the University of Minho. Master in Informatics from the Faculty of Sciences of the University of Lisbon. He also has a degree in Computer Engineering from COCITE. He is a consultant in Information Systems and Architectures, Applications and Technologies.

Arnaldo Santos is a Professor of the Department of Sciences and Technologies of Universidade Aberta. Invited Professor at the Department of Communication and Art of the Aveiro University. He is the Vice-director of Doctor's Degree in Web Science and Technology. His current research interests are focused on Digital Learning Systems and Contents and Learning Organizations. 28 years' experience in Management in Corporate Sector, where he was Communication and Learning Director.

***

José Bidarra has a PhD in Educational Communications by Universidade Aberta (the Portuguese Open University), where he is currently Professor with Habilitation in the Department of Science and Technology. For many years he was head of the Informatics, Physics and Technology Section (SIFT) and has been director of Master and PhD programs. He is also co-author of the virtual pedagogical model used at Universidade Aberta. His current research interests focus mainly on the application of multimedia and digital media in distance education, including ebooks, games and simulations. Many of his master and doctorate students are developing new methodologies to engage learners in valuable experiences with digital media. Most of the research is conducted at Universidade Aberta and at CIAC (Center for the Arts and Communication Research, University of Algarve); other research includes a Honorary Fellowship at the Games, Learning, and Society research unit,

University of Wisconsin – Madison (USA), and frequent collaborations with European universities and networks: TU Graz, OU-NL, OU-UK, EADTU, EMPOWER, SmartLearning DK.

Tomas Blažauskas is a professor in the Software Engineering department of the Faculty of Informatics. His scientific interests are multimodal interfaces, smart wellbeing technologies, augmented and virtual reality systems, and gamification in e-learning. He is a principal investigator of the researchers' group called "Multimodal Human-Computer Interfaces". He is a co-author of more than 70 research articles, two books and one patent. Various solutions designed by his research group were demonstrated in more than 20 exhibitions and other events.

Rita Butkienė is an associate professor, dean of the Faculty of Informatics at the Kaunas University of Technology (KTU). She received her Ph.D. in Informatics Engineering from KTU in 2002. Her research interests include information system engineering, ontologies, semantic technologies, and databases. She has over 20 years' experience in student teaching. She is deeply interested in the Education domain, in the application of information and communication technologies in learning and teaching.

L. Čeponienė is an associate professor at Department of Information Systems, Faculty of Informatics, Kaunas University of Technology. She received her BSc, MSc, and PhD in Informatics Engineering from Kaunas University of Technology. She is an author and co-author of more than 30 research papers and several methodological books.

Daina Gudoniene is an associate professor leading the researchers group on Smart educational technologies and applications; she is a researcher and methodology specialist, lectured at Faculty of Informatics. Her research area is Smart educational technologies and applications: models, systems, platforms, and architecture. The author and co-author of more than 60 research papers and 8 Books.

Lúcia Moreira holds a PhD in Information and Communication in Digital Platforms from the University of Aveiro and the University of Porto. She has authored and co-authored books and publications on User Experience and eLearning and participated in R&D projects for Digital Society. Her research interests mainly revolve around knowledge management, communication technologies for digital learning and health, usability, and user experience. With over 19 years of experience in the fields of telecommunications, knowledge management, user experience and digital transformation, she has successfully led and developed areas and teams that focus on activating human capital through knowledge, process improvement, service and experience design.

Ujjal Mukherjee holds a Ph.D. and serves as a professor in Organizational Behavior and Human Resource Management at the Institute of Public Enterprises in Hyderabad. He has over 14 years of experience in academia, previously serving as a Professor and Area Head at the Faculty of Management Studies, CMS B School, Jain University. In addition to teaching, he has contributed as Co-Chairman of the PhD and Research Committee and Editor-in-Chief of the Jain Journal of Management and Commerce Review. Dr. Mukherjee is also a member of the Research Advisory Committee at RV Institute of Management. He holds academic qualifications, including a Ph.D. in HR and an MBA in HR, along with a UGC-NET certification. He is a Certified Happiness Coach from "The Berkeley Well-Being Institute, California" and completed a Certificate in University Teaching from Newcastle University, Australia. Dr. Mukherjee brings over 4 years of industry experience and 5+ years of entrepreneurial experience to his portfolio, making significant contributions to management and human resources fields.

Cláudia Neves has been an assistant professor at the Universidade Aberta since 2010, where she teaches courses in the Department of Education and Distance Learning. Since 2017, she has been coordinator of the Master's Degree in Educational Administration and Management, where she has supervised several dissertations. But her experience has also included teaching at FCSH/UNL during the years 2010/2012. Her research interests are anchored in the Laboratory of Education and Distance Learning (LE@D) and center around Educational Policies and new forms of regulation of education in the national and international context, with special emphasis on the role of the European Union in defining the educational policy of its member states. Currently, his research seeks to explore and deepen training scenarios in digital environments especially oriented towards the management and leadership of schools in Portugal and Europe and the exploration of complexity theories in educational administration and management.

Alvaro Pistono has a PhD in Web Science and Technology from the UTAD/Open University, Engineer and Master of Science from the Military Engineering Institute, specialist and scholar of Educational Technology for over 20 years. He has a postgraduate qualification in Distance Education Planning, Implementation and Management from the Fluminense Federal University.

Henrik Køhler Simonsen is External Lecturer at Department of Management, Society and Communication at Copenhagen Business School, Visiting Professor at

Saint Paul Business School and Head of Learning at the Danish Insurance Academy. Henrik Køhler Simonsen holds an MA in International Business Communication, a PhD in Corporate Lexicography, an MBA in Emergent Management, an Army Leadership Diploma and an SME Board Certificate. His research interests include digital learning, digital business models, information management and AI. Henrik Køhler Simonsen has published extensively within these fields and is author, co-author and editor of more than 100 books and journal articles. Henrik Køhler Simonsen's professional skills lie within development and management of digital learning, business development and AI in education. Henrik Køhler Simonsen has successfully managed two corporate turnarounds and established digital learning ecosystems in the pharmaceutical industry and the insurance industry.

Evelina Stanevičienė is a lecturer and junior researcher at Kaunas University of Technology Faculty of Informatics. In 2019, she successfully defended her doctoral thesis on the application of hybrid genetic algorithms for the grey pattern problem. The researcher's main research interests are related to hybrid heuristic algorithms and optimization problems. She is a member of the scientific group Application of Artificial Intelligence and Image Processing Methods in Multimedia.

Divya Suresh is an adept scholar with an undergraduate degree specializing in Psychology, Sociology, and Economics and has further honed her skills as a research intern at Jain (Deemed-to-be University). The researcher has worked on research projects related to consumers rationality and her future areas of research are poised to include organizational psychology and behavioural economics.

Index

A

C

D

E

www.ingramcontent.com/pod-product-compliance
Lightning Source LLC
LaVergne TN
LVHW080644011026
849160LV00014B/1321